THE SUMMIT IS HIGH, AND THE PATH LONG. HOWEVER...!
IF YOU DON'T TAKE A BREAK ABOUT NOW...
...DON'T YOU THINK YOUR TRUE NATURE WILL BE REVEALED?
LOOK AT ME! SEE?
WHEEZ-
PANT-

VOLUME 20

AFTER ALL THAT'S BEEN SAID AND DONE, IT'S FINALLY VOLUME 20. IT TOOK FOUR YEARS TO GET HERE, AND THAT'S MORE THAN ENOUGH...ACTUALLY I'M NOWHERE NEAR SATISFIED. I HAVE A HUNGER THAT HAS YET TO BE SATISFIED! I WANT TO DRAW BETTER PICTURES. I WANT TO WRITE MORE INTRIGUING STORIES. I WANT
'E BIRTH TO MORE ATTRACTIVE
:TERS. I KNOW I'M BEING GREEDY,
:AN'T STOP BEING A MANGA
THIS IS JUST THE BEGINNING!

Rurouni Kenshin, which has found fans not only in Japan but around the world, first made its appearance in 1992, as an original short story in ***Weekly Shonen Jump Special***. Later rewritten and published as a regular, continuing ***Jump*** series in 1994, ***Rurouni Kenshin*** ended serialization in 1999 but continued in popularity, as evidenced by the 2000 publication of ***Yahiko no Sakabatô*** ("Yahiko's Reversed-Edge Sword") in ***Weekly Shonen Jump***. His most current work, ***Busô Renkin*** ("Armored Alchemist"), began publication in June 2003, also in ***Jump***.

RUROUNI KENSHIN
VOL. 20: REMEMBRANCE
The SHONEN JUMP Graphic Novel Edition

STORY AND ART BY
NOBUHIRO WATSUKI

English Adaptation/Gerard Jones
Translation/Kenichiro Yagi
Touch-Up Art & Lettering/Steve Dutro
Design/Matt Hinrichs
Editor/Kit Fox

Managing Editor/Elizabeth Kawasaki
Director of Production/Noboru Watanabe
Vice President of Publishing/Alvin Lu
Executive Vice President & Editor in Chief/Yumi Hoashi
Sr. Director of Acquisitions/Rika Inouye
Vice President of Sales & Marketing/Liza Coppola
Publisher/Hyoe Narita

Printed in the U.S.A.

Published by VIZ Media, LLC
P.O. Box 77010
San Francisco, CA 94107

SHONEN JUMP Graphic Novel Edition
10 9 8 7 6 5 4 3 2 1
First printing, October 2005

viz media
www.viz.com

RATED T+ FOR OLDER TEEN

PARENTAL ADVISORY
RUROUNI KENSHIN is rated T+ for Older Teen and is recommended for ages 16 and up. This volume contains realistic violence and alcohol and tobacco usage.

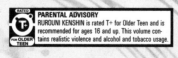

Rurouni Kenshin™

STORY & ART BY
NOBUHIRO WATSUKI

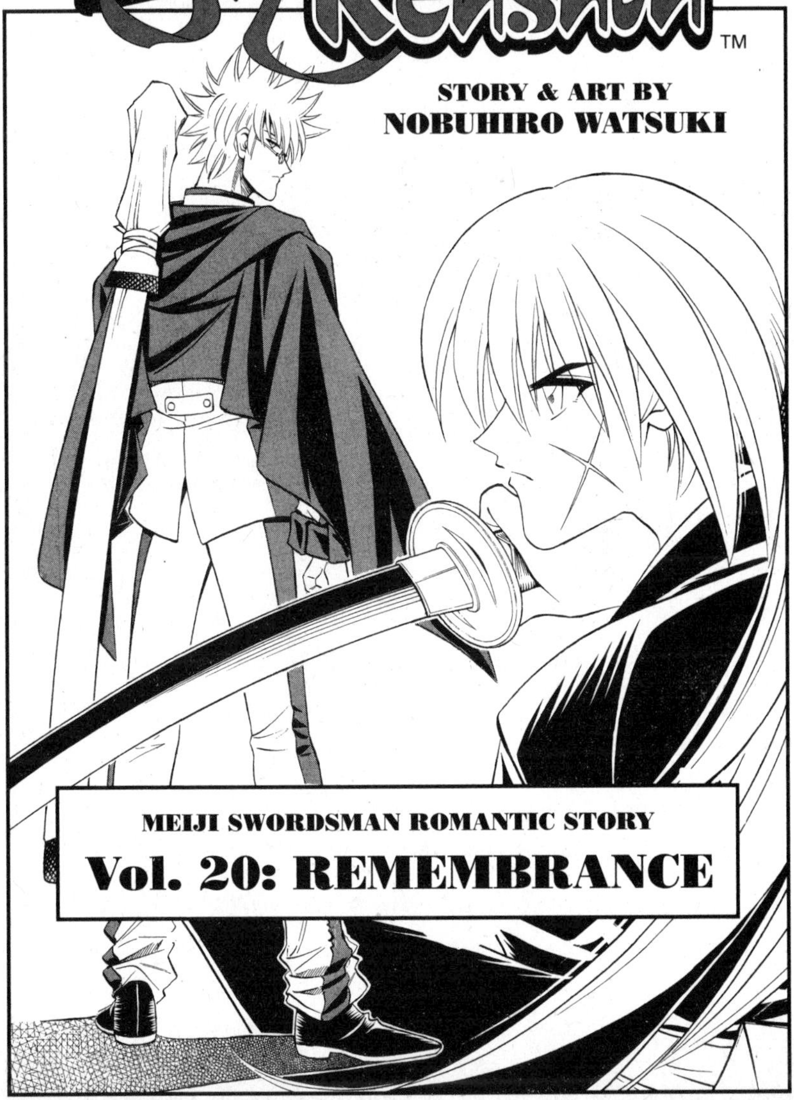

MEIJI SWORDSMAN ROMANTIC STORY

Vol. 20: REMEMBRANCE

CAST

緋村剣心（人斬り抜刀斎）
Himura Kenshin
(Hitokiri Battōsai)
神谷 薫
Kamiya Kaoru
桂 小五郎
Katsura Kogorō
相楽左之助
Sagara Sanosuke
雪代 縁（子供時代）
Yukishiro Enishi (childhood)
明神弥彦
Myōjin Yahiko

Once he was *hitokiri*, an assassin, called Battōsai. His name was legend among the pro-Imperialist or "patriot" warriors who launched the Meiji Era. Now, Himura Kenshin is *rurouni*, a wanderer, and carries a reversed-edge *sakabatō* to prohibit himself from killing.

雪代（緋村）巴

Yukishiro (Himura) Tomoe

THUS FAR

Having finally thwarted Shishio Makoto's plan to conquer Japan, Kenshin and his friends return to Tokyo. While Sanosuke seeks treatment for his injured hand, the others return to everyday life at Kamiya Dojo. But the peace is short-lived, as warriors who hold grudges against Battōsai gather to exact a form of revenge they call *Jinchū*—if the heavens will not cast judgment, they themselves will. Akabeko is destroyed by an Armstrong cannon fired from Ueno Mountain, and simultaneous attacks are unleashed against Maekawa Dojo and police chief Uramura's house. Kenshin anguishes over the harm that falls on others from his past as a *hitokiri*. The mastermind of the revenge, Yukishiro Enishi, appears before Kenshin and announces that he will strike Kamiya Dojo in ten days. Kenshin begins to see images of Tomoe, Yukishiro's sister—a woman whose life was fraught with tragedy. Kenshin falls into despair as he tries to find a way to pay for his crimes, but after seeing Yahiko, Kaoru, and the rest standing courageously against the danger, he knows he must fight to protect the present. He begins to tell everyone of his past...

The time is Bakumatsu. Kenshin has been wielding his sword for the "New Era" under Katsura Kogorō of Chōshū. One night, he defends himself against an assassin sent by the *shōgunate*—but a woman he helped at a pub witnesses the scene!

CONTENTS

RUROUNI KENSHIN
Meiji Swordsman Romantic Story
BOOK TWENTY: REMEMBRANCE

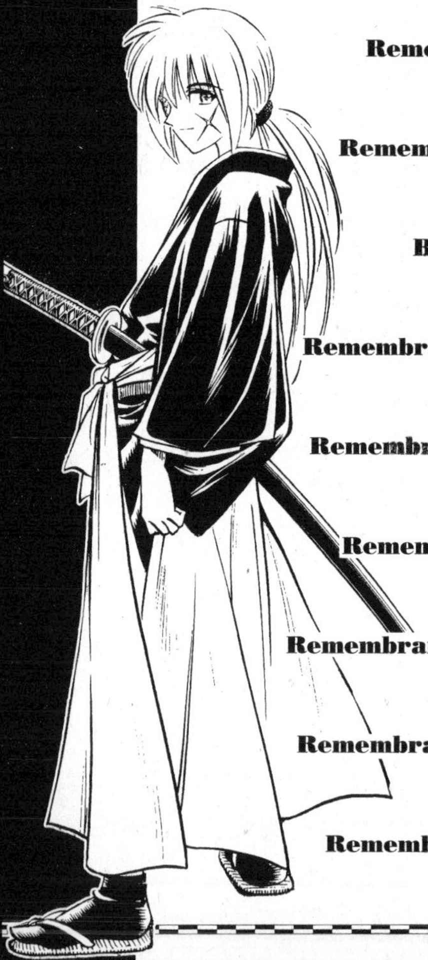

Act 168
Remembrance 4: Yukishiro Tomoe

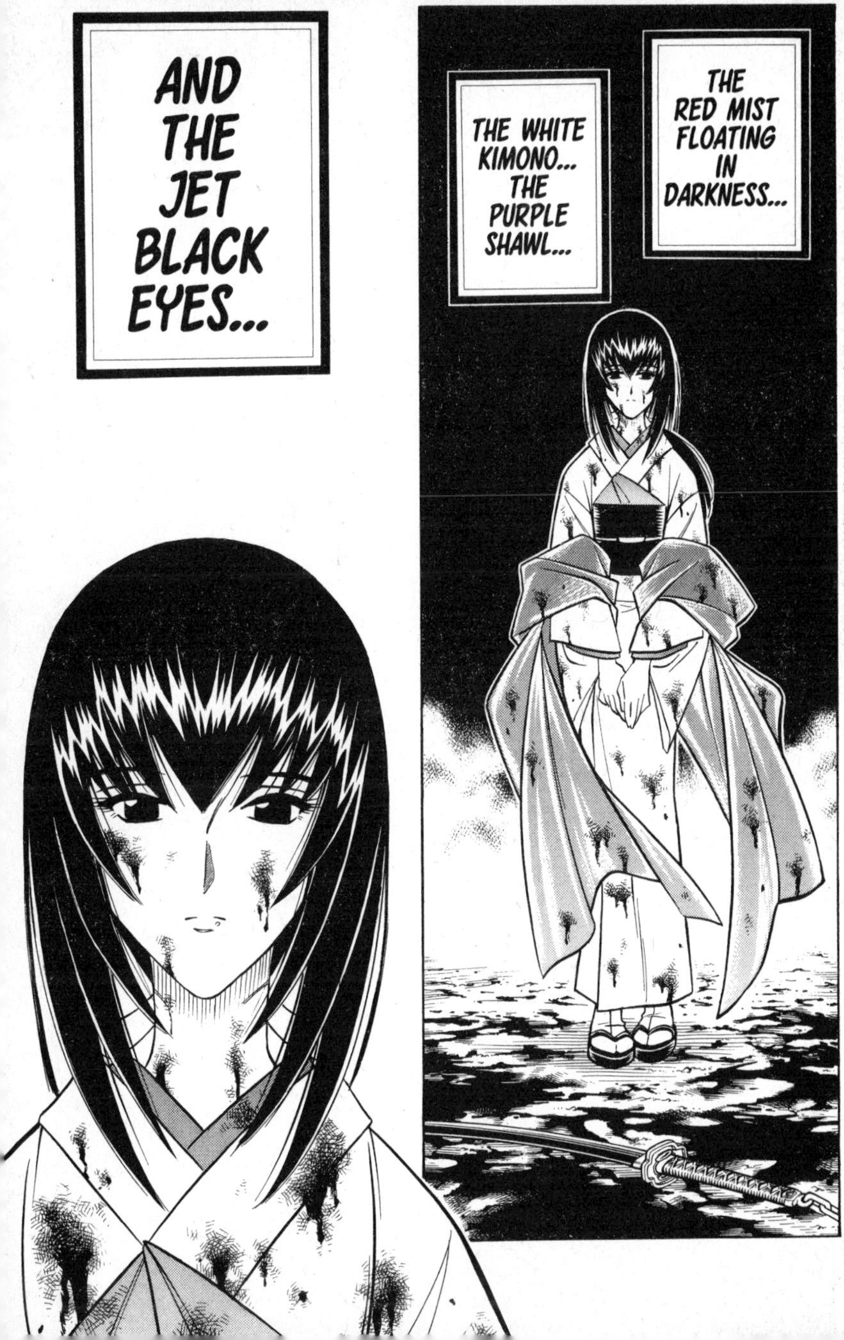
THE RED MIST FLOATING IN DARKNESS...
THE WHITE KIMONO... THE PURPLE SHAWL...
AND THE JET BLACK EYES...

Act 168

Remembrance 4: Yukishiro Tomoe

READ THIS WAY

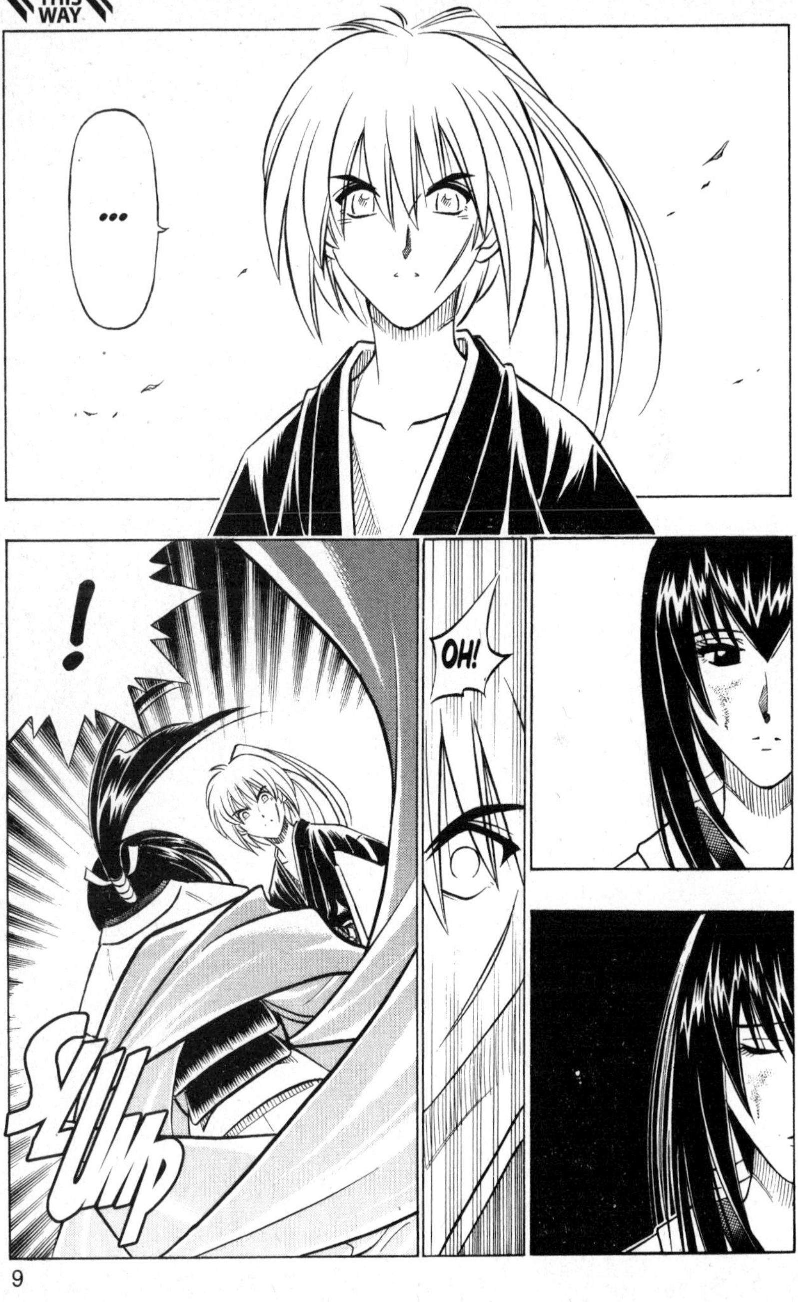
...
OH!
!
SLUMP

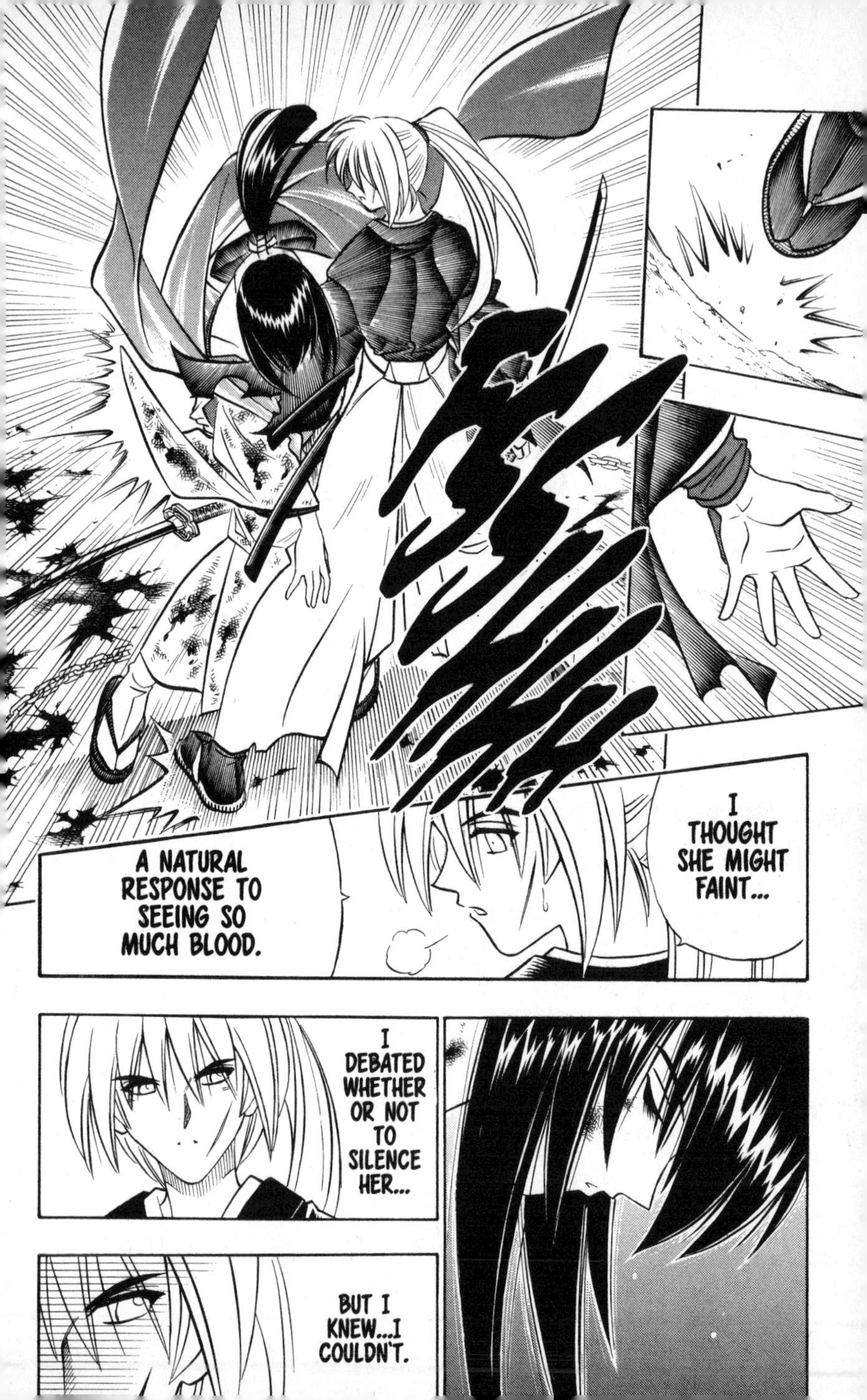
I THOUGHT SHE MIGHT FAINT...
A NATURAL RESPONSE TO SEEING SO MUCH BLOOD.
I DEBATED WHETHER OR NOT TO SILENCE HER...
BUT I KNEW...I COULDN'T.

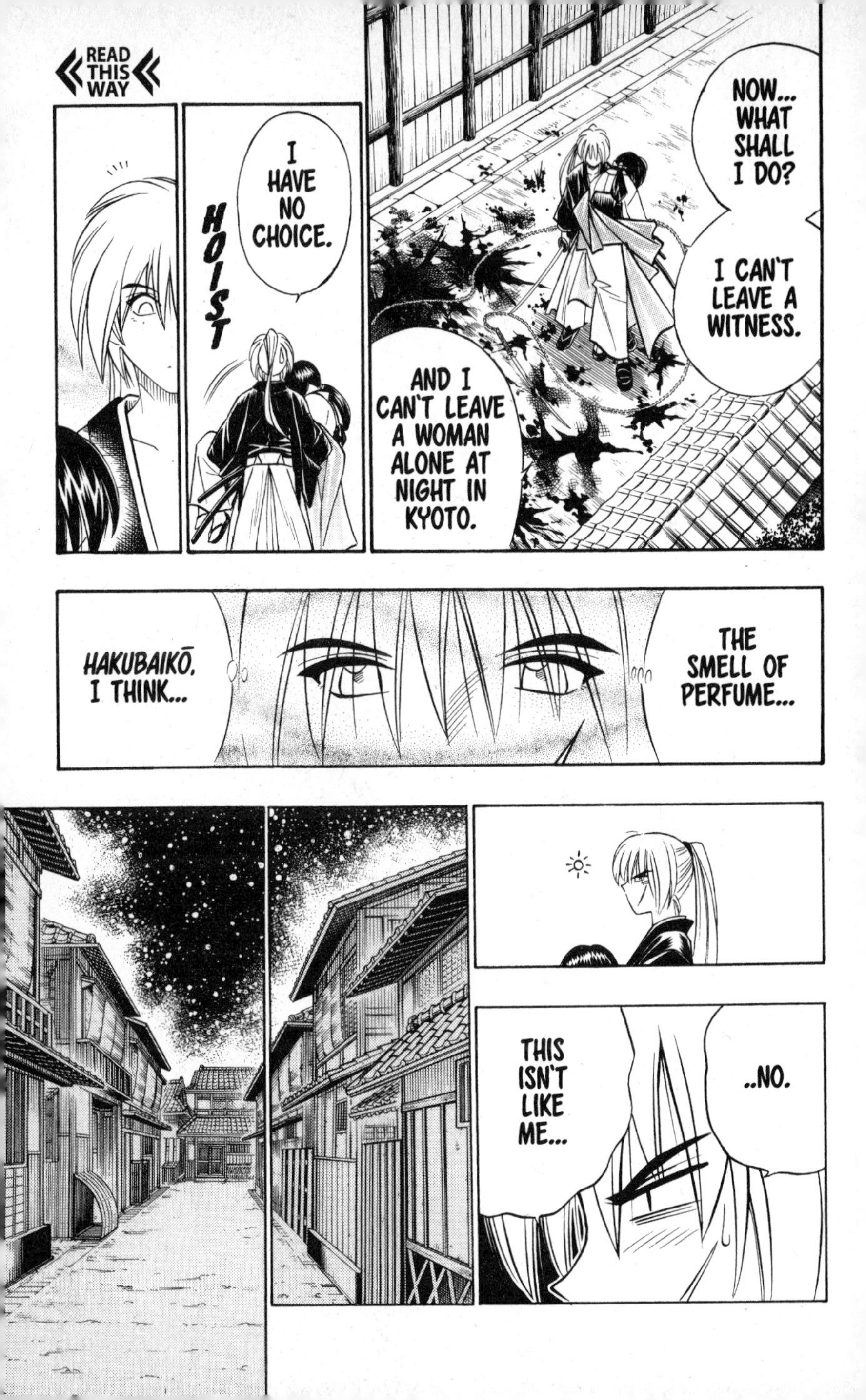
READ THIS WAY
NOW... WHAT SHALL I DO?
I CAN'T LEAVE A WITNESS.
AND I CAN'T LEAVE A WOMAN ALONE AT NIGHT IN KYOTO.
I HAVE NO CHOICE.
HOIST
THE SMELL OF PERFUME...
HAKUBAIKŌ, I THINK...
..NO.
THIS ISN'T LIKE ME...

KOHAGIYA INN

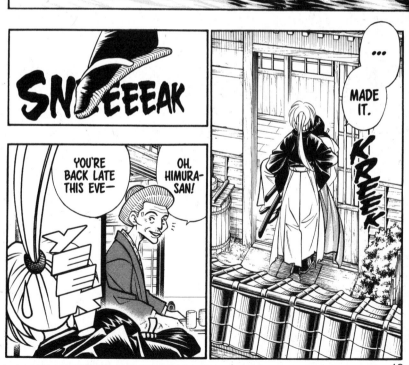

SN EEEEAK

...

MADE IT.

KREEK

YOU'RE BACK LATE THIS EVE—

OH, HIMURA-SAN!

12

READ THIS WAY

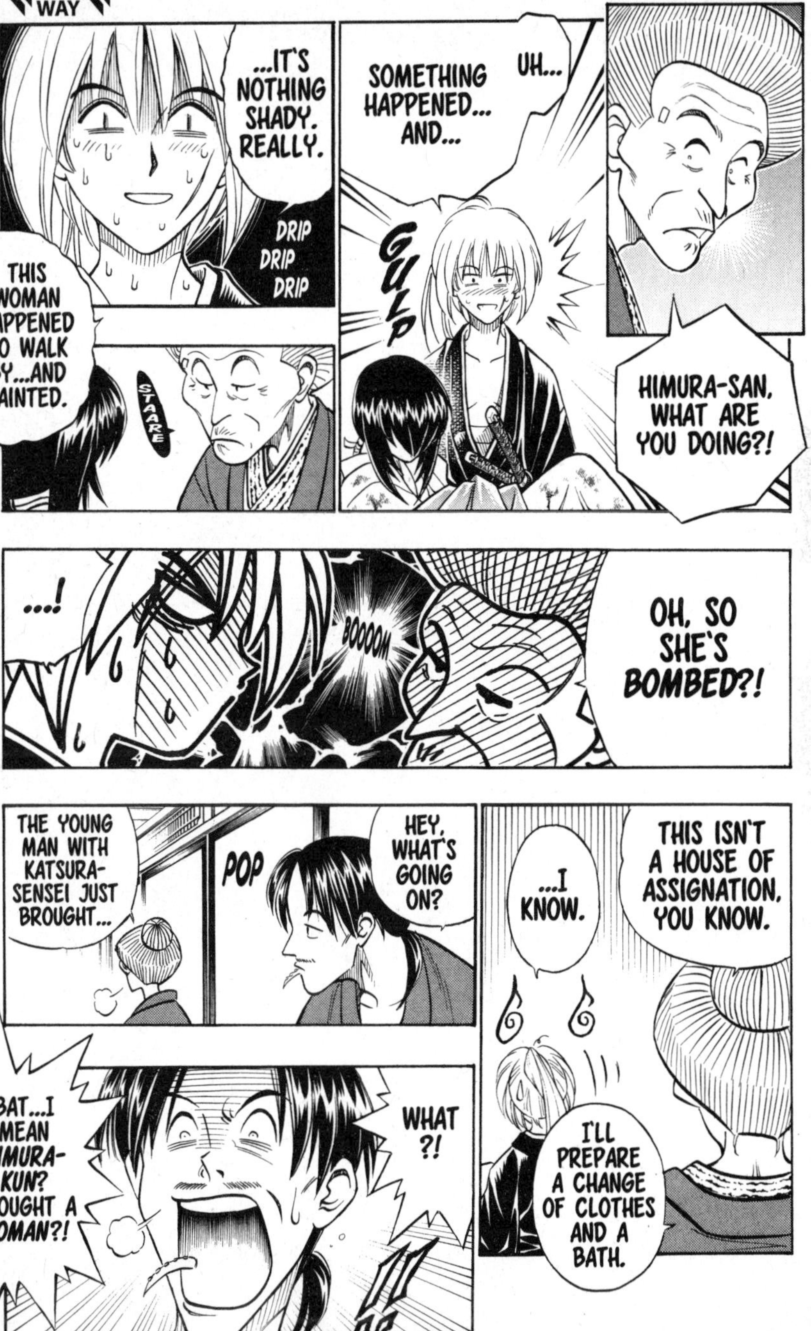
HIMURA-SAN, WHAT ARE YOU DOING?!
UH...
SOMETHING HAPPENED... AND...
GULP
...IT'S NOTHING SHADY. REALLY.
DRIP DRIP DRIP
THIS WOMAN HAPPENED TO WALK BY...AND FAINTED.
STAARE
OH, SO SHE'S BOMBED?!
BOOOOM
...!
THIS ISN'T A HOUSE OF ASSIGNATION, YOU KNOW.
...I KNOW.
I'LL PREPARE A CHANGE OF CLOTHES AND A BATH.
HEY, WHAT'S GOING ON?
POP
THE YOUNG MAN WITH KATSURA-SENSEI JUST BROUGHT...
WHAT ?!
BAT...I MEAN HIMURA-KUN? BROUGHT A WOMAN?!

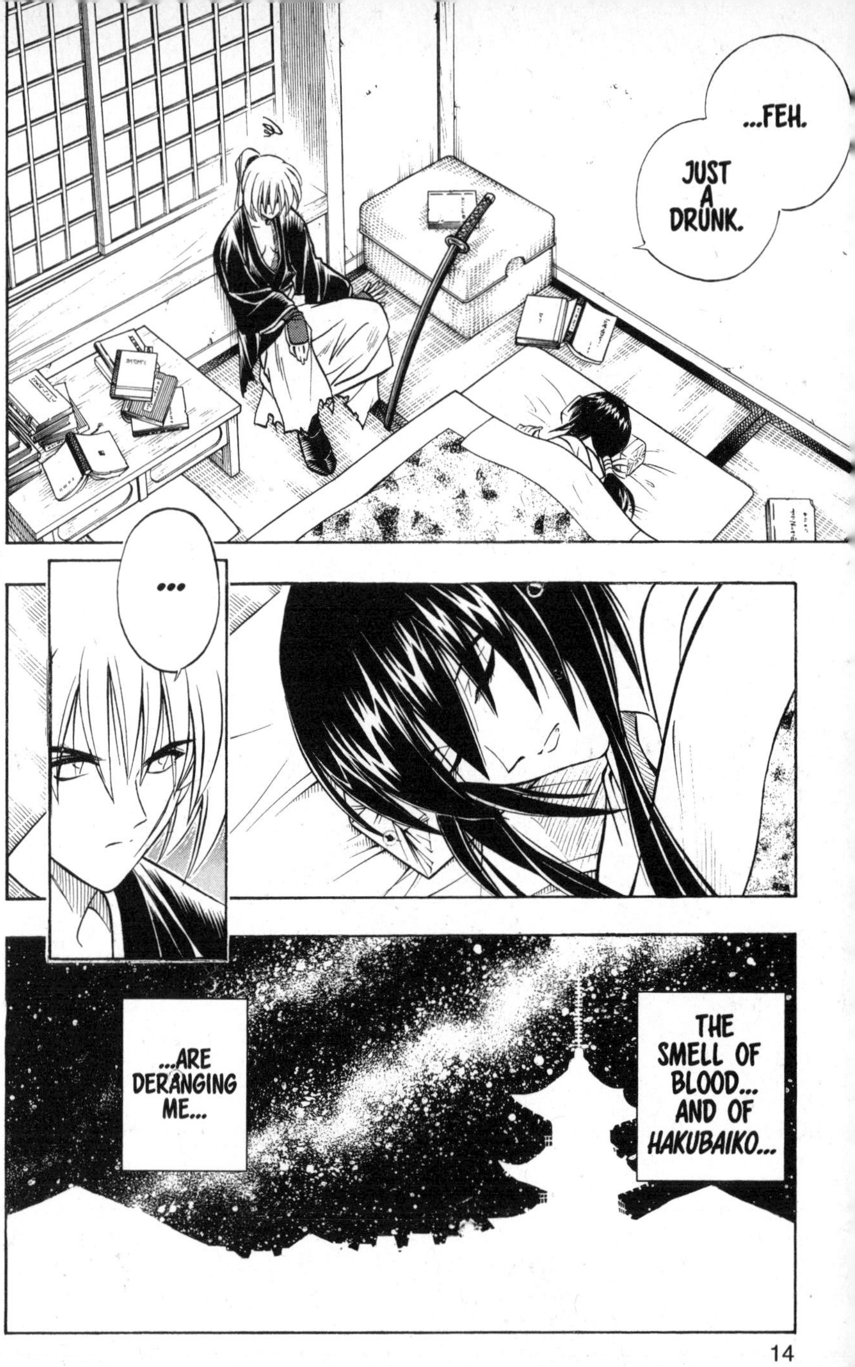
...FEH.
JUST A DRUNK.
...
THE SMELL OF BLOOD... AND OF HAKUBAIKO...
...ARE DERANGING ME...

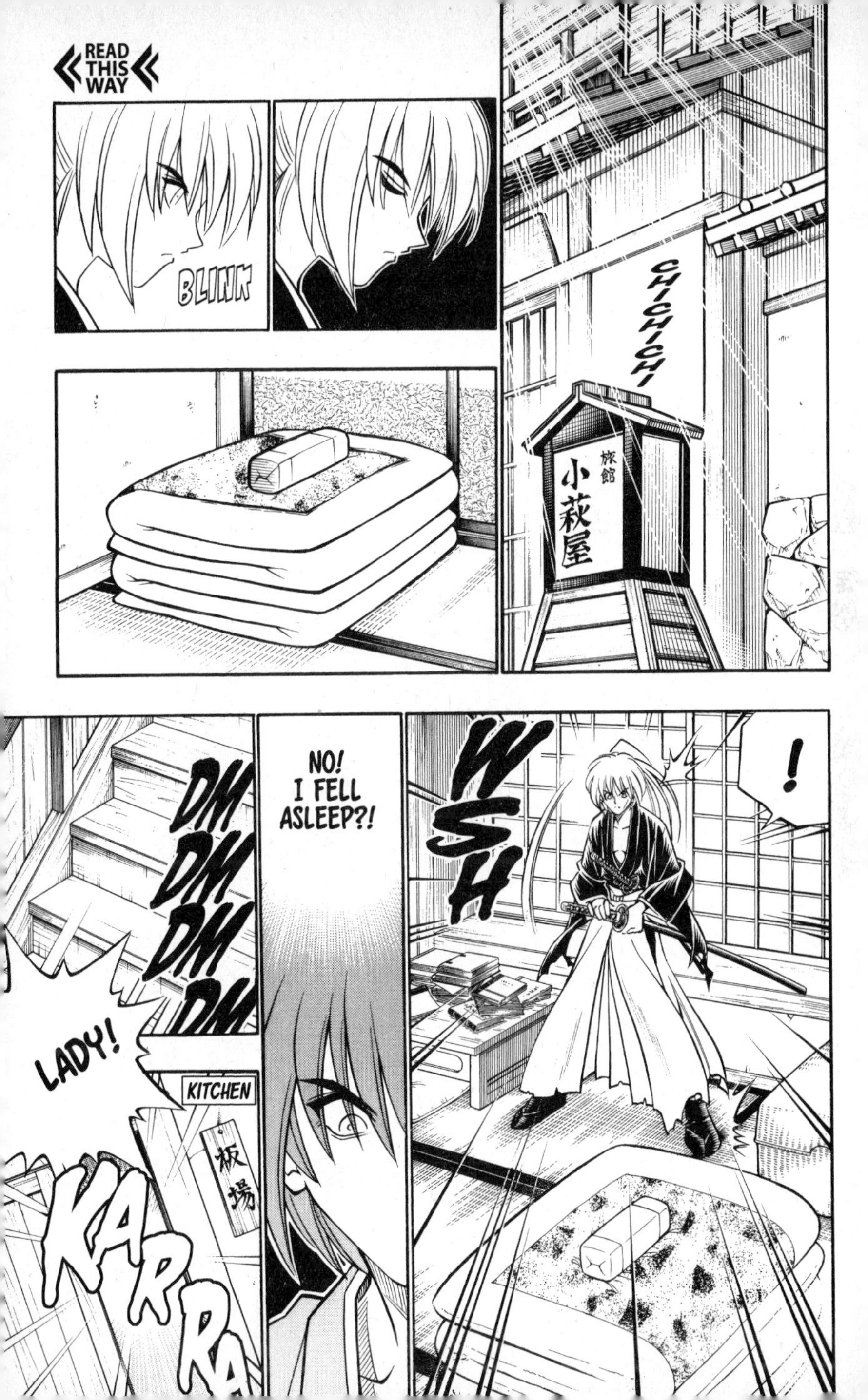
READ THIS WAY
CHICHICHI
旅館
小萩屋
BLINK
!
WSH
NO! I FELL ASLEEP?!
DM DM DM DM
LADY!
KITCHEN
板場
KARRA

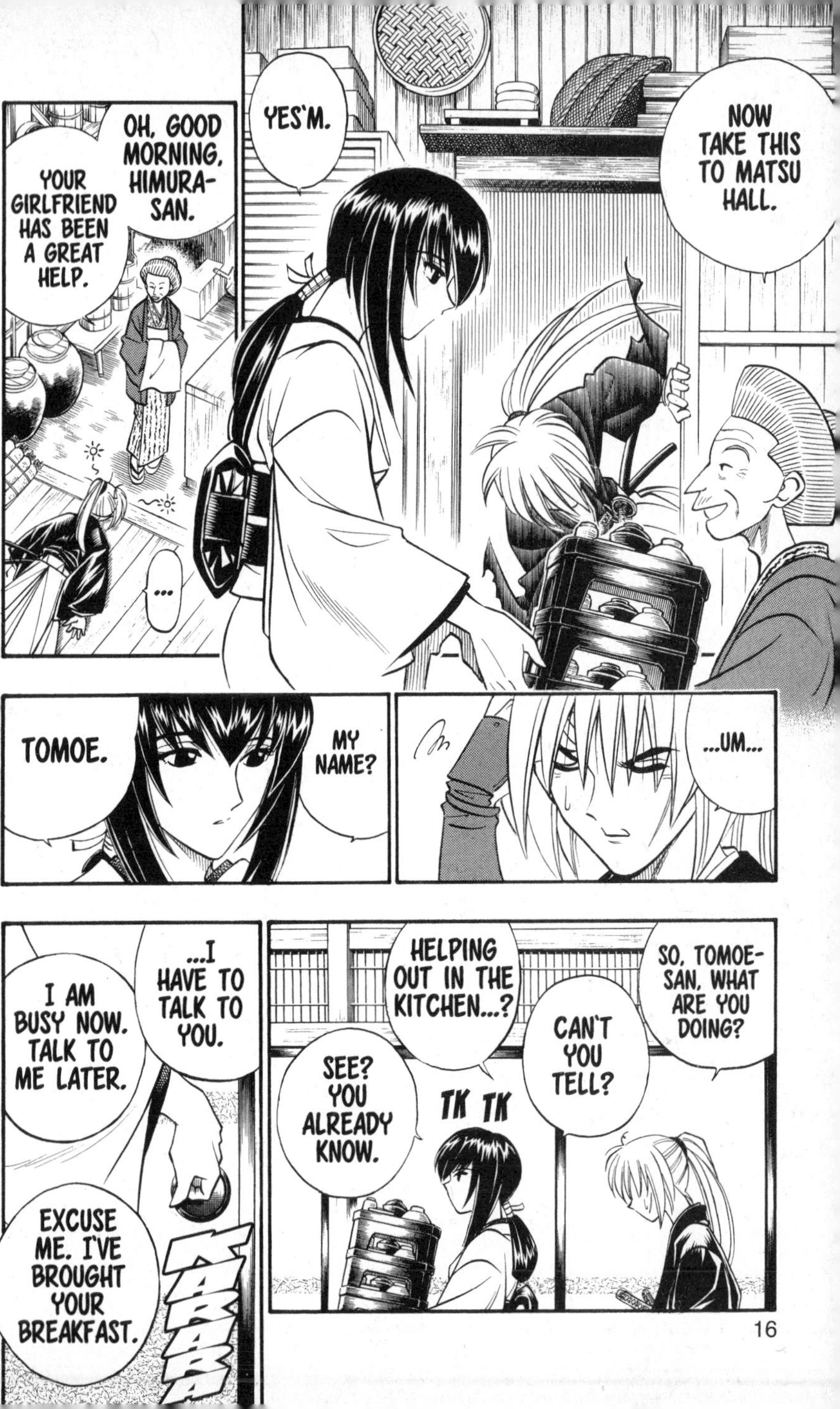
NOW TAKE THIS TO MATSU HALL.
YES'M.
OH, GOOD MORNING, HIMURA-SAN.
YOUR GIRLFRIEND HAS BEEN A GREAT HELP.
...
...UM...
MY NAME?
TOMOE.
SO, TOMOE-SAN, WHAT ARE YOU DOING?
CAN'T YOU TELL?
HELPING OUT IN THE KITCHEN...?
SEE? YOU ALREADY KNOW.
TK TK
...I HAVE TO TALK TO YOU.
I AM BUSY NOW. TALK TO ME LATER.
EXCUSE ME. I'VE BROUGHT YOUR BREAKFAST.

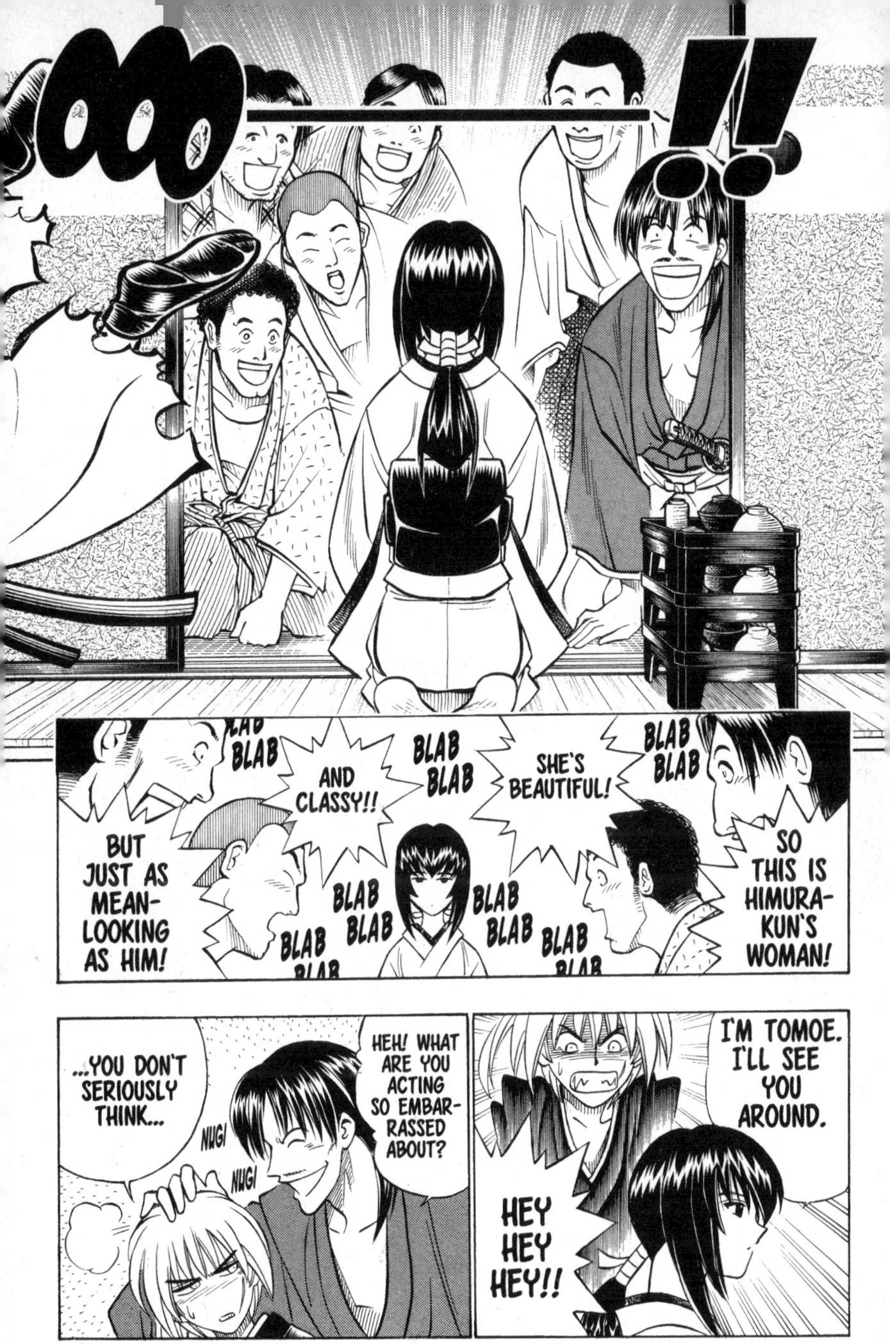
OOOO!!
SO THIS IS HIMURA-KUN'S WOMAN!
BLAB BLAB
BLAB
SHE'S BEAUTIFUL!
BLAB BLAB
BLAB BLAB
AND CLASSY!!
BLAB BLAB
BLAB
BLAB
BUT JUST AS MEAN-LOOKING AS HIM!
I'M TOMOE. I'LL SEE YOU AROUND.
HEY HEY HEY!!
HEH! WHAT ARE YOU ACTING SO EMBARRASSED ABOUT?
NUGI
NUGI
...YOU DON'T SERIOUSLY THINK...

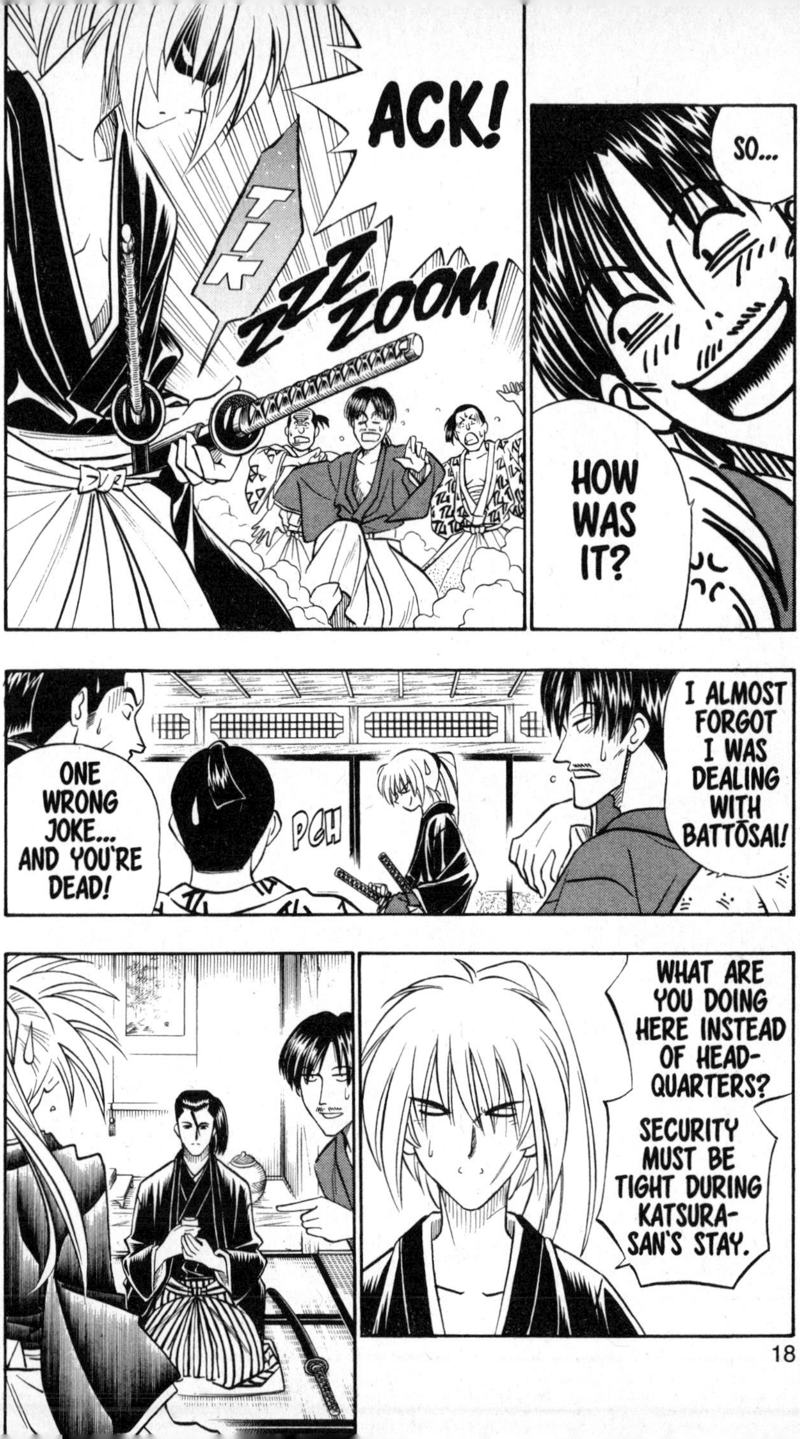
SO...
HOW WAS IT?
ACK!
TIK
ZZZZ ZOOM
I ALMOST FORGOT I WAS DEALING WITH BATTŌSAI!
PCH
ONE WRONG JOKE... AND YOU'RE DEAD!
WHAT ARE YOU DOING HERE INSTEAD OF HEAD-QUARTERS?
SECURITY MUST BE TIGHT DURING KATSURA-SAN'S STAY.

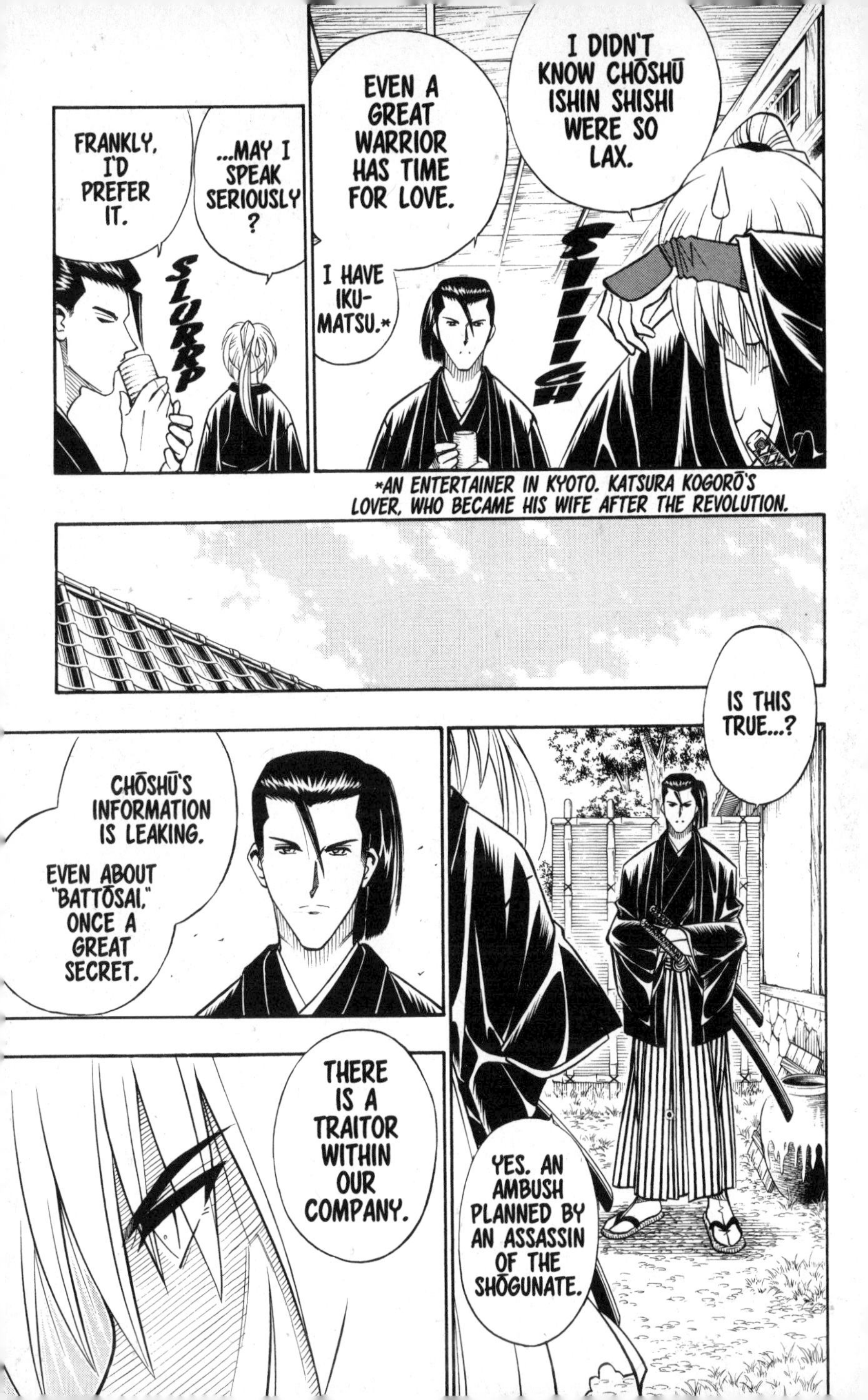
I DIDN'T KNOW CHŌSHŪ ISHIN SHISHI WERE SO LAX.
SIIIIGH
EVEN A GREAT WARRIOR HAS TIME FOR LOVE.
I HAVE IKU-MATSU.*
...MAY I SPEAK SERIOUSLY?
FRANKLY, I'D PREFER IT.
SLURRP
IS THIS TRUE...?
CHŌSHŪ'S INFORMATION IS LEAKING.
EVEN ABOUT "BATTŌSAI," ONCE A GREAT SECRET.
YES. AN AMBUSH PLANNED BY AN ASSASSIN OF THE SHŌGUNATE.
THERE IS A TRAITOR WITHIN OUR COMPANY.

*AN ENTERTAINER IN KYOTO. KATSURA KOGORŌ'S LOVER, WHO BECAME HIS WIFE AFTER THE REVOLUTION.

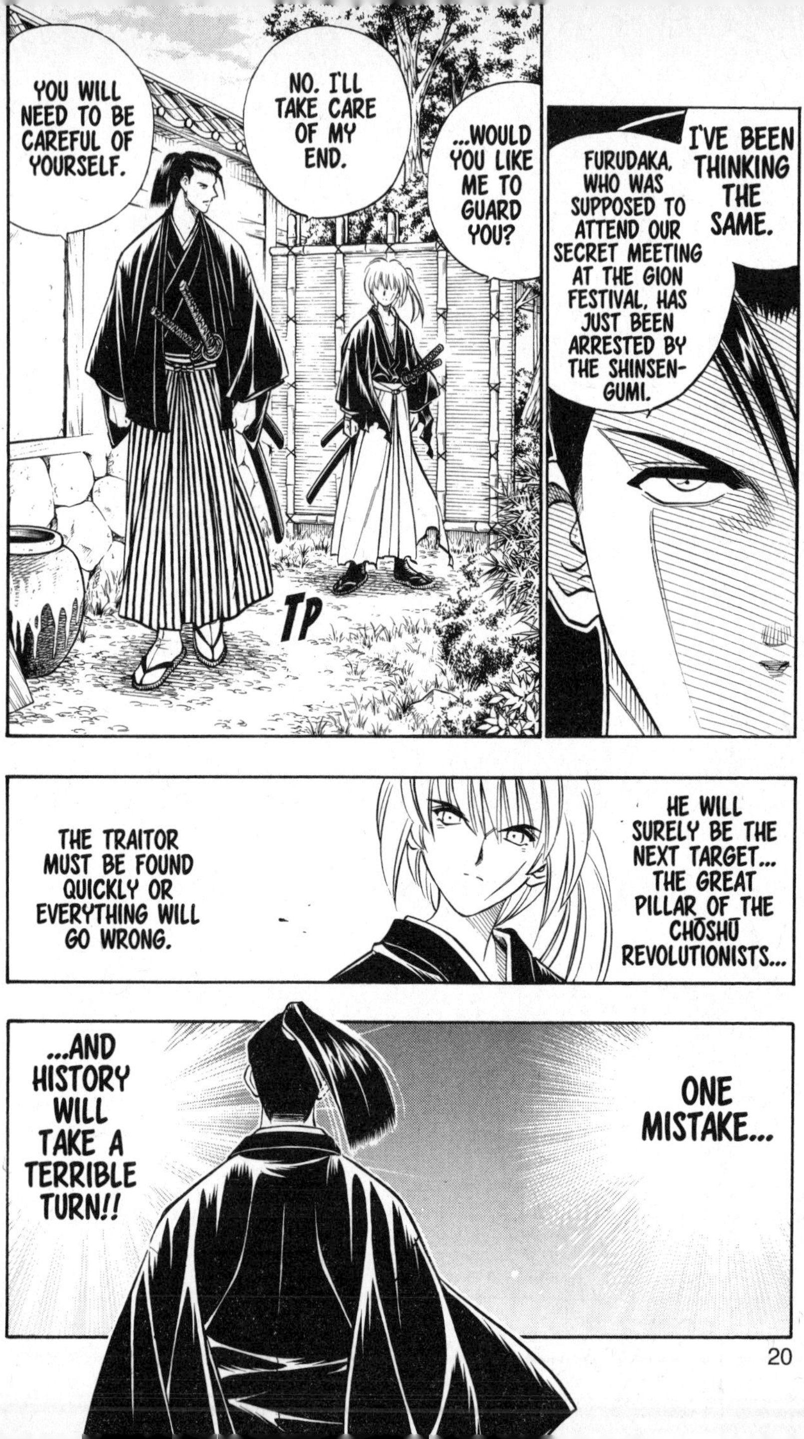
I'VE BEEN THINKING THE SAME.
FURUDAKA, WHO WAS SUPPOSED TO ATTEND OUR SECRET MEETING AT THE GION FESTIVAL, HAS JUST BEEN ARRESTED BY THE SHINSEN-GUMI.
...WOULD YOU LIKE ME TO GUARD YOU?
NO. I'LL TAKE CARE OF MY END.
YOU WILL NEED TO BE CAREFUL OF YOURSELF.
TP
HE WILL SURELY BE THE NEXT TARGET... THE GREAT PILLAR OF THE CHŌSHŪ REVOLUTIONISTS...
THE TRAITOR MUST BE FOUND QUICKLY OR EVERYTHING WILL GO WRONG.
ONE MISTAKE...
...AND HISTORY WILL TAKE A TERRIBLE TURN!!

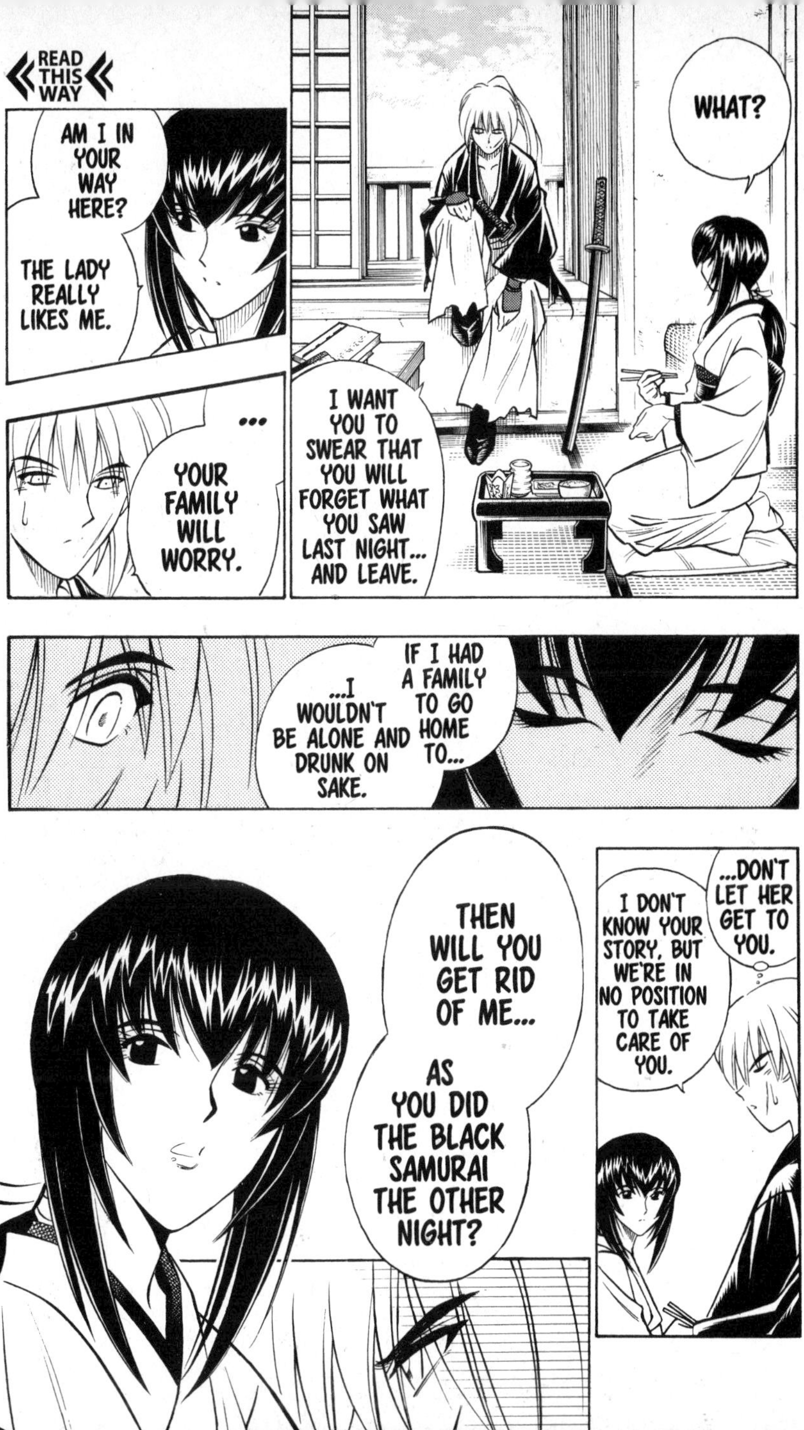
READ THIS WAY
WHAT?
I WANT YOU TO SWEAR THAT YOU WILL FORGET WHAT YOU SAW LAST NIGHT... AND LEAVE.
AM I IN YOUR WAY HERE?
THE LADY REALLY LIKES ME.
...
YOUR FAMILY WILL WORRY.
IF I HAD A FAMILY TO GO HOME TO...
...I WOULDN'T BE ALONE AND DRUNK ON SAKE.
...DON'T LET HER GET TO YOU.
I DON'T KNOW YOUR STORY, BUT WE'RE IN NO POSITION TO TAKE CARE OF YOU.
THEN WILL YOU GET RID OF ME...
AS YOU DID THE BLACK SAMURAI THE OTHER NIGHT?

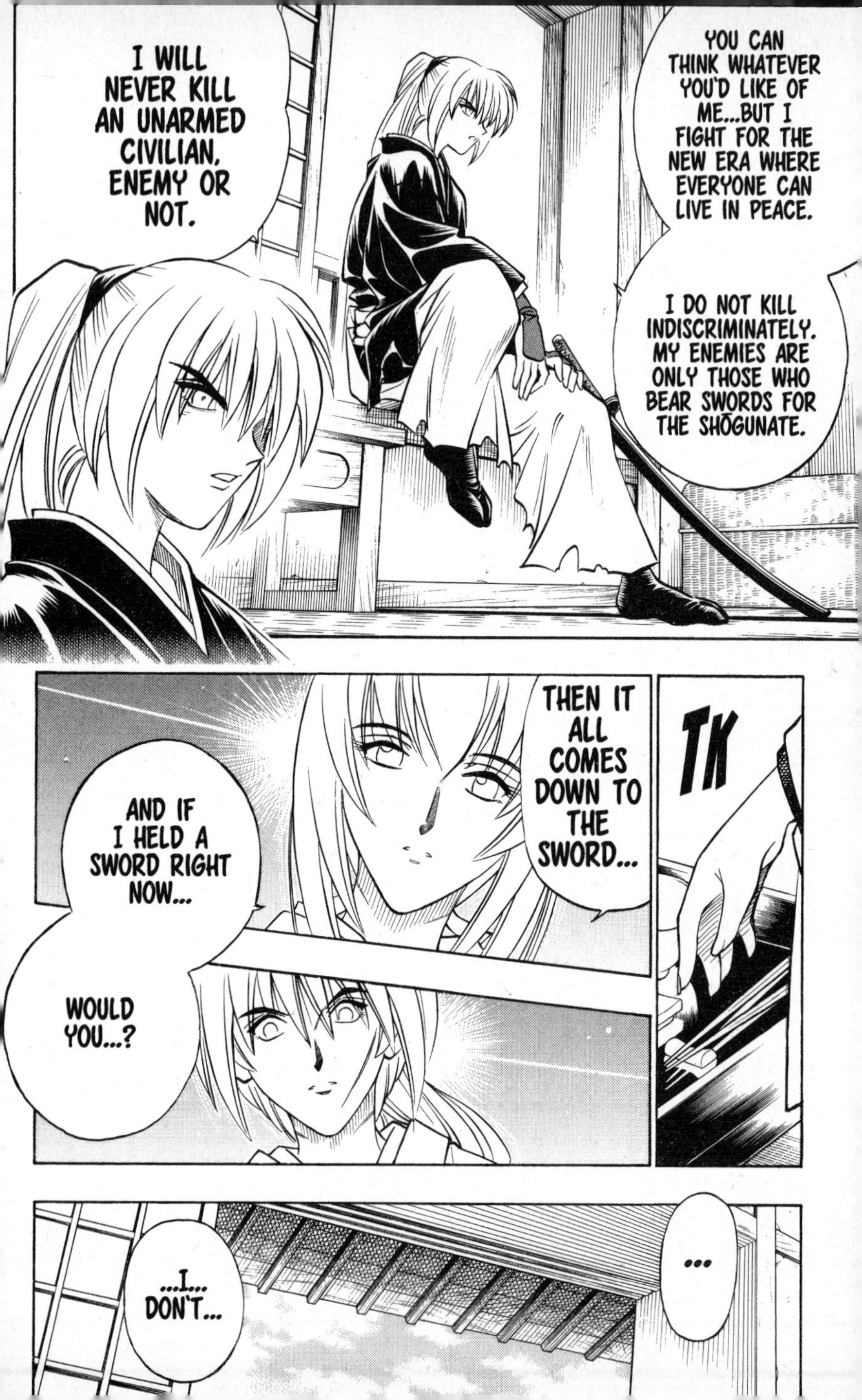
YOU CAN THINK WHATEVER YOU'D LIKE OF ME...BUT I FIGHT FOR THE NEW ERA WHERE EVERYONE CAN LIVE IN PEACE.
I DO NOT KILL INDISCRIMINATELY. MY ENEMIES ARE ONLY THOSE WHO BEAR SWORDS FOR THE SHŌGUNATE.
I WILL NEVER KILL AN UNARMED CIVILIAN, ENEMY OR NOT.
TK
THEN IT ALL COMES DOWN TO THE SWORD...
AND IF I HELD A SWORD RIGHT NOW...
WOULD YOU...?
...
...I... DON'T...

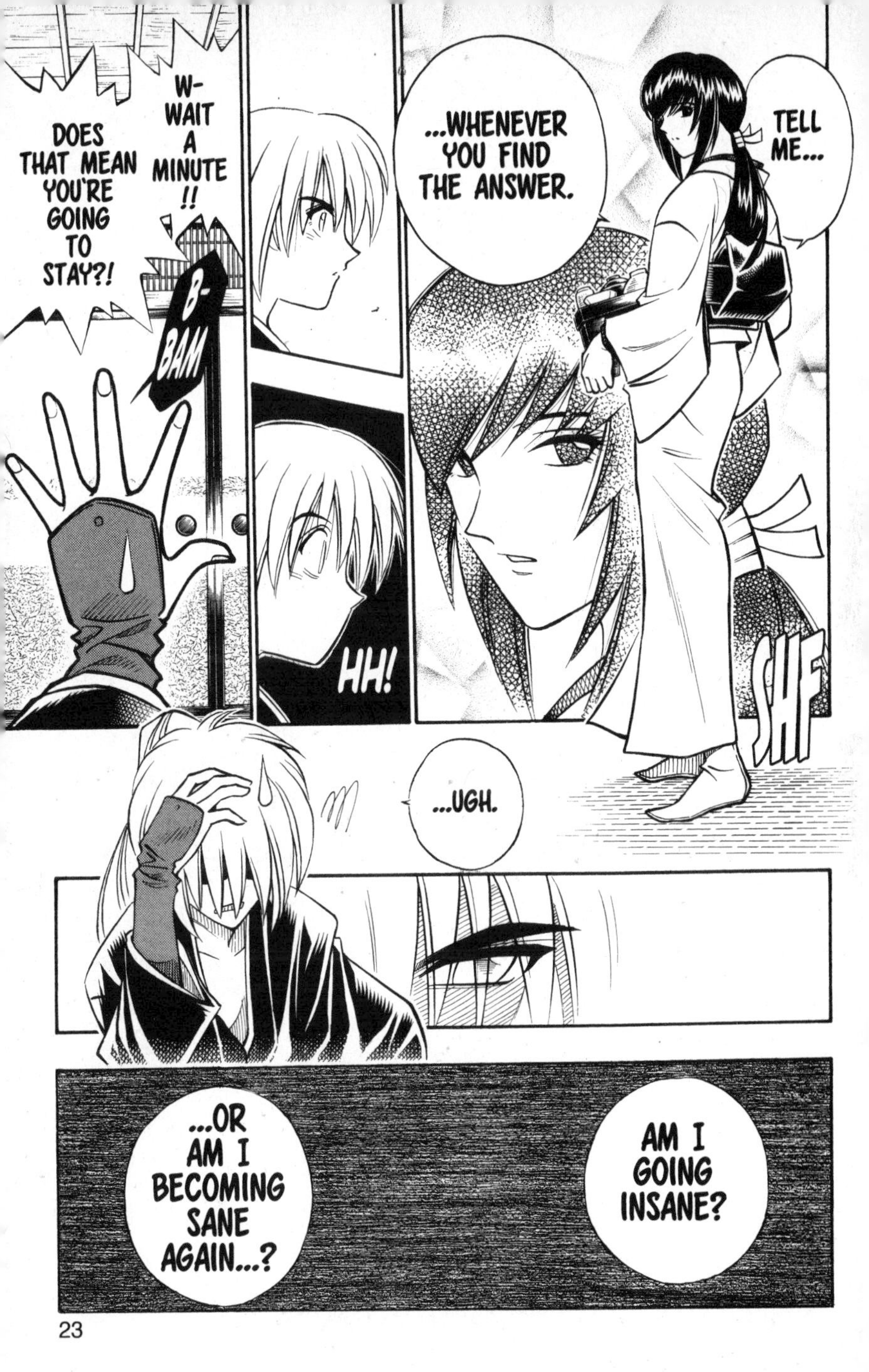
TELL ME...
...WHENEVER YOU FIND THE ANSWER.
SHF
HH!
W-WAIT A MINUTE!!
DOES THAT MEAN YOU'RE GOING TO STAY?!
B-BAM
...UGH.
AM I GOING INSANE?
...OR AM I BECOMING SANE AGAIN...?

Rurouni Kenshin

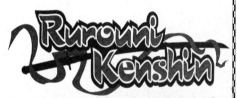

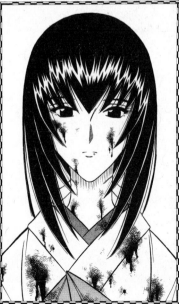

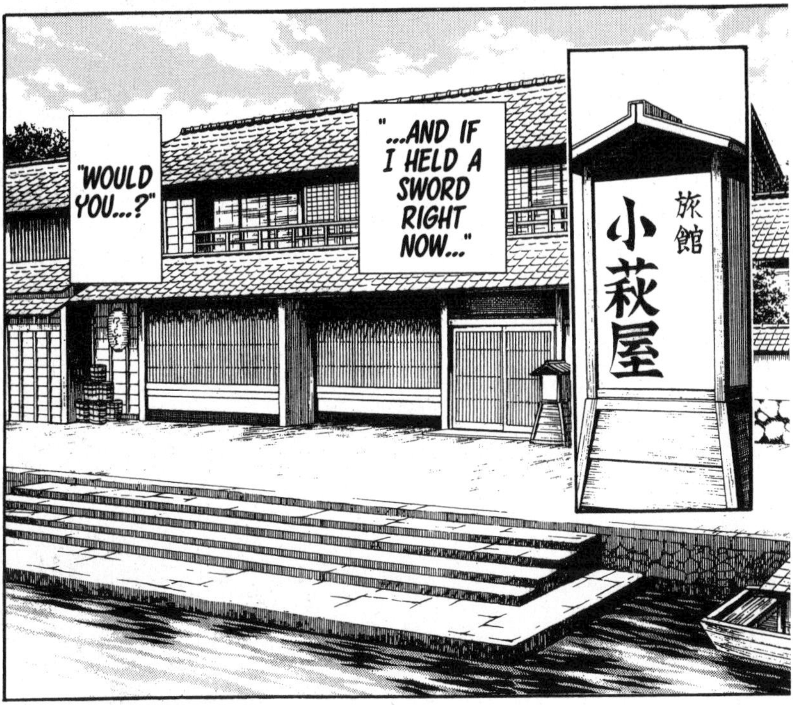
旅館
小萩屋
"...AND IF I HELD A SWORD RIGHT NOW..."
"WOULD YOU...?"

Act 169
Remembrance 5: Madness

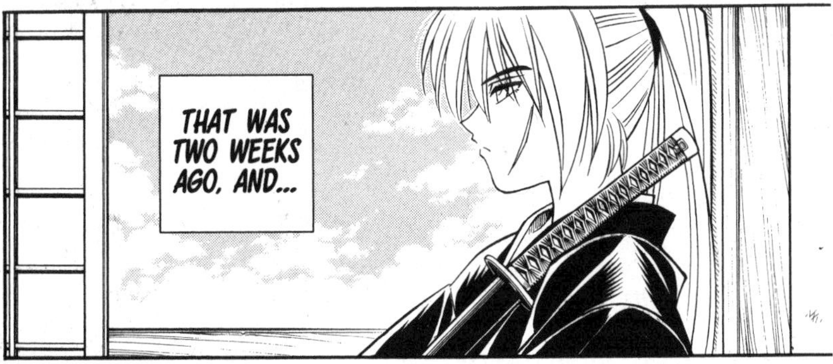
THAT WAS TWO WEEKS AGO, AND...

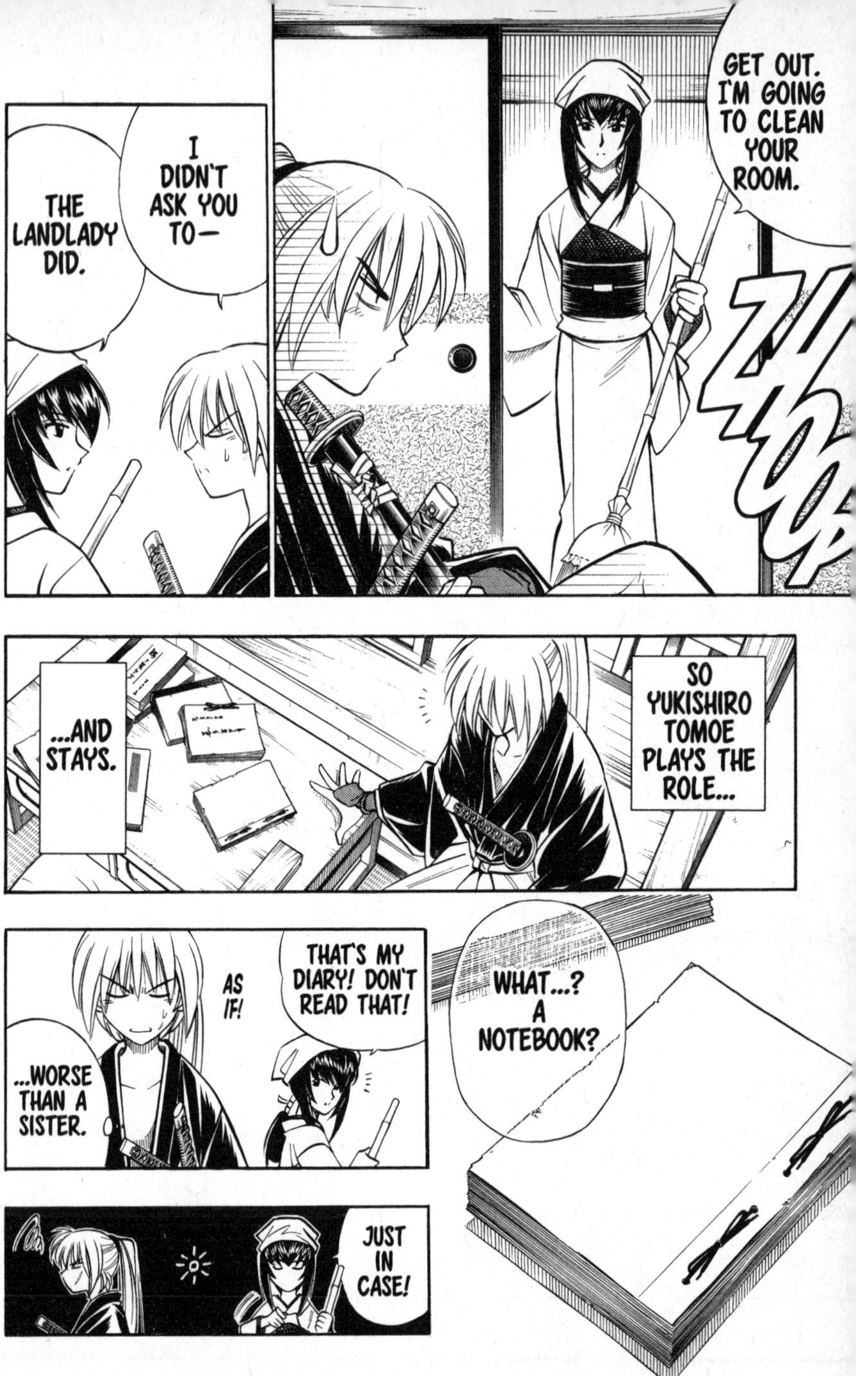
GET OUT. I'M GOING TO CLEAN YOUR ROOM.
ZHOOP
I DIDN'T ASK YOU TO—
THE LANDLADY DID.
SO YUKISHIRO TOMOE PLAYS THE ROLE...
...AND STAYS.
WHAT...? A NOTEBOOK?
THAT'S MY DIARY! DON'T READ THAT!
AS IF!
...WORSE THAN A SISTER.
JUST IN CASE!

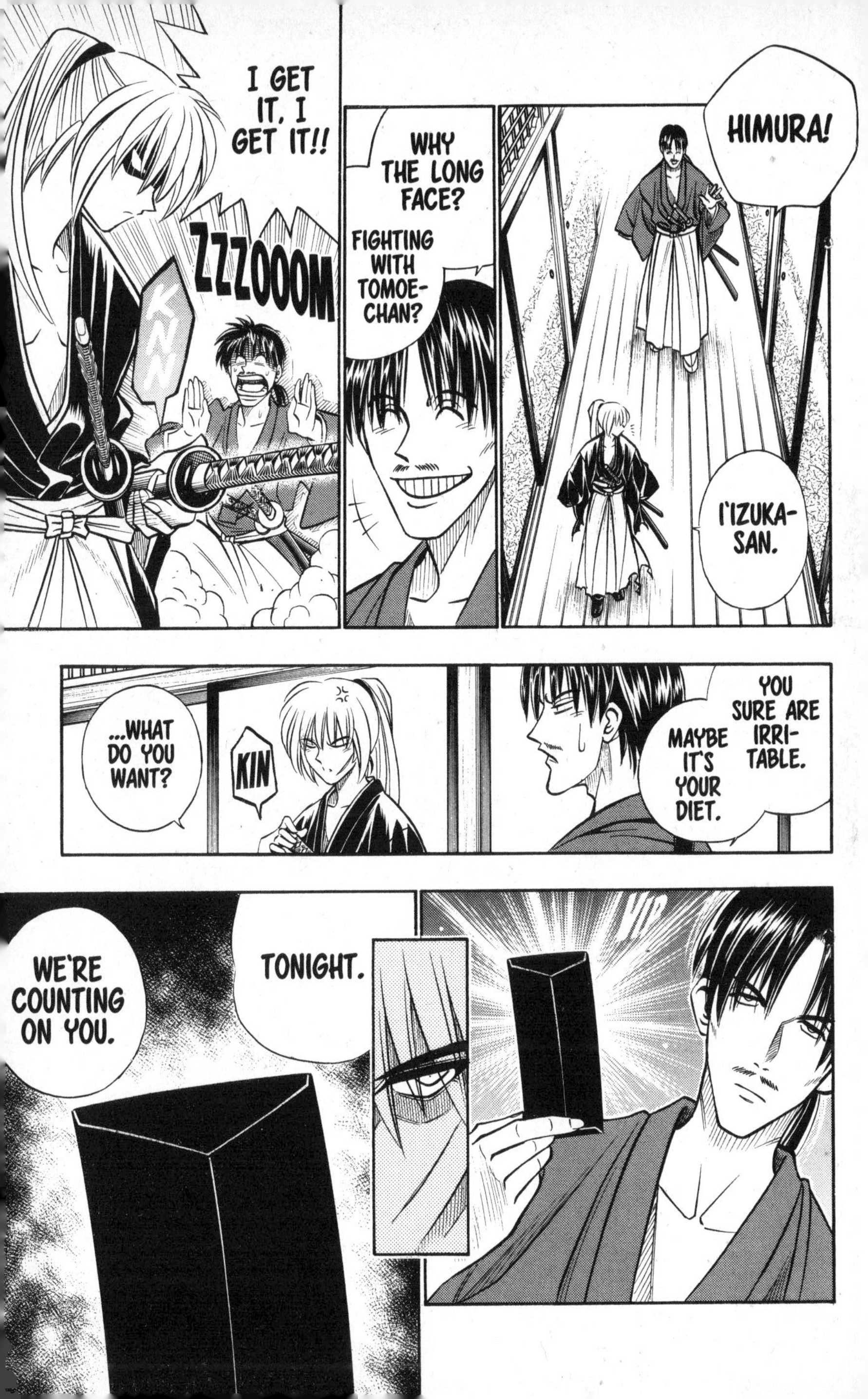
HIMURA!
I'IZUKA-SAN.
WHY THE LONG FACE?
FIGHTING WITH TOMOE-CHAN?
I GET IT, I GET IT!!
ZZZOOOM
YOU SURE ARE IRRI-TABLE.
MAYBE IT'S YOUR DIET.
KIN
...WHAT DO YOU WANT?
TONIGHT.
WE'RE COUNTING ON YOU.

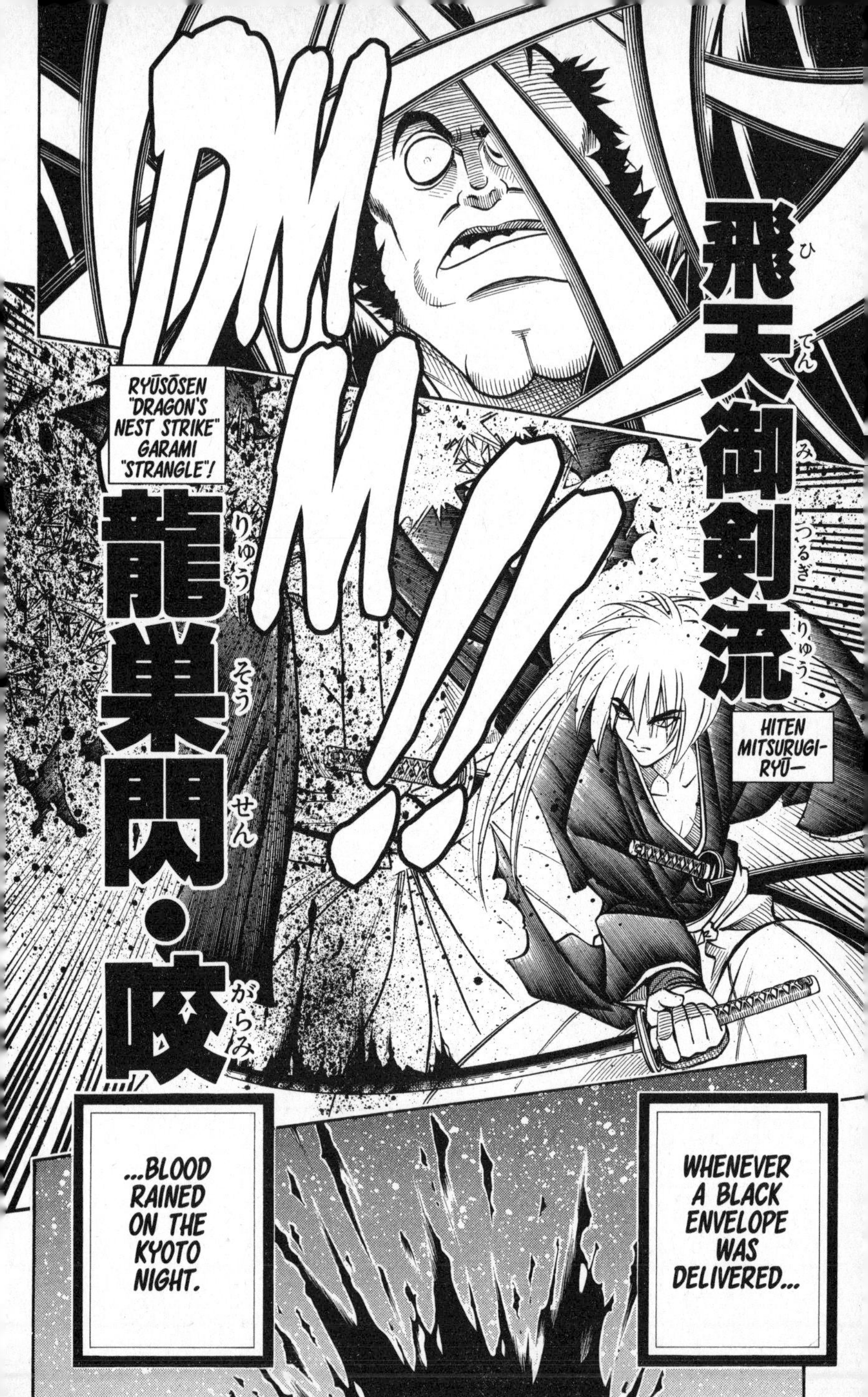
飛天御剣流
HITEN MITSURUGI-RYŪ—
RYŪSŌSEN "DRAGON'S NEST STRIKE" GARAMI "STRANGLE"!
龍巣閃・咬
WHENEVER A BLACK ENVELOPE WAS DELIVERED...
...BLOOD RAINED ON THE KYOTO NIGHT.

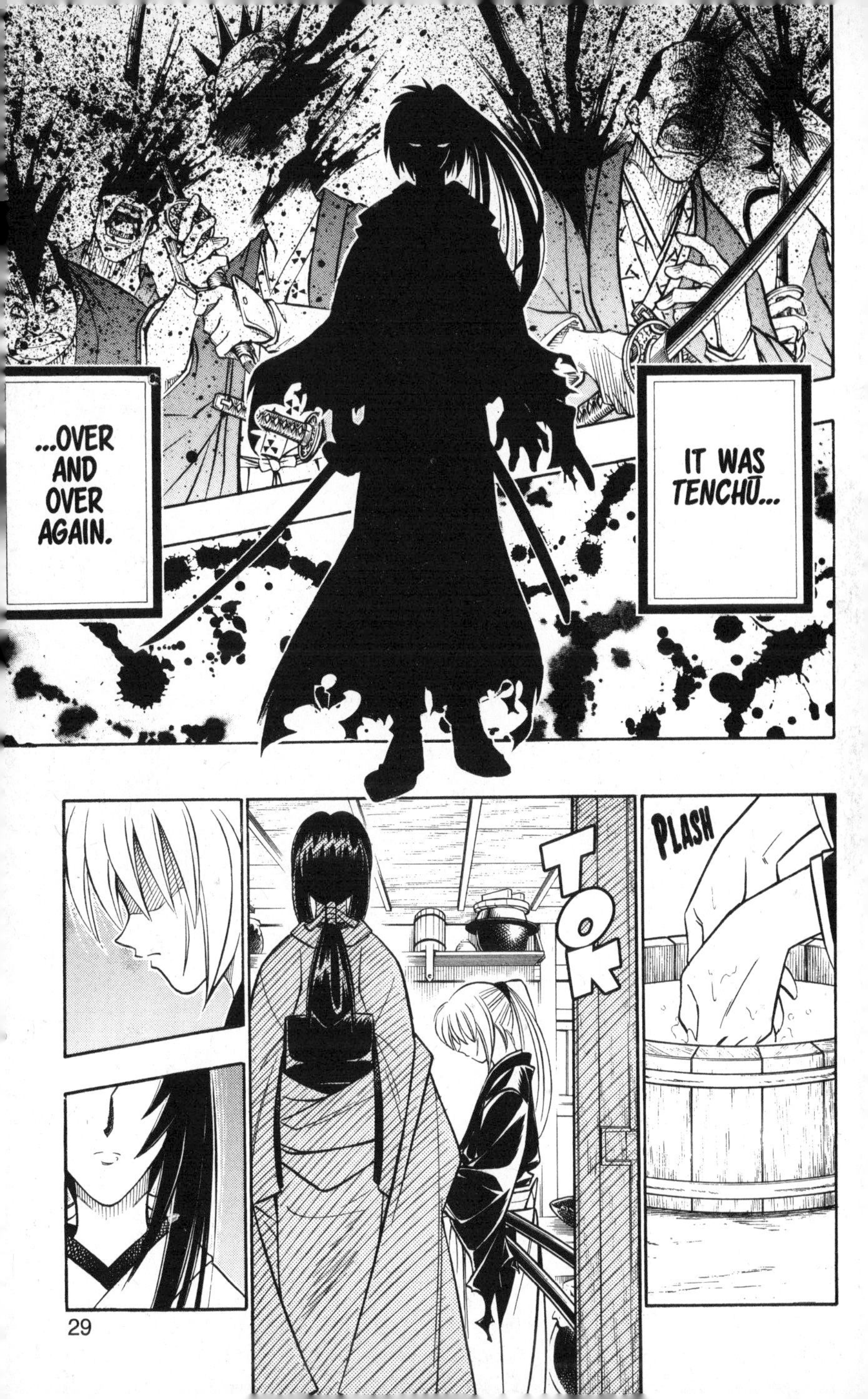
IT WAS TENCHŪ...
...OVER AND OVER AGAIN.
PLASH
TOK

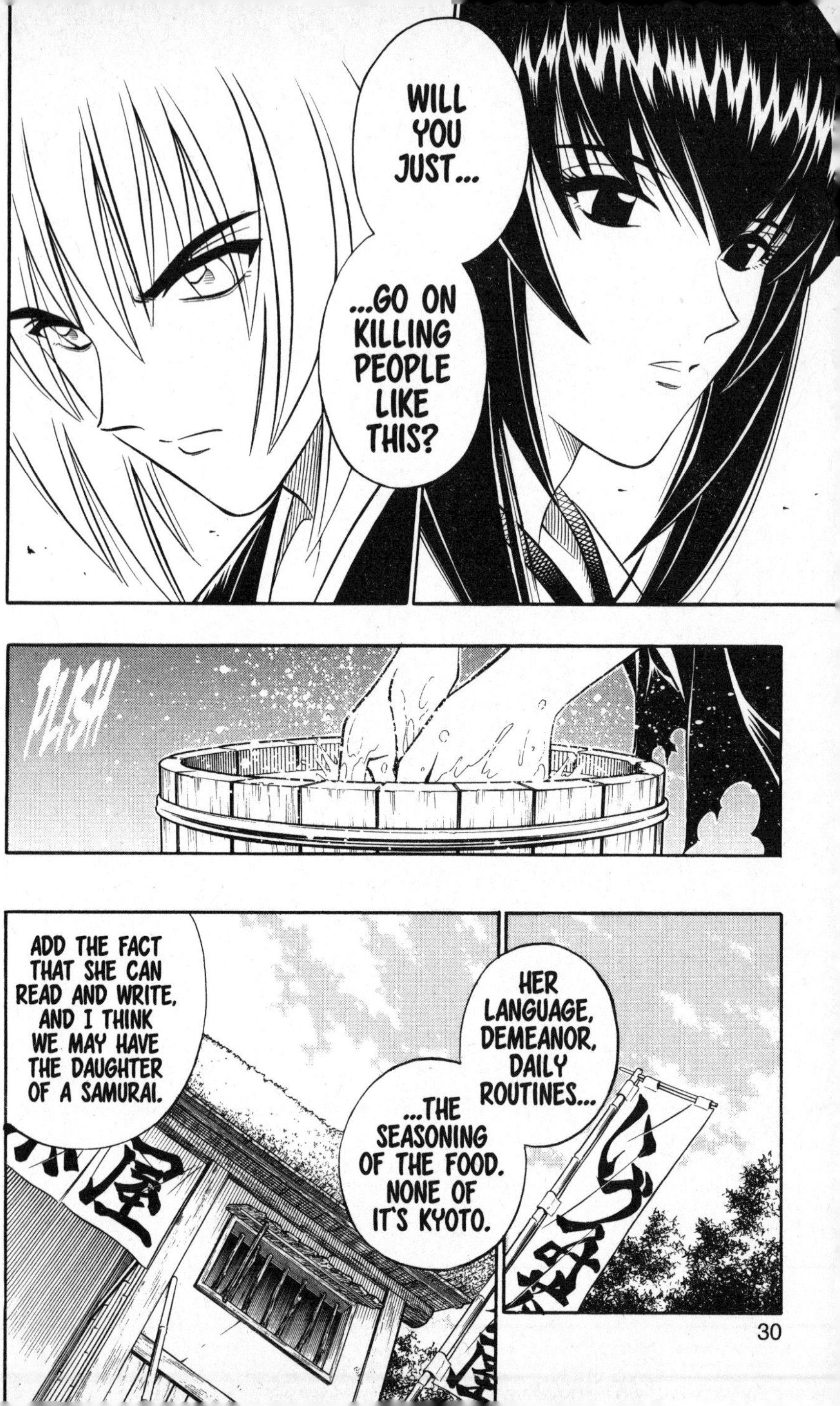
WILL YOU JUST...
...GO ON KILLING PEOPLE LIKE THIS?
HER LANGUAGE, DEMEANOR, DAILY ROUTINES...
...THE SEASONING OF THE FOOD. NONE OF IT'S KYOTO.
ADD THE FACT THAT SHE CAN READ AND WRITE, AND I THINK WE MAY HAVE THE DAUGHTER OF A SAMURAI.

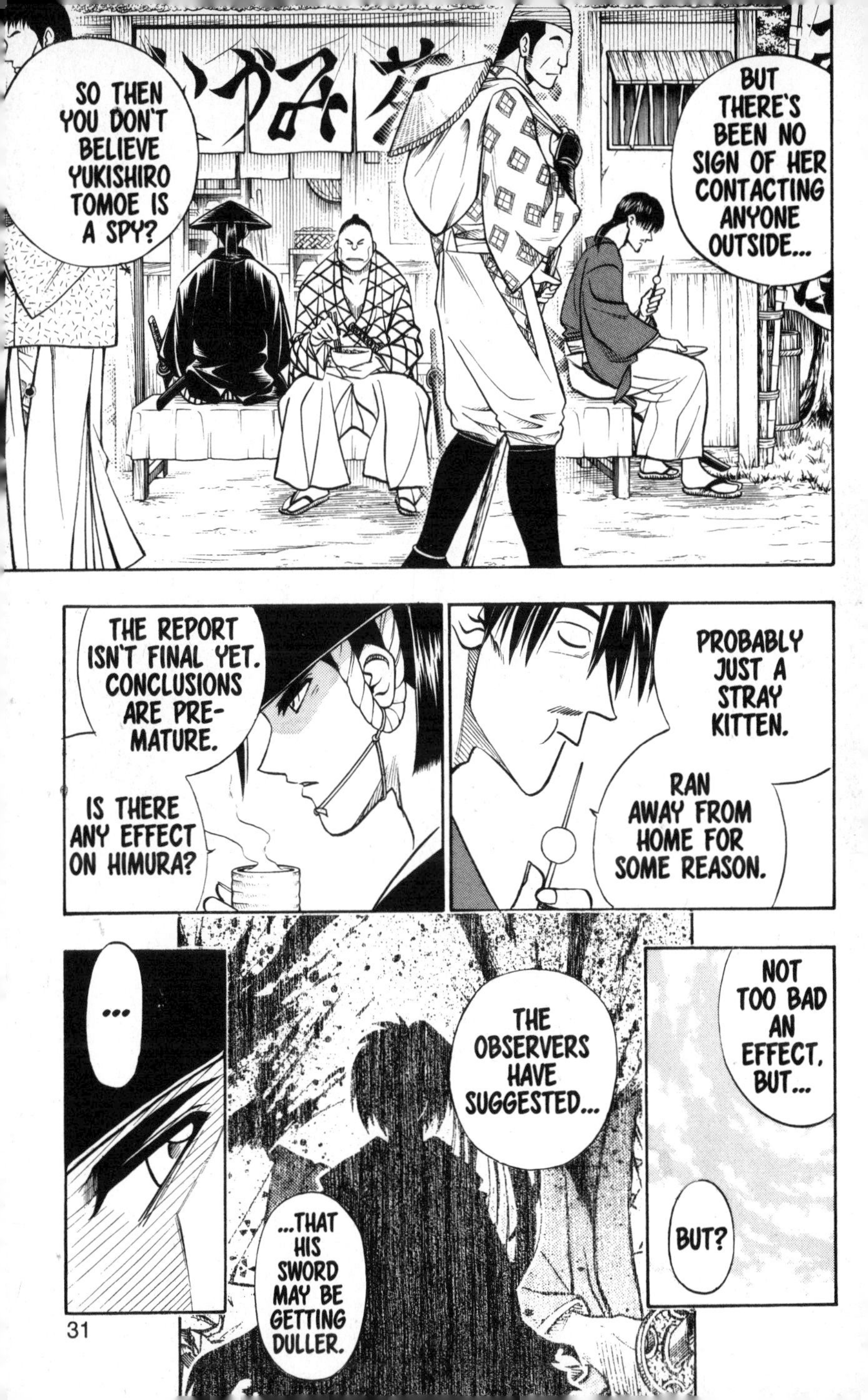
BUT THERE'S BEEN NO SIGN OF HER CONTACTING ANYONE OUTSIDE...
SO THEN YOU DON'T BELIEVE YUKISHIRO TOMOE IS A SPY?
PROBABLY JUST A STRAY KITTEN.
RAN AWAY FROM HOME FOR SOME REASON.
THE REPORT ISN'T FINAL YET. CONCLUSIONS ARE PRE-MATURE.
IS THERE ANY EFFECT ON HIMURA?
NOT TOO BAD AN EFFECT, BUT...
BUT?
THE OBSERVERS HAVE SUGGESTED...
...THAT HIS SWORD MAY BE GETTING DULLER.
...

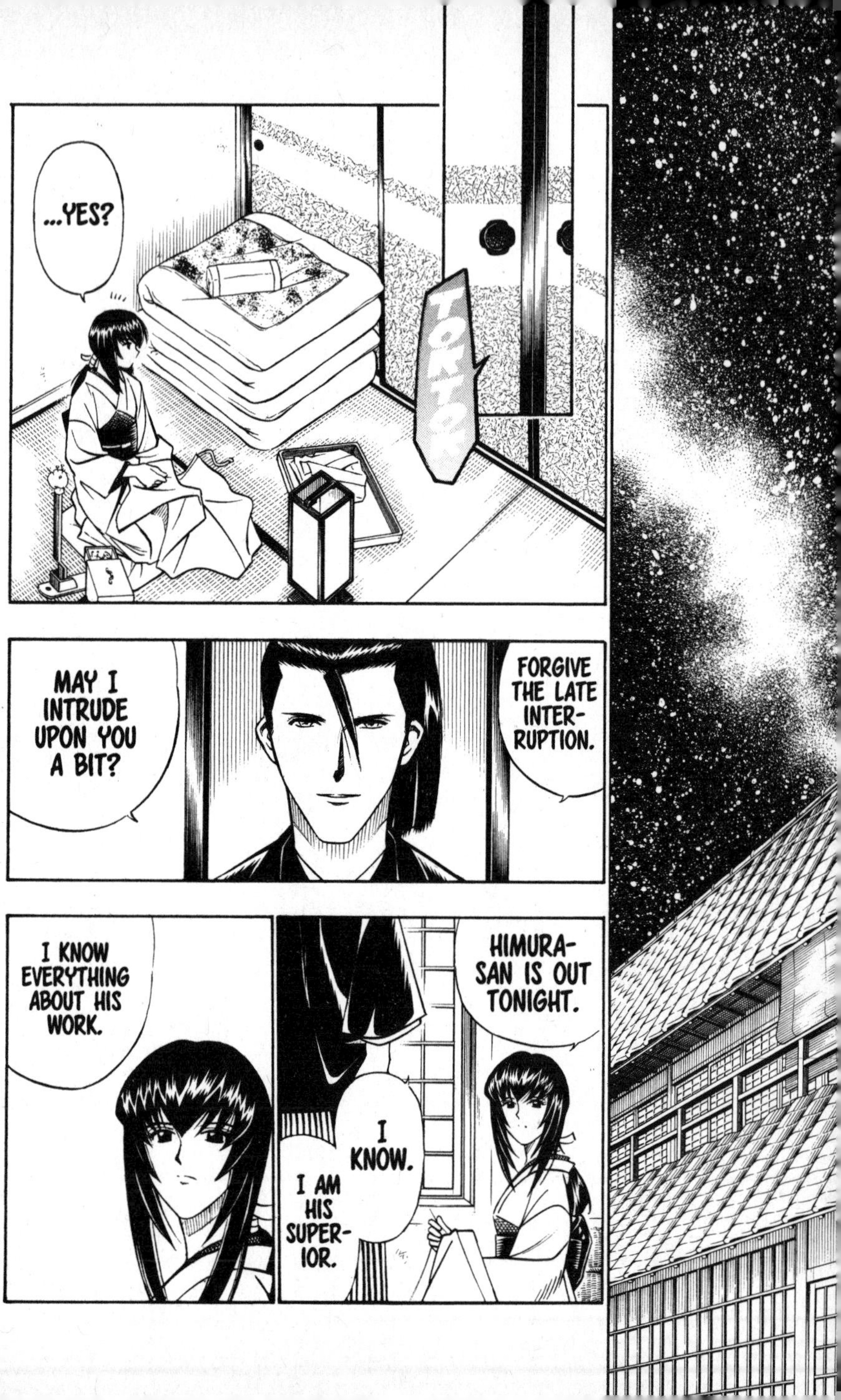
TOKTOK
...YES?
FORGIVE THE LATE INTER-RUPTION.
MAY I INTRUDE UPON YOU A BIT?
HIMURA-SAN IS OUT TONIGHT.
I KNOW.
I AM HIS SUPER-IOR.
I KNOW EVERYTHING ABOUT HIS WORK.

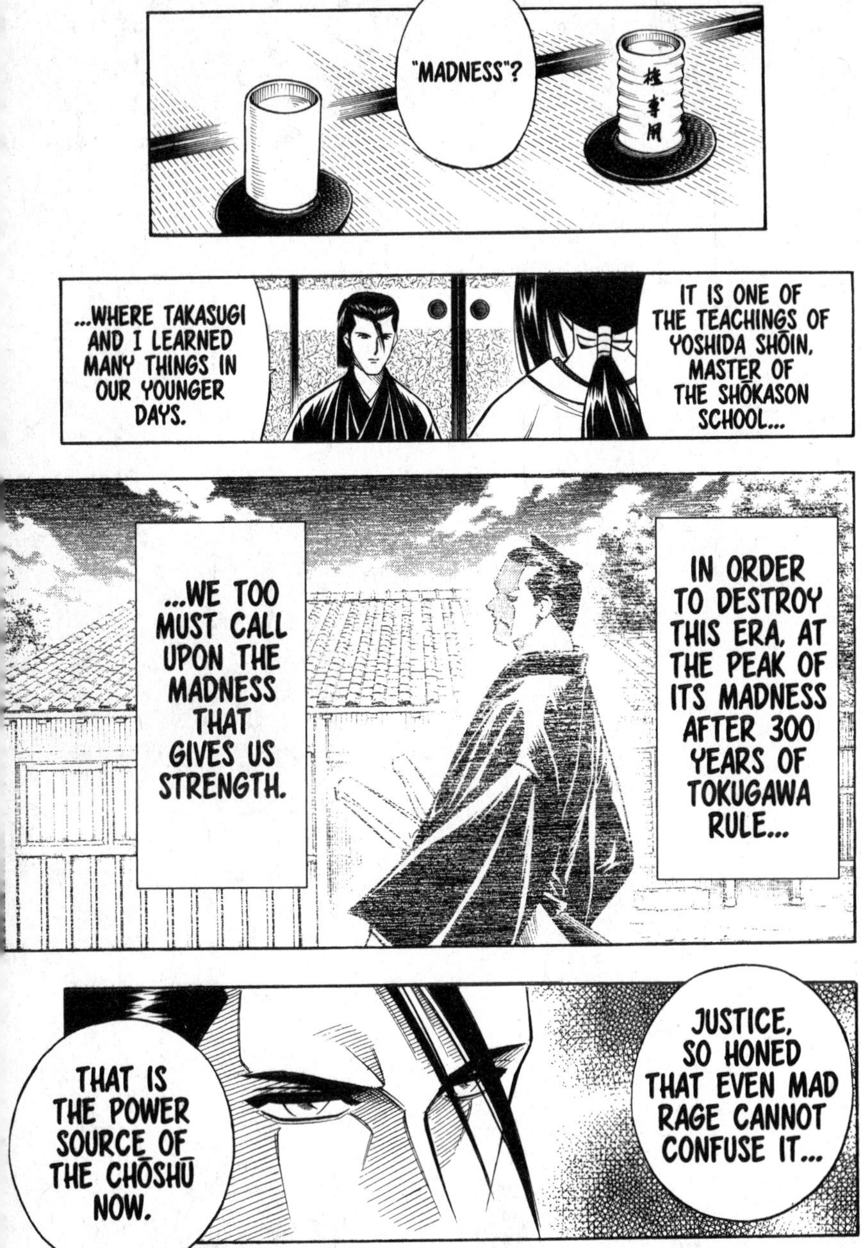
"MADNESS"?
IT IS ONE OF THE TEACHINGS OF YOSHIDA SHŌIN, MASTER OF THE SHŌKASON SCHOOL...
...WHERE TAKASUGI AND I LEARNED MANY THINGS IN OUR YOUNGER DAYS.
IN ORDER TO DESTROY THIS ERA, AT THE PEAK OF ITS MADNESS AFTER 300 YEARS OF TOKUGAWA RULE...
...WE TOO MUST CALL UPON THE MADNESS THAT GIVES US STRENGTH.
JUSTICE, SO HONED THAT EVEN MAD RAGE CANNOT CONFUSE IT...
THAT IS THE POWER SOURCE OF THE CHŌSHŪ NOW.

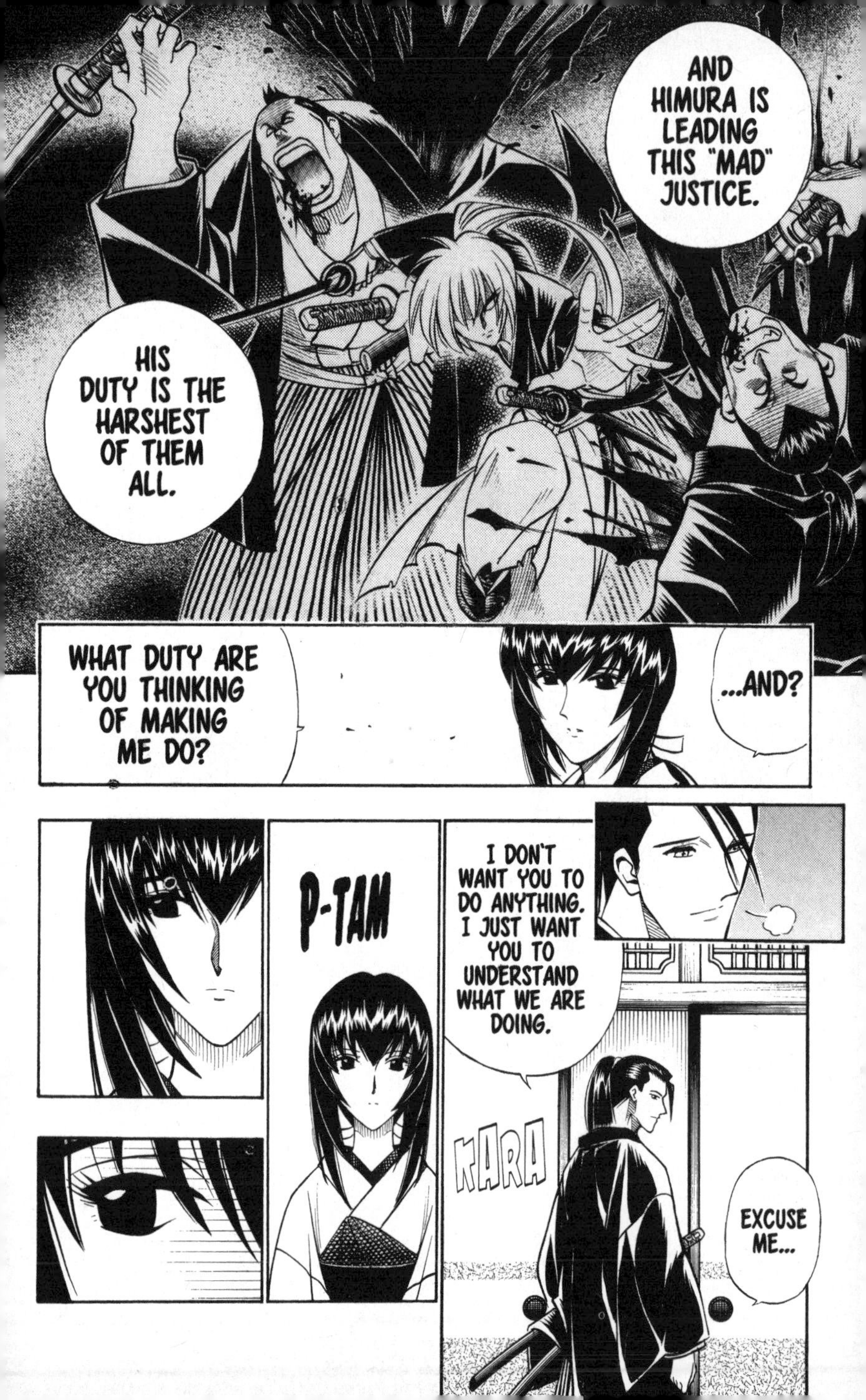
AND HIMURA IS LEADING THIS "MAD" JUSTICE.
HIS DUTY IS THE HARSHEST OF THEM ALL.
...AND?
WHAT DUTY ARE YOU THINKING OF MAKING ME DO?
I DON'T WANT YOU TO DO ANYTHING. I JUST WANT YOU TO UNDERSTAND WHAT WE ARE DOING.
KARA
EXCUSE ME...
P-TAM

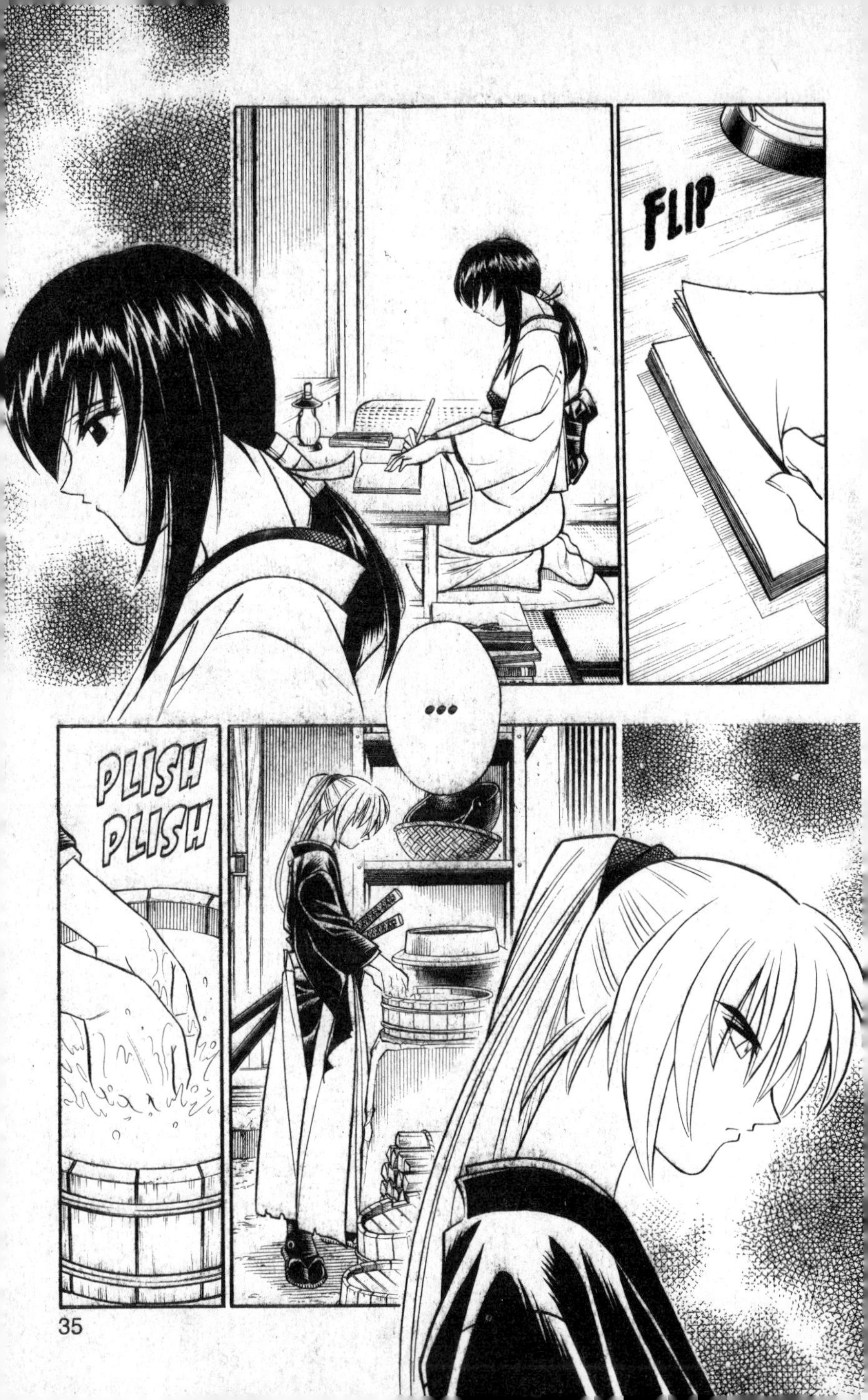
FLIP
...
PLISH PLISH

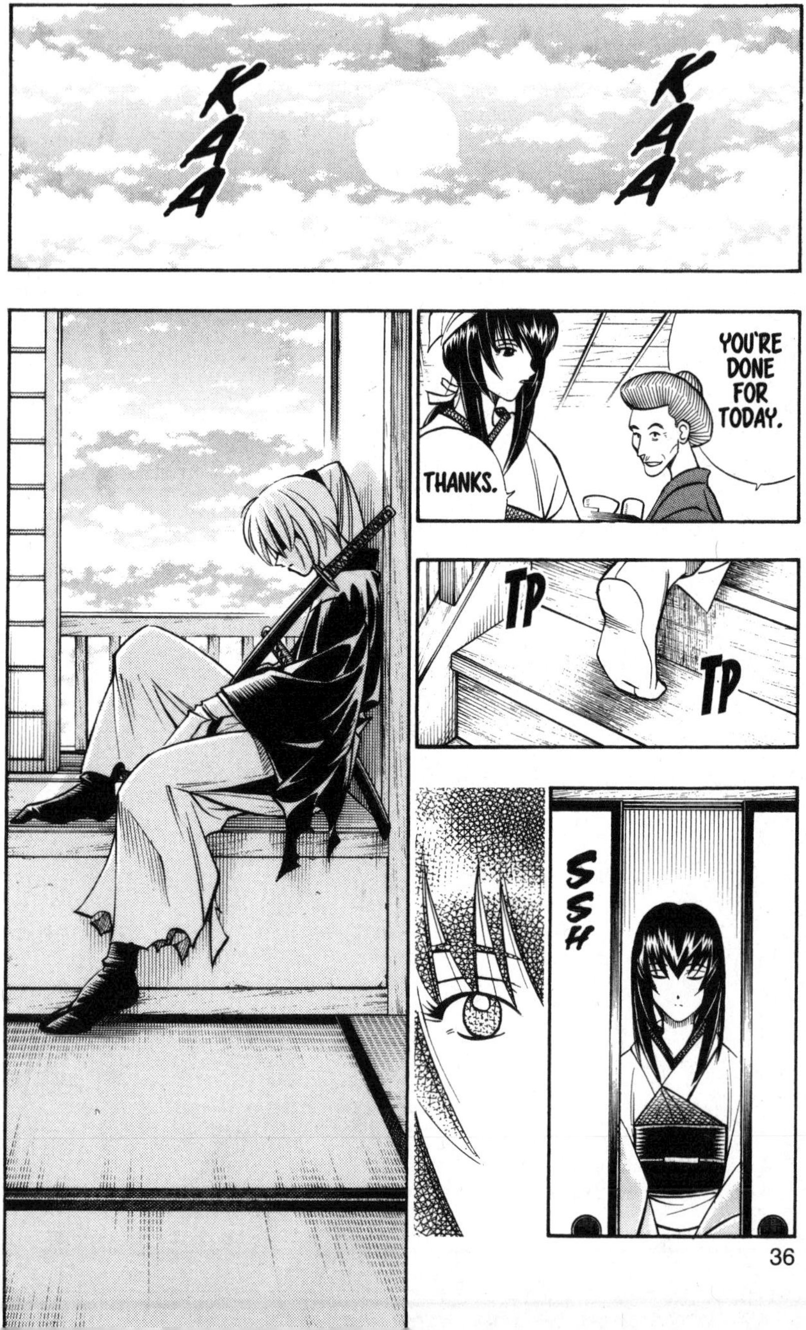
KAAA
KAAA
YOU'RE DONE FOR TODAY.
THANKS.
TP
TP
SSH

READ THIS WAY

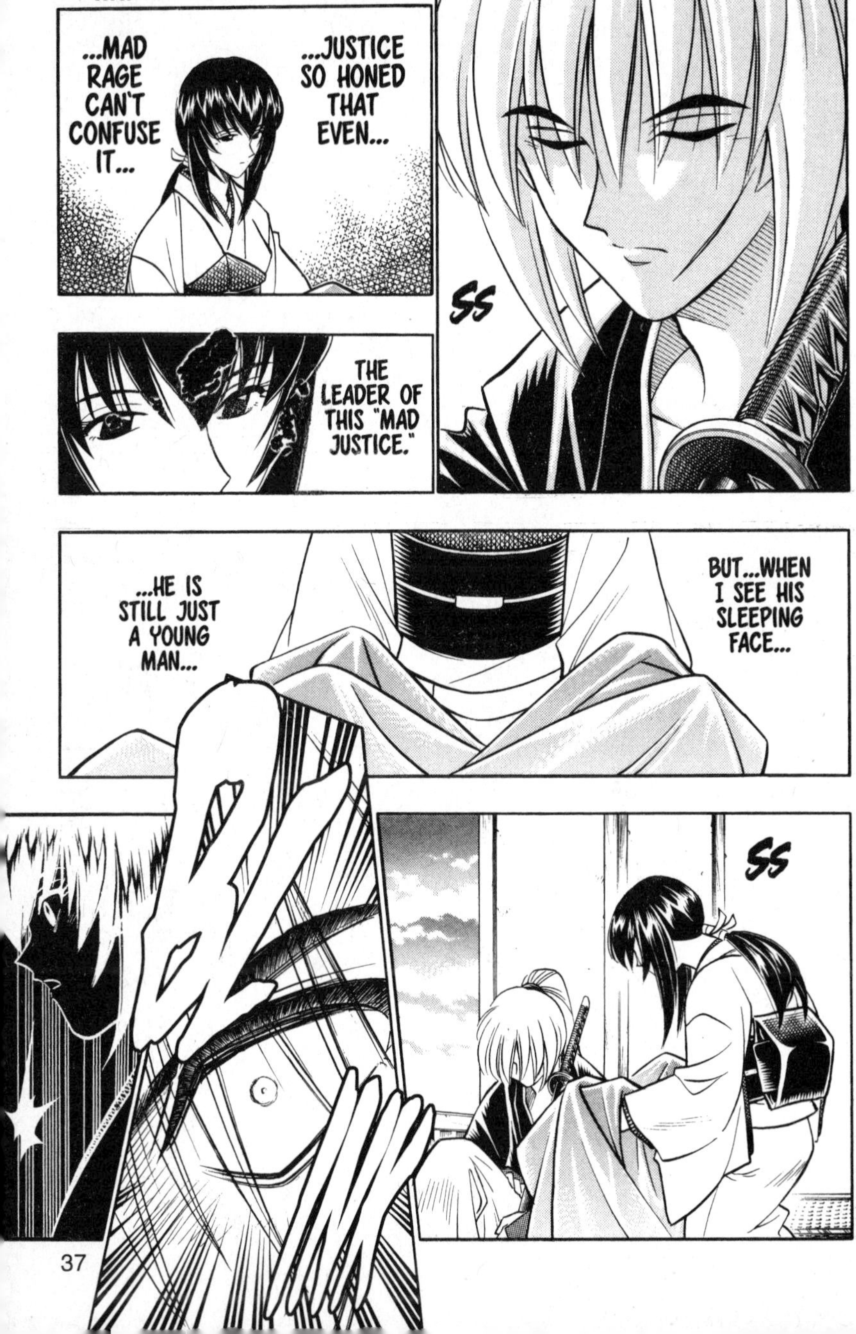
SS
...JUSTICE SO HONED THAT EVEN...
...MAD RAGE CAN'T CONFUSE IT...
THE LEADER OF THIS "MAD JUSTICE."
BUT...WHEN I SEE HIS SLEEPING FACE...
...HE IS STILL JUST A YOUNG MAN...
SS

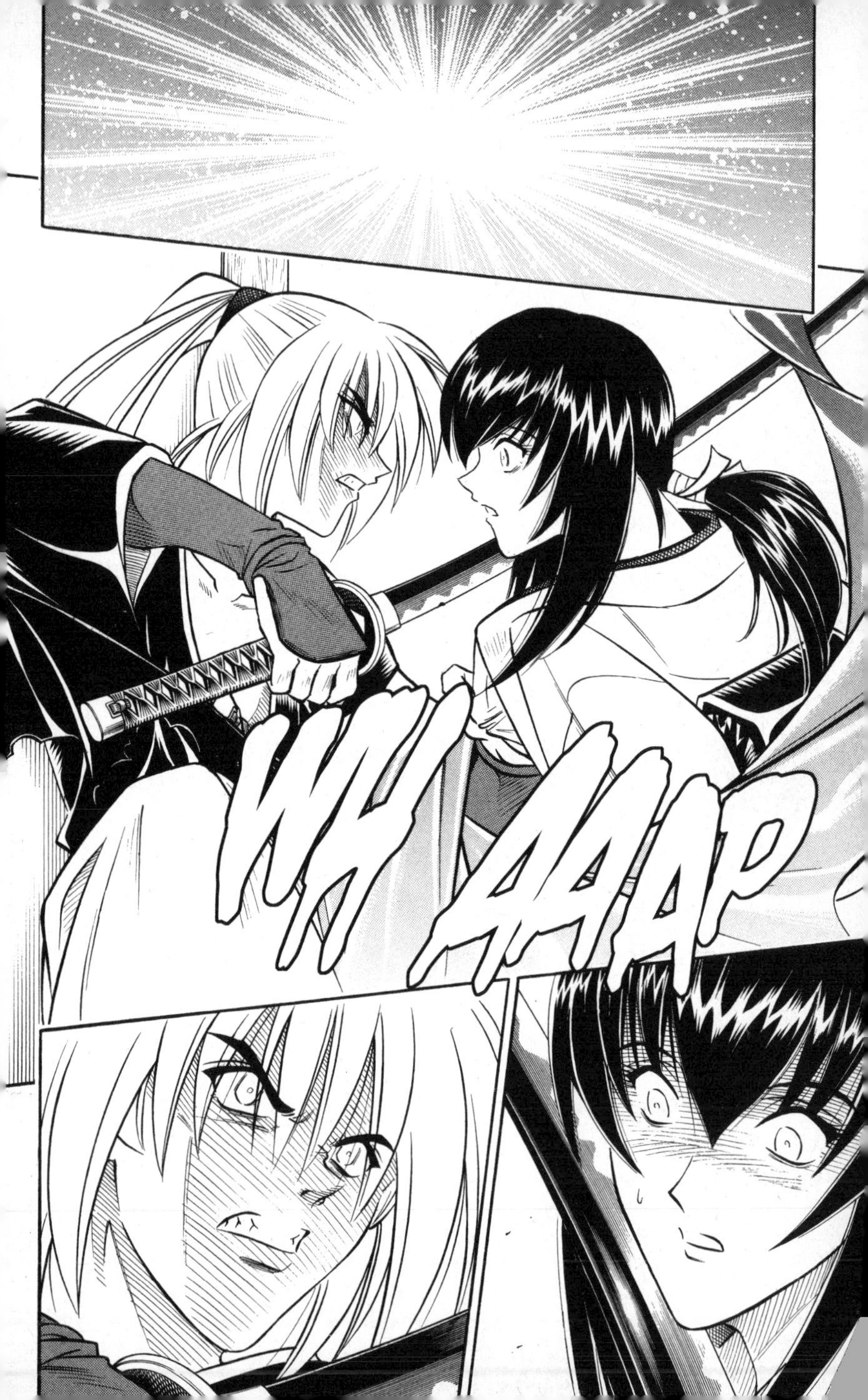
WHAAAP

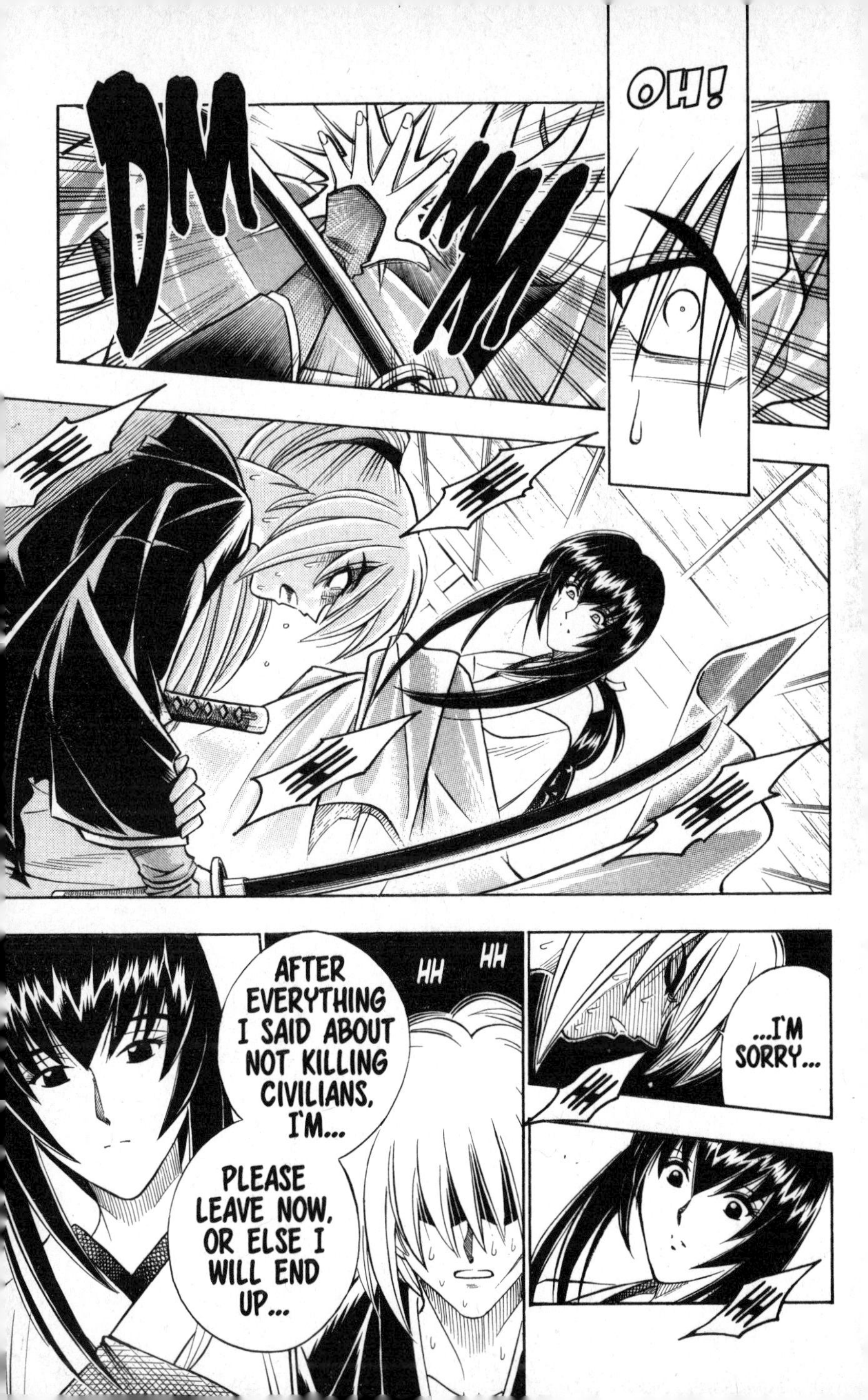

OH!
DM
MM
...I'M SORRY...
HH
HH
AFTER EVERYTHING I SAID ABOUT NOT KILLING CIVILIANS, I'M...
PLEASE LEAVE NOW, OR ELSE I WILL END UP...

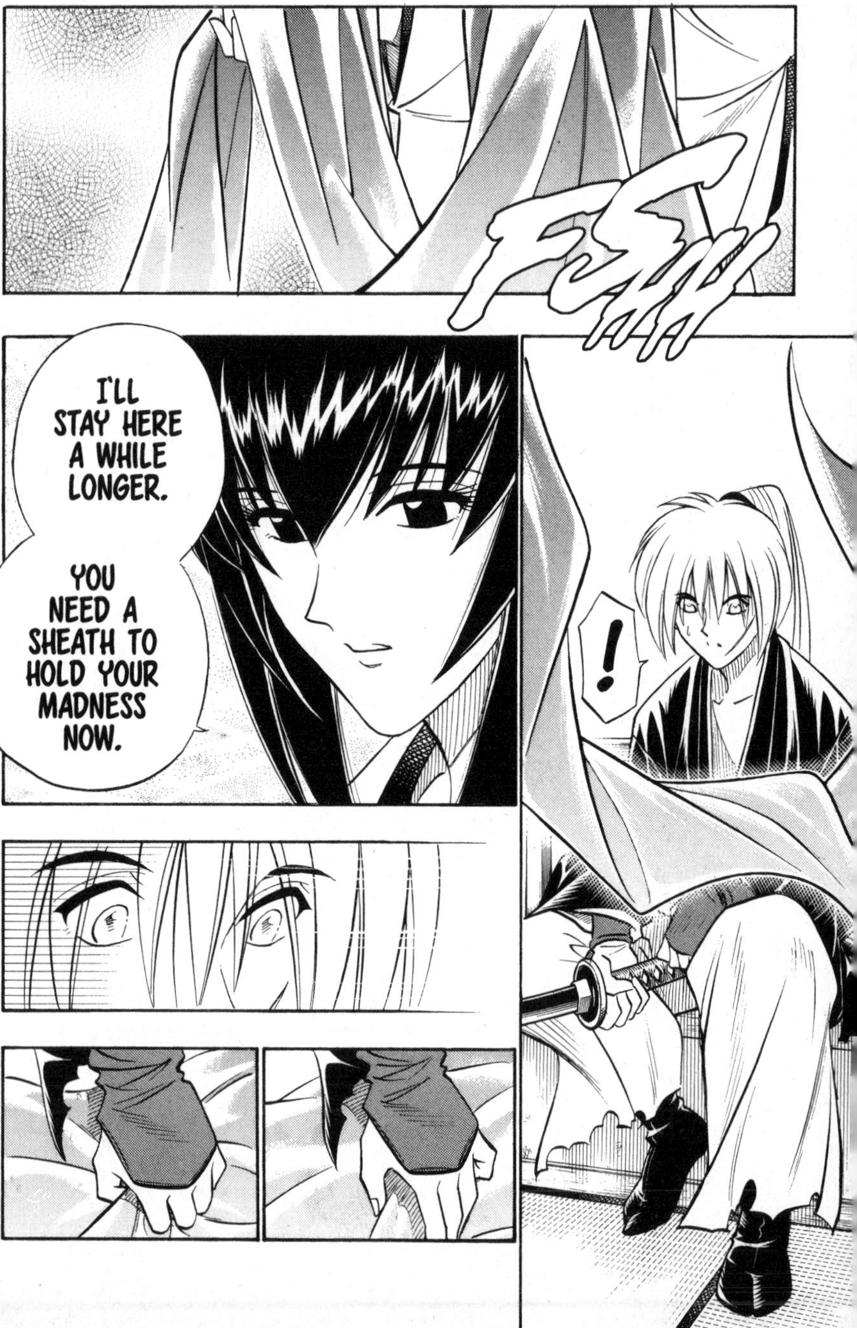
FSHH
!
I'LL STAY HERE A WHILE LONGER.
YOU NEED A SHEATH TO HOLD YOUR MADNESS NOW.

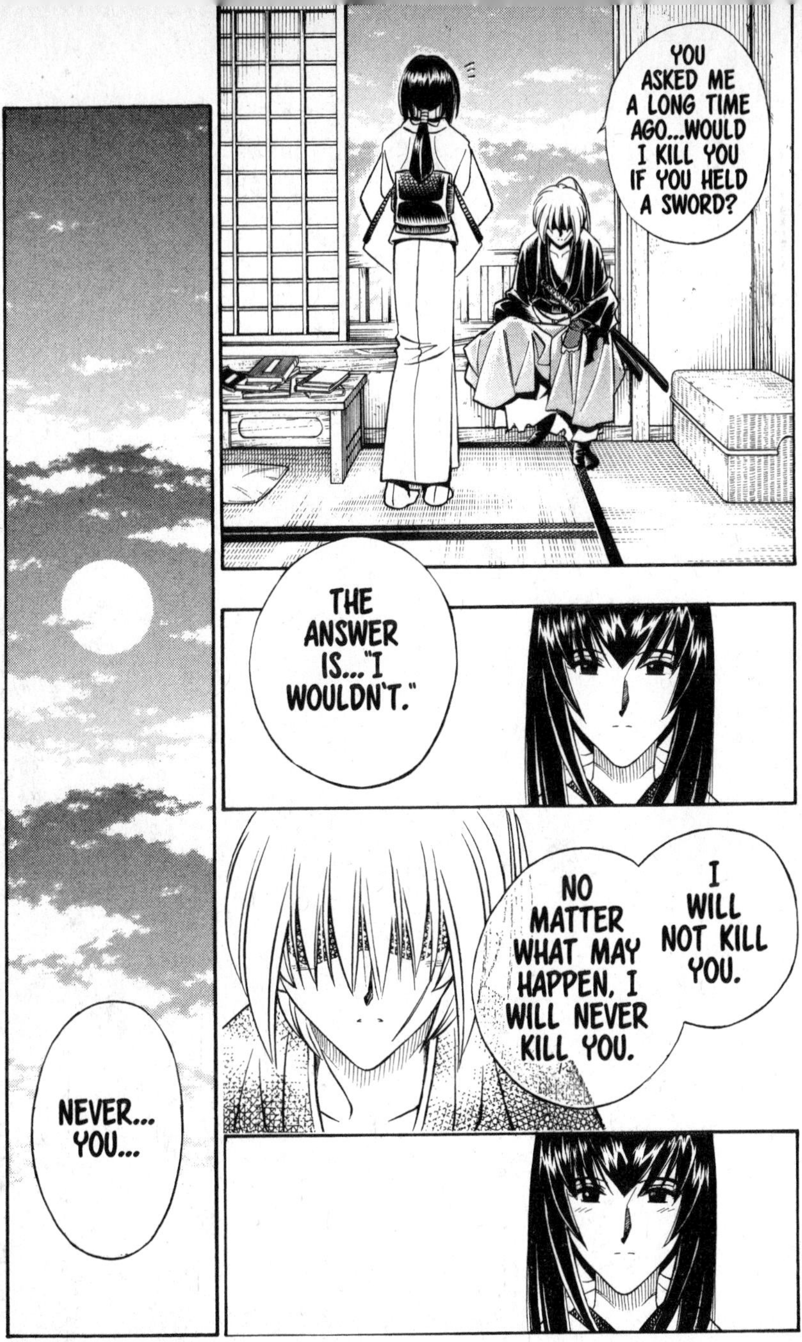
YOU ASKED ME A LONG TIME AGO...WOULD I KILL YOU IF YOU HELD A SWORD?
THE ANSWER IS..."I WOULDN'T."
I WILL NOT KILL YOU.
NO MATTER WHAT MAY HAPPEN, I WILL NEVER KILL YOU.
NEVER... YOU...

Rurouni Kenshin

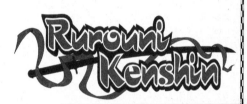

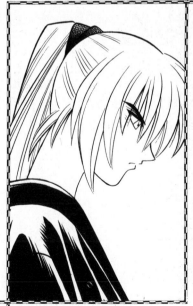

Act 170

Remembrance 6: Chaos: Genji

伸宏
和月

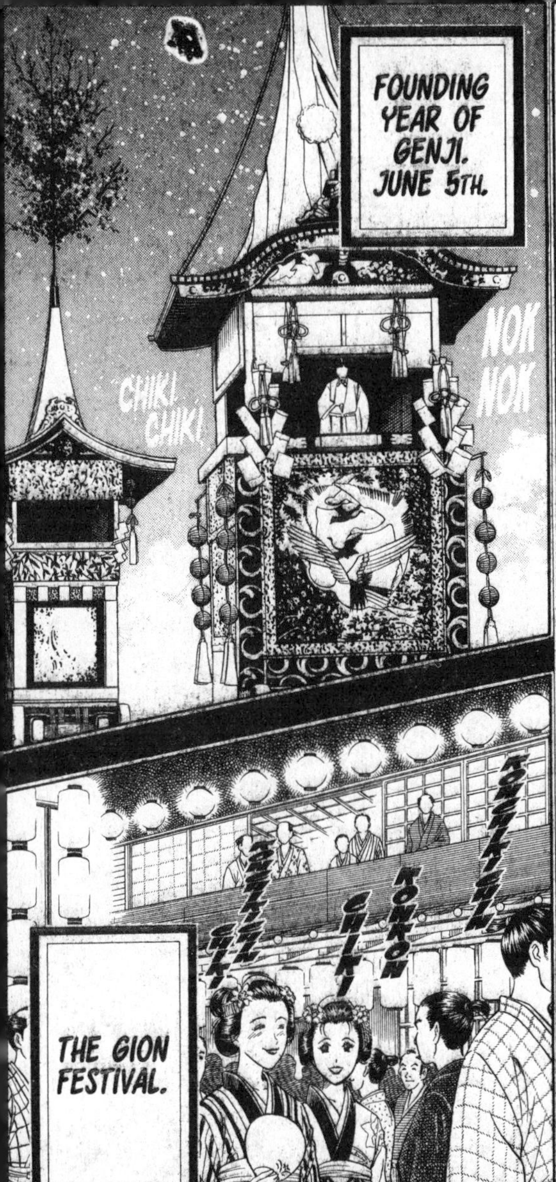
FOUNDING YEAR OF GENJI. JUNE 5TH.
NOK NOK
CHIKI CHIKI
KONCHIKICHIN
KONKON
CHIKI
KONCHIKICHIN
CHIKI
THE GION FESTIVAL.

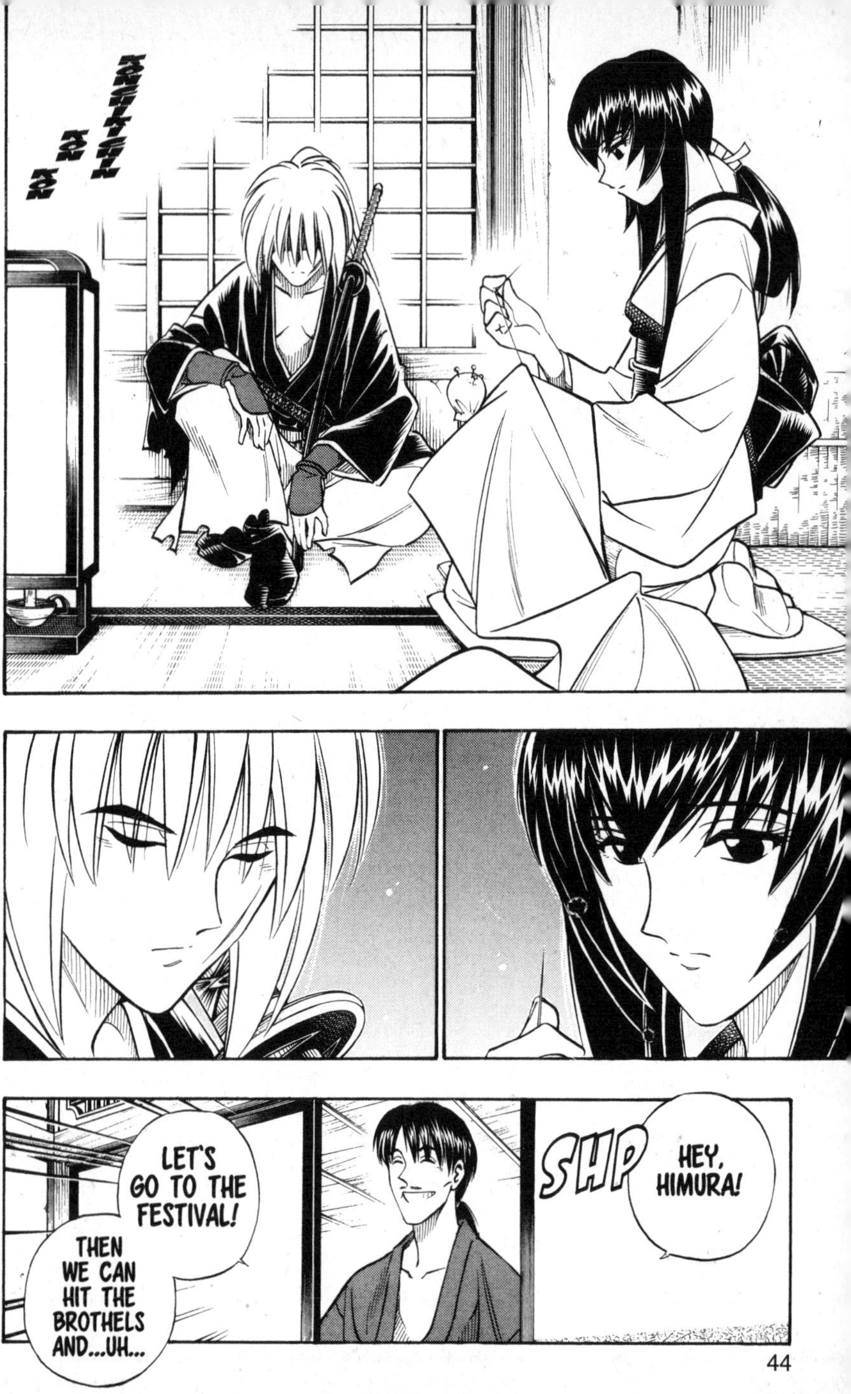
KONCHIKICHIN
KON KON
SHP
HEY, HIMURA!
LET'S GO TO THE FESTIVAL!
THEN WE CAN HIT THE BROTHELS AND...UH...

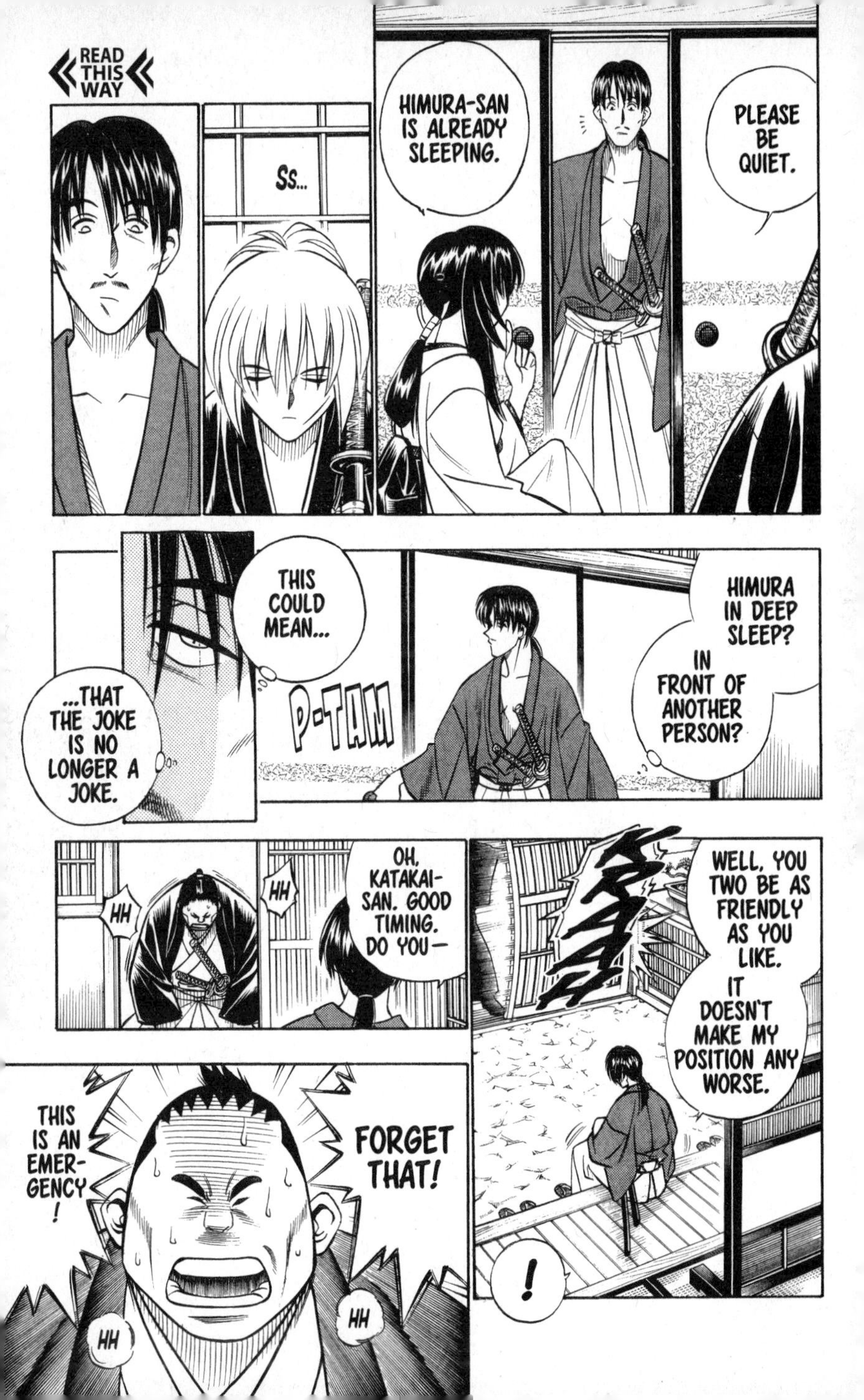
READ THIS WAY
PLEASE BE QUIET.
HIMURA-SAN IS ALREADY SLEEPING.
Ss...
HIMURA IN DEEP SLEEP?
IN FRONT OF ANOTHER PERSON?
P-TAM
THIS COULD MEAN...
...THAT THE JOKE IS NO LONGER A JOKE.
WELL, YOU TWO BE AS FRIENDLY AS YOU LIKE.
IT DOESN'T MAKE MY POSITION ANY WORSE.
!
OH, KATAKAI-SAN. GOOD TIMING. DO YOU—
HH
HH
FORGET THAT!
THIS IS AN EMERGENCY!
HH
HH

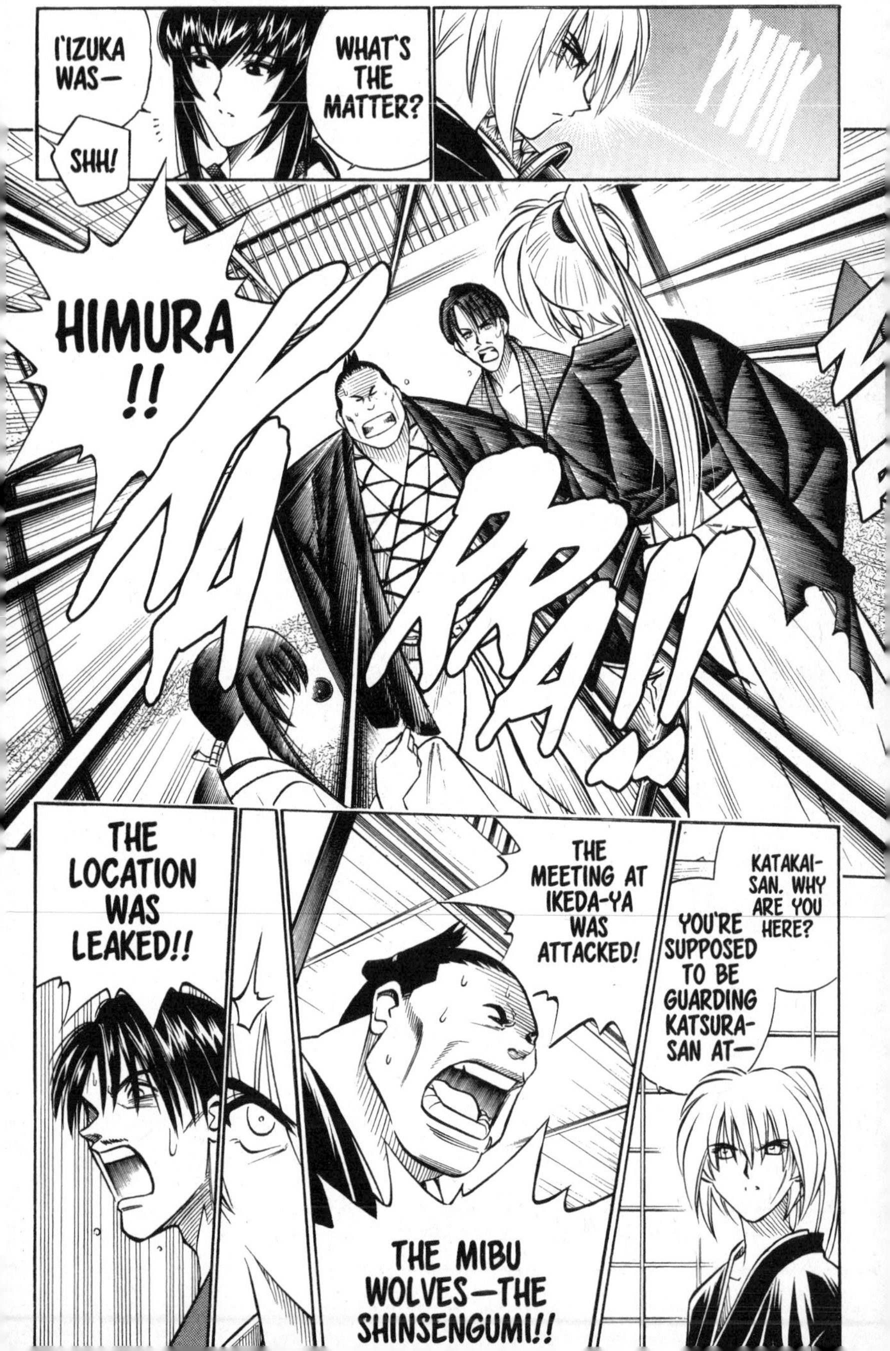
WHAT'S THE MATTER?
I'IZUKA WAS—
SHH!
HIMURA!!
KATAKAI-SAN. WHY ARE YOU HERE?
YOU'RE SUPPOSED TO BE GUARDING KATSURA-SAN AT—
THE MEETING AT IKEDA-YA WAS ATTACKED!
THE MIBU WOLVES—THE SHINSENGUMI!!
THE LOCATION WAS LEAKED!!

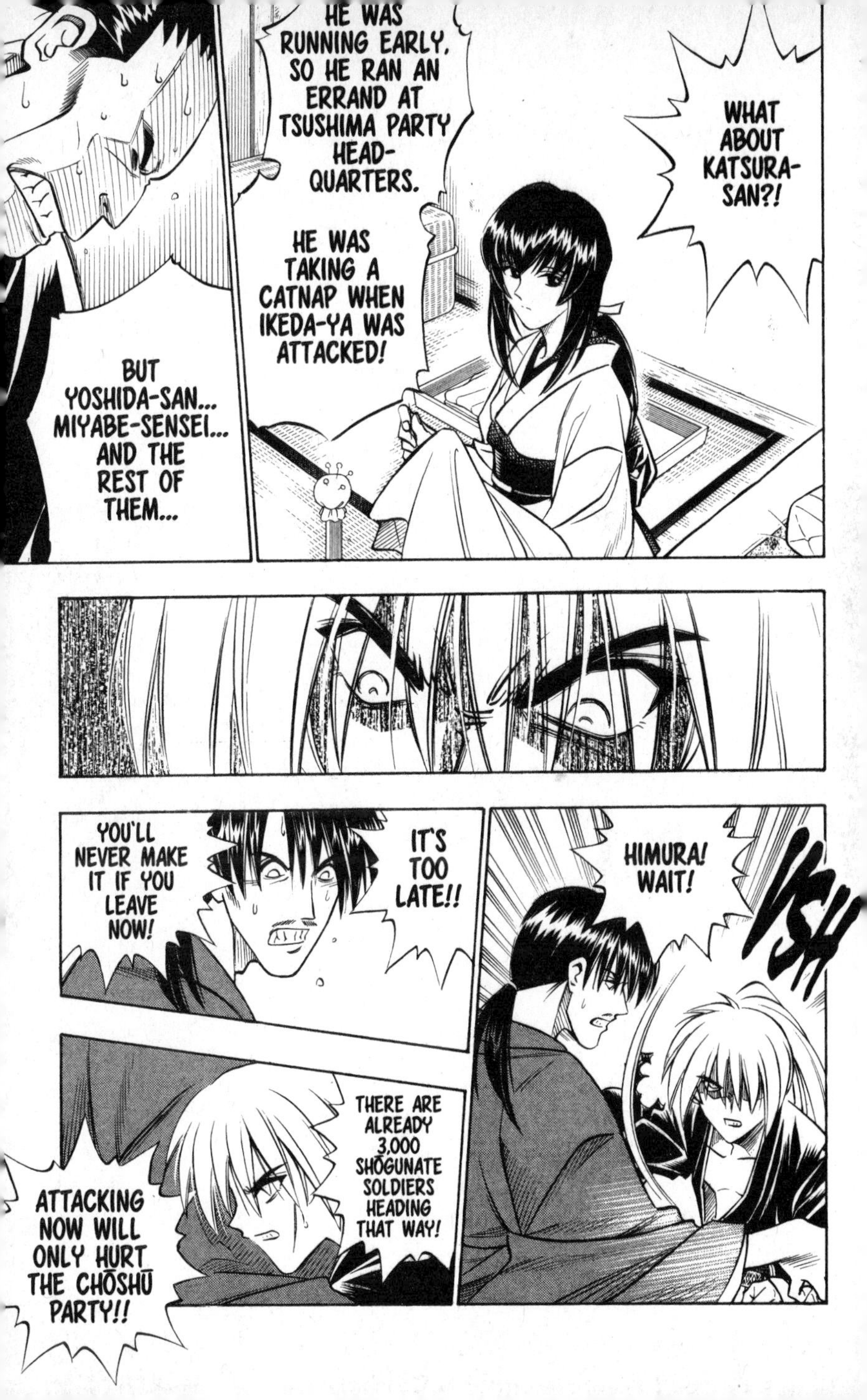
WHAT ABOUT KATSURA-SAN?!
HE WAS RUNNING EARLY, SO HE RAN AN ERRAND AT TSUSHIMA PARTY HEAD-QUARTERS.
HE WAS TAKING A CATNAP WHEN IKEDA-YA WAS ATTACKED!
BUT YOSHIDA-SAN... MIYABE-SENSEI... AND THE REST OF THEM...
HIMURA! WAIT!
VSH
IT'S TOO LATE!!
YOU'LL NEVER MAKE IT IF YOU LEAVE NOW!
THERE ARE ALREADY 3,000 SHŌGUNATE SOLDIERS HEADING THAT WAY!
ATTACKING NOW WILL ONLY HURT THE CHŌSHŪ PARTY!!

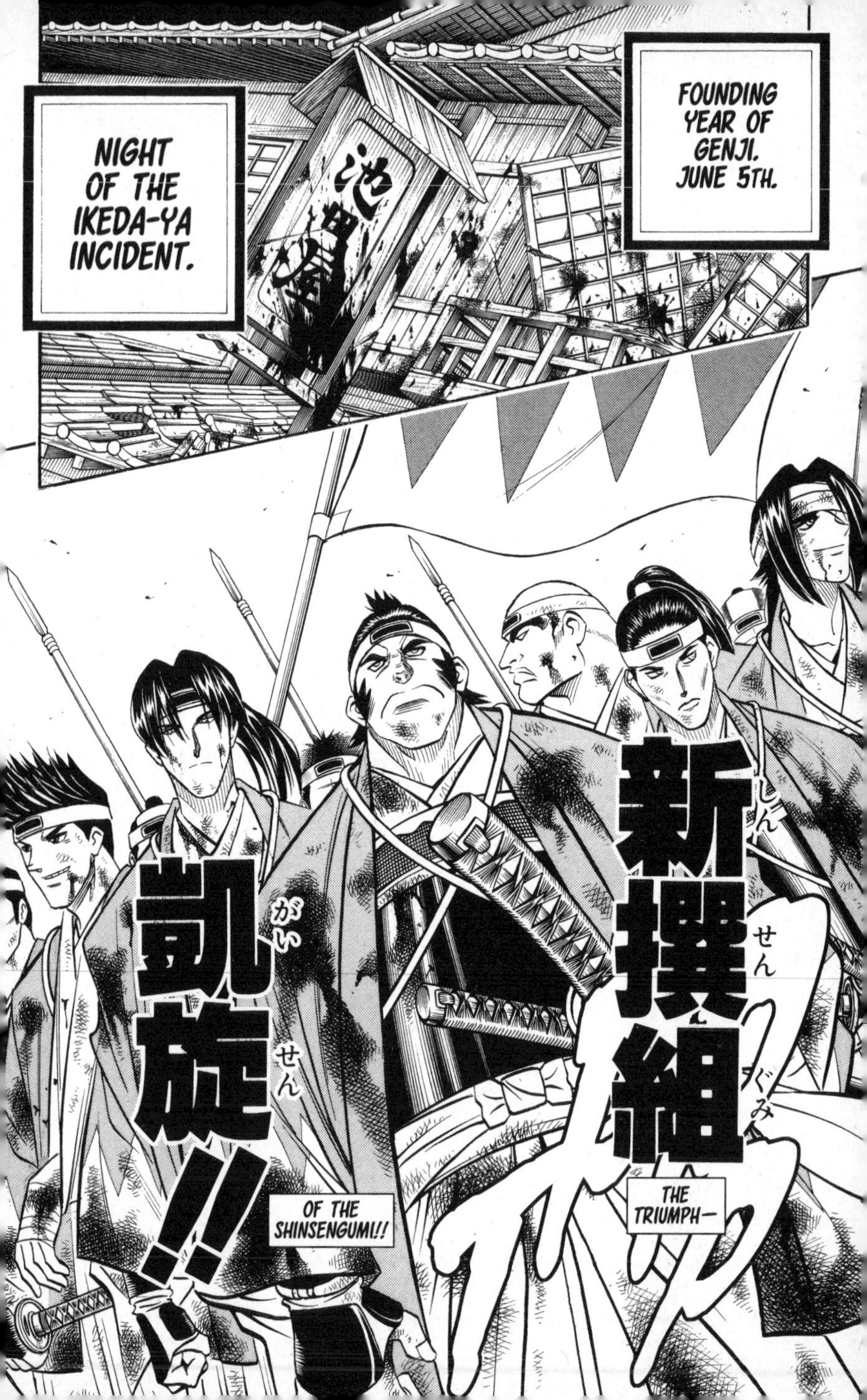
FOUNDING YEAR OF GENJI. JUNE 5TH.
池田屋
NIGHT OF THE IKEDA-YA INCIDENT.
新撰組
THE TRIUMPH—
凱旋!!
OF THE SHINSENGUMI!!

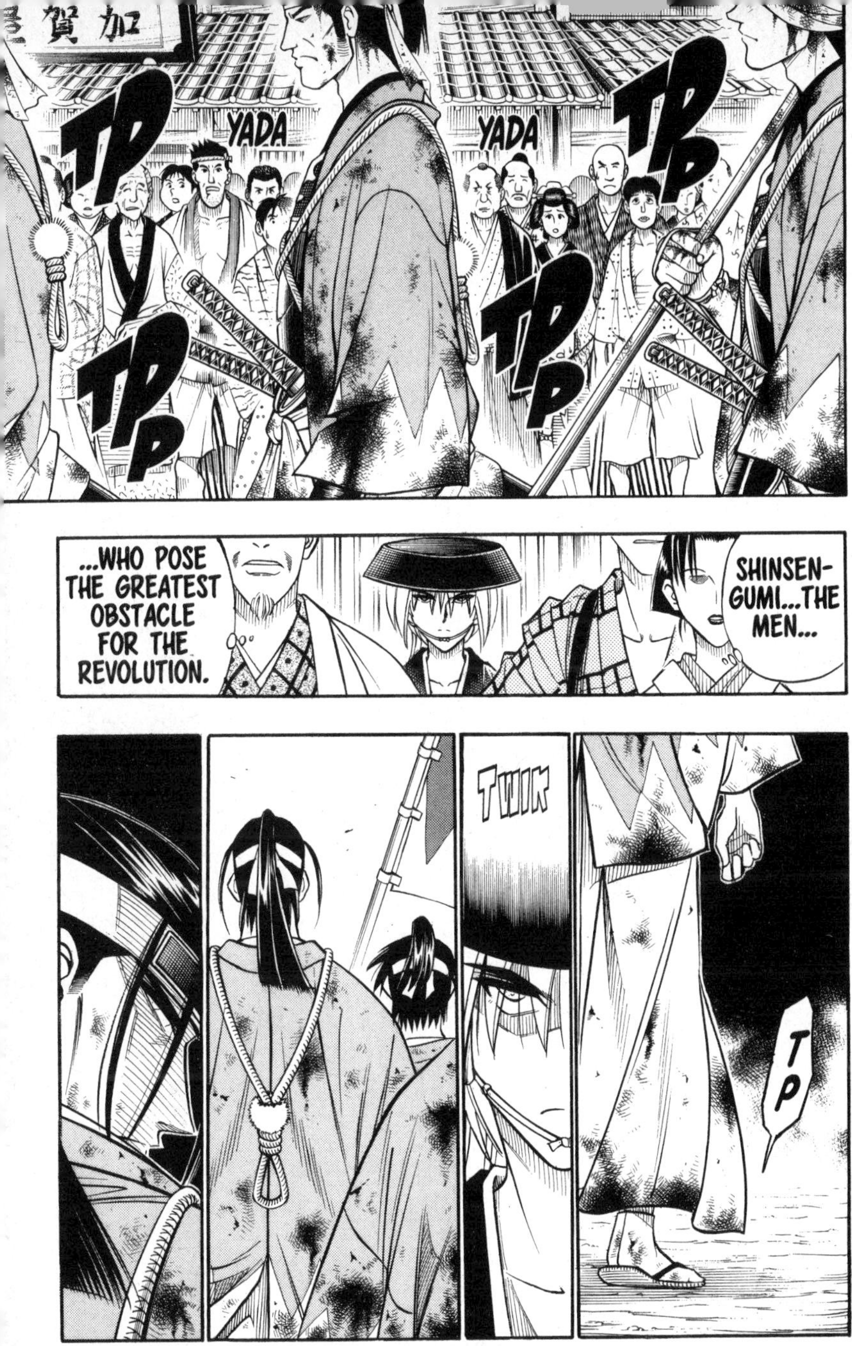
TPP
YADA
TPP
YADA
TP
TPP
SHINSEN-GUMI...THE MEN...
...WHO POSE THE GREATEST OBSTACLE FOR THE REVOLUTION.
TP
TWIK

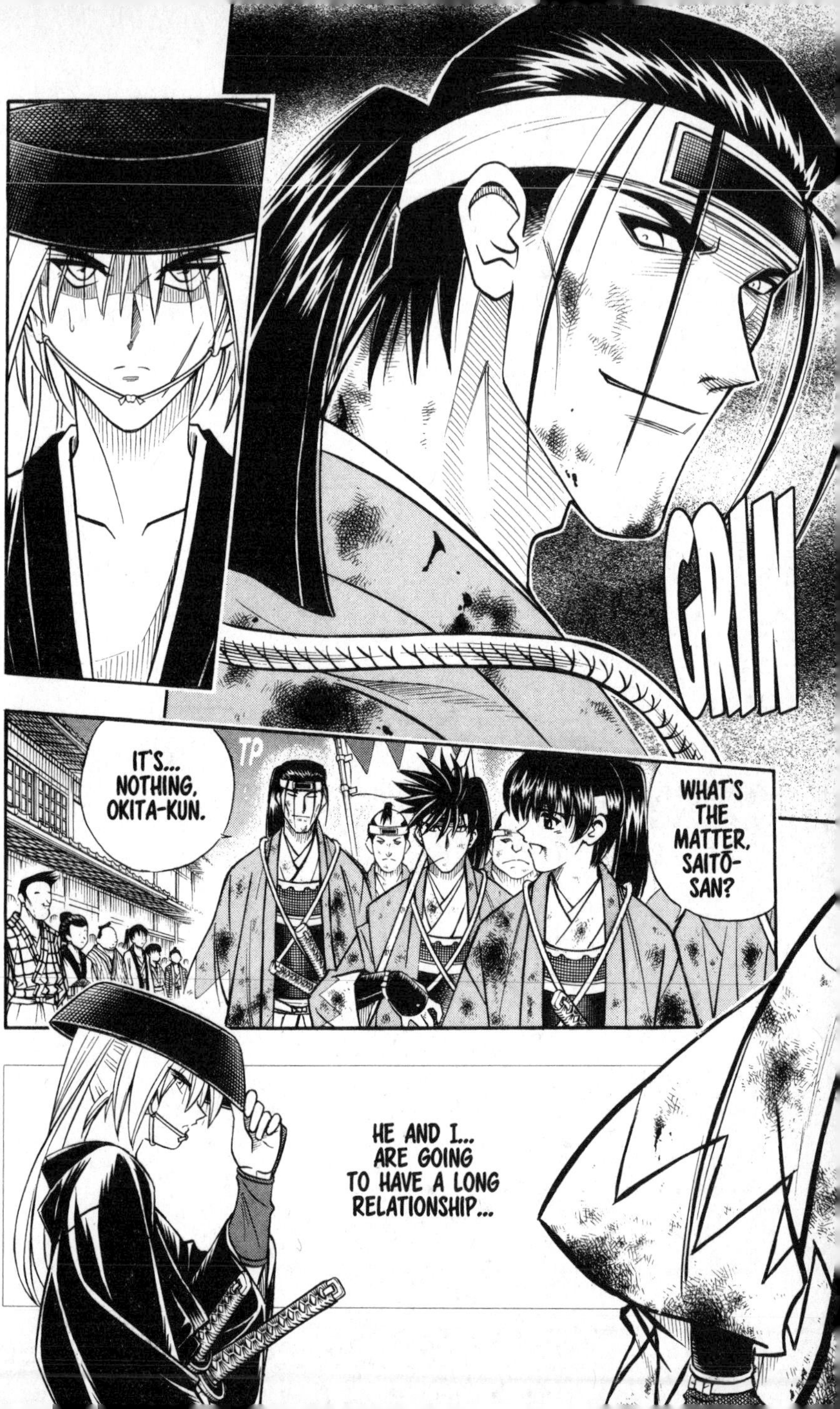
GRIN
WHAT'S THE MATTER, SAITŌ-SAN?
TP
IT'S... NOTHING, OKITA-KUN.
HE AND I... ARE GOING TO HAVE A LONG RELATIONSHIP...

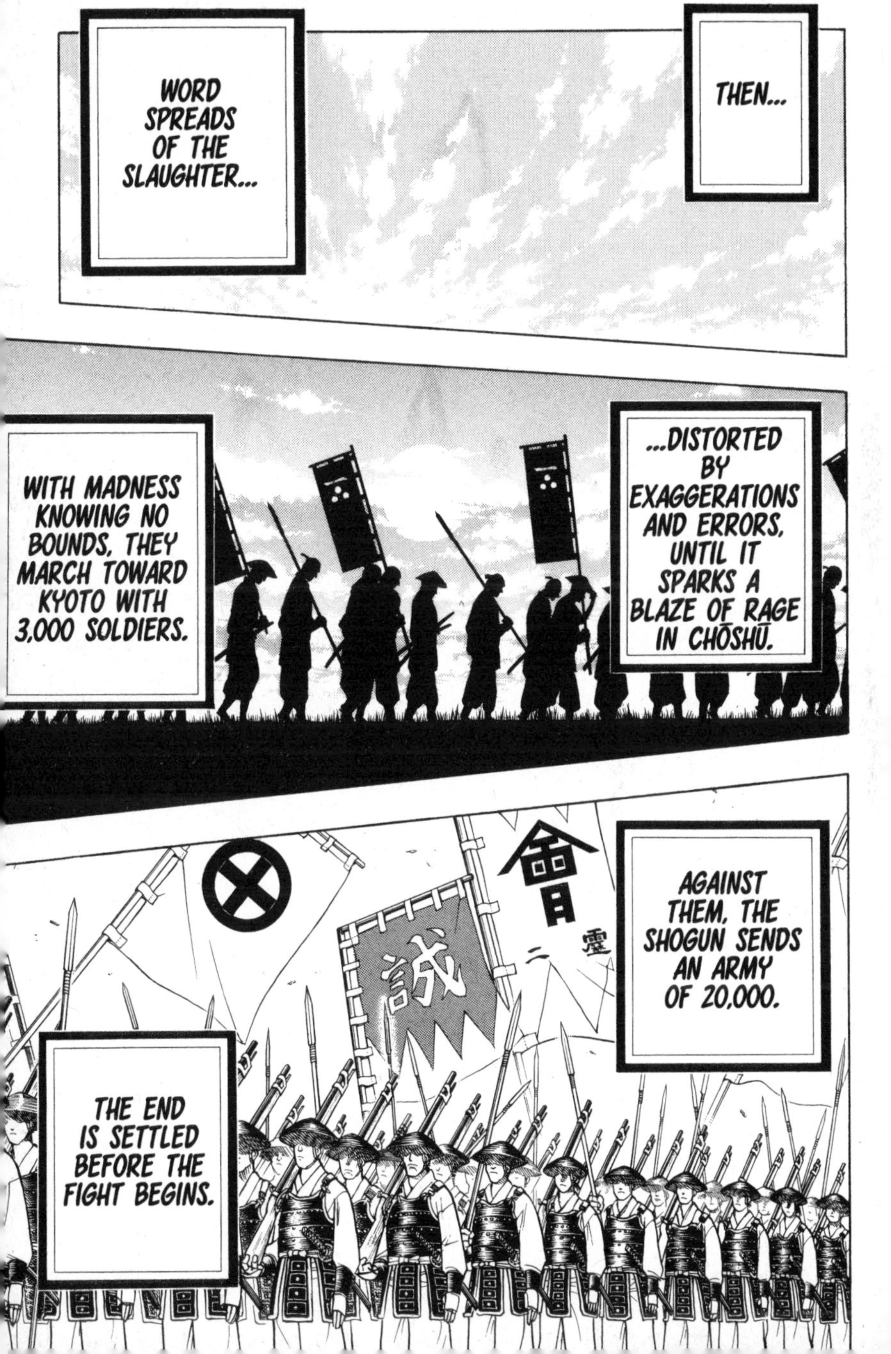
THEN...
WORD SPREADS OF THE SLAUGHTER...
...DISTORTED BY EXAGGERATIONS AND ERRORS, UNTIL IT SPARKS A BLAZE OF RAGE IN CHŌSHŪ.
WITH MADNESS KNOWING NO BOUNDS, THEY MARCH TOWARD KYOTO WITH 3,000 SOLDIERS.
AGAINST THEM, THE SHOGUN SENDS AN ARMY OF 20,000.
THE END IS SETTLED BEFORE THE FIGHT BEGINS.

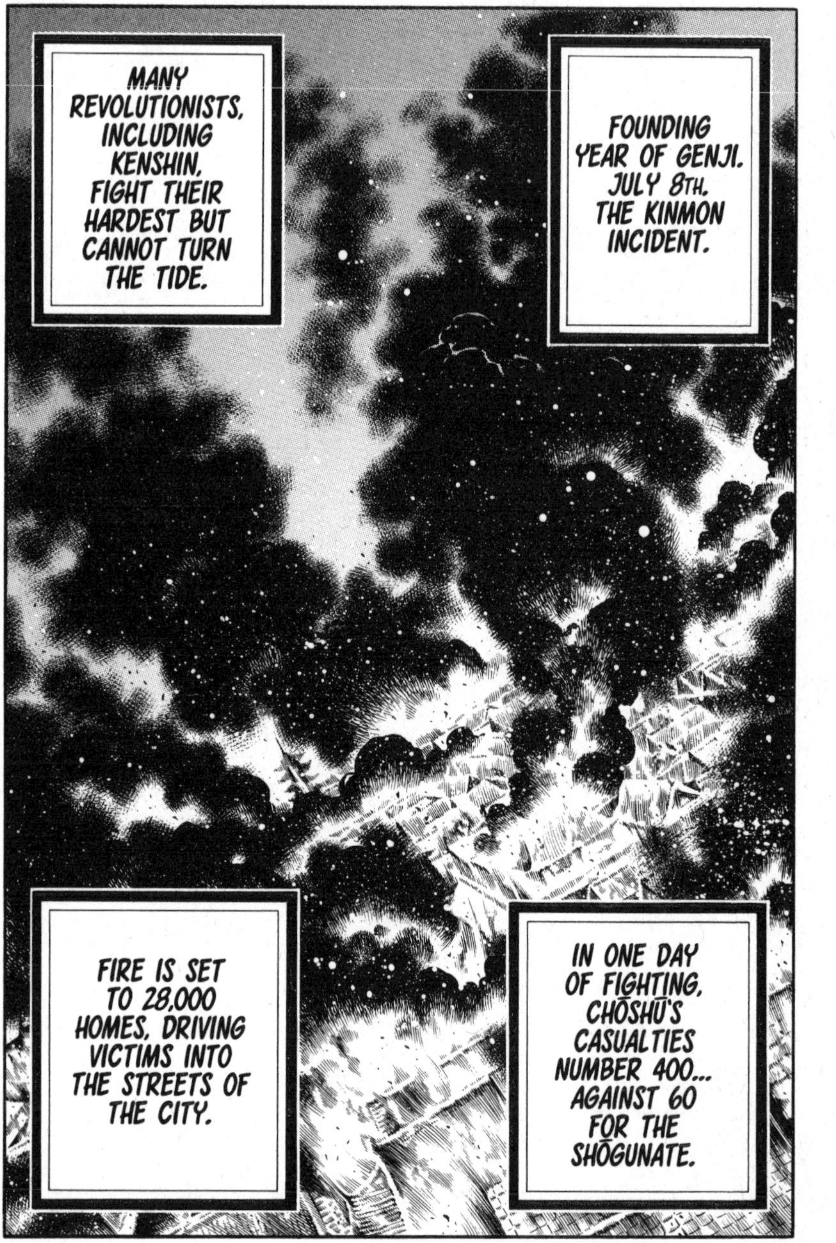
FOUNDING YEAR OF GENJI. JULY 8TH. THE KINMON INCIDENT.
MANY REVOLUTIONISTS, INCLUDING KENSHIN, FIGHT THEIR HARDEST BUT CANNOT TURN THE TIDE.
IN ONE DAY OF FIGHTING, CHŌSHŪ'S CASUALTIES NUMBER 400... AGAINST 60 FOR THE SHŌGUNATE.
FIRE IS SET TO 28,000 HOMES, DRIVING VICTIMS INTO THE STREETS OF THE CITY.

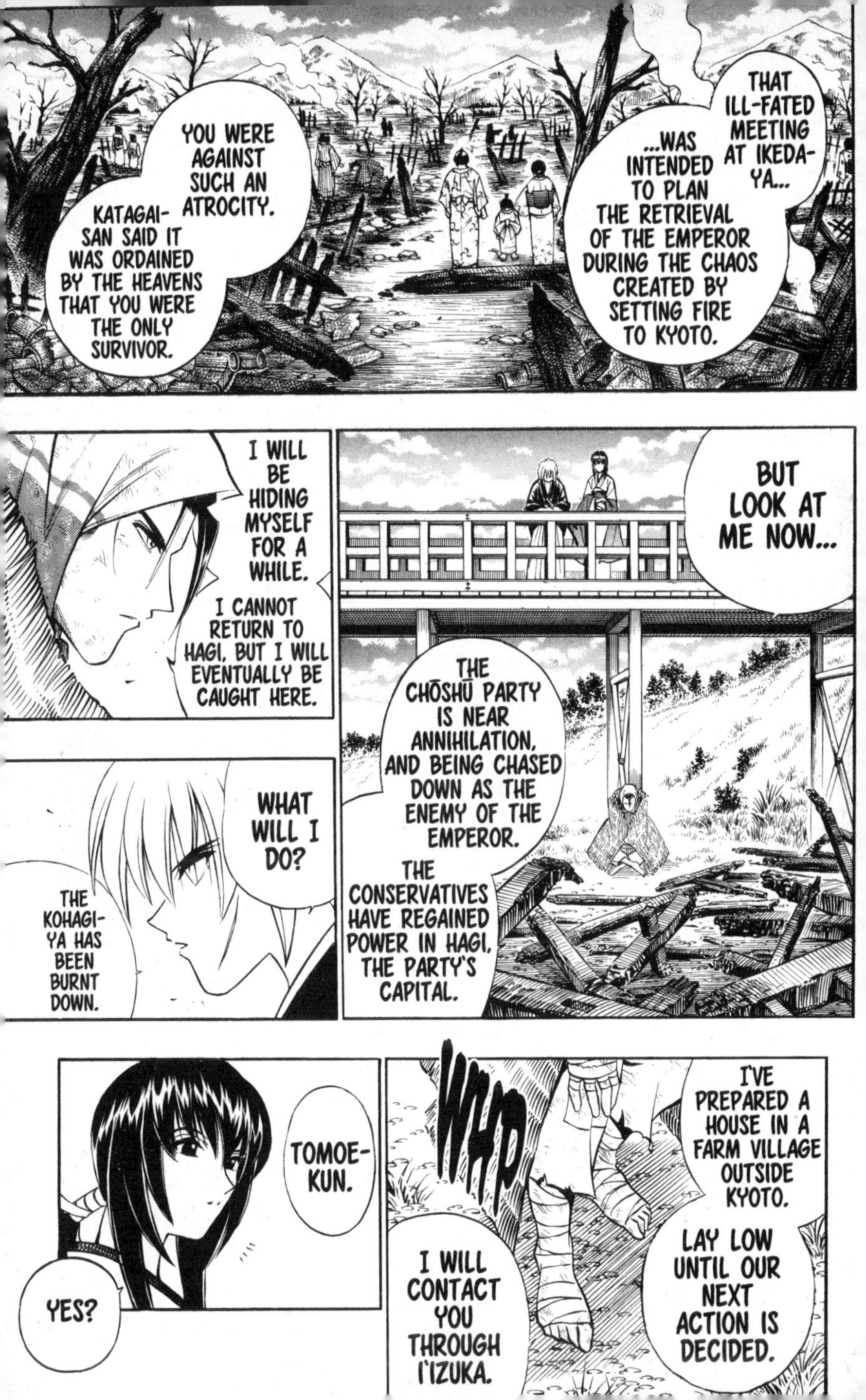
THAT ILL-FATED MEETING AT IKEDA-YA...
...WAS INTENDED TO PLAN THE RETRIEVAL OF THE EMPEROR DURING THE CHAOS CREATED BY SETTING FIRE TO KYOTO.
YOU WERE AGAINST SUCH AN ATROCITY.
KATAGAI-SAN SAID IT WAS ORDAINED BY THE HEAVENS THAT YOU WERE THE ONLY SURVIVOR.
BUT LOOK AT ME NOW...
THE CHŌSHŪ PARTY IS NEAR ANNIHILATION, AND BEING CHASED DOWN AS THE ENEMY OF THE EMPEROR.
THE CONSERVATIVES HAVE REGAINED POWER IN HAGI, THE PARTY'S CAPITAL.
I WILL BE HIDING MYSELF FOR A WHILE.
I CANNOT RETURN TO HAGI, BUT I WILL EVENTUALLY BE CAUGHT HERE.
WHAT WILL I DO?
THE KOHAGI-YA HAS BEEN BURNT DOWN.
I'VE PREPARED A HOUSE IN A FARM VILLAGE OUTSIDE KYOTO.
WHIP
LAY LOW UNTIL OUR NEXT ACTION IS DECIDED.
I WILL CONTACT YOU THROUGH I'IZUKA.
TOMOE-KUN.
YES?

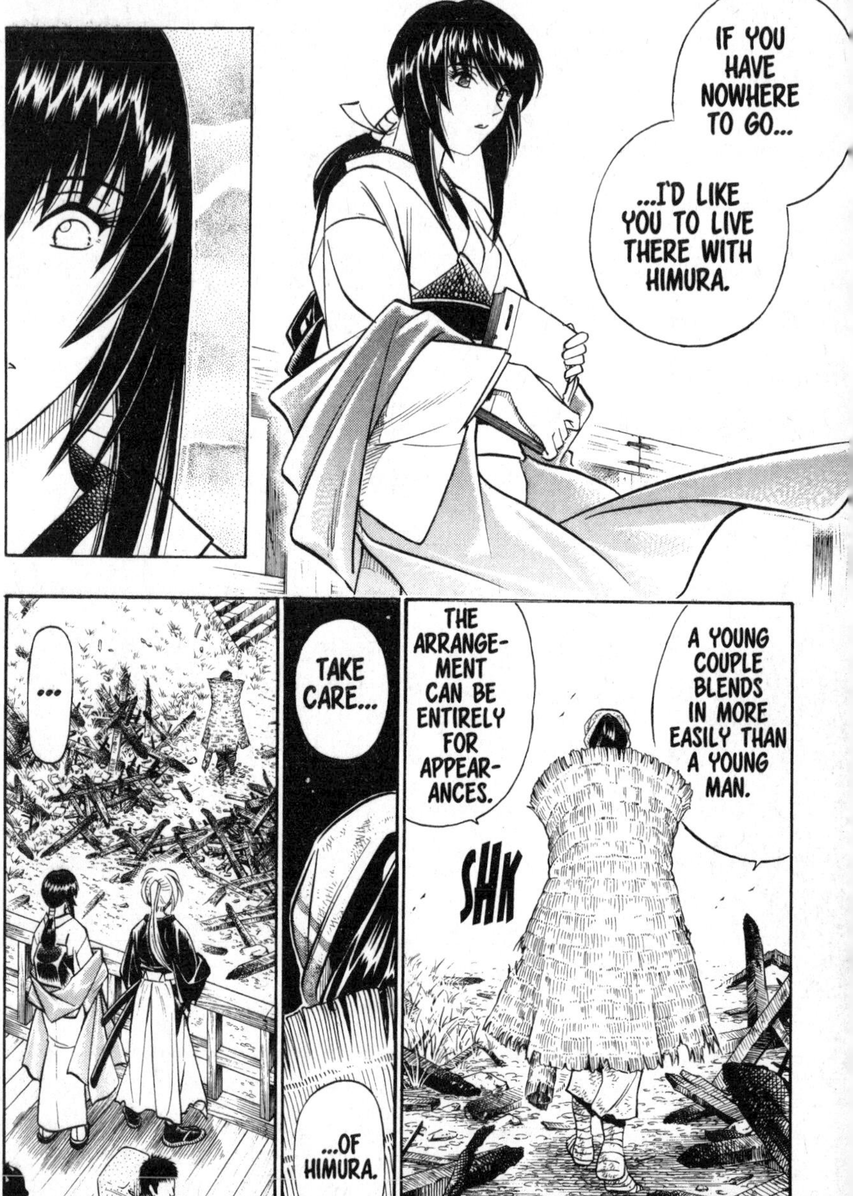
IF YOU HAVE NOWHERE TO GO...
...I'D LIKE YOU TO LIVE THERE WITH HIMURA.
A YOUNG COUPLE BLENDS IN MORE EASILY THAN A YOUNG MAN.
THE ARRANGE-MENT CAN BE ENTIRELY FOR APPEAR-ANCES.
SHK
TAKE CARE...
...OF HIMURA.
...

READ THIS WAY

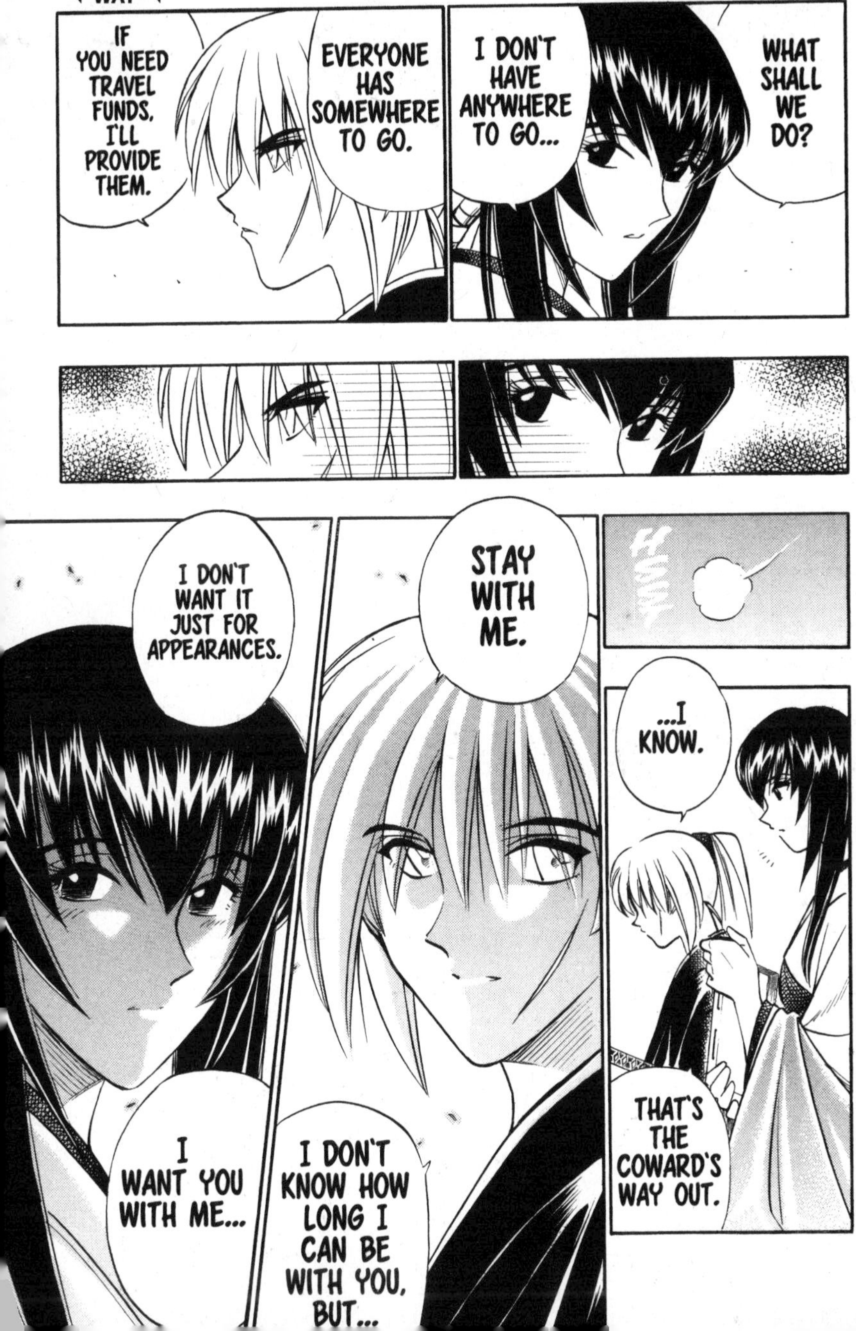
WHAT SHALL WE DO?
I DON'T HAVE ANYWHERE TO GO...
EVERYONE HAS SOMEWHERE TO GO.
IF YOU NEED TRAVEL FUNDS, I'LL PROVIDE THEM.
...I KNOW.
THAT'S THE COWARD'S WAY OUT.
STAY WITH ME.
I DON'T KNOW HOW LONG I CAN BE WITH YOU, BUT...
I DON'T WANT IT JUST FOR APPEARANCES.
I WANT YOU WITH ME...

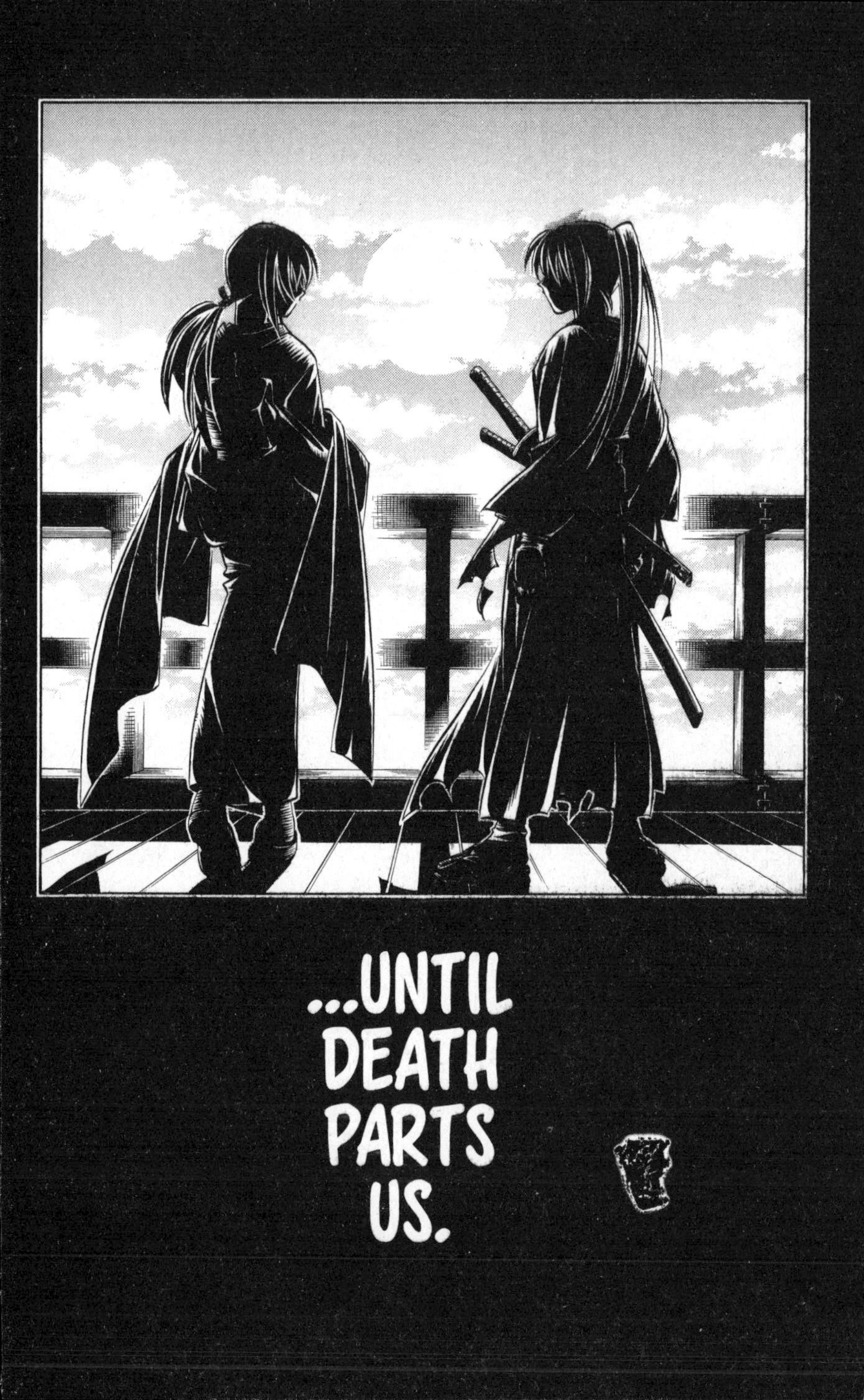
...UNTIL DEATH PARTS US.

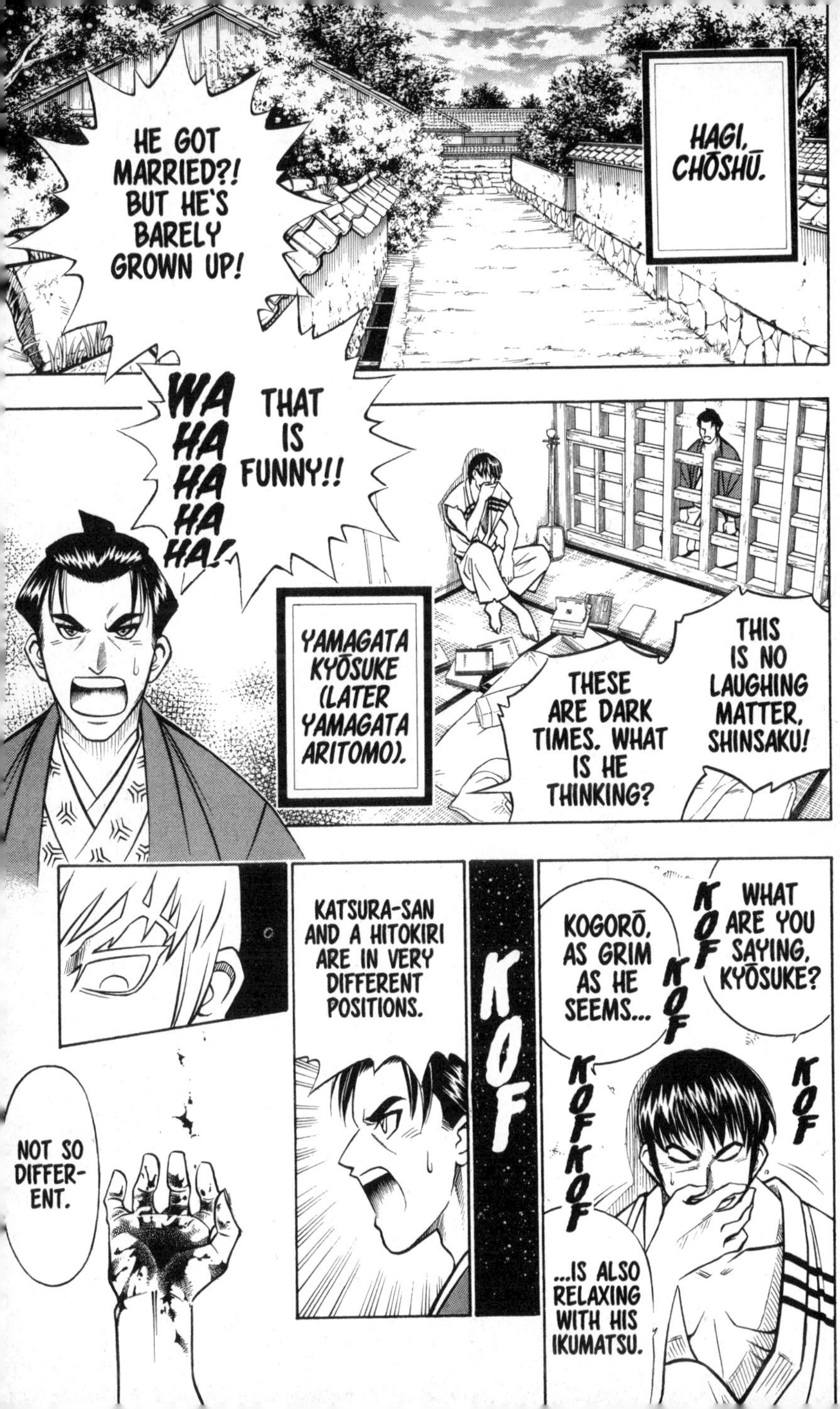
HAGI, CHŌSHŪ.
HE GOT MARRIED?! BUT HE'S BARELY GROWN UP!
WAHAHAHAHAHA!
THAT IS FUNNY!!
THIS IS NO LAUGHING MATTER, SHINSAKU!
THESE ARE DARK TIMES. WHAT IS HE THINKING?
YAMAGATA KYŌSUKE (LATER YAMAGATA ARITOMO).
KOF KOF
WHAT ARE YOU SAYING, KYŌSUKE?
KOF KOF
KOGORŌ, AS GRIM AS HE SEEMS...
KOF KOF KOF KOF
...IS ALSO RELAXING WITH HIS IKUMATSU.
KOF
KATSURA-SAN AND A HITOKIRI ARE IN VERY DIFFERENT POSITIONS.
NOT SO DIFFERENT.

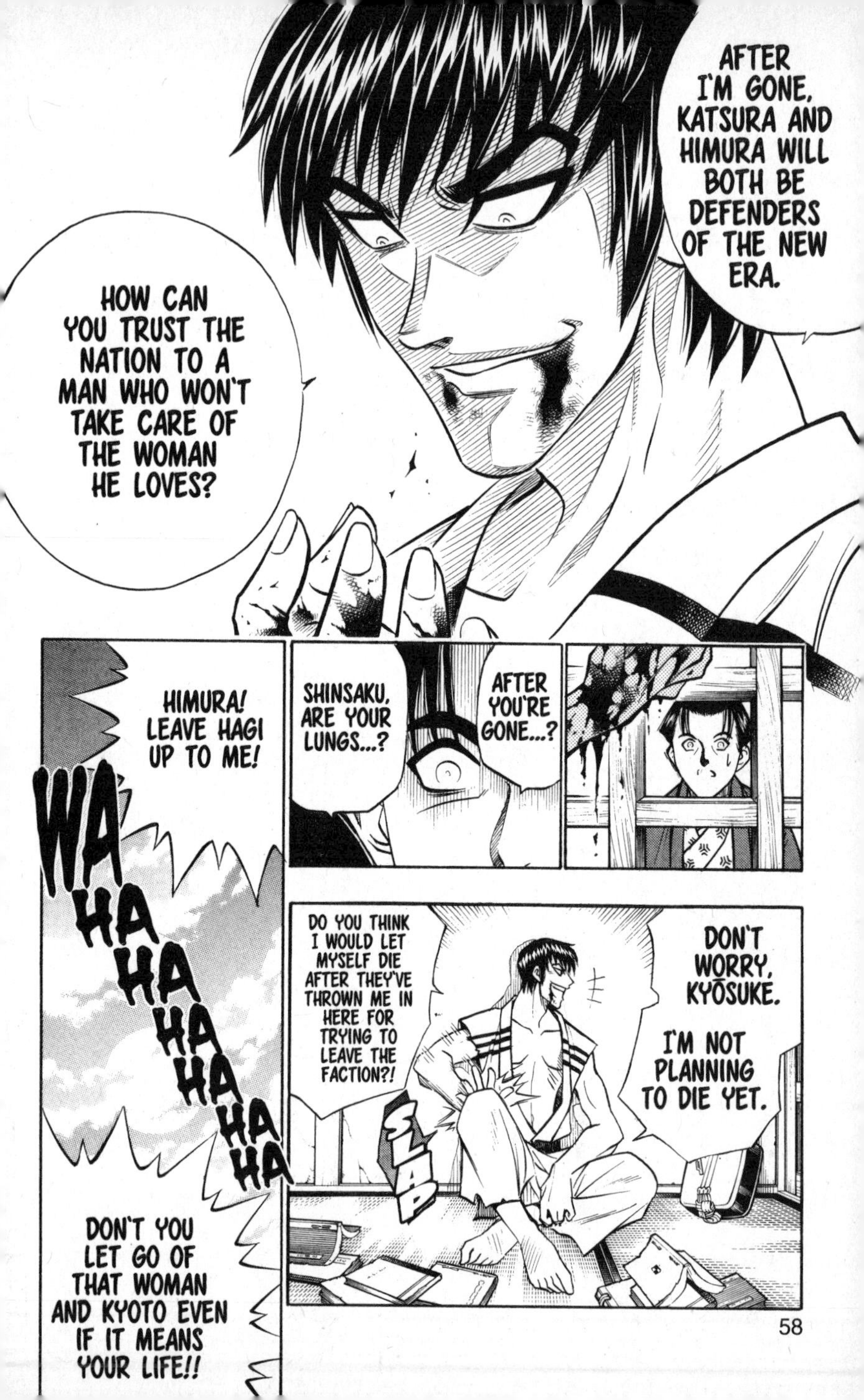
AFTER I'M GONE, KATSURA AND HIMURA WILL BOTH BE DEFENDERS OF THE NEW ERA.
HOW CAN YOU TRUST THE NATION TO A MAN WHO WON'T TAKE CARE OF THE WOMAN HE LOVES?
AFTER YOU'RE GONE...?
SHINSAKU, ARE YOUR LUNGS...?
DON'T WORRY, KYŌSUKE.
I'M NOT PLANNING TO DIE YET.
DO YOU THINK I WOULD LET MYSELF DIE AFTER THEY'VE THROWN ME IN HERE FOR TRYING TO LEAVE THE FACTION?!
SLAP
HIMURA! LEAVE HAGI UP TO ME!
WA HA HA HA HA HA HA HA HA
DON'T YOU LET GO OF THAT WOMAN AND KYOTO EVEN IF IT MEANS YOUR LIFE!!

READ THIS WAY

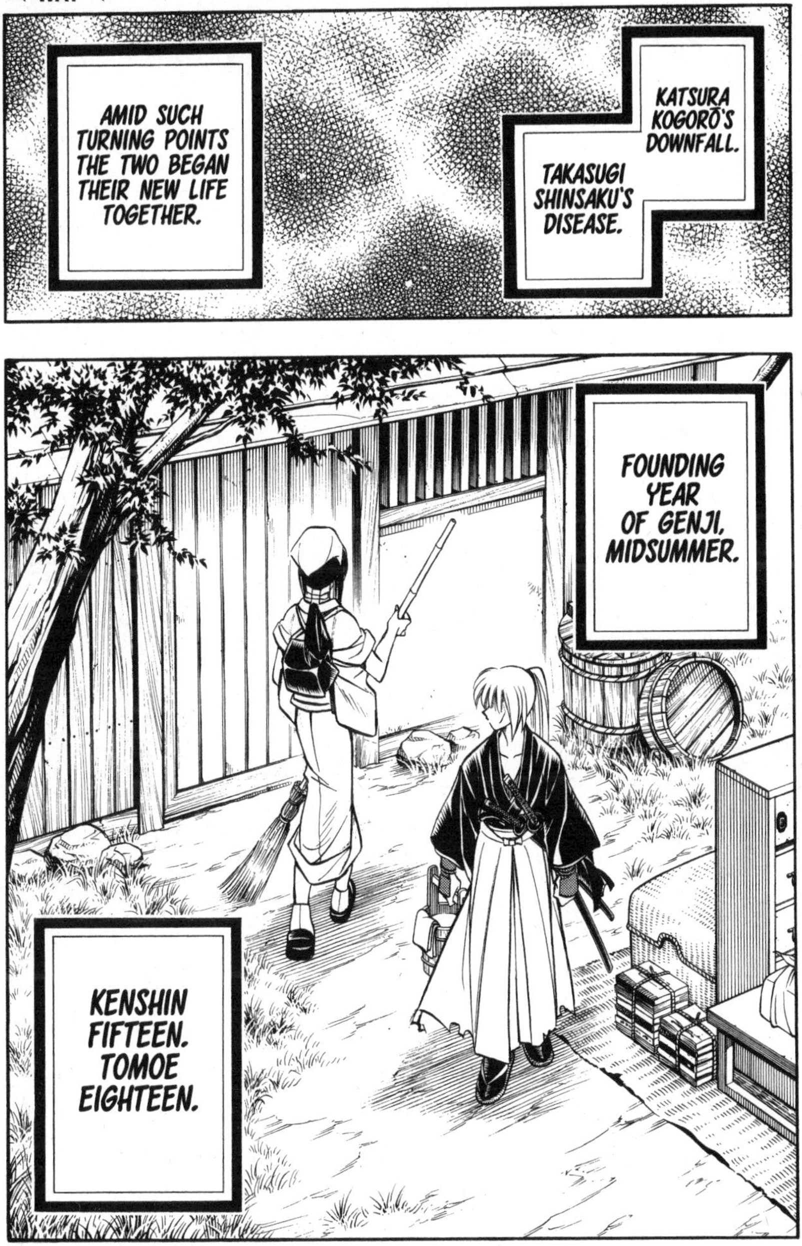

KATSURA KOGORŌ'S DOWNFALL.
TAKASUGI SHINSAKU'S DISEASE.
AMID SUCH TURNING POINTS THE TWO BEGAN THEIR NEW LIFE TOGETHER.
FOUNDING YEAR OF GENJI, MIDSUMMER.
KENSHIN FIFTEEN. TOMOE EIGHTEEN.

Rurouni Kenshin

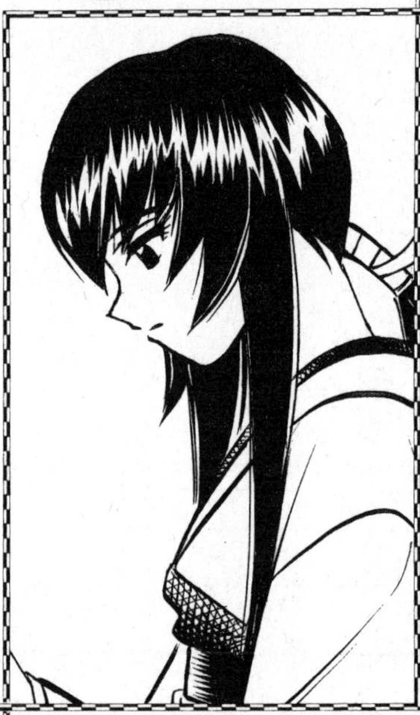

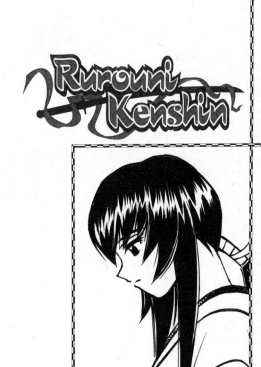

Act 171 Brief Intermission

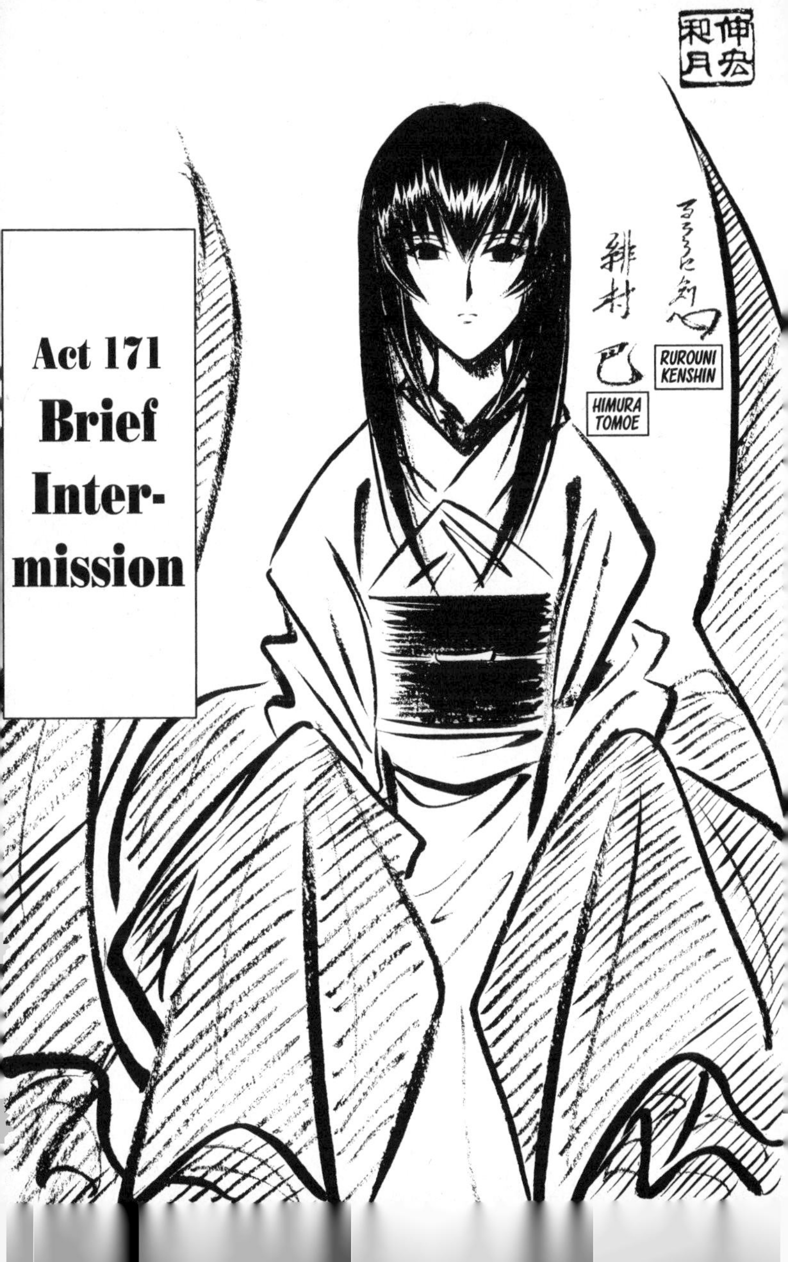

るろうに剣心
RUROUNI KENSHIN
緋村巴
HIMURA TOMOE

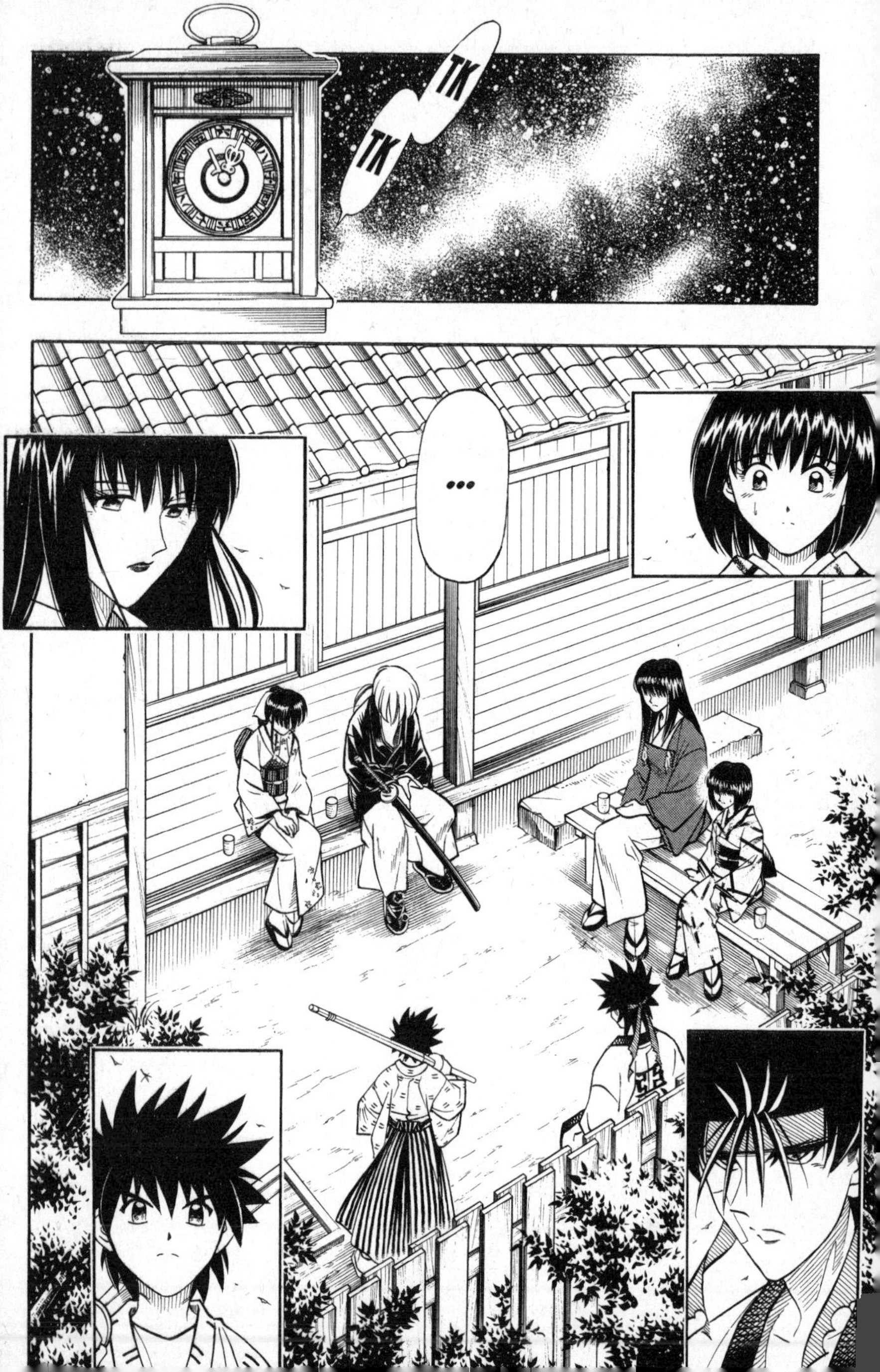
TK TK
...

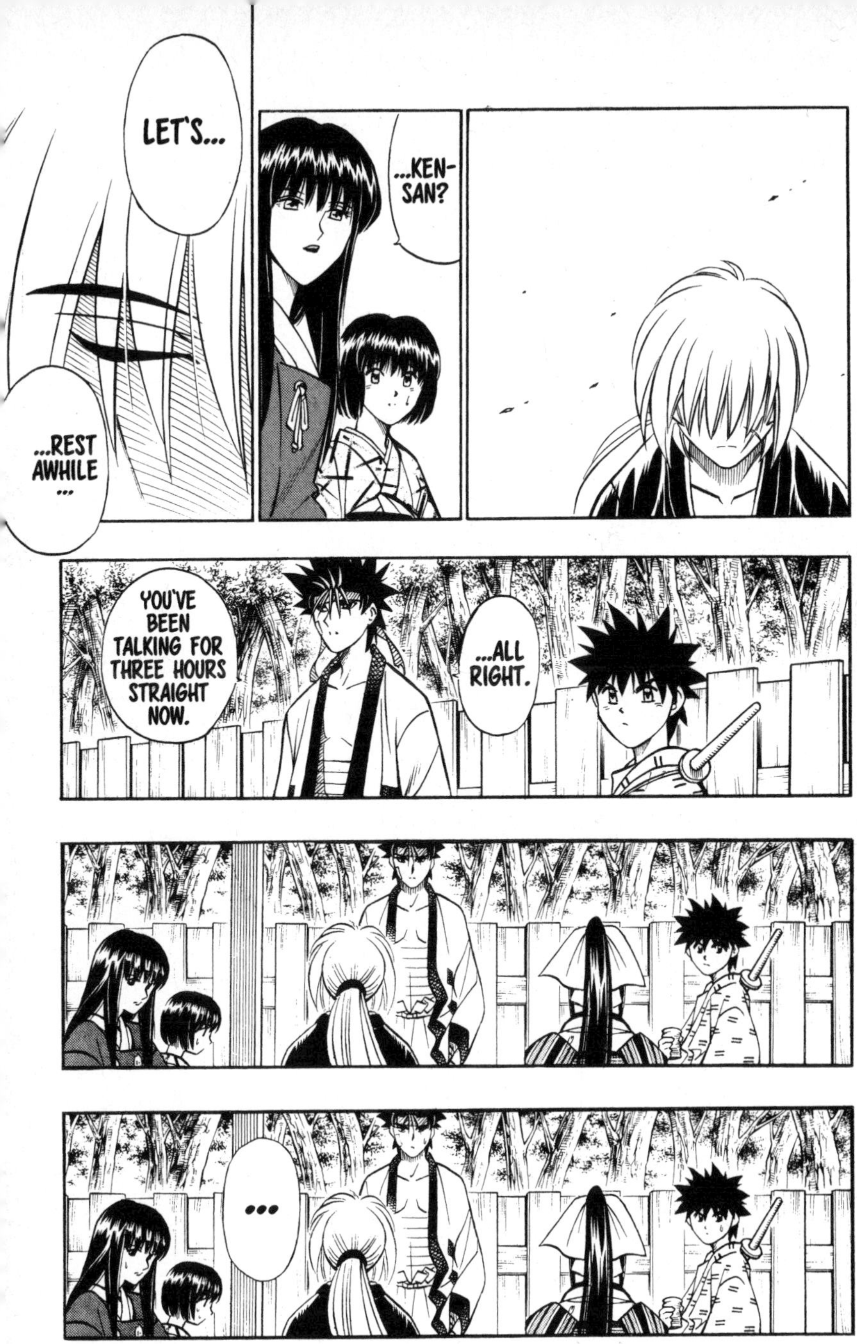
...KEN-SAN?
LET'S...
...REST AWHILE ...
...ALL RIGHT.
YOU'VE BEEN TALKING FOR THREE HOURS STRAIGHT NOW.
...

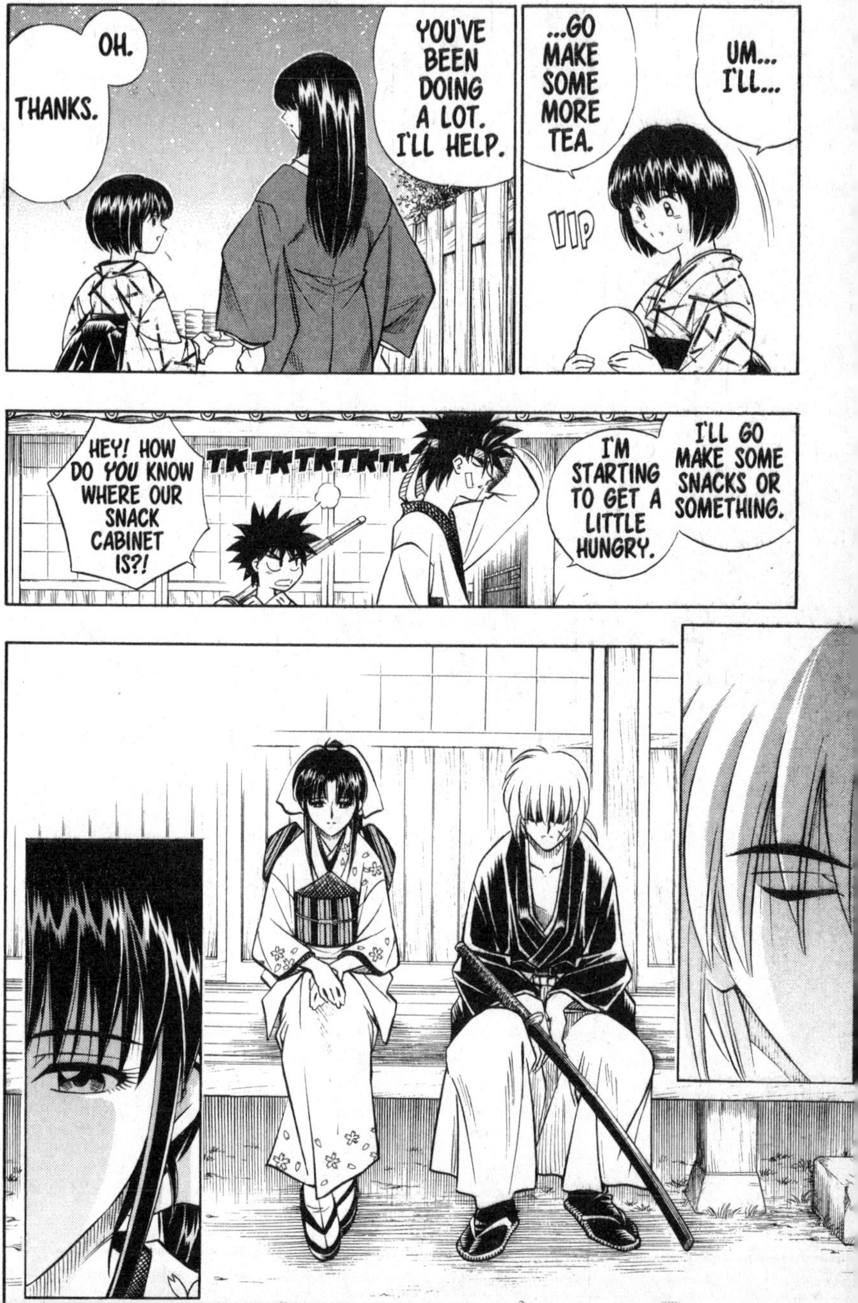
UM... I'LL...
...GO MAKE SOME MORE TEA.
VIP
YOU'VE BEEN DOING A LOT. I'LL HELP.
OH.
THANKS.
I'LL GO MAKE SOME SNACKS OR SOMETHING.
I'M STARTING TO GET A LITTLE HUNGRY.
TKTKTKTKTK
HEY! HOW DO YOU KNOW WHERE OUR SNACK CABINET IS?!

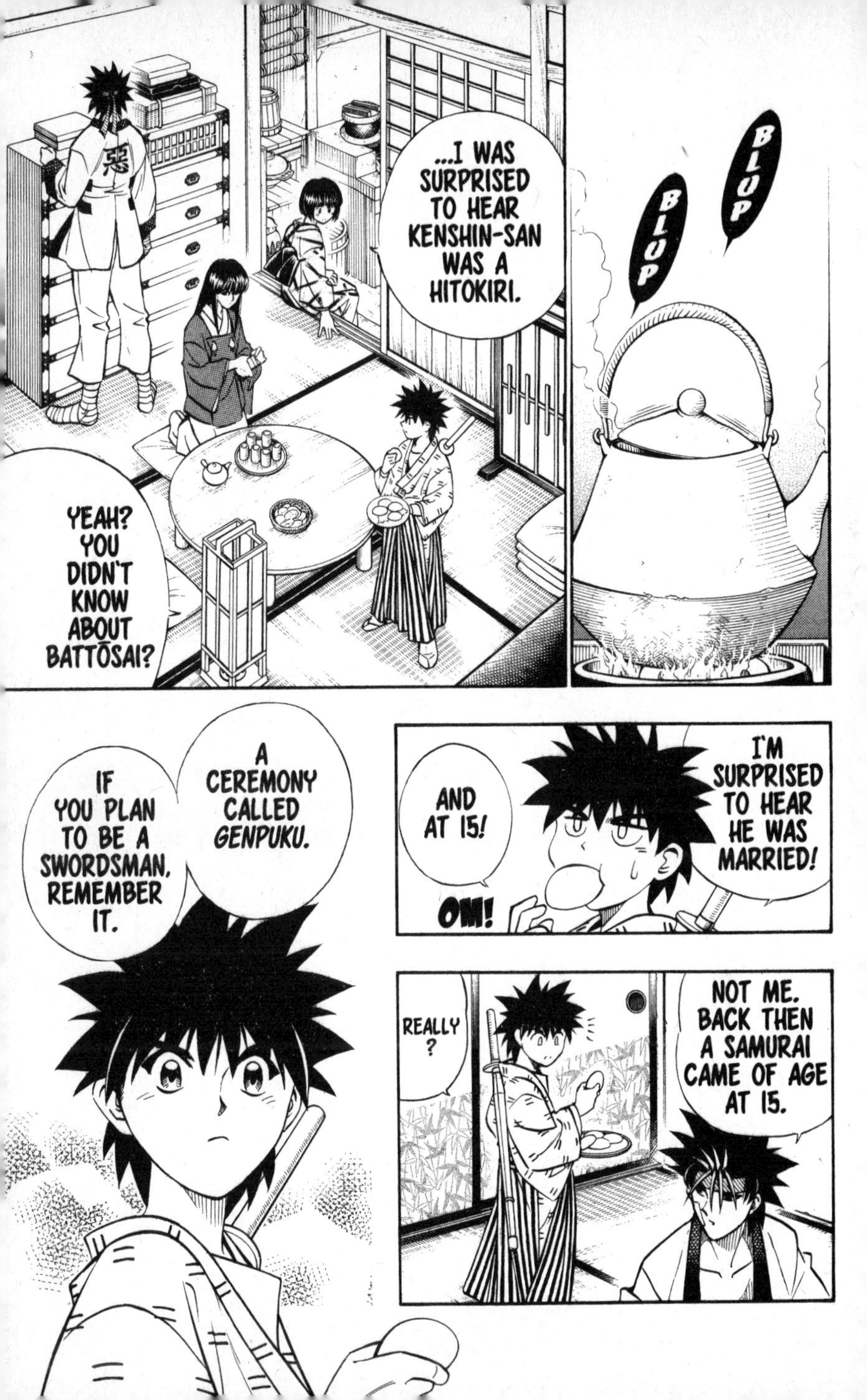
BLUP
BLUP
...I WAS SURPRISED TO HEAR KENSHIN-SAN WAS A HITOKIRI.
YEAH? YOU DIDN'T KNOW ABOUT BATTŌSAI?
I'M SURPRISED TO HEAR HE WAS MARRIED!
AND AT 15!
OM!
NOT ME. BACK THEN A SAMURAI CAME OF AGE AT 15.
REALLY?
A CEREMONY CALLED GENPUKU.
IF YOU PLAN TO BE A SWORDSMAN, REMEMBER IT.

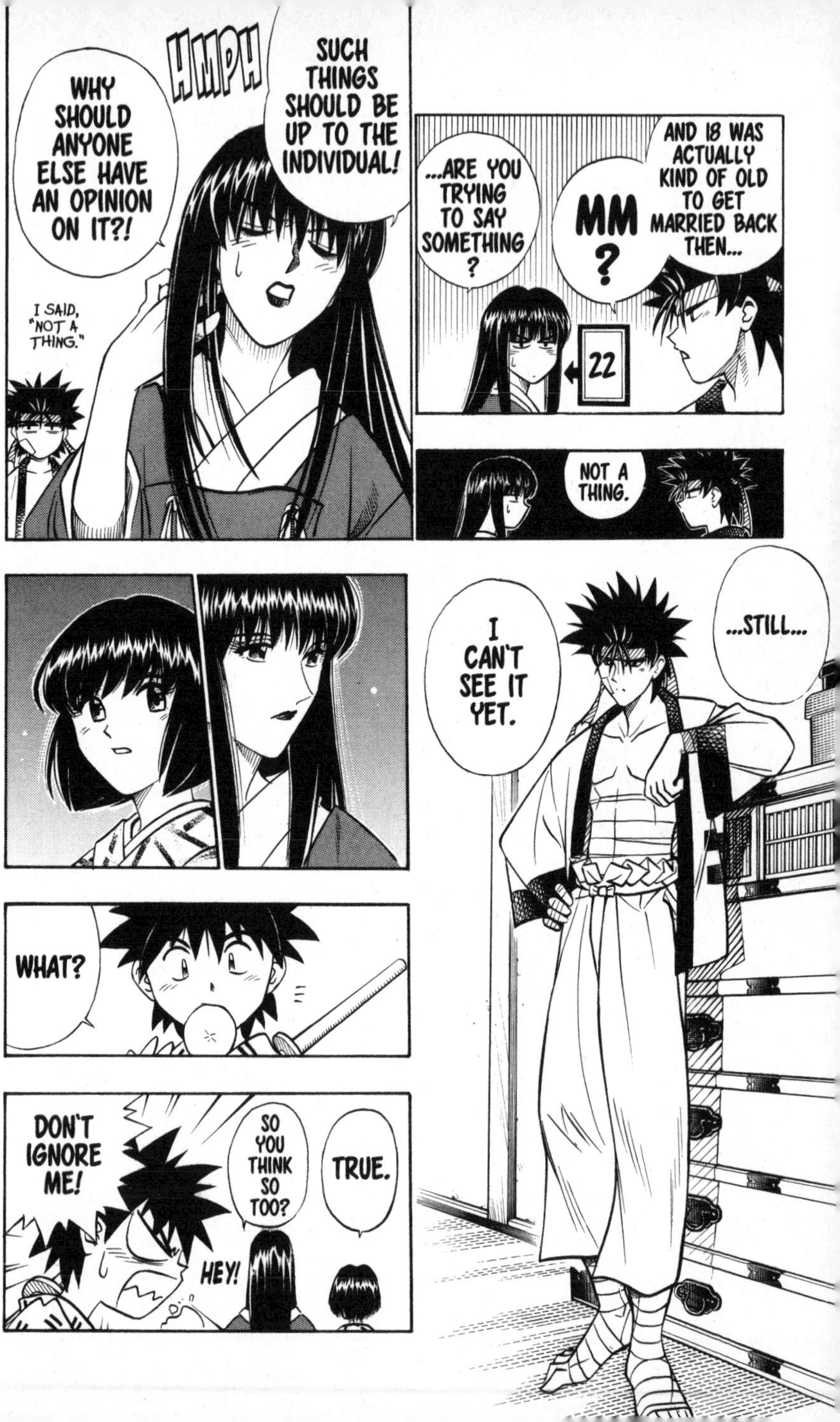
AND 18 WAS ACTUALLY KIND OF OLD TO GET MARRIED BACK THEN...
MM?
...ARE YOU TRYING TO SAY SOMETHING?
22
NOT A THING.
SUCH THINGS SHOULD BE UP TO THE INDIVIDUAL!
HMPH
WHY SHOULD ANYONE ELSE HAVE AN OPINION ON IT?!
I SAID, "NOT A THING."
...STILL...
I CAN'T SEE IT YET.
WHAT?
TRUE.
SO YOU THINK SO TOO?
DON'T IGNORE ME!
HEY!

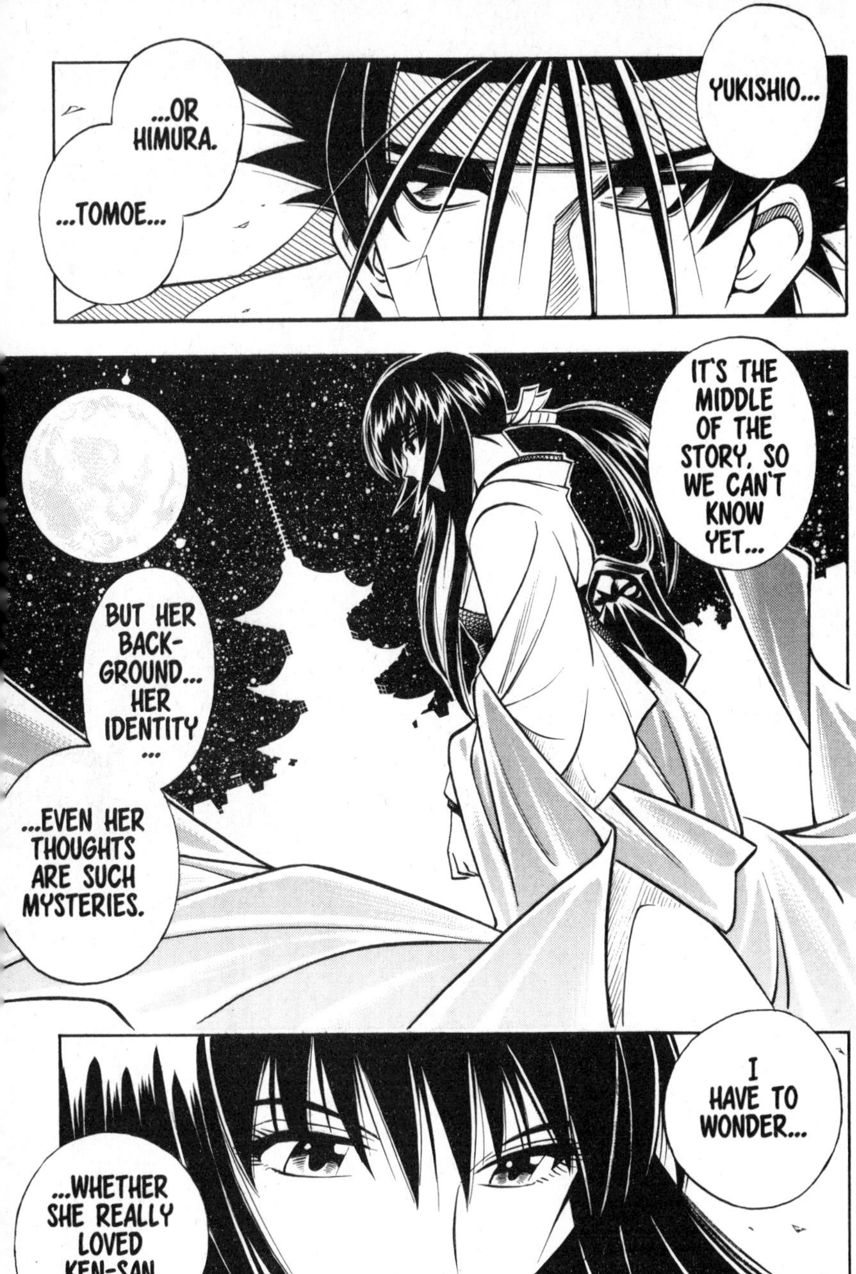
YUKISHIO...
...OR HIMURA.
...TOMOE...
IT'S THE MIDDLE OF THE STORY, SO WE CAN'T KNOW YET...
BUT HER BACK-GROUND... HER IDENTITY...
...EVEN HER THOUGHTS ARE SUCH MYSTERIES.
I HAVE TO WONDER...
...WHETHER SHE REALLY LOVED KEN-SAN OR NOT.

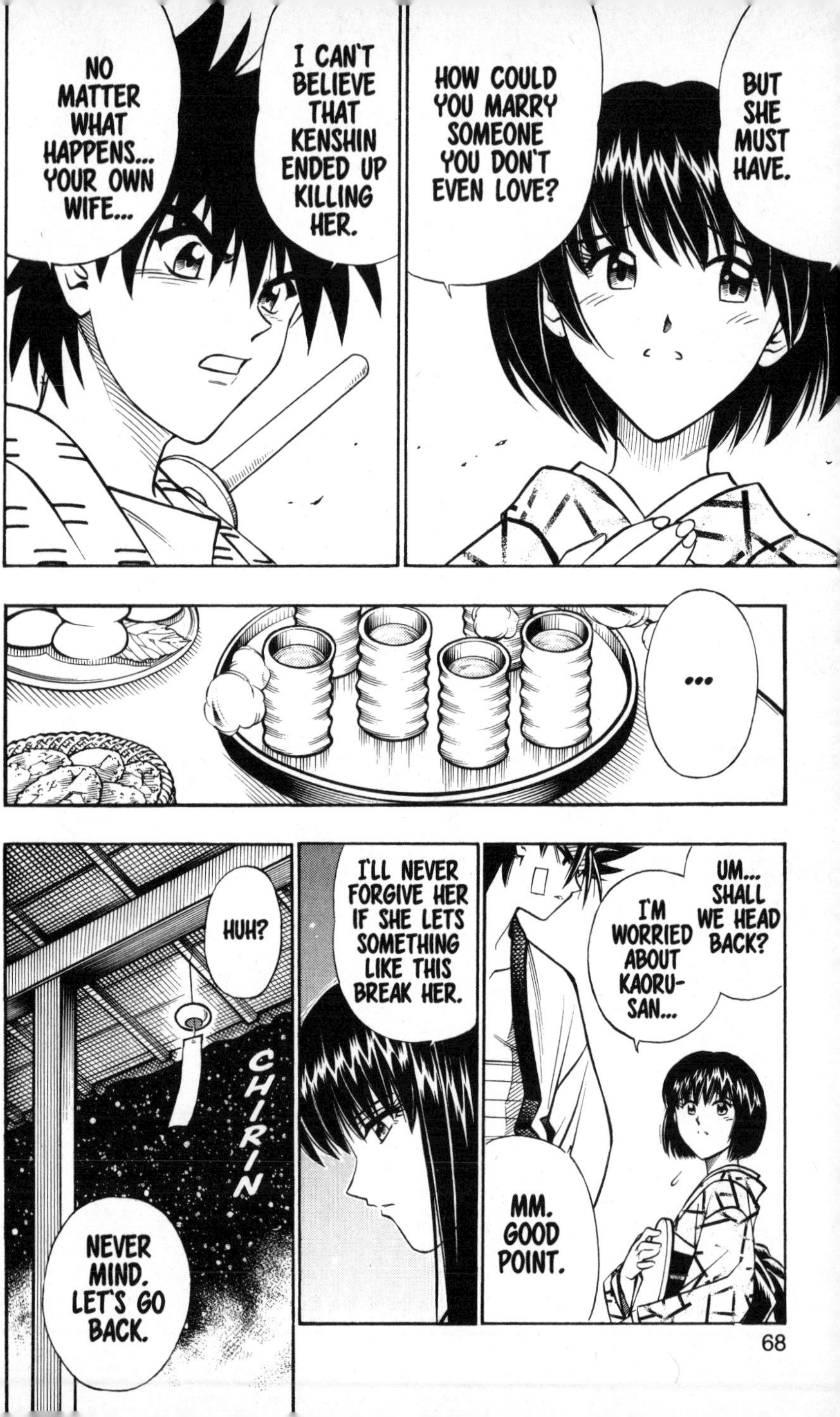
BUT SHE MUST HAVE.
HOW COULD YOU MARRY SOMEONE YOU DON'T EVEN LOVE?
I CAN'T BELIEVE THAT KENSHIN ENDED UP KILLING HER.
NO MATTER WHAT HAPPENS... YOUR OWN WIFE...
...
UM... SHALL WE HEAD BACK?
I'M WORRIED ABOUT KAORU-SAN...
MM. GOOD POINT.
I'LL NEVER FORGIVE HER IF SHE LETS SOMETHING LIKE THIS BREAK HER.
HUH?
CHIRIN
NEVER MIND. LET'S GO BACK.

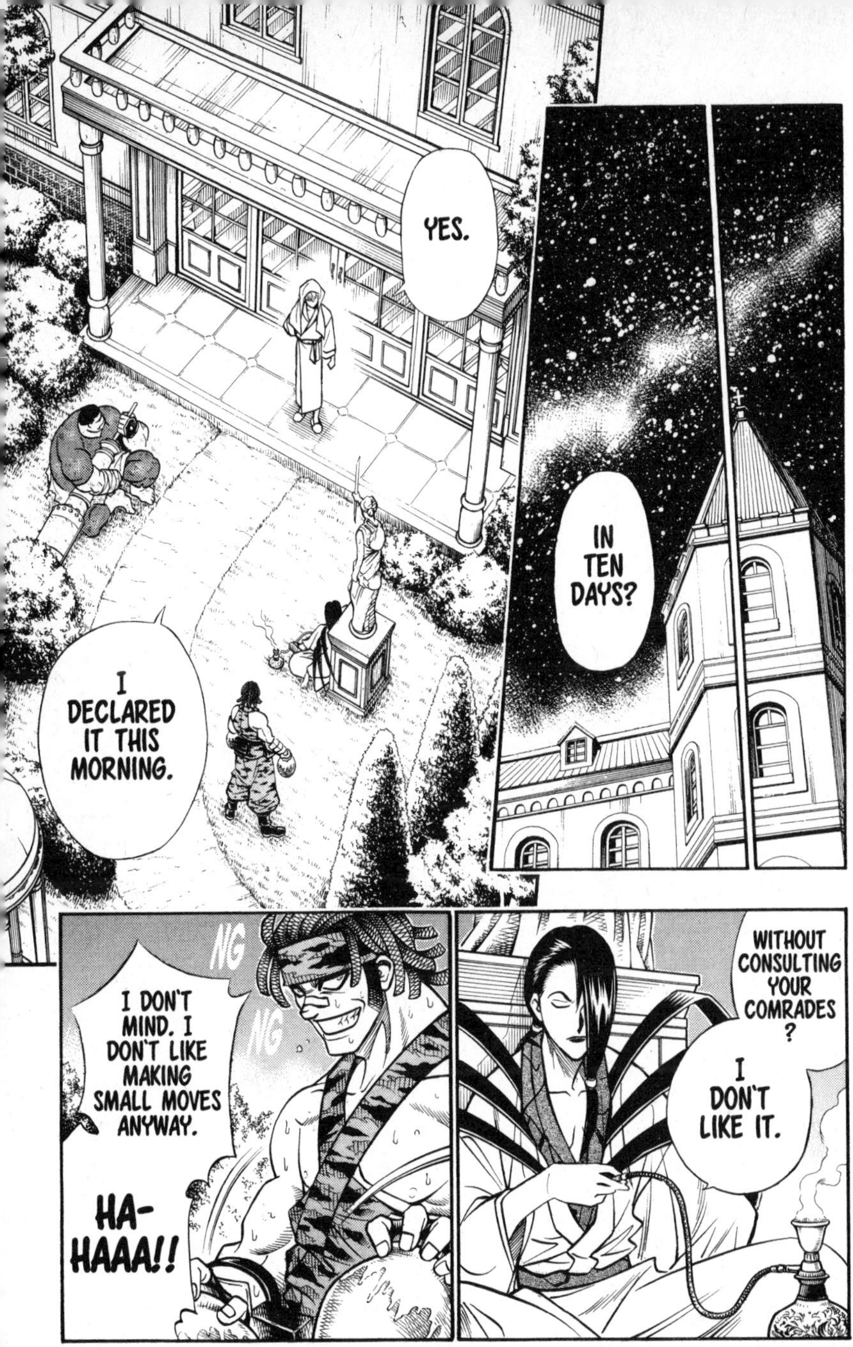
IN TEN DAYS?
YES.
I DECLARED IT THIS MORNING.
WITHOUT CONSULTING YOUR COMRADES?
I DON'T LIKE IT.
NG
NG
I DON'T MIND. I DON'T LIKE MAKING SMALL MOVES ANYWAY.
HA-HAAA!!

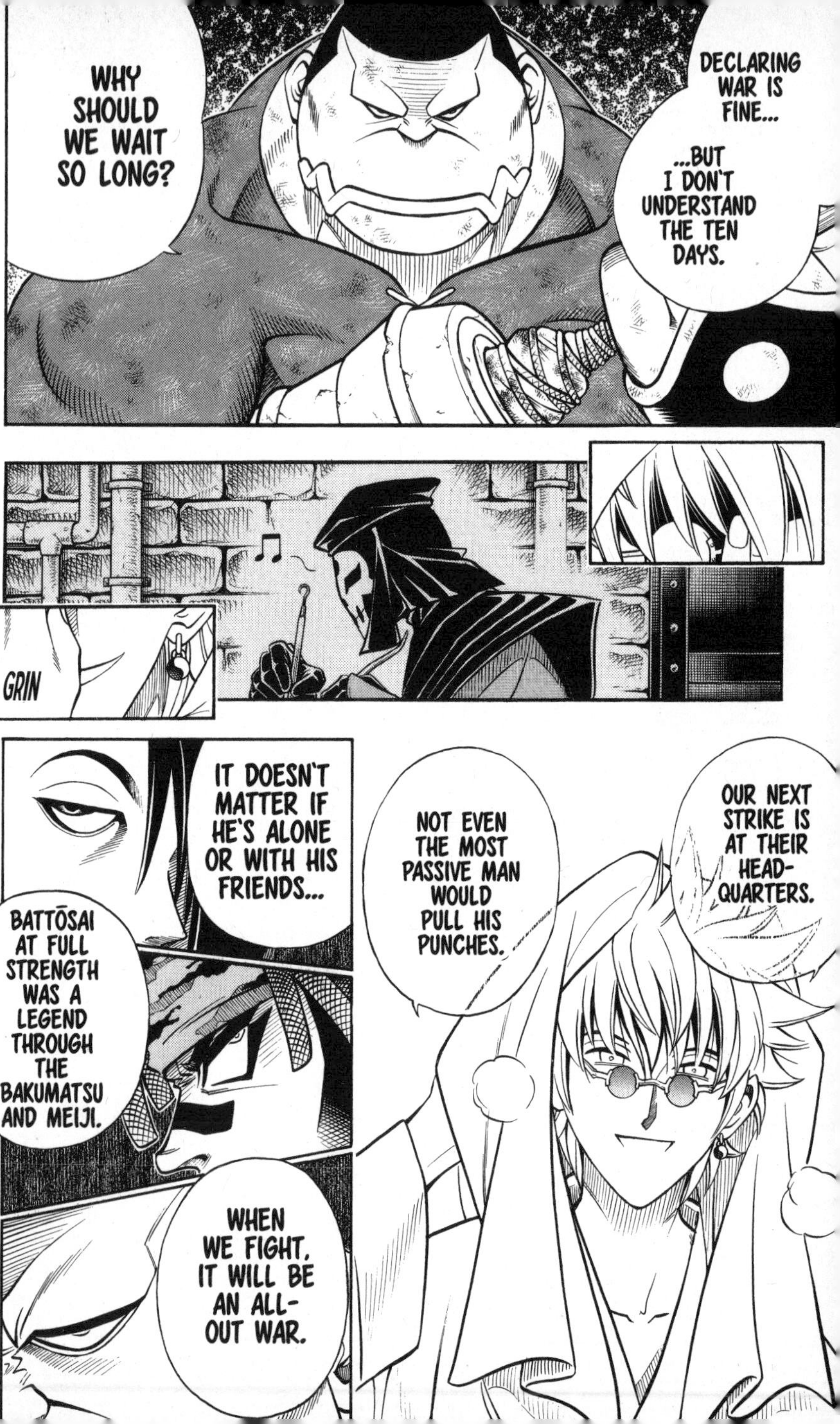
DECLARING WAR IS FINE...
...BUT I DON'T UNDERSTAND THE TEN DAYS.
WHY SHOULD WE WAIT SO LONG?
GRIN
OUR NEXT STRIKE IS AT THEIR HEAD-QUARTERS.
NOT EVEN THE MOST PASSIVE MAN WOULD PULL HIS PUNCHES.
IT DOESN'T MATTER IF HE'S ALONE OR WITH HIS FRIENDS...
BATTŌSAI AT FULL STRENGTH WAS A LEGEND THROUGH THE BAKUMATSU AND MEIJI.
WHEN WE FIGHT, IT WILL BE AN ALL-OUT WAR.

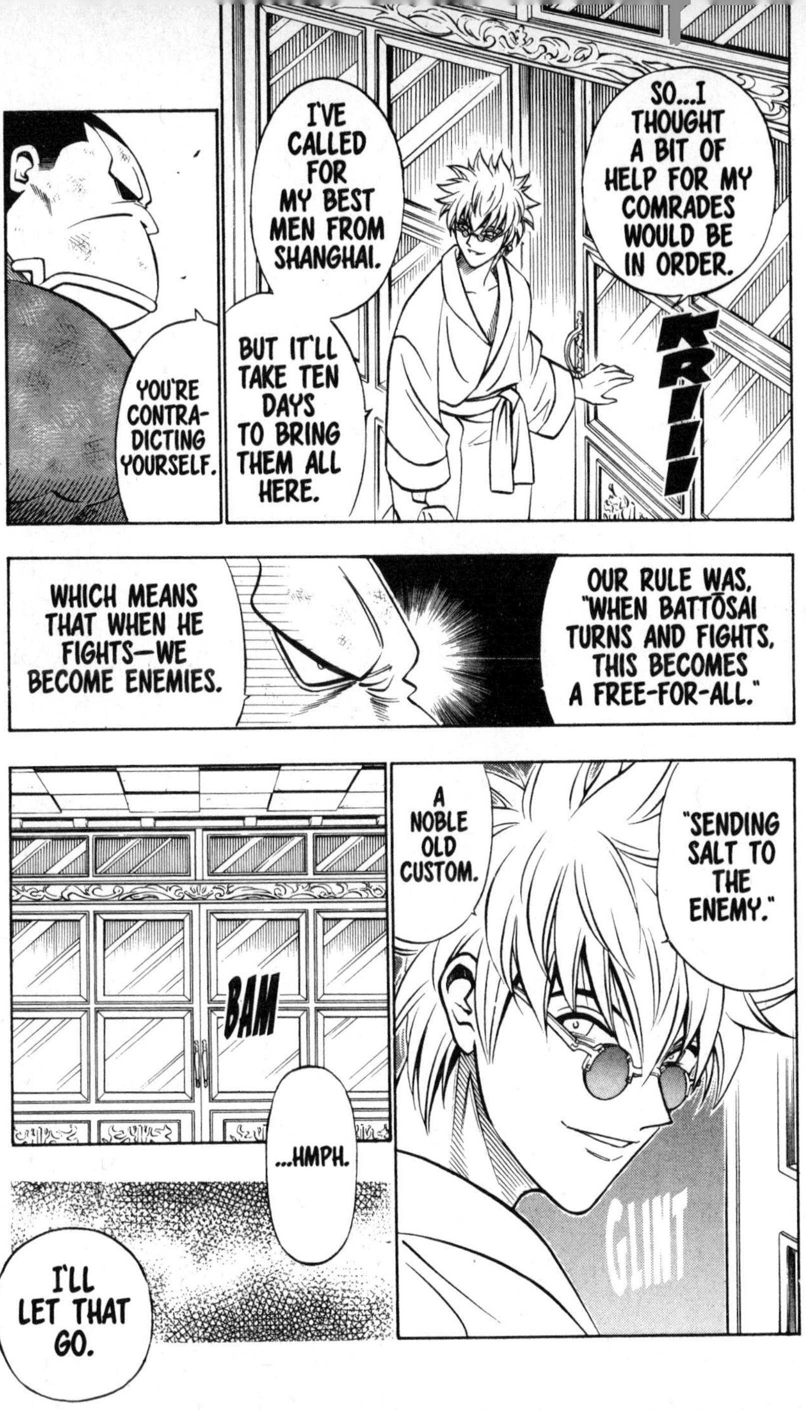
SO...I THOUGHT A BIT OF HELP FOR MY COMRADES WOULD BE IN ORDER.
KRII
I'VE CALLED FOR MY BEST MEN FROM SHANGHAI.
BUT IT'LL TAKE TEN DAYS TO BRING THEM ALL HERE.
YOU'RE CONTRA-DICTING YOURSELF.
OUR RULE WAS, "WHEN BATTŌSAI TURNS AND FIGHTS, THIS BECOMES A FREE-FOR-ALL."
WHICH MEANS THAT WHEN HE FIGHTS—WE BECOME ENEMIES.
"SENDING SALT TO THE ENEMY."
A NOBLE OLD CUSTOM.
GLINT
BAM
...HMPH.
I'LL LET THAT GO.

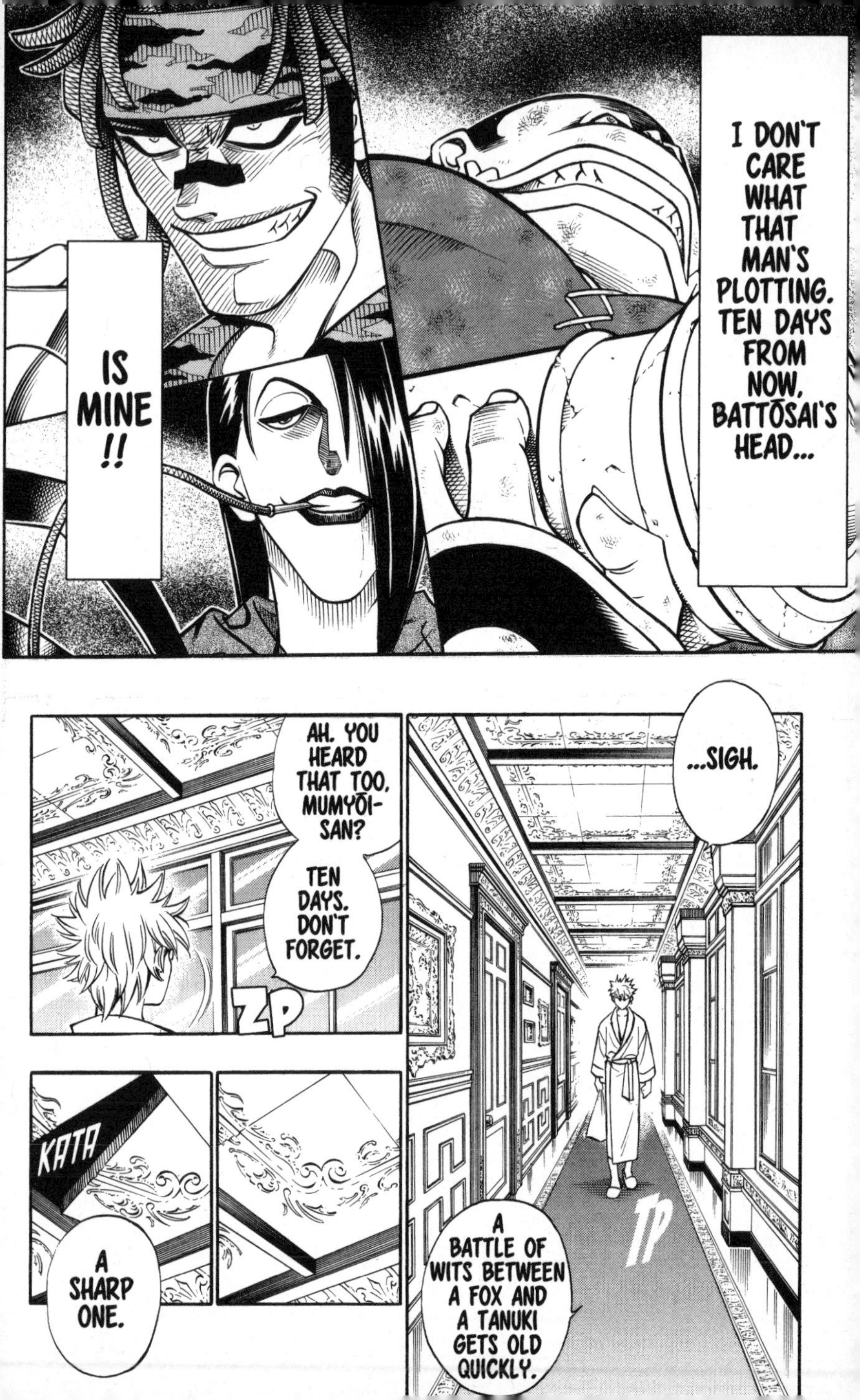
I DON'T CARE WHAT THAT MAN'S PLOTTING. TEN DAYS FROM NOW, BATTŌSAI'S HEAD...
IS MINE!!
...SIGH.
TP
A BATTLE OF WITS BETWEEN A FOX AND A TANUKI GETS OLD QUICKLY.
AH. YOU HEARD THAT TOO, MUMYŌI-SAN?
TEN DAYS. DON'T FORGET.
ZP
KATA
A SHARP ONE.

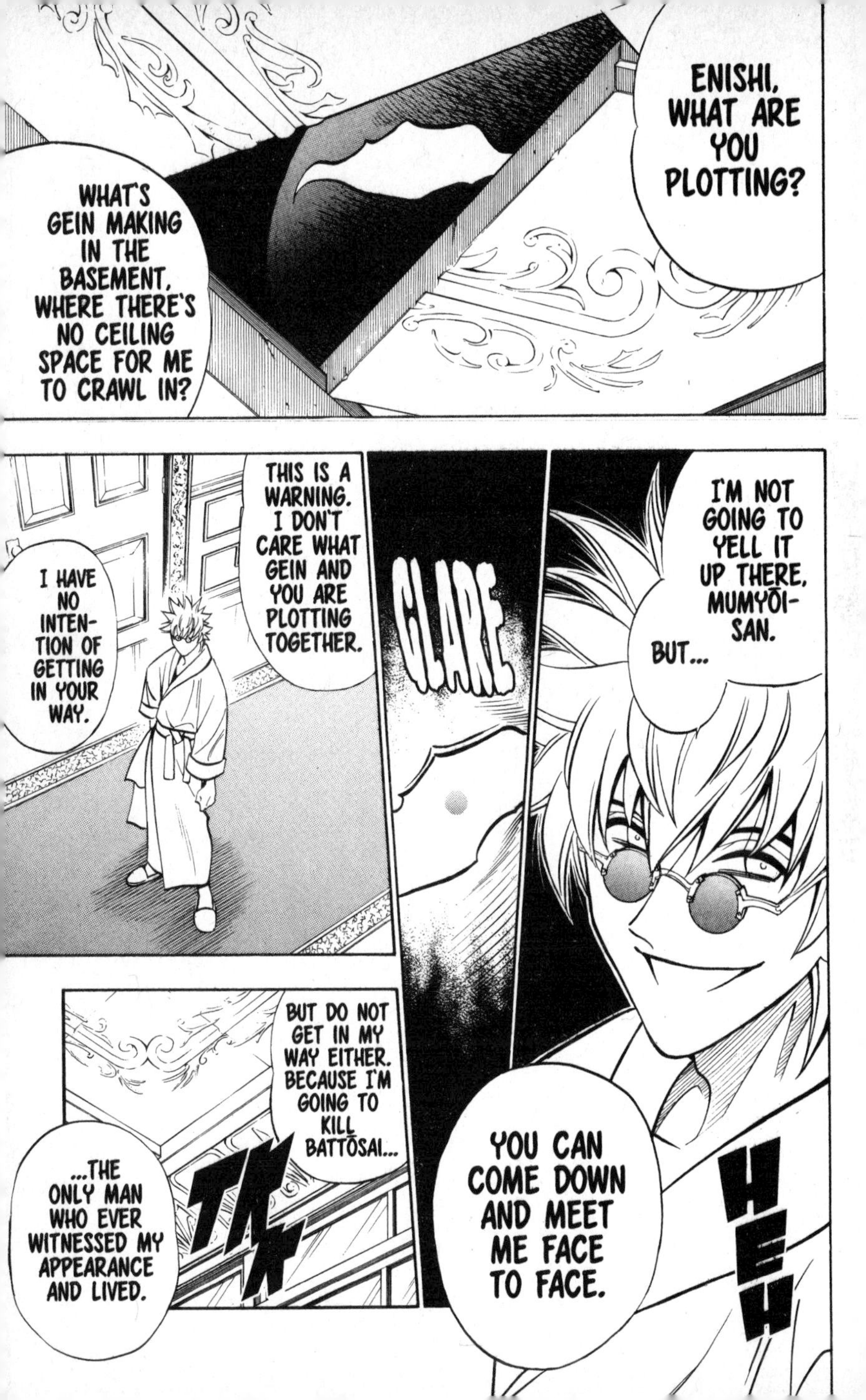
ENISHI, WHAT ARE YOU PLOTTING?
WHAT'S GEIN MAKING IN THE BASEMENT, WHERE THERE'S NO CEILING SPACE FOR ME TO CRAWL IN?
I'M NOT GOING TO YELL IT UP THERE, MUMYŌI-SAN.
BUT...
YOU CAN COME DOWN AND MEET ME FACE TO FACE.
HEH
GLARE
THIS IS A WARNING. I DON'T CARE WHAT GEIN AND YOU ARE PLOTTING TOGETHER.
I HAVE NO INTENTION OF GETTING IN YOUR WAY.
BUT DO NOT GET IN MY WAY EITHER. BECAUSE I'M GOING TO KILL BATTŌSAI...
...THE ONLY MAN WHO EVER WITNESSED MY APPEARANCE AND LIVED.

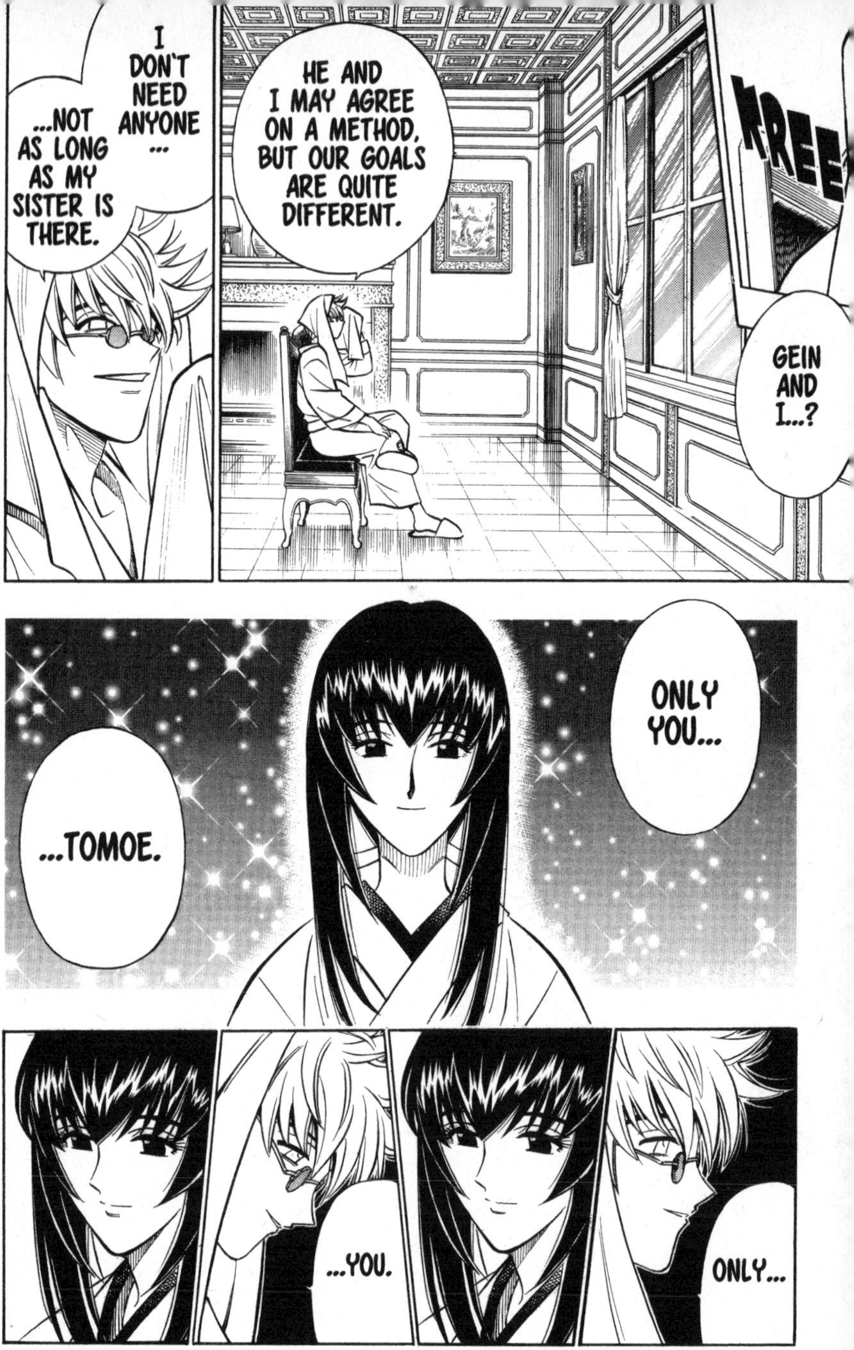
KREE
GEIN AND I...?
HE AND I MAY AGREE ON A METHOD, BUT OUR GOALS ARE QUITE DIFFERENT.
I DON'T NEED ANYONE...
...NOT AS LONG AS MY SISTER IS THERE.
ONLY YOU...
...TOMOE.
ONLY...
...YOU.

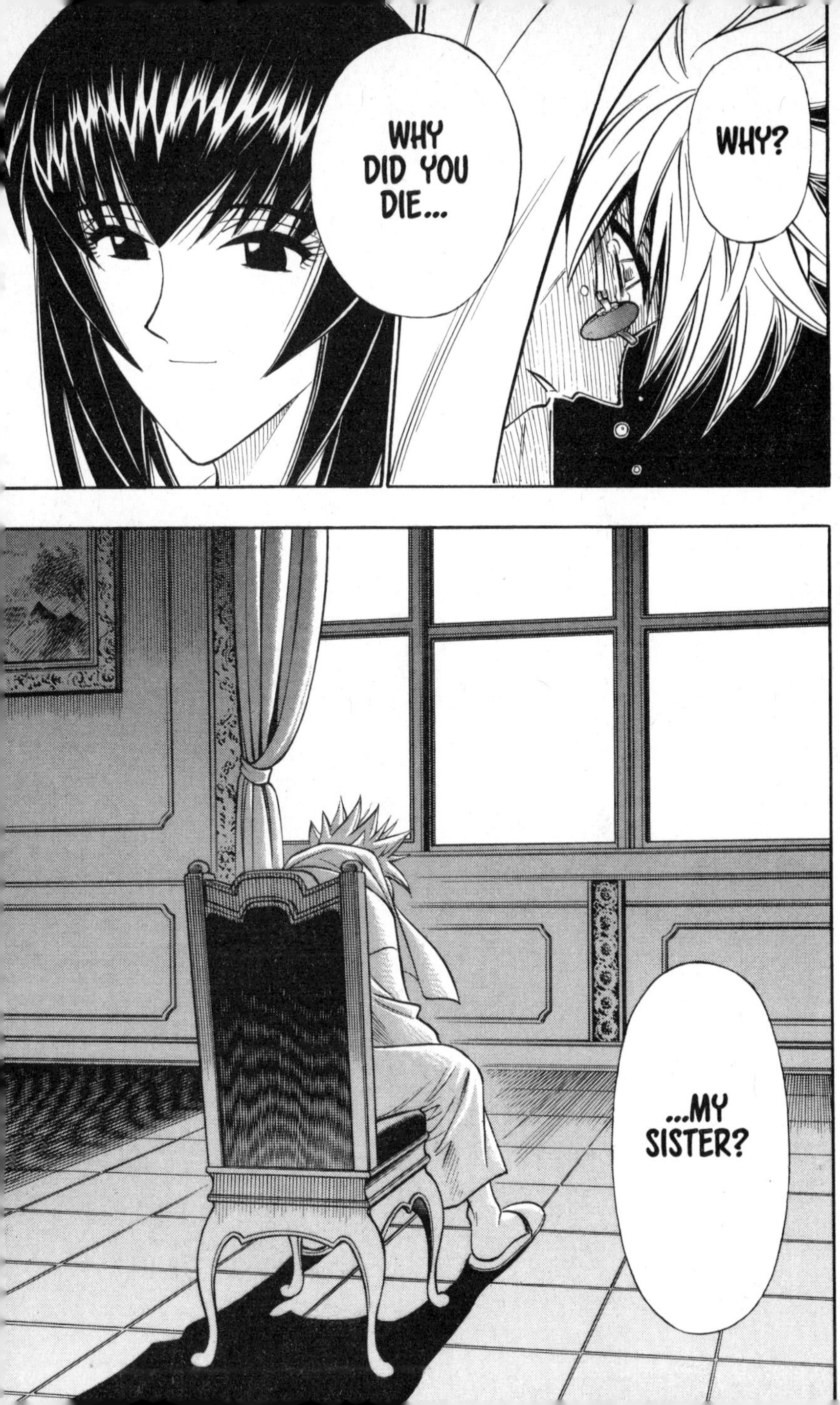
WHY?
WHY DID YOU DIE...
...MY SISTER?

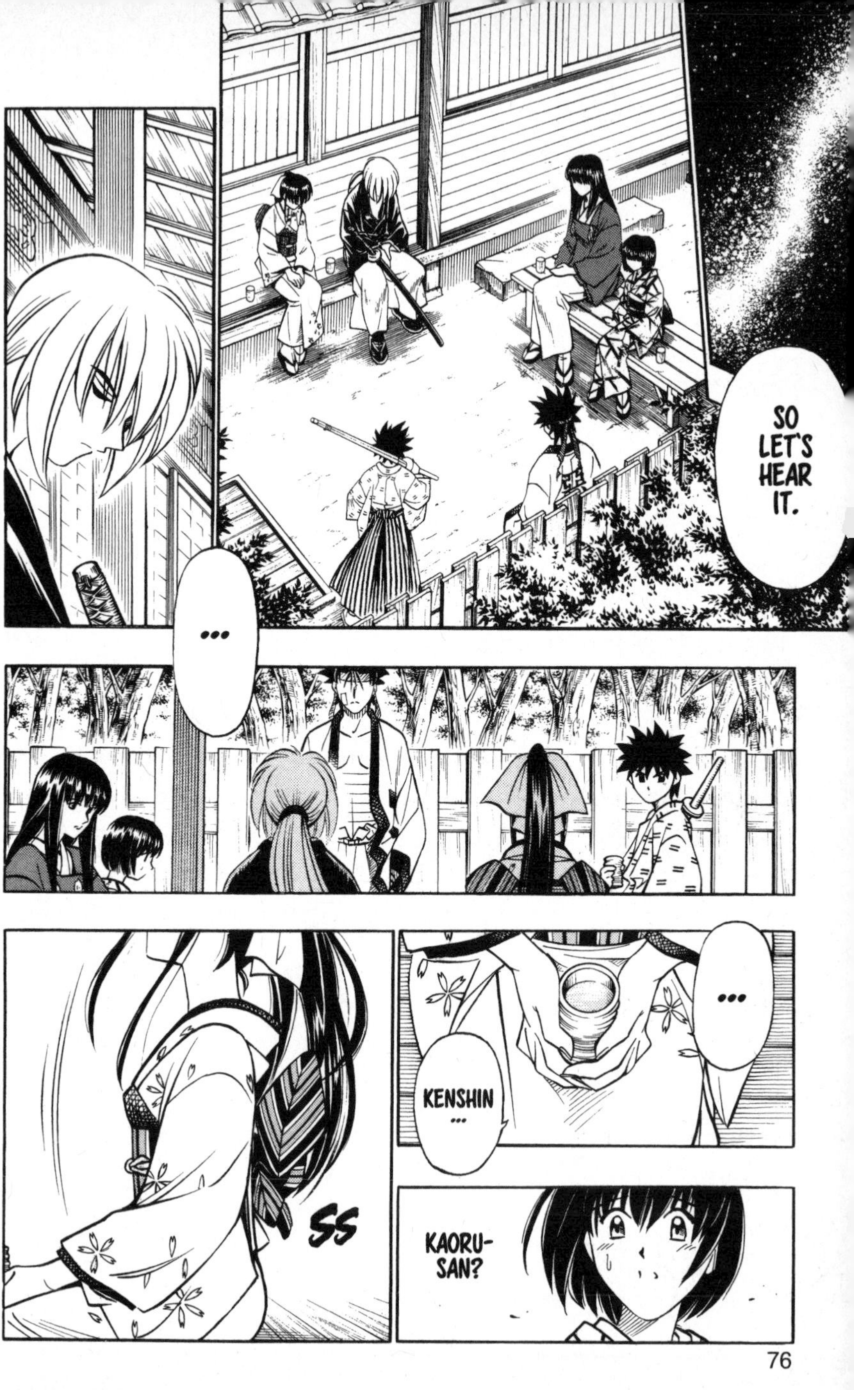
SO LET'S HEAR IT.
...
...
KENSHIN ...
KAORU-SAN?
SS

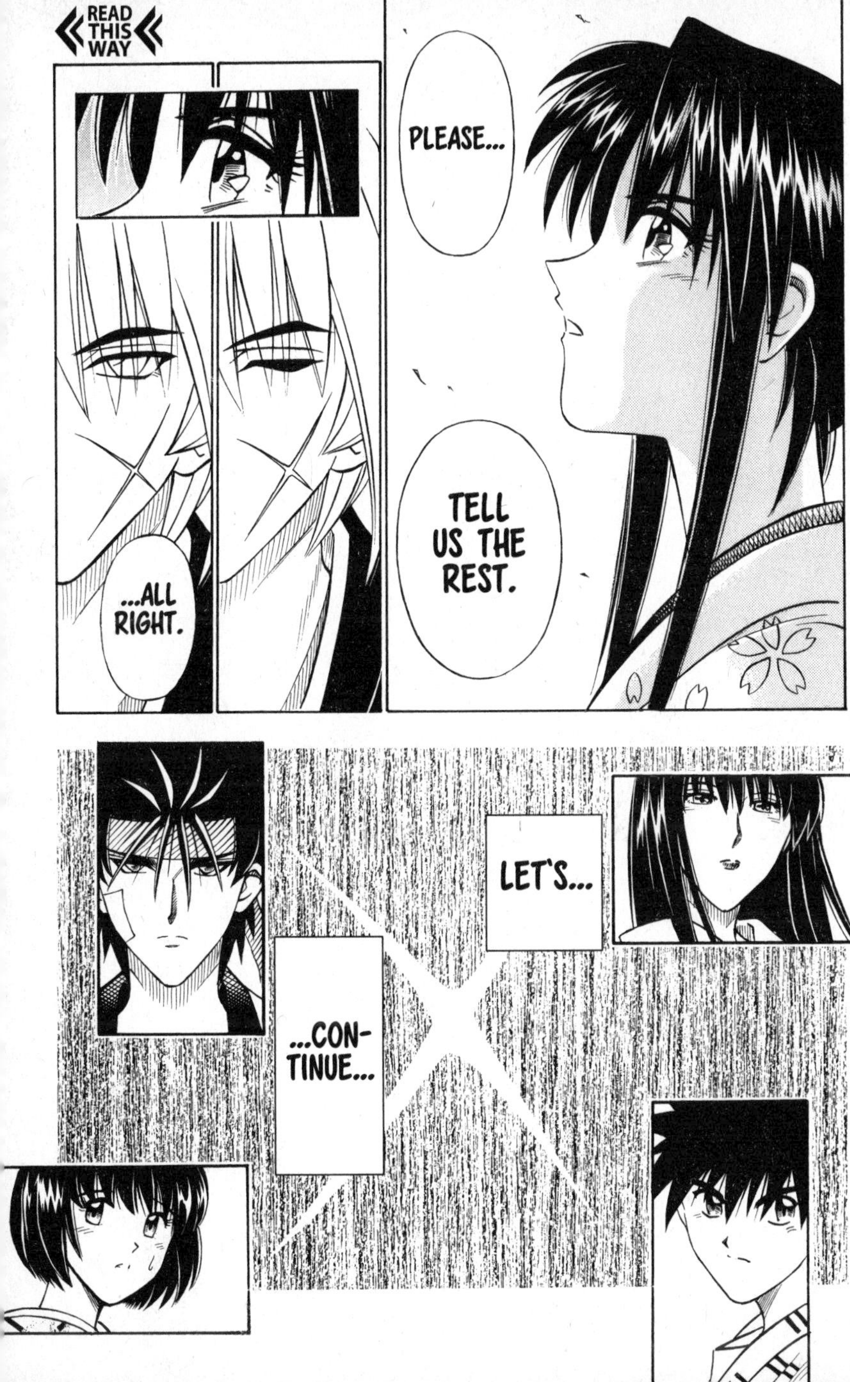
READ THIS WAY
PLEASE...
TELL US THE REST.
...ALL RIGHT.
LET'S...
...CON-TINUE...

Act 172
Remembrance 7: By the Farmlands

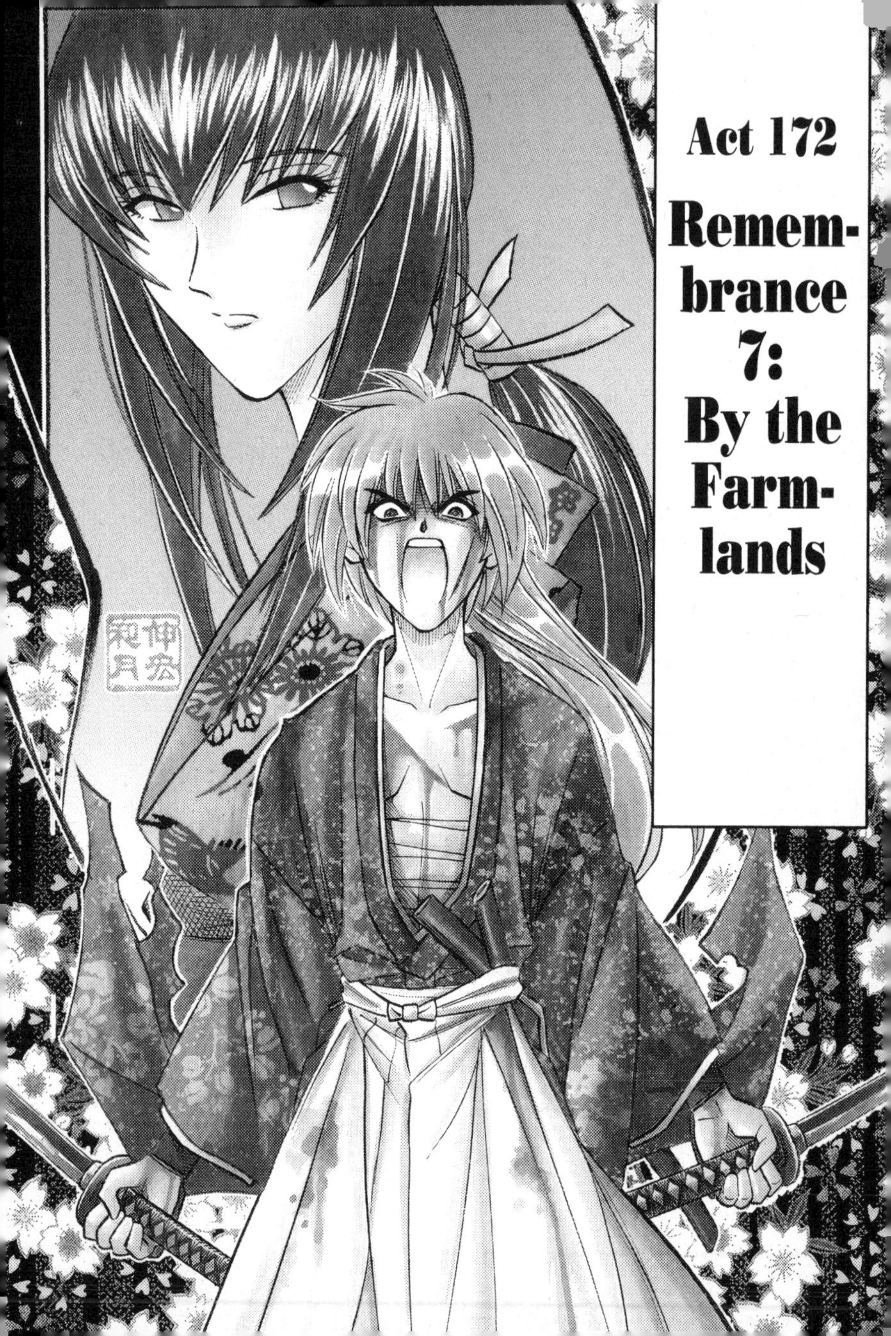

READ THIS WAY

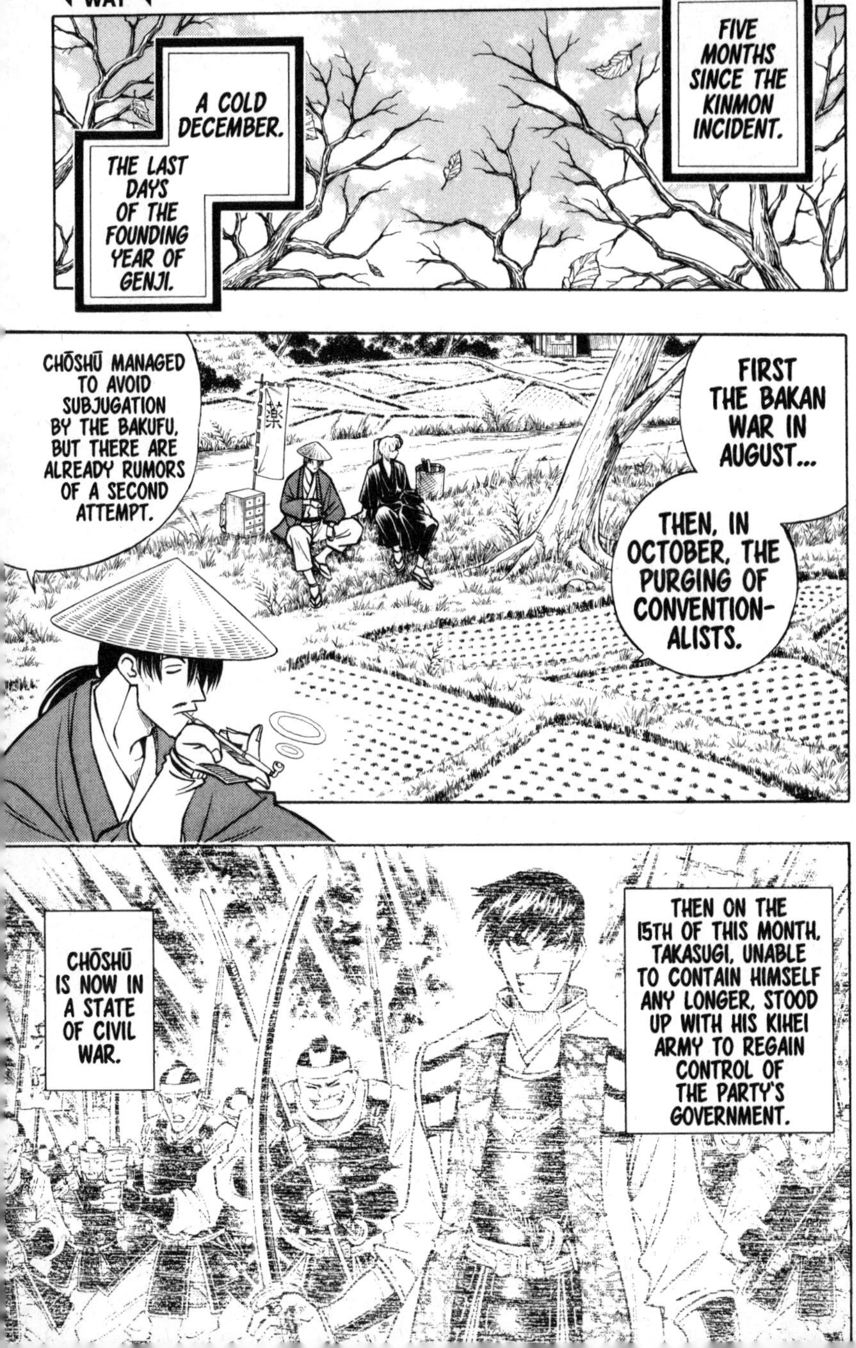
FIVE MONTHS SINCE THE KINMON INCIDENT.
A COLD DECEMBER.
THE LAST DAYS OF THE FOUNDING YEAR OF GENJI.
FIRST THE BAKAN WAR IN AUGUST...
THEN, IN OCTOBER, THE PURGING OF CONVENTION-ALISTS.
CHŌSHŪ MANAGED TO AVOID SUBJUGATION BY THE BAKUFU, BUT THERE ARE ALREADY RUMORS OF A SECOND ATTEMPT.
THEN ON THE 15TH OF THIS MONTH, TAKASUGI, UNABLE TO CONTAIN HIMSELF ANY LONGER, STOOD UP WITH HIS KIHEI ARMY TO REGAIN CONTROL OF THE PARTY'S GOVERNMENT.
CHŌSHŪ IS NOW IN A STATE OF CIVIL WAR.

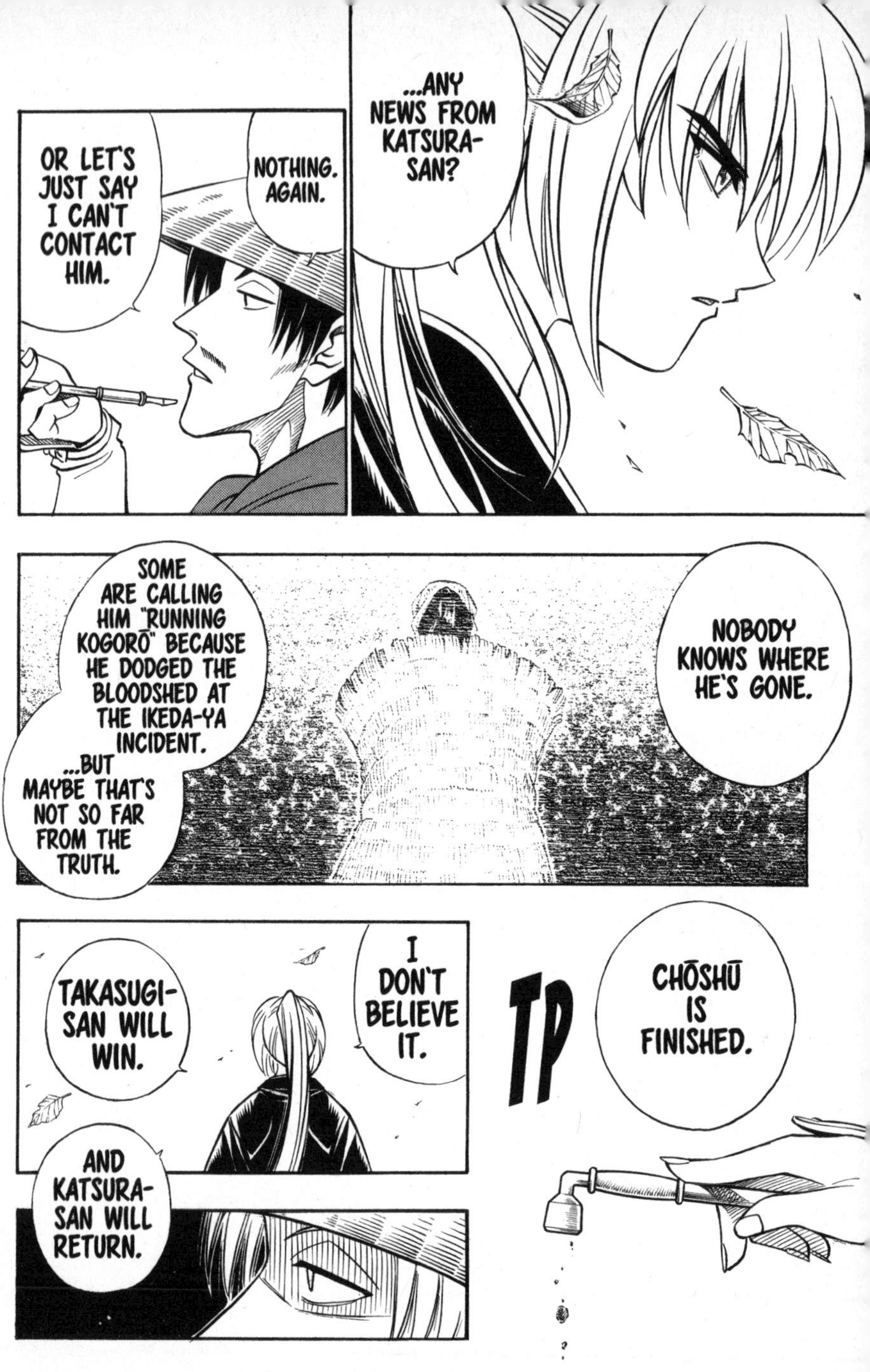
...ANY NEWS FROM KATSURA-SAN?
NOTHING. AGAIN.
OR LET'S JUST SAY I CAN'T CONTACT HIM.
NOBODY KNOWS WHERE HE'S GONE.
SOME ARE CALLING HIM "RUNNING KOGORŌ" BECAUSE HE DODGED THE BLOODSHED AT THE IKEDA-YA INCIDENT.
...BUT MAYBE THAT'S NOT SO FAR FROM THE TRUTH.
TP
CHŌSHŪ IS FINISHED.
I DON'T BELIEVE IT.
TAKASUGI-SAN WILL WIN.
AND KATSURA-SAN WILL RETURN.

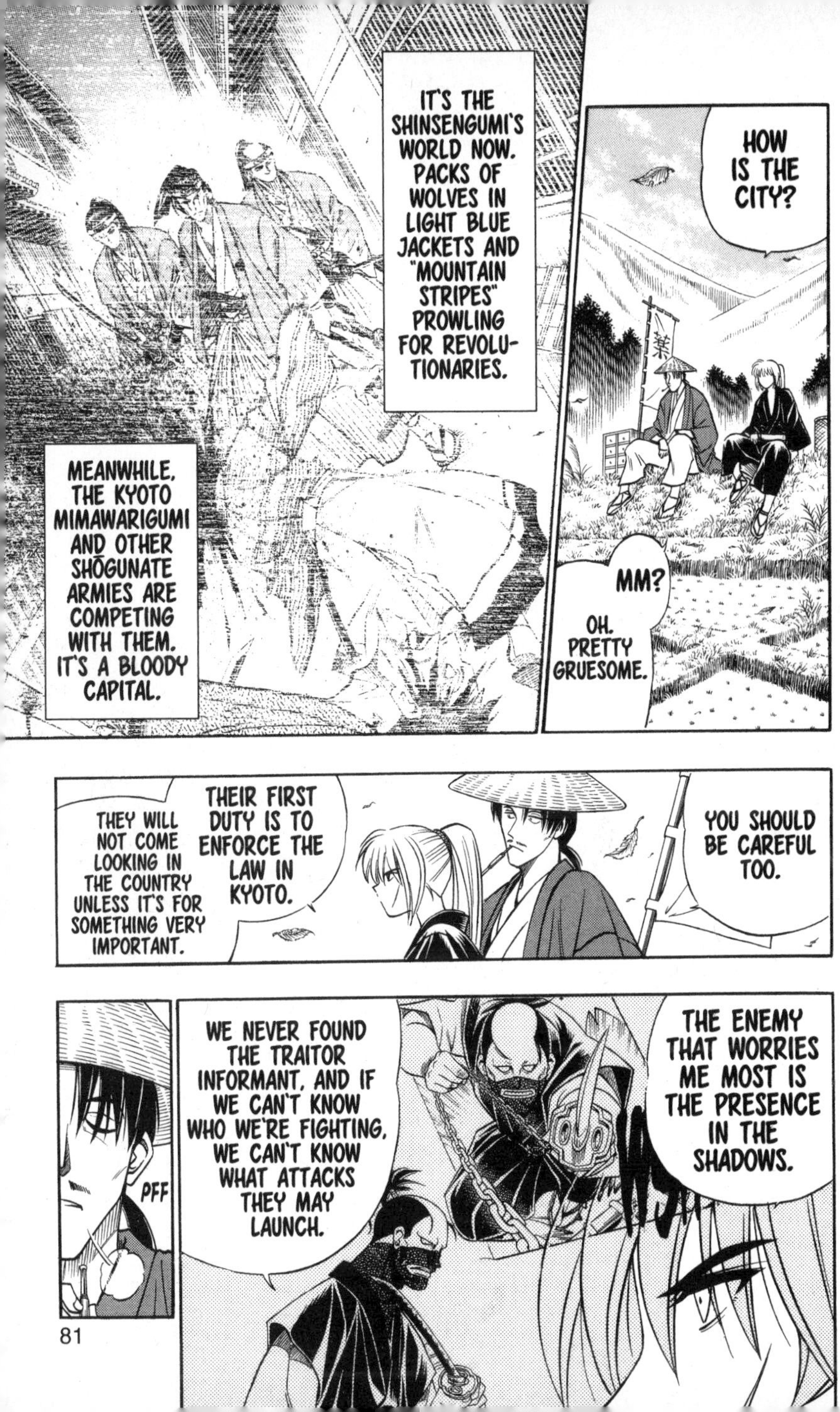
HOW IS THE CITY?
MM?
OH. PRETTY GRUESOME.
IT'S THE SHINSENGUMI'S WORLD NOW. PACKS OF WOLVES IN LIGHT BLUE JACKETS AND "MOUNTAIN STRIPES" PROWLING FOR REVOLUTIONARIES.
MEANWHILE, THE KYOTO MIMAWARIGUMI AND OTHER SHŌGUNATE ARMIES ARE COMPETING WITH THEM. IT'S A BLOODY CAPITAL.
YOU SHOULD BE CAREFUL TOO.
THEIR FIRST DUTY IS TO ENFORCE THE LAW IN KYOTO.
THEY WILL NOT COME LOOKING IN THE COUNTRY UNLESS IT'S FOR SOMETHING VERY IMPORTANT.
THE ENEMY THAT WORRIES ME MOST IS THE PRESENCE IN THE SHADOWS.
WE NEVER FOUND THE TRAITOR INFORMANT, AND IF WE CAN'T KNOW WHO WE'RE FIGHTING, WE CAN'T KNOW WHAT ATTACKS THEY MAY LAUNCH.
PFF

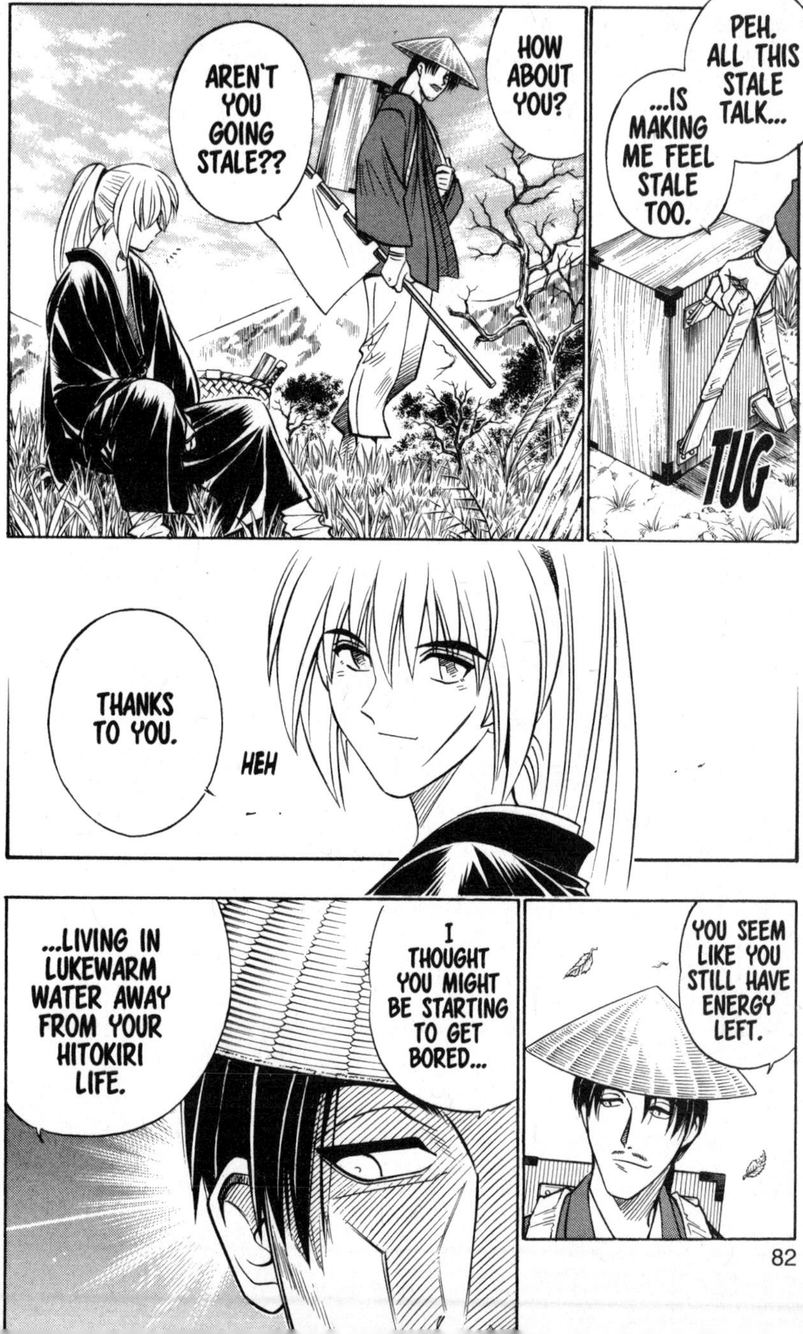
PEH. ALL THIS STALE TALK...
...IS MAKING ME FEEL STALE TOO.
TUG
HOW ABOUT YOU?
AREN'T YOU GOING STALE??
THANKS TO YOU.
HEH
YOU SEEM LIKE YOU STILL HAVE ENERGY LEFT.
I THOUGHT YOU MIGHT BE STARTING TO GET BORED...
...LIVING IN LUKEWARM WATER AWAY FROM YOUR HITOKIRI LIFE.

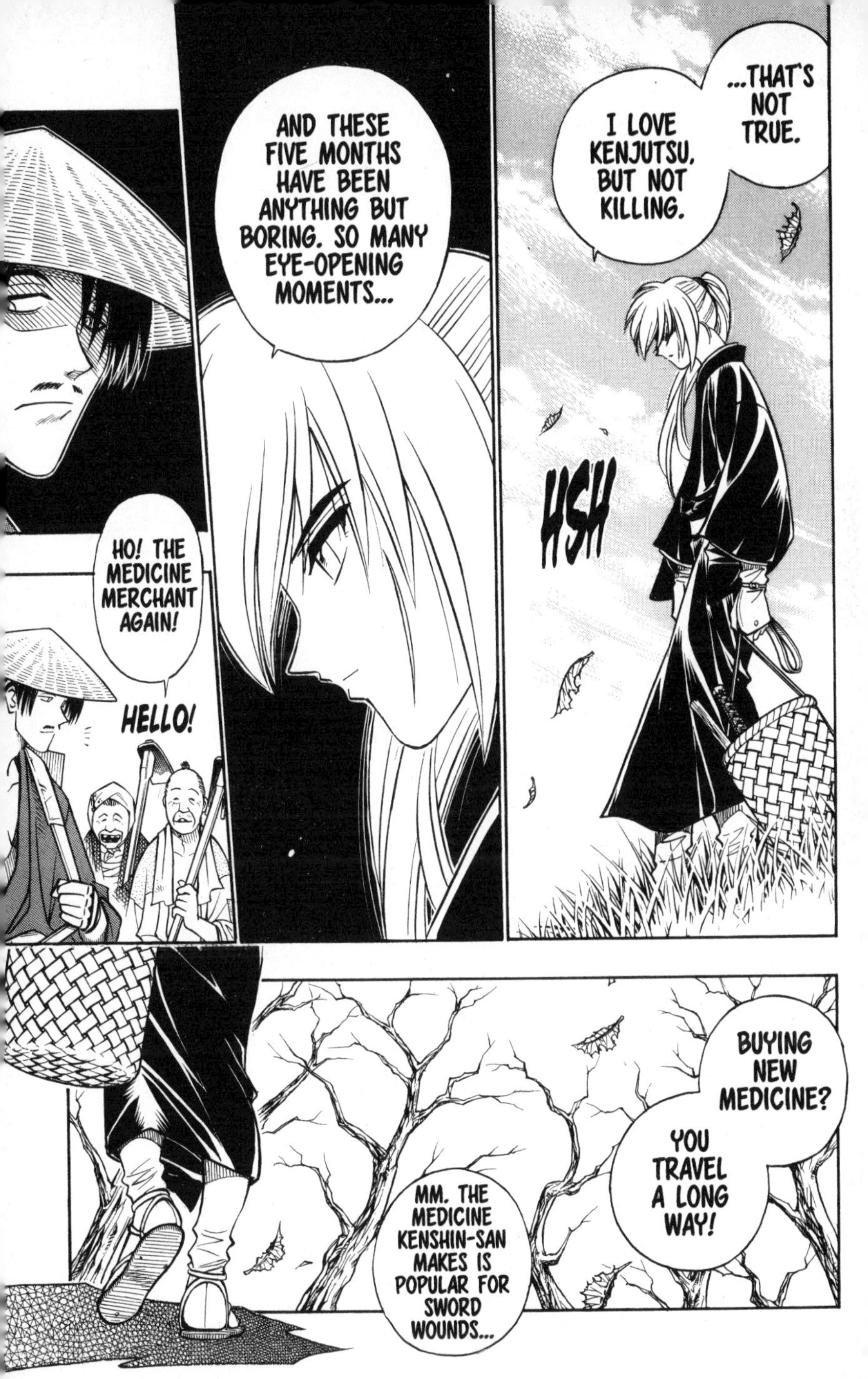
...THAT'S NOT TRUE.
I LOVE KENJUTSU, BUT NOT KILLING.
HSH
AND THESE FIVE MONTHS HAVE BEEN ANYTHING BUT BORING. SO MANY EYE-OPENING MOMENTS...
HO! THE MEDICINE MERCHANT AGAIN!
HELLO!
BUYING NEW MEDICINE?
YOU TRAVEL A LONG WAY!
MM. THE MEDICINE KENSHIN-SAN MAKES IS POPULAR FOR SWORD WOUNDS...

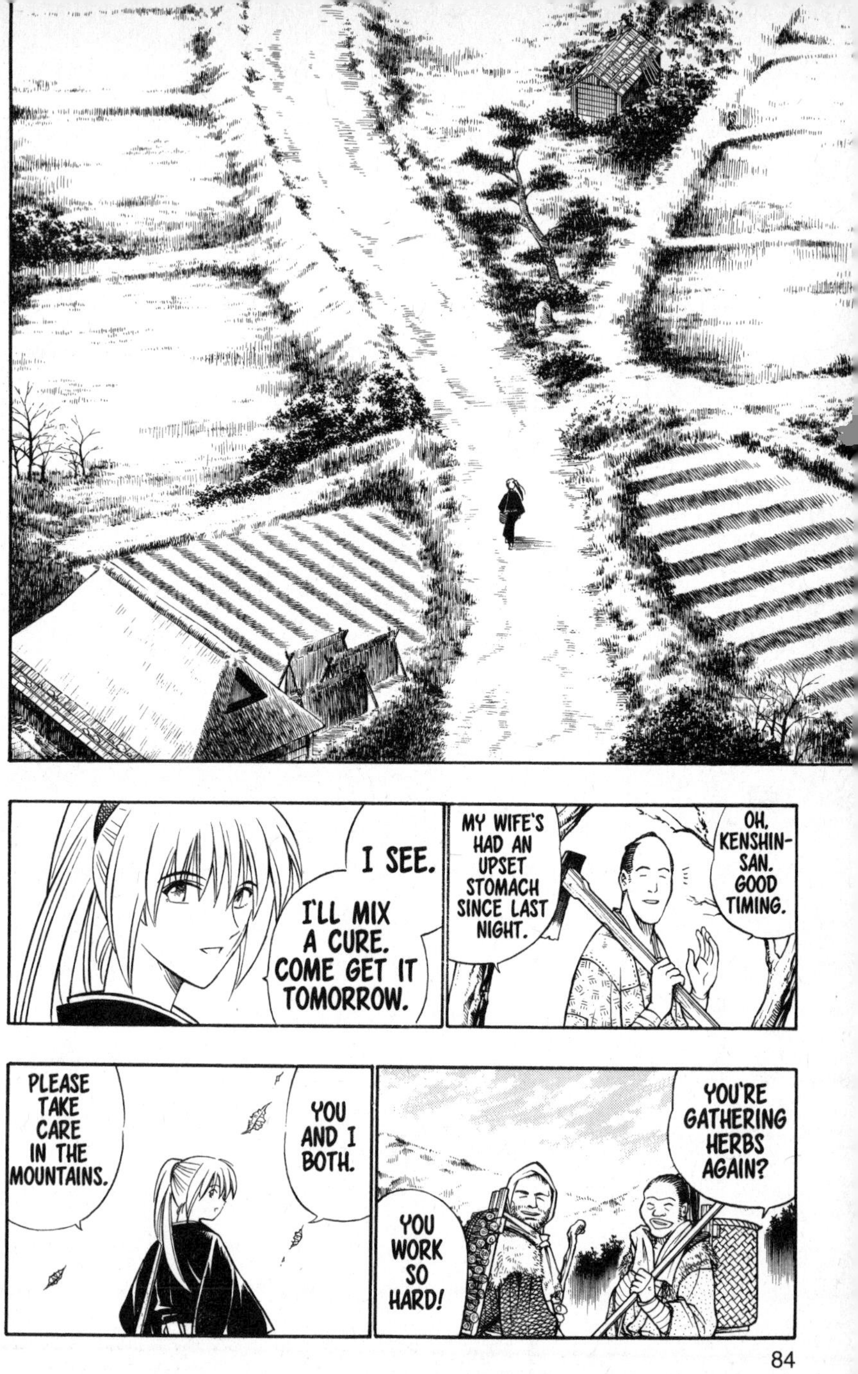
OH, KENSHIN-SAN. GOOD TIMING.
MY WIFE'S HAD AN UPSET STOMACH SINCE LAST NIGHT.
I SEE.
I'LL MIX A CURE. COME GET IT TOMORROW.
YOU'RE GATHERING HERBS AGAIN?
YOU WORK SO HARD!
YOU AND I BOTH.
PLEASE TAKE CARE IN THE MOUNTAINS.

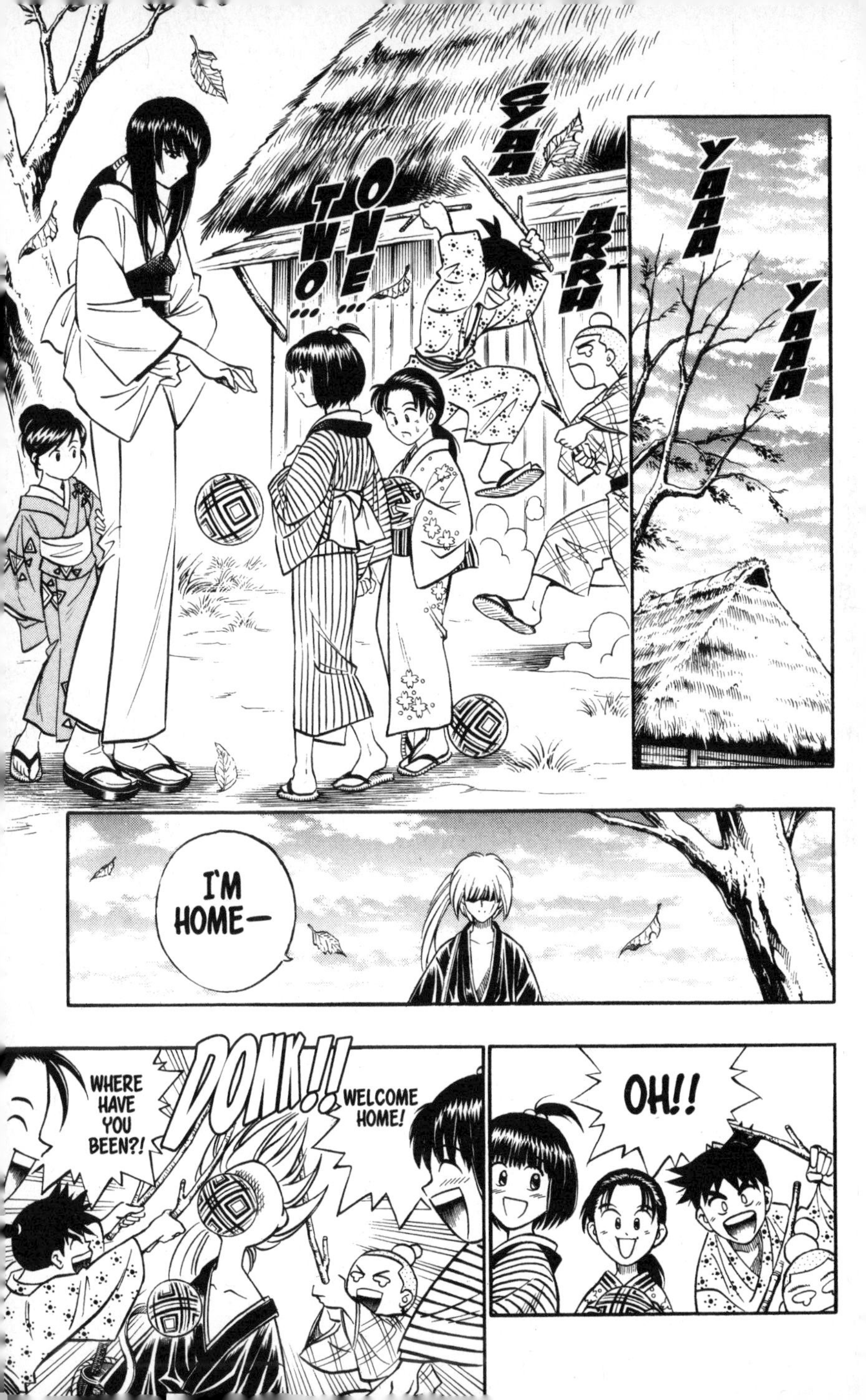
YAAA
YAAA
GYAA
ARRH
ONE...
TWO...
I'M HOME—
OH!!
WELCOME HOME!
DONK!!
WHERE HAVE YOU BEEN?!

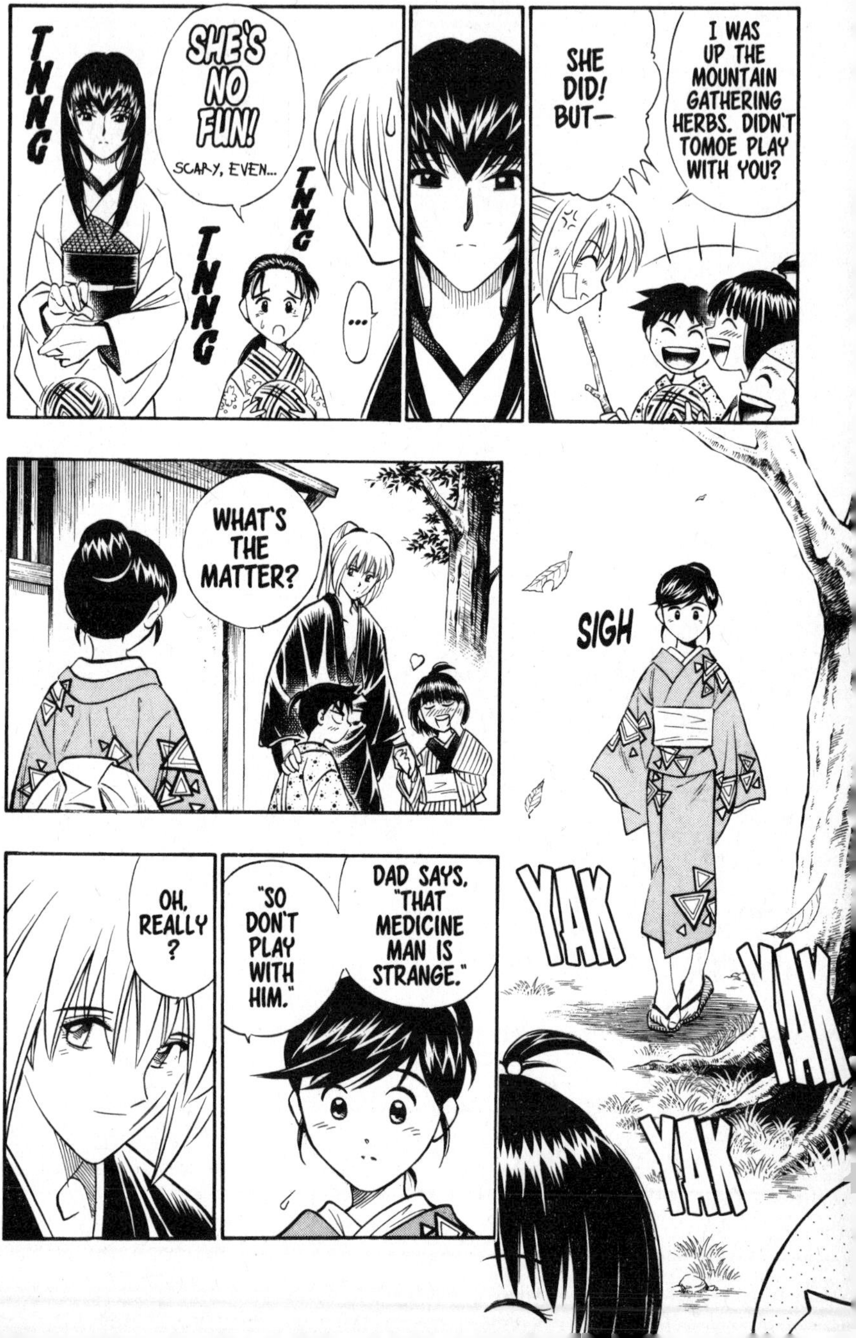
I WAS UP THE MOUNTAIN GATHERING HERBS. DIDN'T TOMOE PLAY WITH YOU?
SHE DID! BUT—
...
SHE'S NO FUN!
SCARY, EVEN...
TNNG
TNNG
TNNG
SIGH
YAK
YAK
YAK
WHAT'S THE MATTER?
DAD SAYS, "THAT MEDICINE MAN IS STRANGE."
"SO DON'T PLAY WITH HIM."
OH, REALLY?

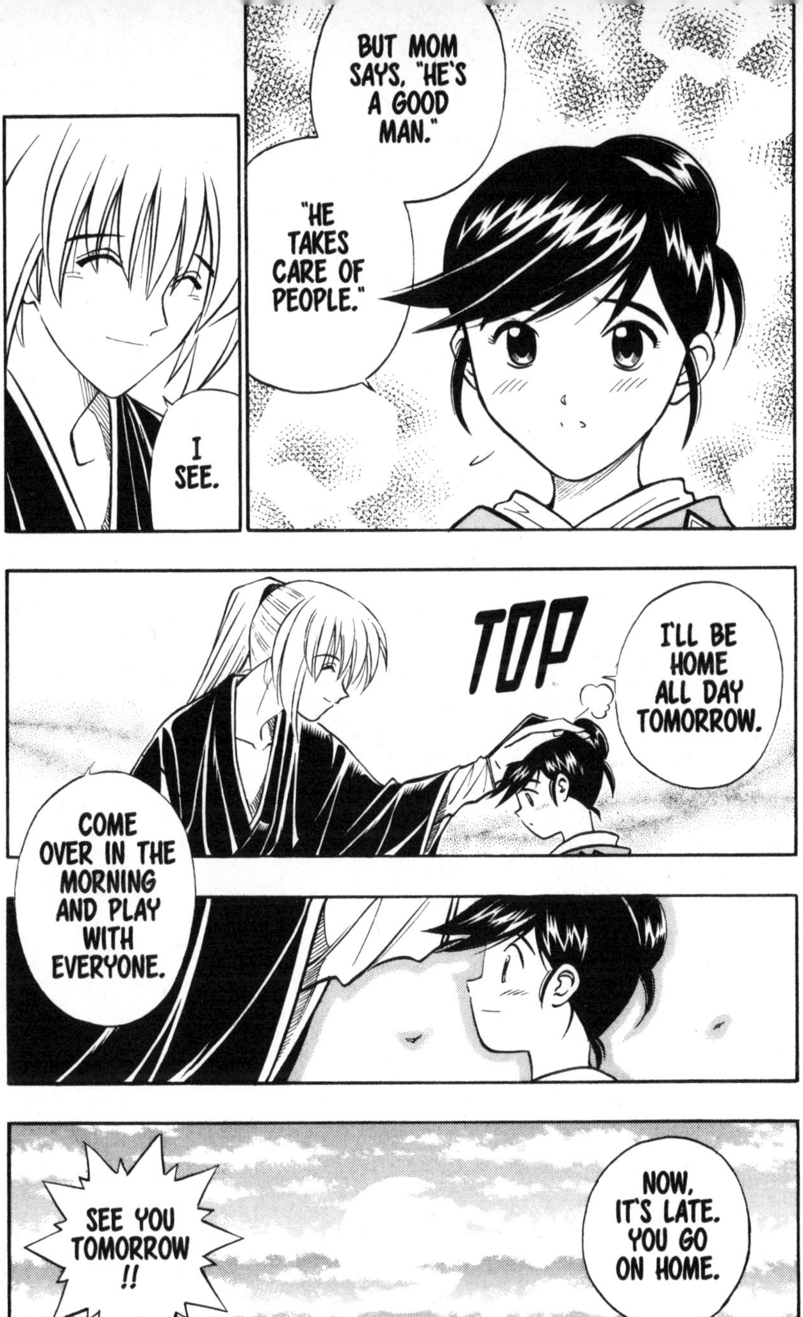
BUT MOM SAYS, "HE'S A GOOD MAN."
"HE TAKES CARE OF PEOPLE."
I SEE.
TOP
I'LL BE HOME ALL DAY TOMORROW.
COME OVER IN THE MORNING AND PLAY WITH EVERYONE.
NOW, IT'S LATE. YOU GO ON HOME.
SEE YOU TOMORROW !!

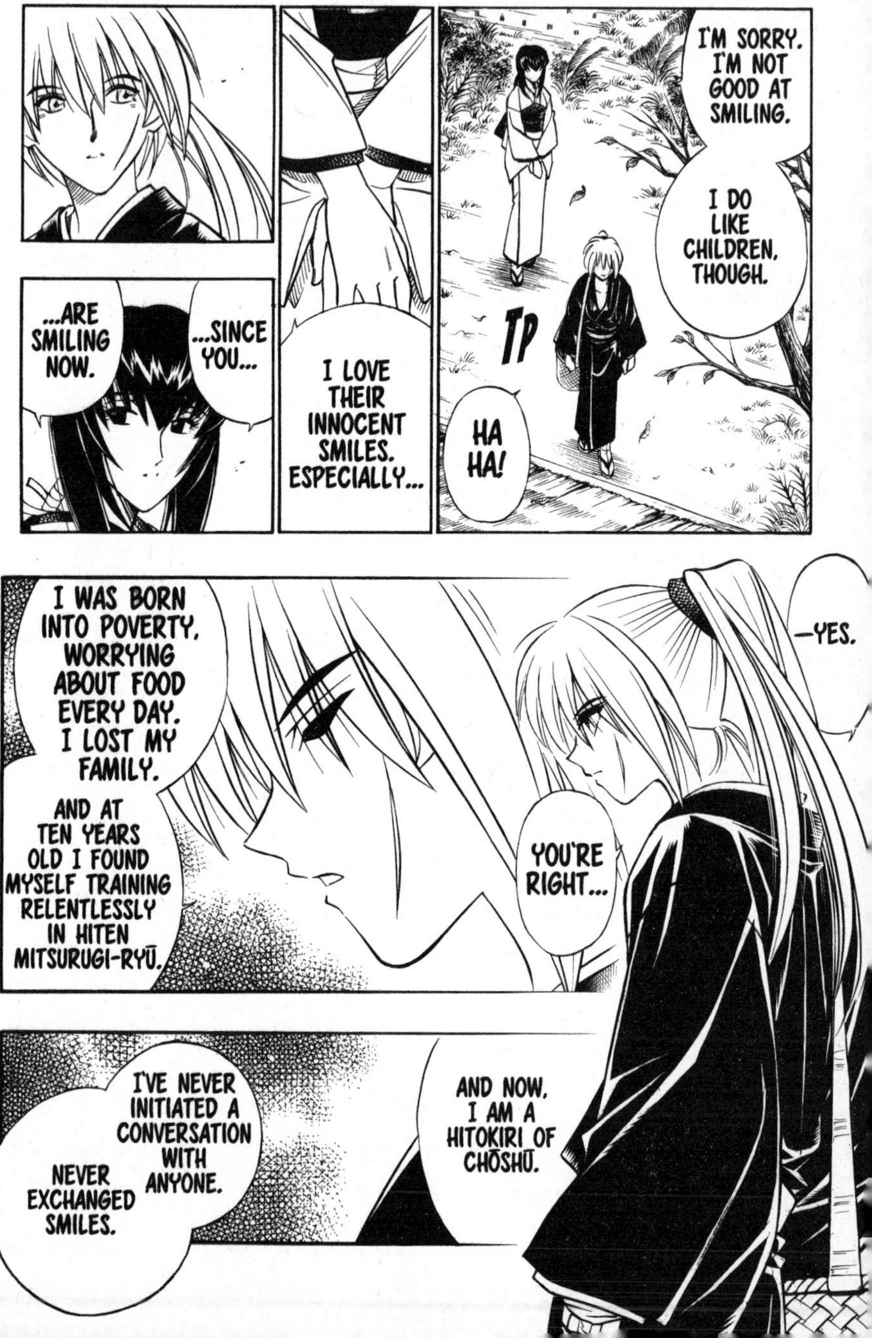
I'M SORRY. I'M NOT GOOD AT SMILING.
I DO LIKE CHILDREN, THOUGH.
TP
HA HA!
I LOVE THEIR INNOCENT SMILES. ESPECIALLY...
...SINCE YOU...
...ARE SMILING NOW.
—YES.
YOU'RE RIGHT...
I WAS BORN INTO POVERTY, WORRYING ABOUT FOOD EVERY DAY. I LOST MY FAMILY.
AND AT TEN YEARS OLD I FOUND MYSELF TRAINING RELENTLESSLY IN HITEN MITSURUGI-RYŪ.
AND NOW, I AM A HITOKIRI OF CHŌSHŪ.
I'VE NEVER INITIATED A CONVERSATION WITH ANYONE.
NEVER EXCHANGED SMILES.

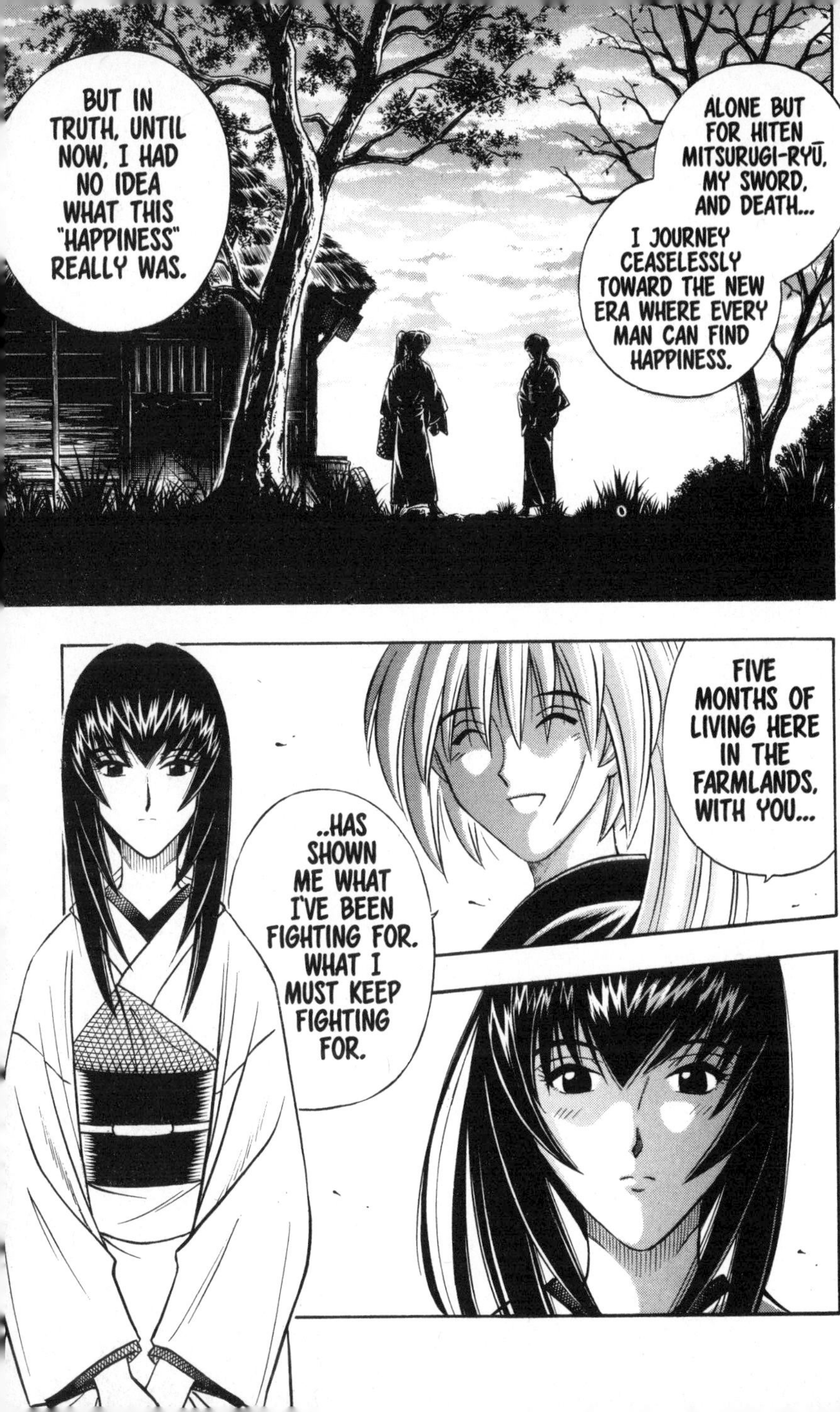
ALONE BUT FOR HITEN MITSURUGI-RYŪ, MY SWORD, AND DEATH...
I JOURNEY CEASELESSLY TOWARD THE NEW ERA WHERE EVERY MAN CAN FIND HAPPINESS.
BUT IN TRUTH, UNTIL NOW, I HAD NO IDEA WHAT THIS "HAPPINESS" REALLY WAS.
FIVE MONTHS OF LIVING HERE IN THE FARMLANDS, WITH YOU...
..HAS SHOWN ME WHAT I'VE BEEN FIGHTING FOR. WHAT I MUST KEEP FIGHTING FOR.

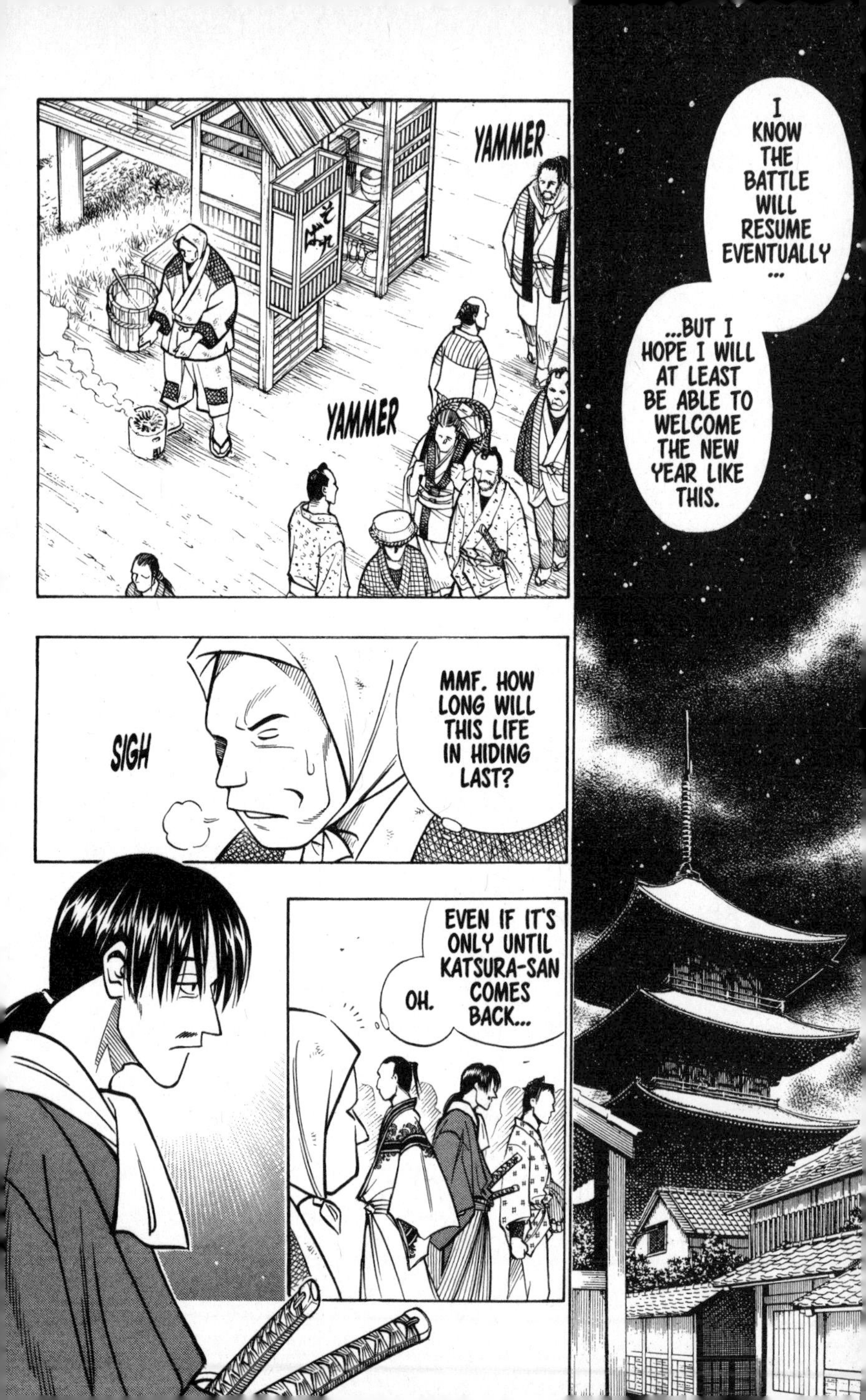
I KNOW THE BATTLE WILL RESUME EVENTUALLY...
...BUT I HOPE I WILL AT LEAST BE ABLE TO WELCOME THE NEW YEAR LIKE THIS.
YAMMER
YAMMER
MMF. HOW LONG WILL THIS LIFE IN HIDING LAST?
SIGH
EVEN IF IT'S ONLY UNTIL KATSURA-SAN COMES BACK...
OH.

READ THIS WAY

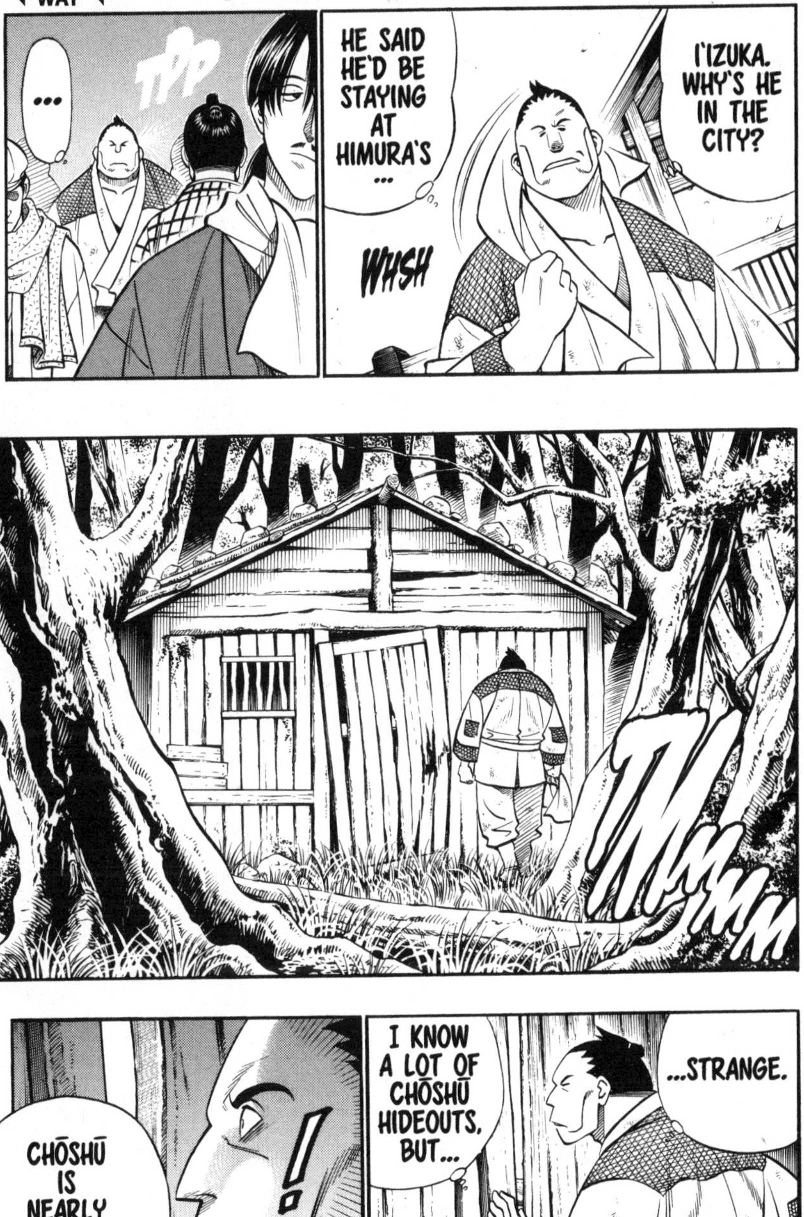
I'IZUKA. WHY'S HE IN THE CITY?
HE SAID HE'D BE STAYING AT HIMURA'S ...
WHSH
TPP
...
TMMMM
...STRANGE.
I KNOW A LOT OF CHŌSHŪ HIDEOUTS, BUT...
!
CHŌSHŪ IS NEARLY FINISHED.

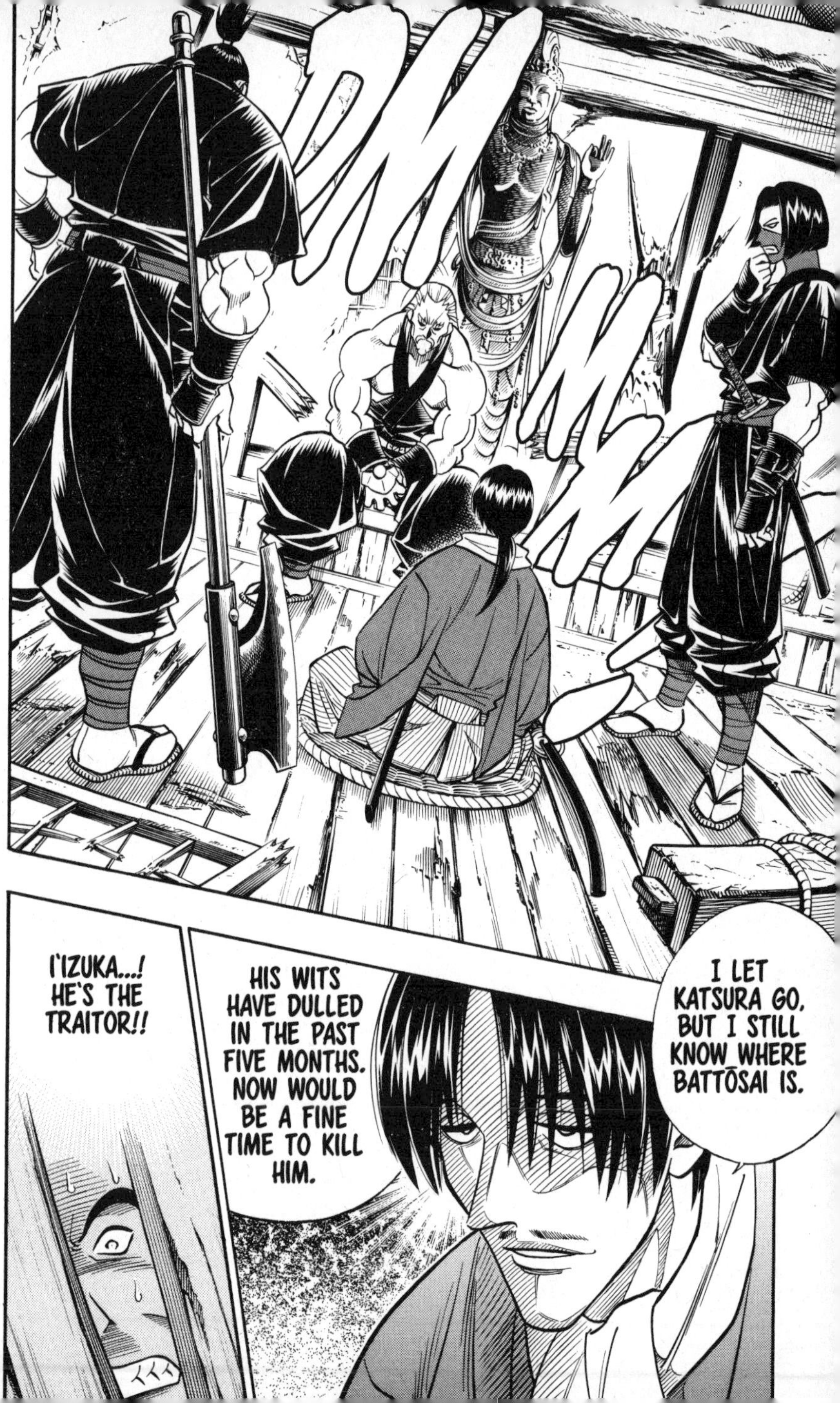
I LET KATSURA GO, BUT I STILL KNOW WHERE BATTŌSAI IS.
HIS WITS HAVE DULLED IN THE PAST FIVE MONTHS. NOW WOULD BE A FINE TIME TO KILL HIM.
I'IZUKA...! HE'S THE TRAITOR!!

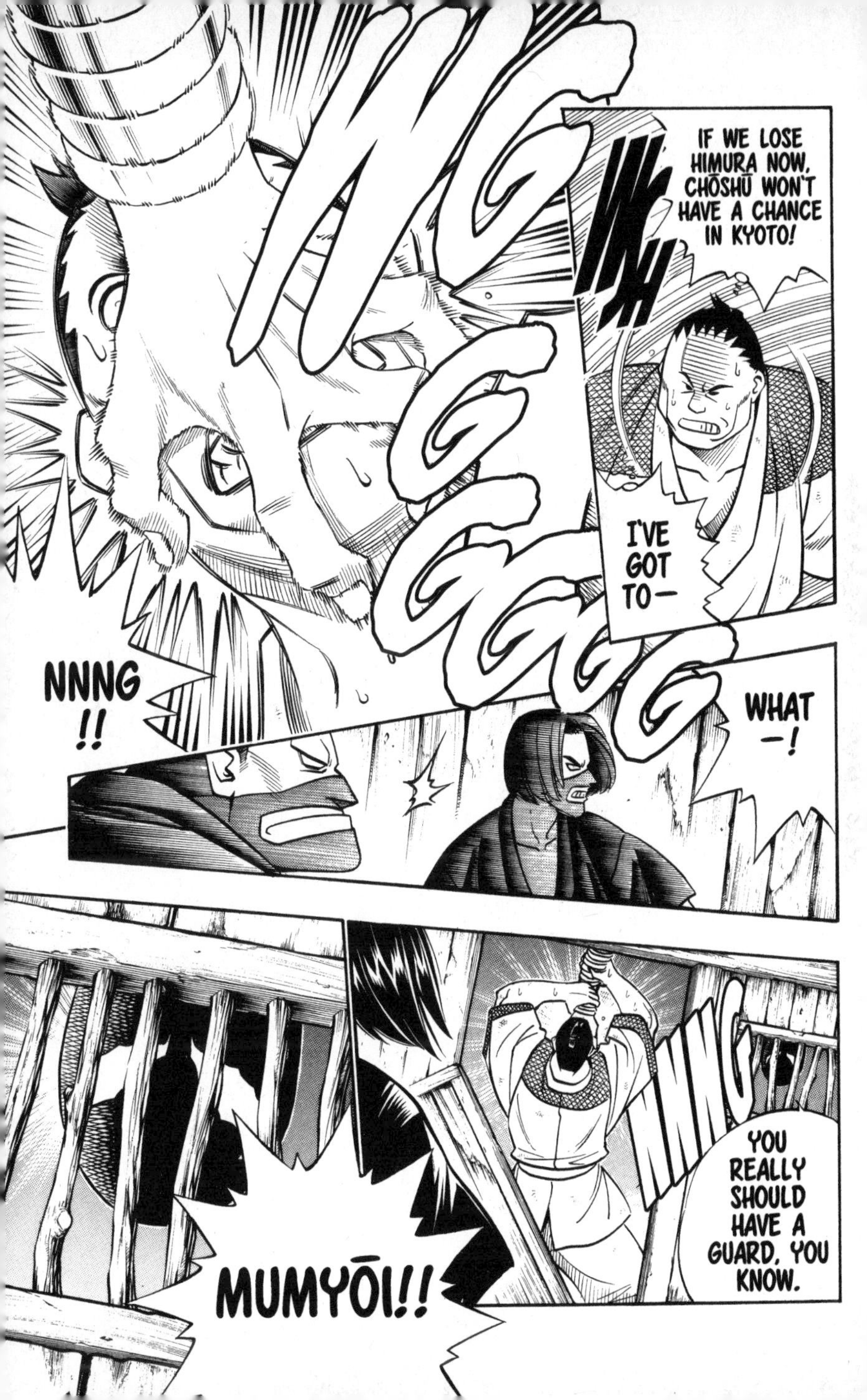
IF WE LOSE HIMURA NOW, CHŌSHŪ WON'T HAVE A CHANCE IN KYOTO!
I'VE GOT TO—
NNNG!!
WHAT—!
YOU REALLY SHOULD HAVE A GUARD, YOU KNOW.
MUMYŌI!!

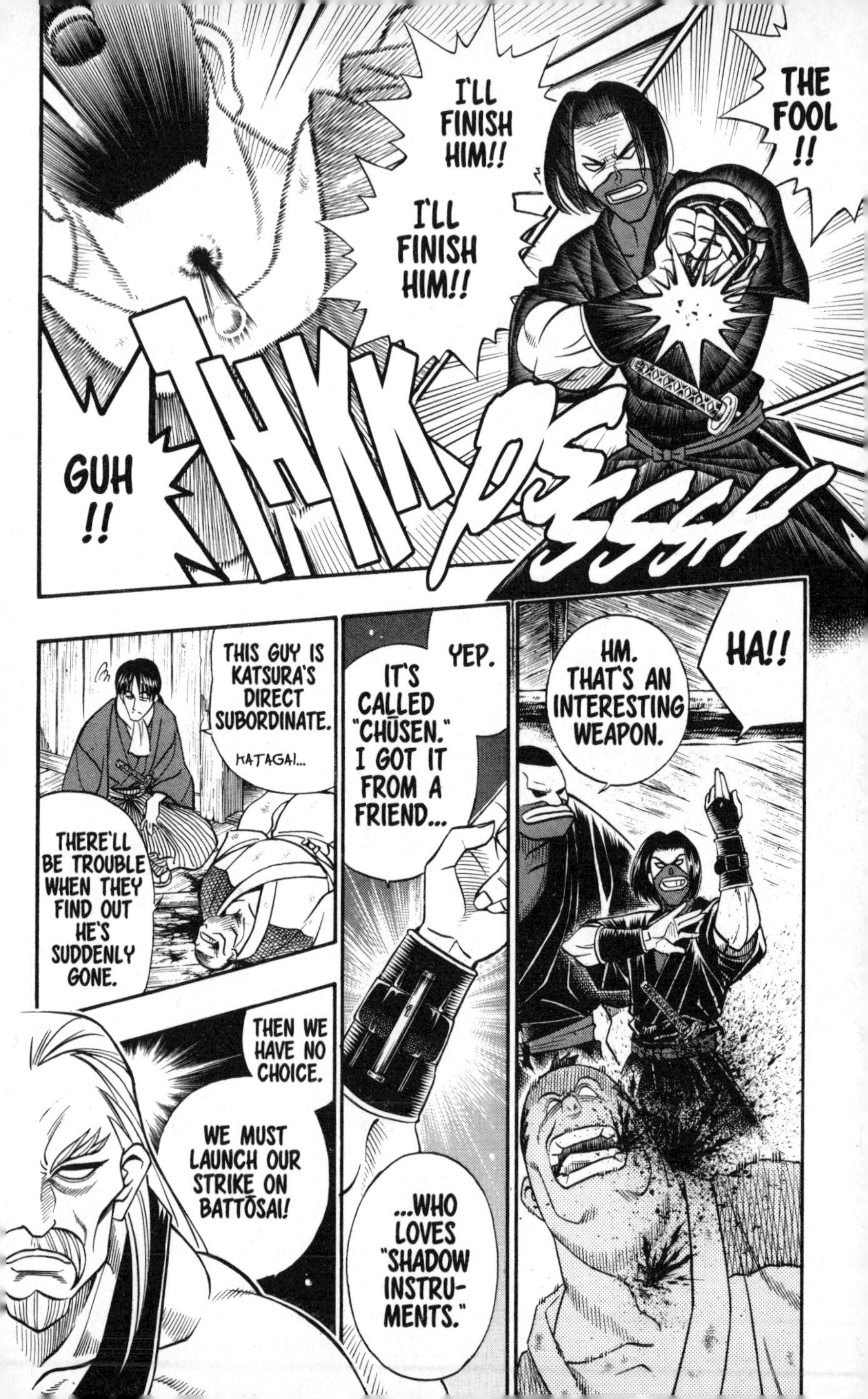
THE FOOL!!
I'LL FINISH HIM!!
I'LL FINISH HIM!!
THKK
PSSSH
GUH!!
HA!!
HM. THAT'S AN INTERESTING WEAPON.
YEP.
IT'S CALLED "CHŪSEN." I GOT IT FROM A FRIEND...
...WHO LOVES "SHADOW INSTRUMENTS."
THIS GUY IS KATSURA'S DIRECT SUBORDINATE.
KATAGAI...
THERE'LL BE TROUBLE WHEN THEY FIND OUT HE'S SUDDENLY GONE.
THEN WE HAVE NO CHOICE.
WE MUST LAUNCH OUR STRIKE ON BATTŌSAI!

READ THIS WAY

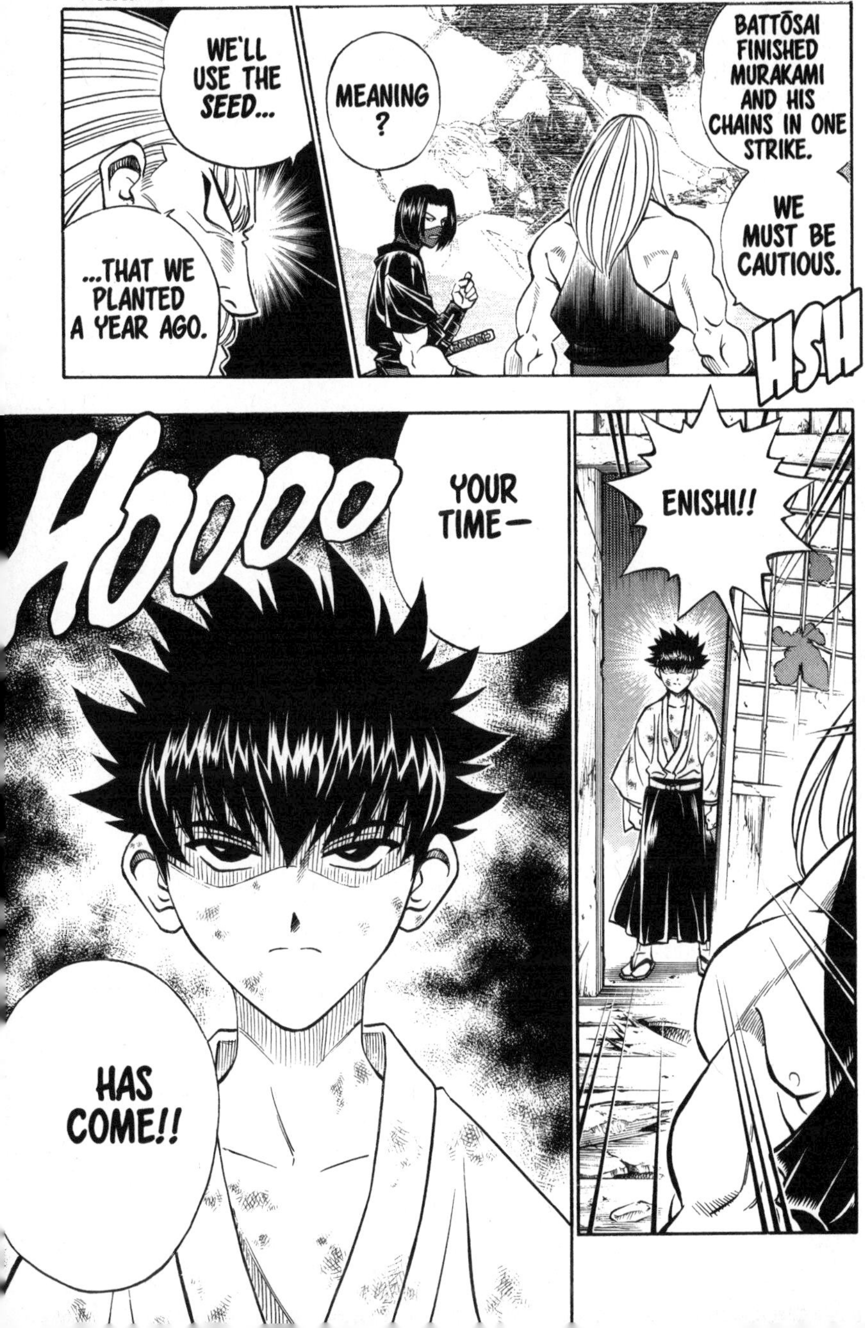
BATTŌSAI FINISHED MURAKAMI AND HIS CHAINS IN ONE STRIKE.
WE MUST BE CAUTIOUS.
HSH
MEANING?
WE'LL USE THE SEED...
...THAT WE PLANTED A YEAR AGO.
ENISHI!!
HOOOO
YOUR TIME—
HAS COME!!

Rurouni Kenshin

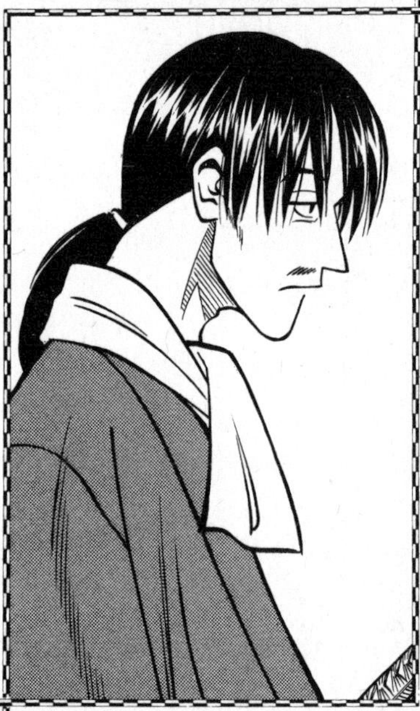

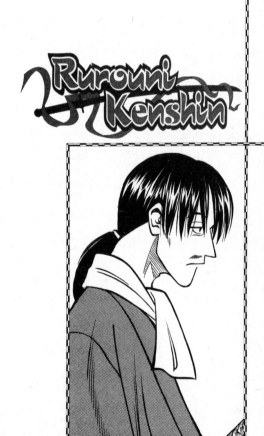

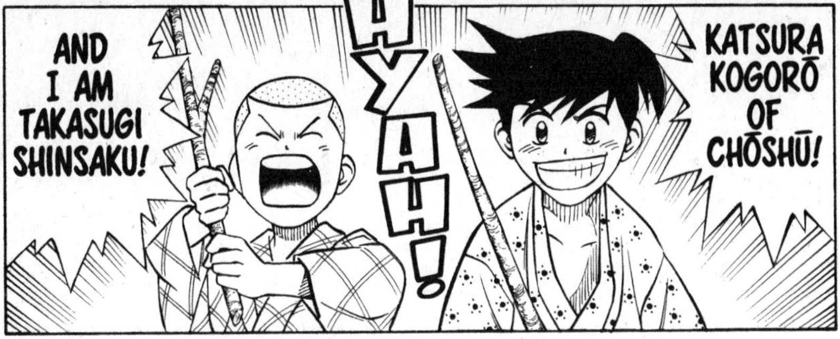
KATSURA KOGORŌ OF CHŌSHŪ!
HYAAH!
AND I AM TAKASUGI SHINSAKU!

Act 173—Remembrance 8: Arrival of Enishi

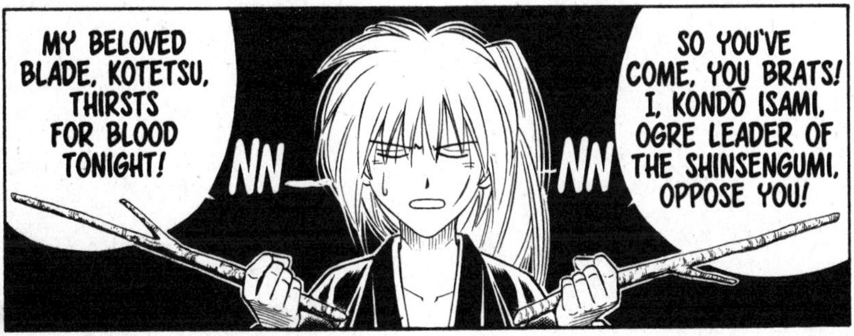
SO YOU'VE COME, YOU BRATS! I, KONDŌ ISAMI, OGRE LEADER OF THE SHINSENGUMI, OPPOSE YOU!
NN—NN
MY BELOVED BLADE, KOTETSU, THIRSTS FOR BLOOD TONIGHT!

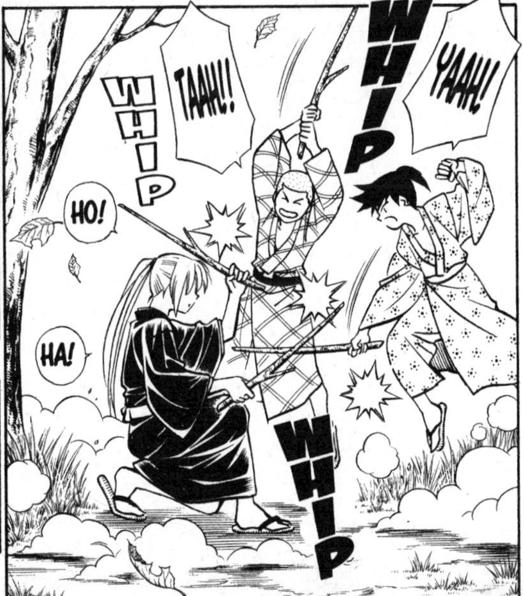
WHIP
YAAH!
TAAH!!
WHIP
HO!
HA!
WHIP

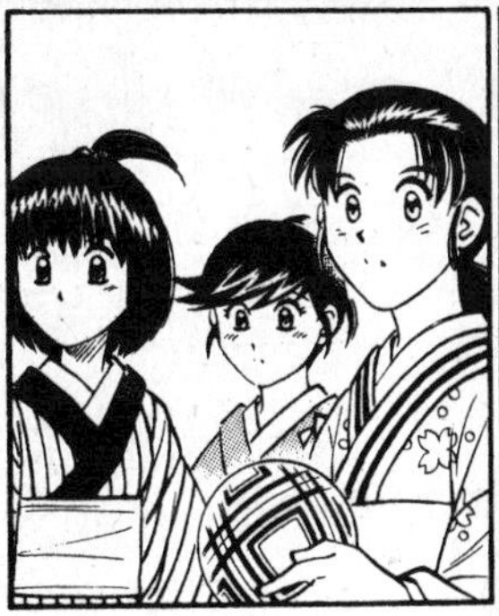

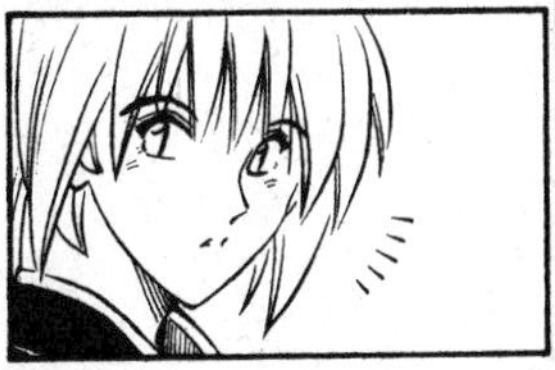

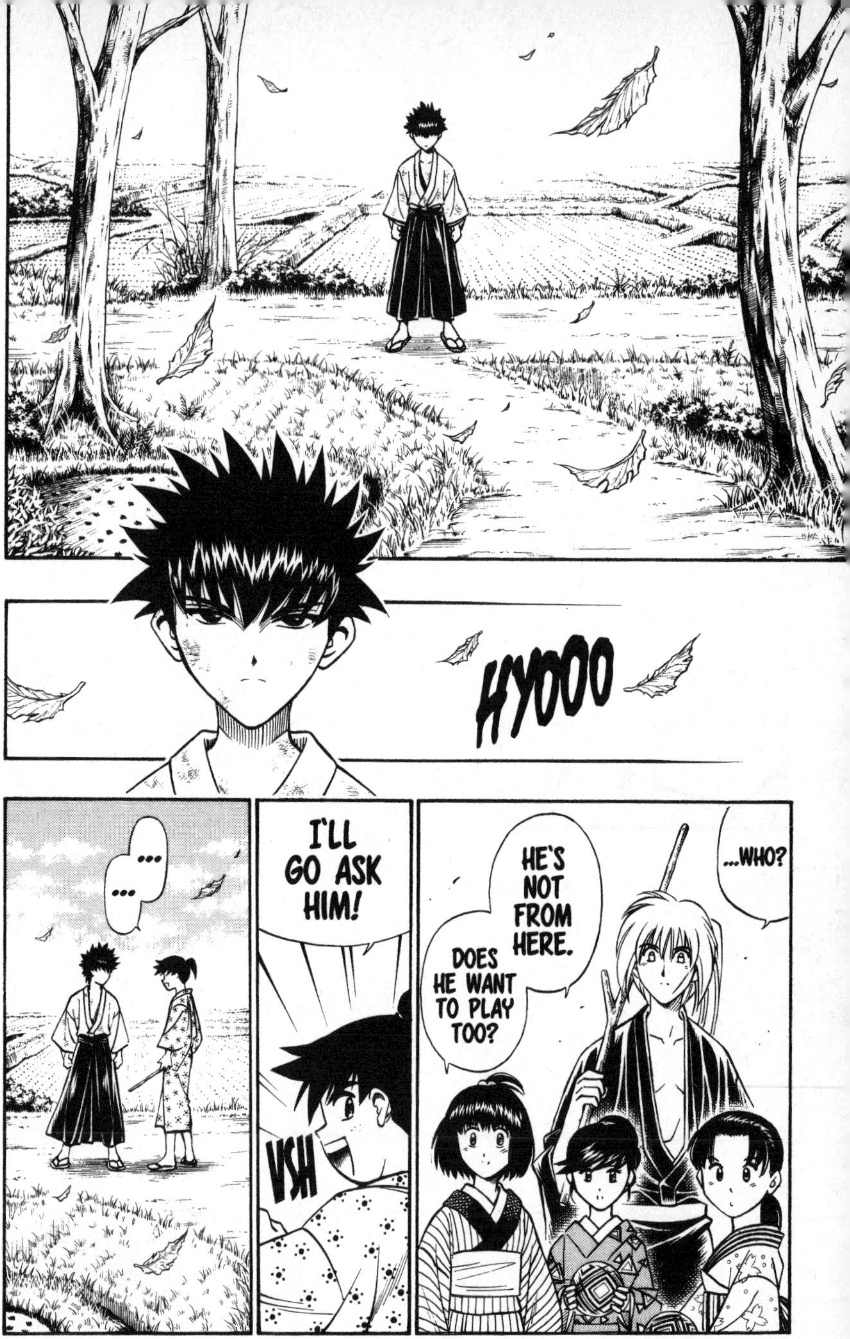
HYOOO
...WHO?
HE'S NOT FROM HERE.
DOES HE WANT TO PLAY TOO?
I'LL GO ASK HIM!
VSH
... ...

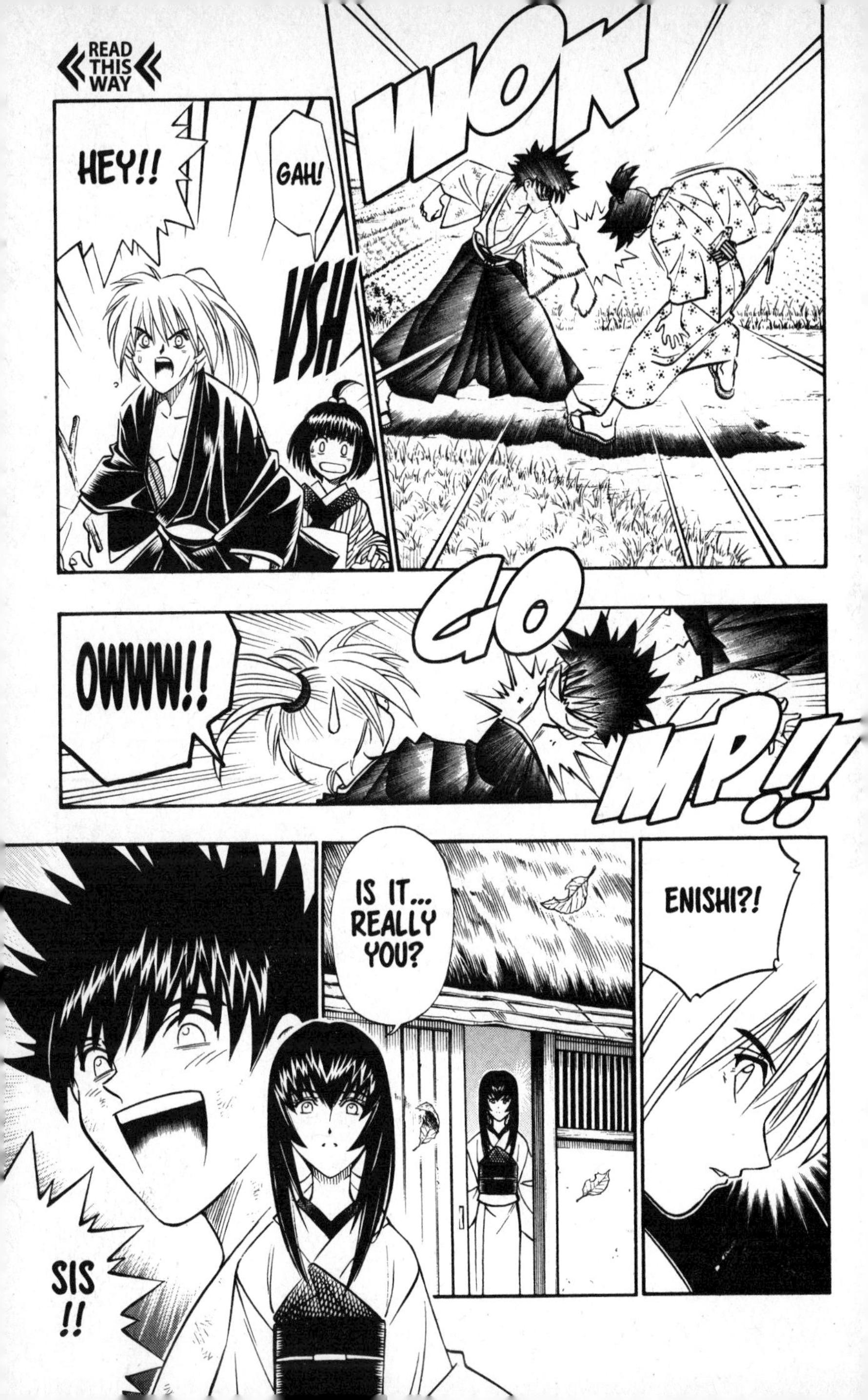
READ THIS WAY
WOK
GAH!
HEY!!
VSH
GO
MP!!
OWWW!!
ENISHI?!
IS IT... REALLY YOU?
SIS !!

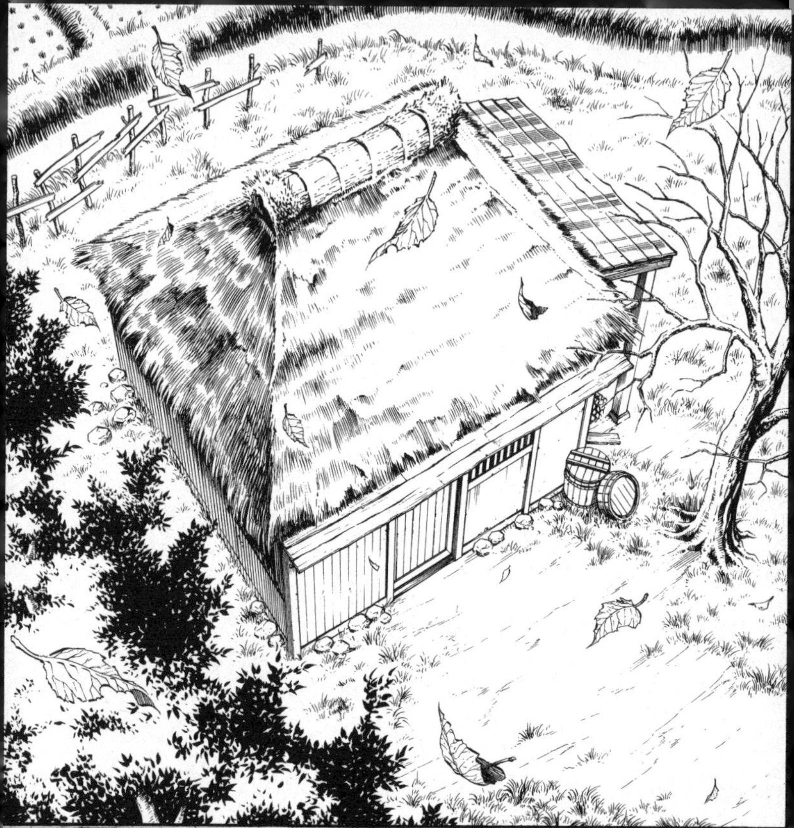

Act 173
Remembrance 8: Arrival of Enishi

伸宏和月

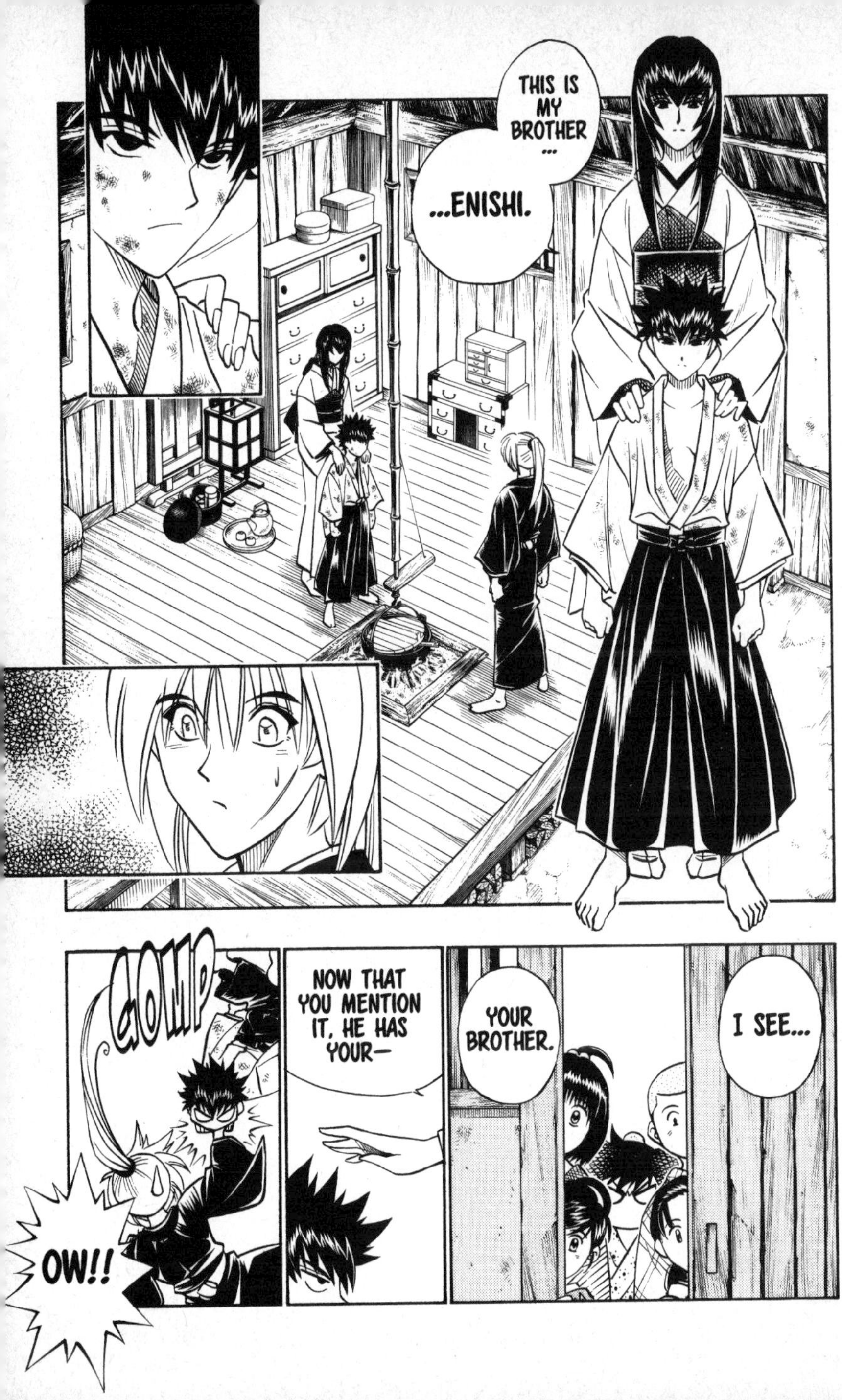
THIS IS MY BROTHER ...
...ENISHI.
I SEE...
YOUR BROTHER.
NOW THAT YOU MENTION IT, HE HAS YOUR—
GOMP
OW!!

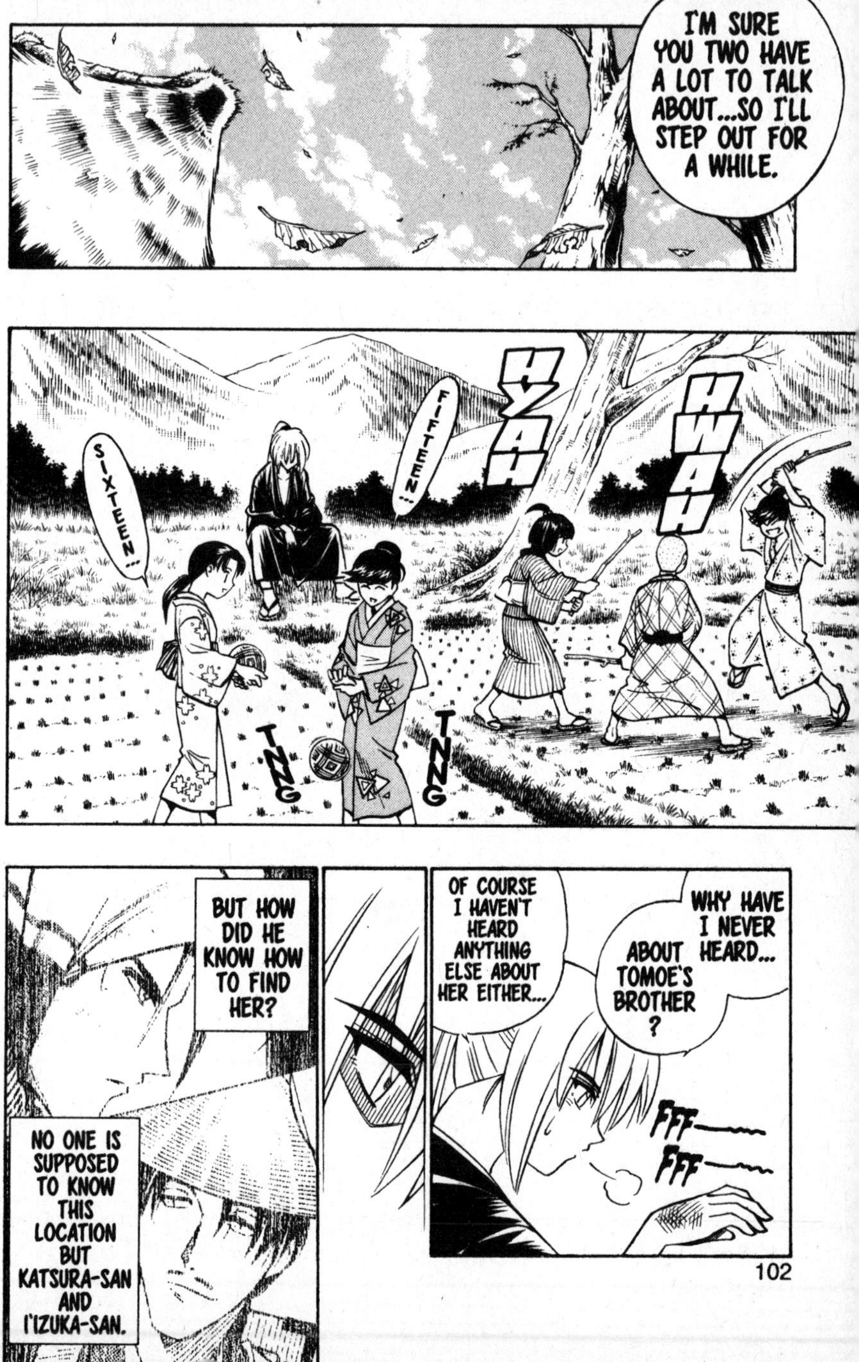
I'M SURE YOU TWO HAVE A LOT TO TALK ABOUT...SO I'LL STEP OUT FOR A WHILE.
HWAH
HYAH
FIFTEEN...
SIXTEEN...
TNNG
TNNG
WHY HAVE I NEVER HEARD...
ABOUT TOMOE'S BROTHER?
OF COURSE I HAVEN'T HEARD ANYTHING ELSE ABOUT HER EITHER...
FFF—
FFF—
BUT HOW DID HE KNOW HOW TO FIND HER?
NO ONE IS SUPPOSED TO KNOW THIS LOCATION BUT KATSURA-SAN AND I'IZUKA-SAN.

READ THIS WAY

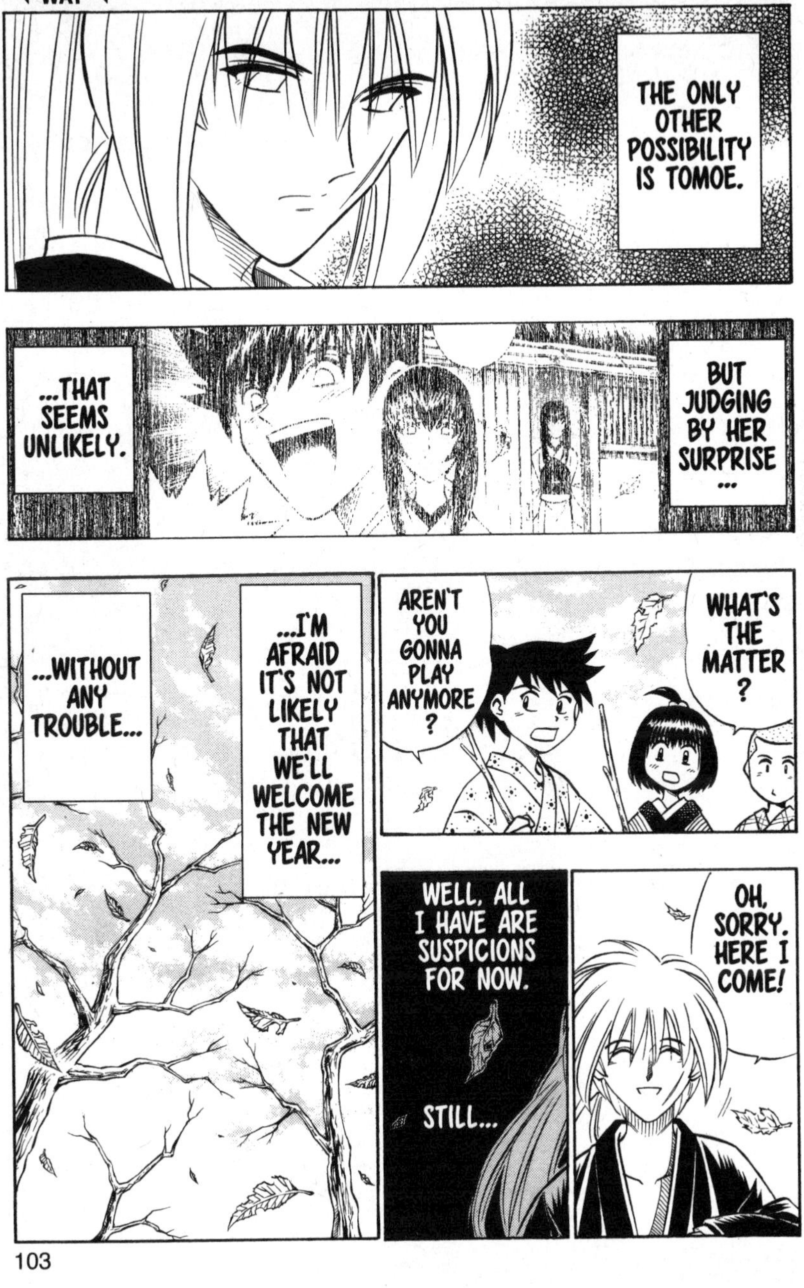
THE ONLY OTHER POSSIBILITY IS TOMOE.
BUT JUDGING BY HER SURPRISE...
...THAT SEEMS UNLIKELY.
WHAT'S THE MATTER?
AREN'T YOU GONNA PLAY ANYMORE?
OH, SORRY. HERE I COME!
WELL, ALL I HAVE ARE SUSPICIONS FOR NOW.
STILL...
...I'M AFRAID IT'S NOT LIKELY THAT WE'LL WELCOME THE NEW YEAR...
...WITHOUT ANY TROUBLE...

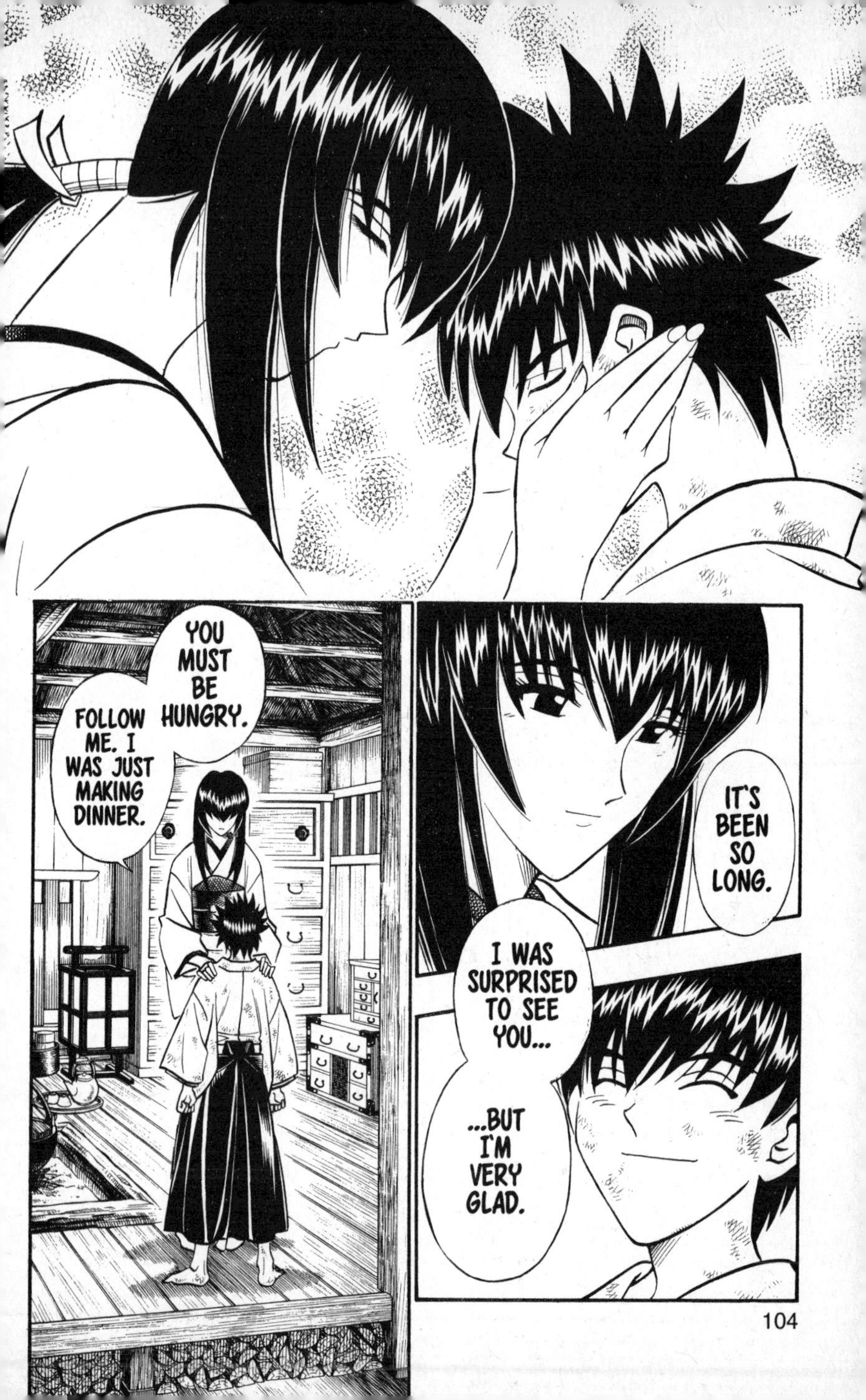
IT'S BEEN SO LONG.
I WAS SURPRISED TO SEE YOU...
...BUT I'M VERY GLAD.
YOU MUST BE HUNGRY.
FOLLOW ME. I WAS JUST MAKING DINNER.

READ THIS WAY

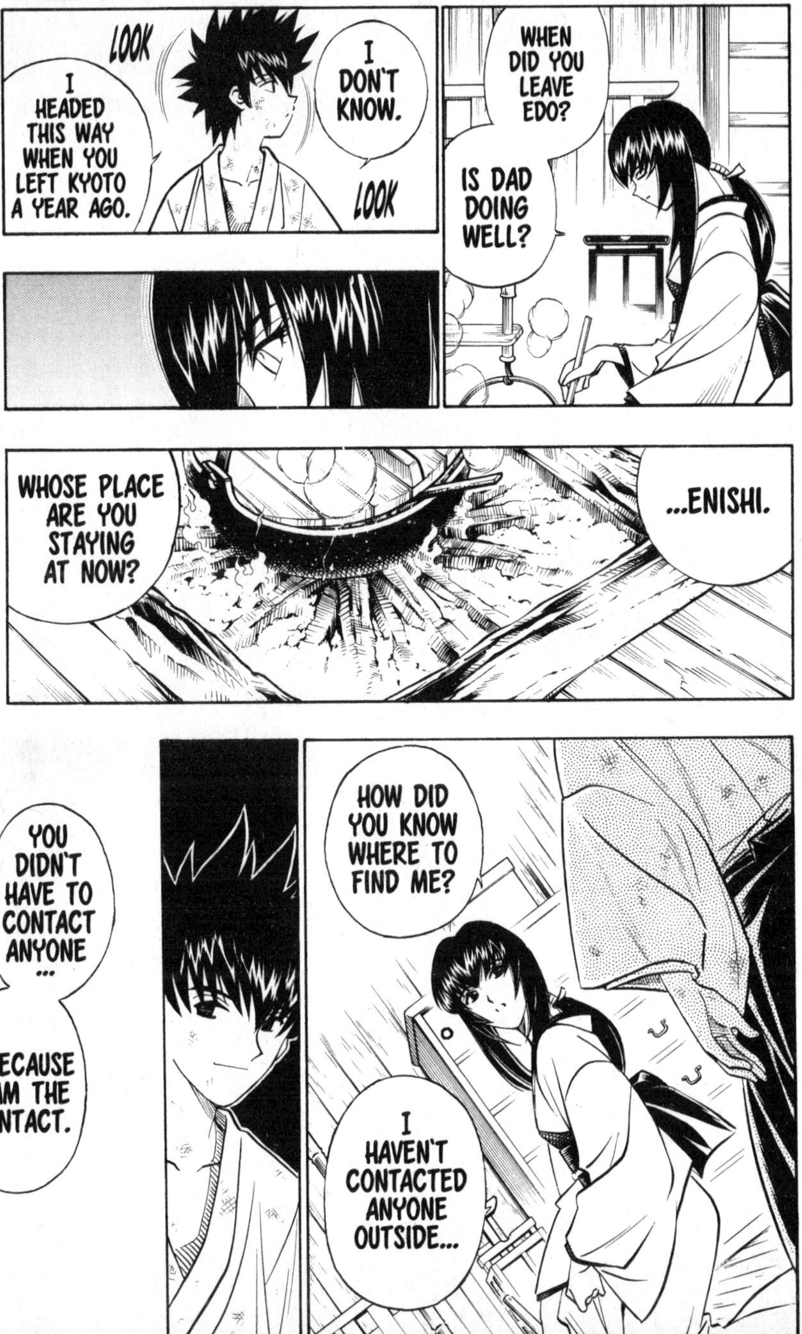
WHEN DID YOU LEAVE EDO?
IS DAD DOING WELL?
I DON'T KNOW.
LOOK
LOOK
I HEADED THIS WAY WHEN YOU LEFT KYOTO A YEAR AGO.
...ENISHI.
WHOSE PLACE ARE YOU STAYING AT NOW?
HOW DID YOU KNOW WHERE TO FIND ME?
I HAVEN'T CONTACTED ANYONE OUTSIDE...
YOU DIDN'T HAVE TO CONTACT ANYONE...
...BECAUSE I AM THE CONTACT.

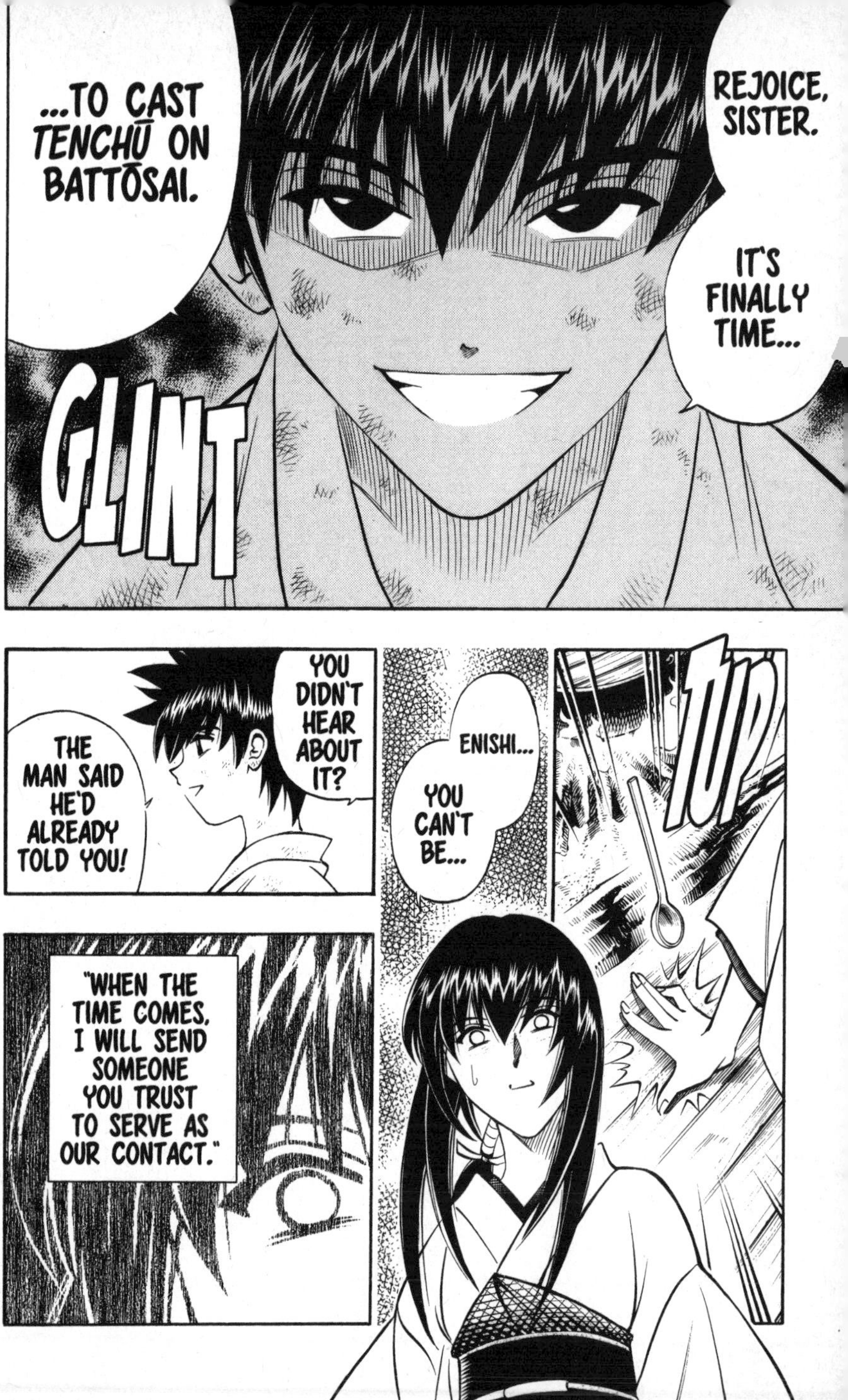
REJOICE, SISTER.
IT'S FINALLY TIME...
...TO CAST TENCHŪ ON BATTŌSAI.
GLINT
TUP
ENISHI...
YOU CAN'T BE...
YOU DIDN'T HEAR ABOUT IT?
THE MAN SAID HE'D ALREADY TOLD YOU!
"WHEN THE TIME COMES, I WILL SEND SOMEONE YOU TRUST TO SERVE AS OUR CONTACT."

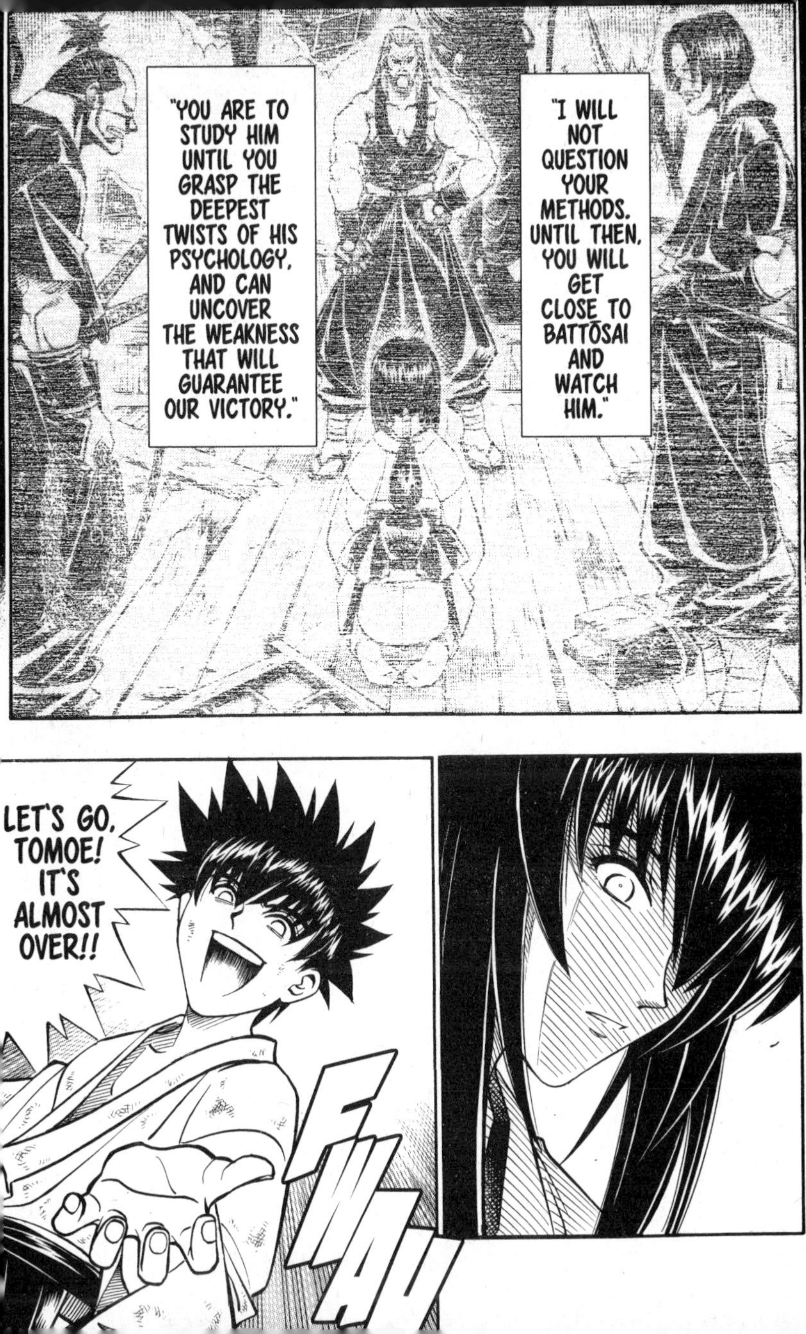
"I WILL NOT QUESTION YOUR METHODS. UNTIL THEN, YOU WILL GET CLOSE TO BATTŌSAI AND WATCH HIM."
"YOU ARE TO STUDY HIM UNTIL YOU GRASP THE DEEPEST TWISTS OF HIS PSYCHOLOGY, AND CAN UNCOVER THE WEAKNESS THAT WILL GUARANTEE OUR VICTORY."
LET'S GO, TOMOE! IT'S ALMOST OVER!!
FWAH

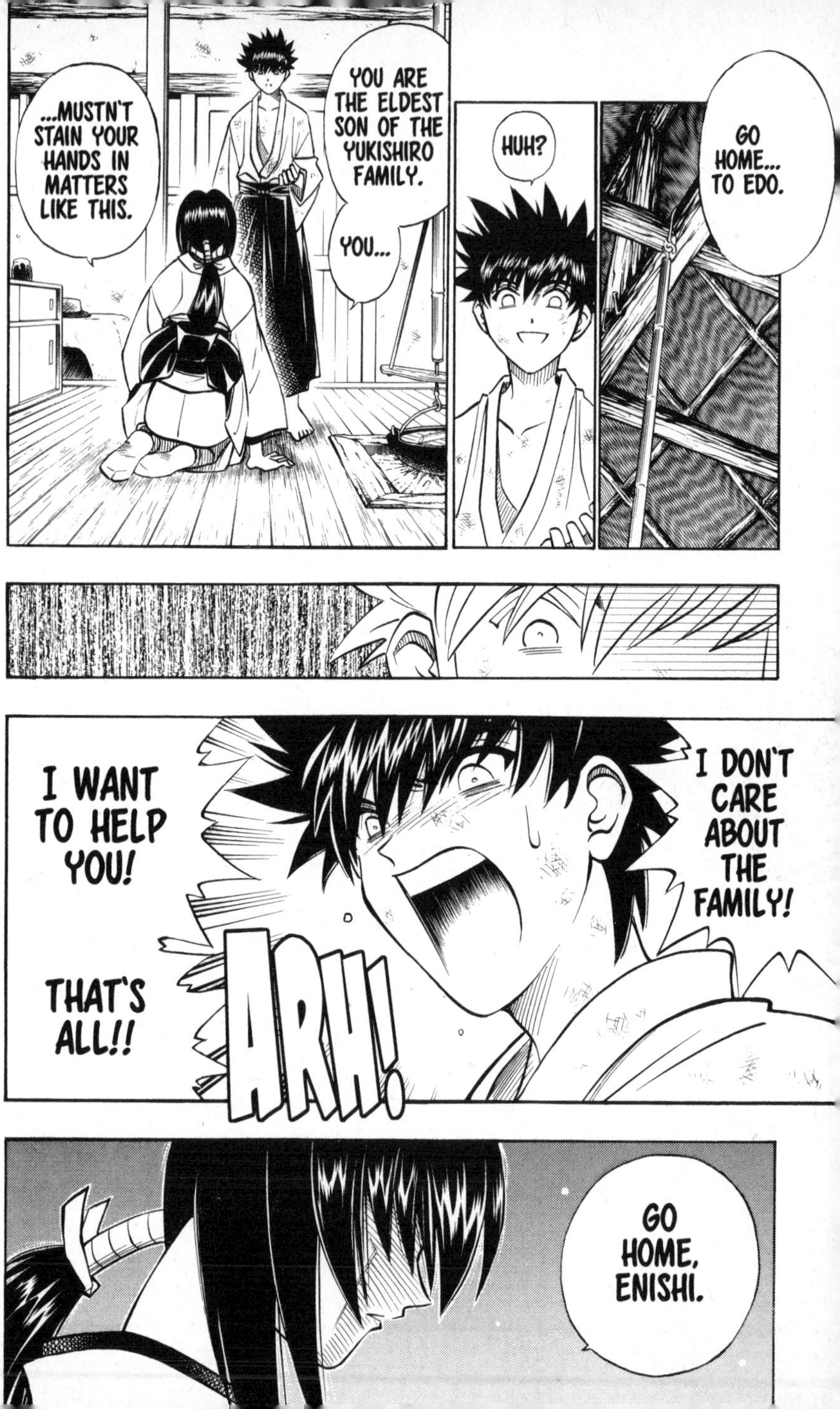
GO HOME... TO EDO.
HUH?
YOU ARE THE ELDEST SON OF THE YUKISHIRO FAMILY.
YOU...
...MUSTN'T STAIN YOUR HANDS IN MATTERS LIKE THIS.
I DON'T CARE ABOUT THE FAMILY!
ARH!
I WANT TO HELP YOU!
THAT'S ALL!!
GO HOME, ENISHI.

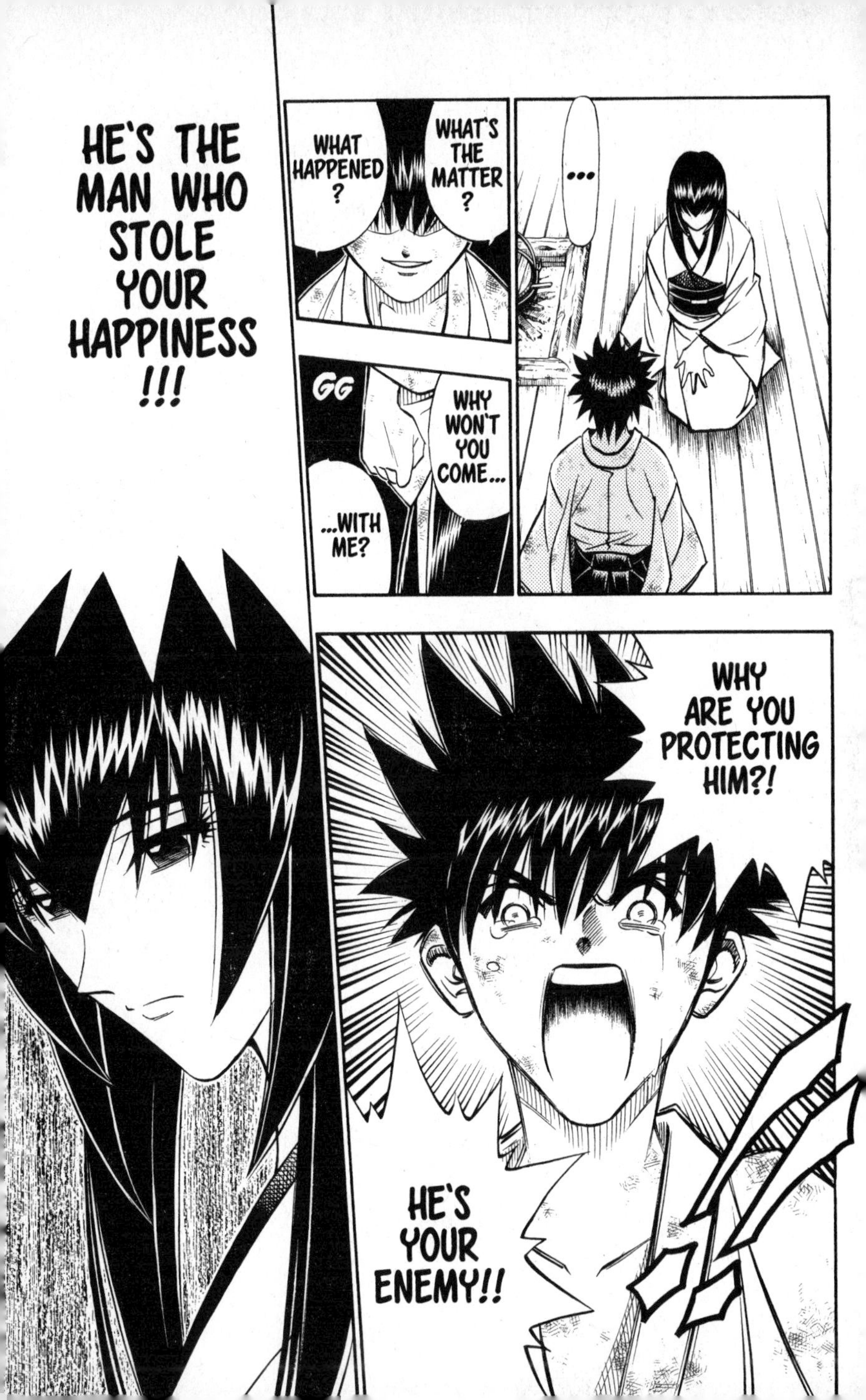
...
WHAT'S THE MATTER?
WHAT HAPPENED?
GG
WHY WON'T YOU COME...
...WITH ME?
WHY ARE YOU PROTECTING HIM?!
HE'S YOUR ENEMY!!
HE'S THE MAN WHO STOLE YOUR HAPPINESS!!!

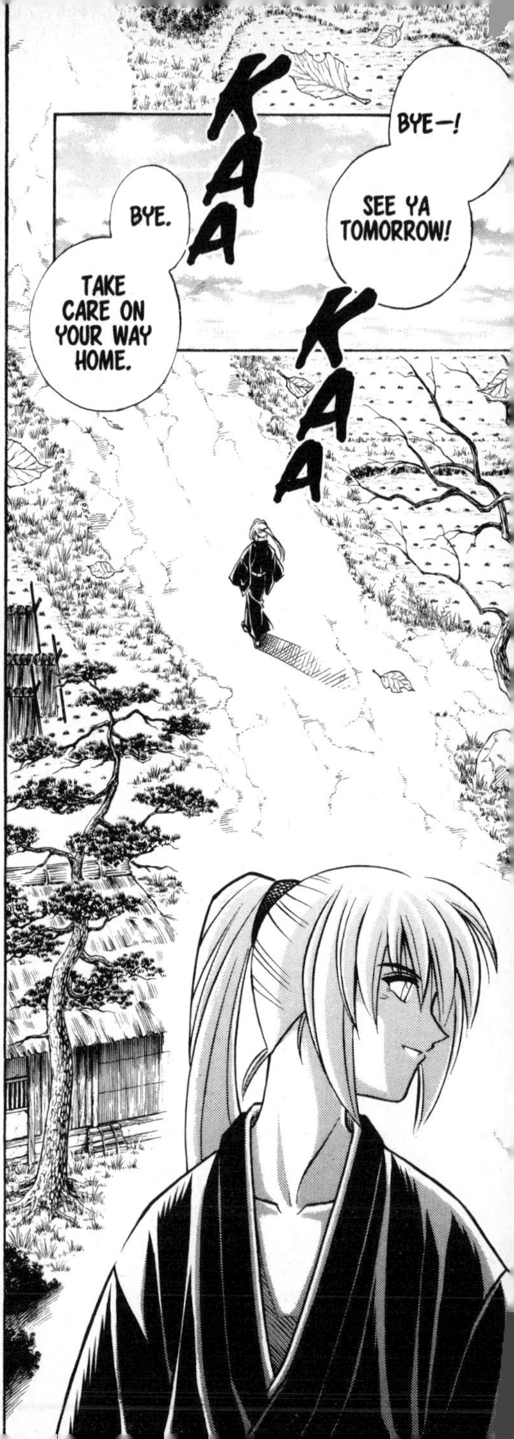
BYE—!
SEE YA TOMORROW!
BYE.
TAKE CARE ON YOUR WAY HOME.
KAA
KAA
KAA
KAA
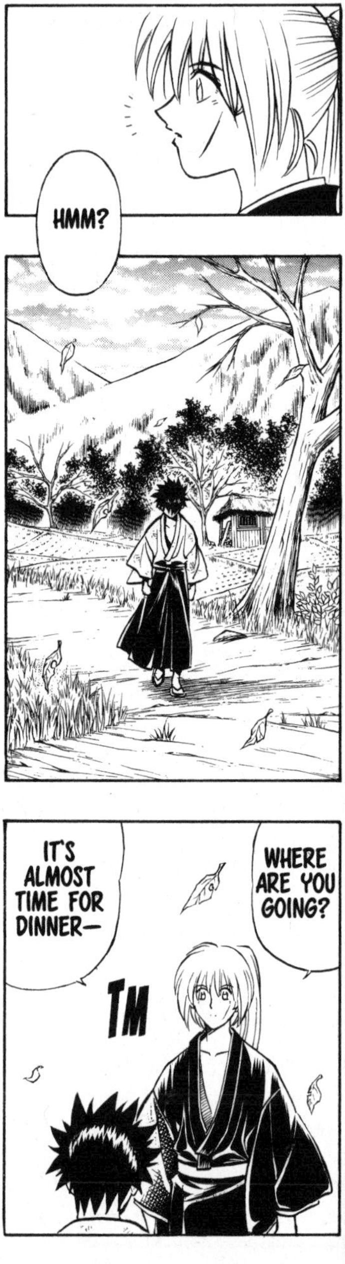
HMM?
WHERE ARE YOU GOING?
IT'S ALMOST TIME FOR DINNER—
TM

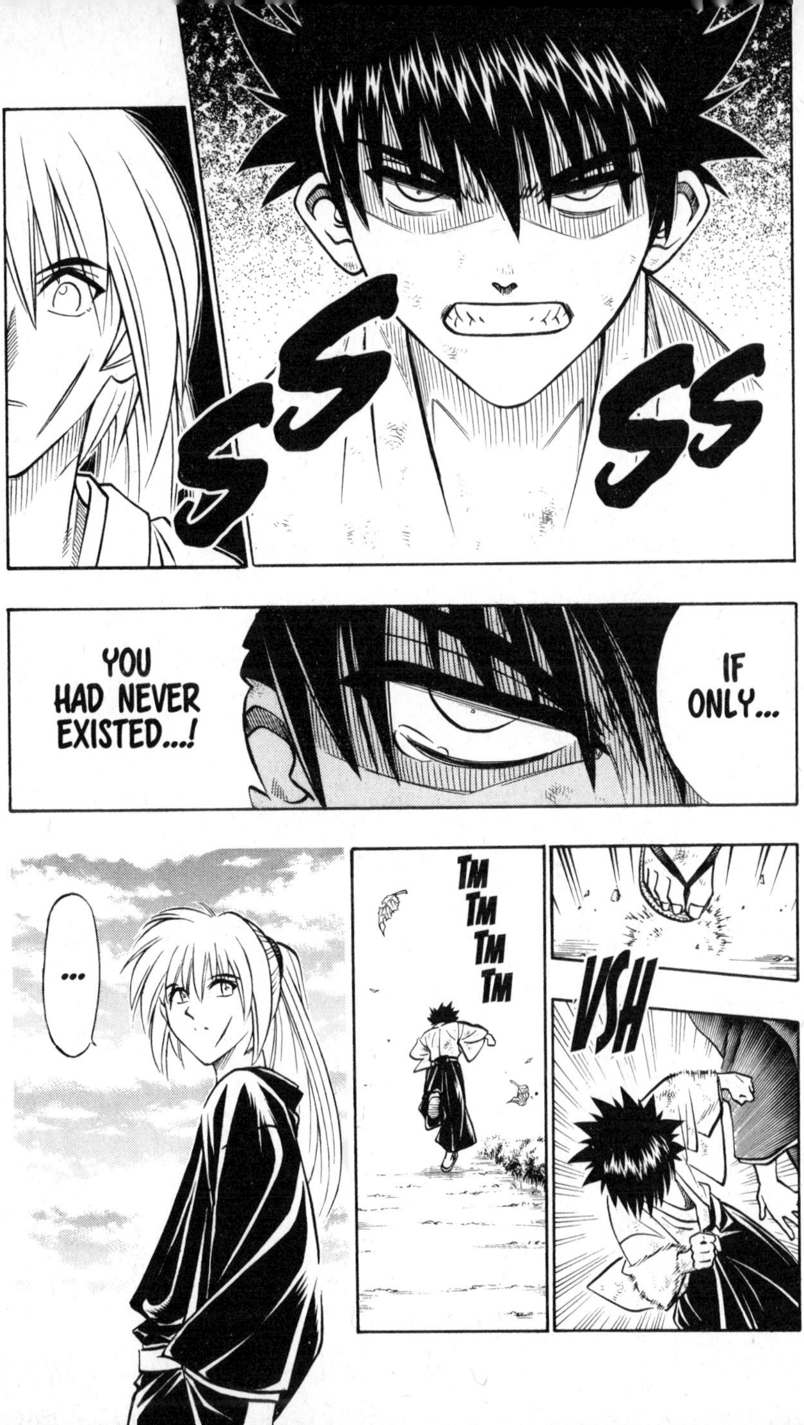
SSSS
IF ONLY...
YOU HAD NEVER EXISTED...!
VSH
TM TM TM TM
...

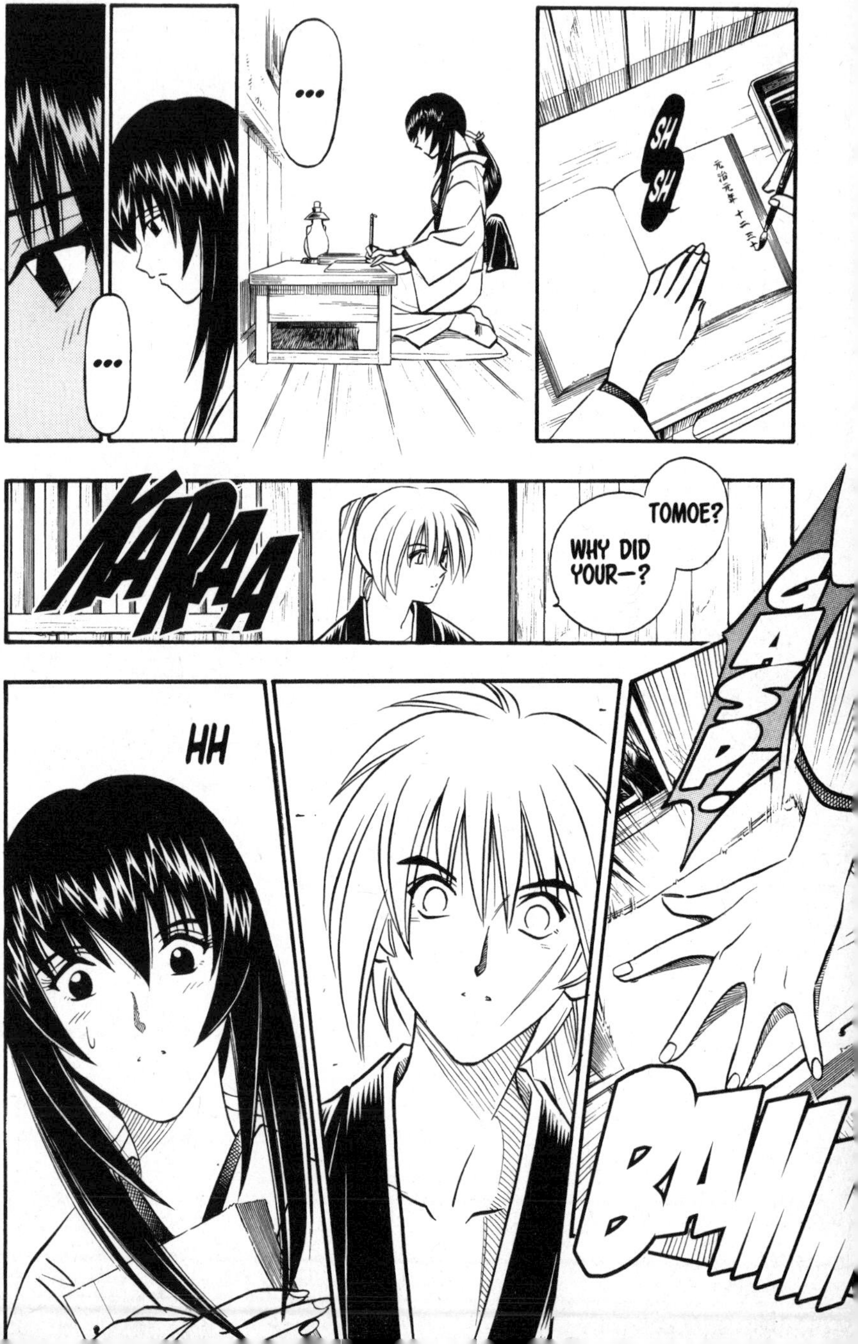
SH SH
元治元年 十二 三十
...
...
TOMOE?
WHY DID YOUR—?
KARAA
GASP!
HH

READ THIS WAY

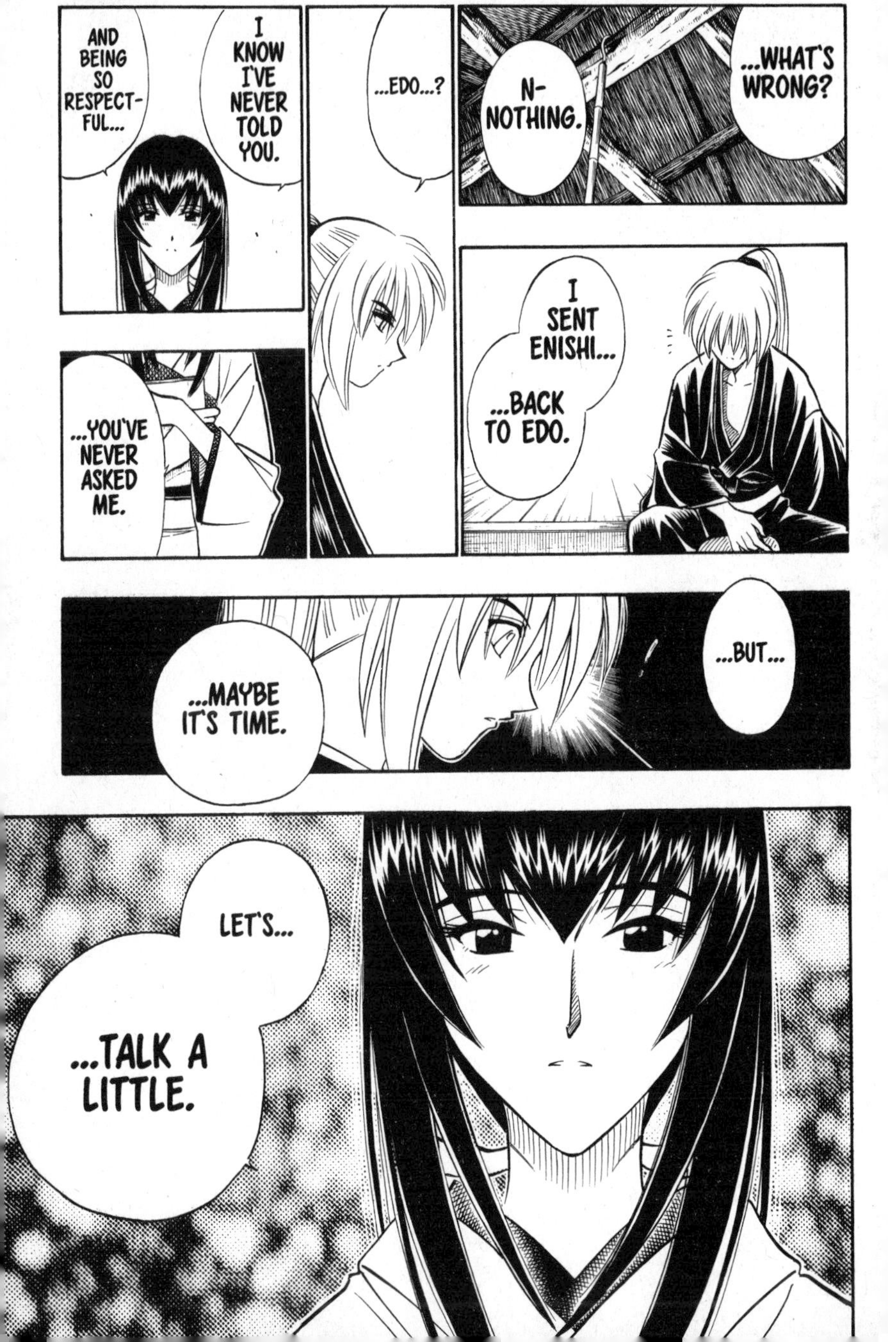
...WHAT'S WRONG?
N-NOTHING.
I SENT ENISHI...
...BACK TO EDO.
...EDO...?
I KNOW I'VE NEVER TOLD YOU.
AND BEING SO RESPECT-FUL...
...YOU'VE NEVER ASKED ME.
...BUT...
...MAYBE IT'S TIME.
LET'S...
...TALK A LITTLE.

Rurouni Kenshin

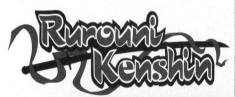

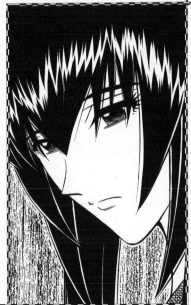

Act 174—Remembrance 9: White Snow

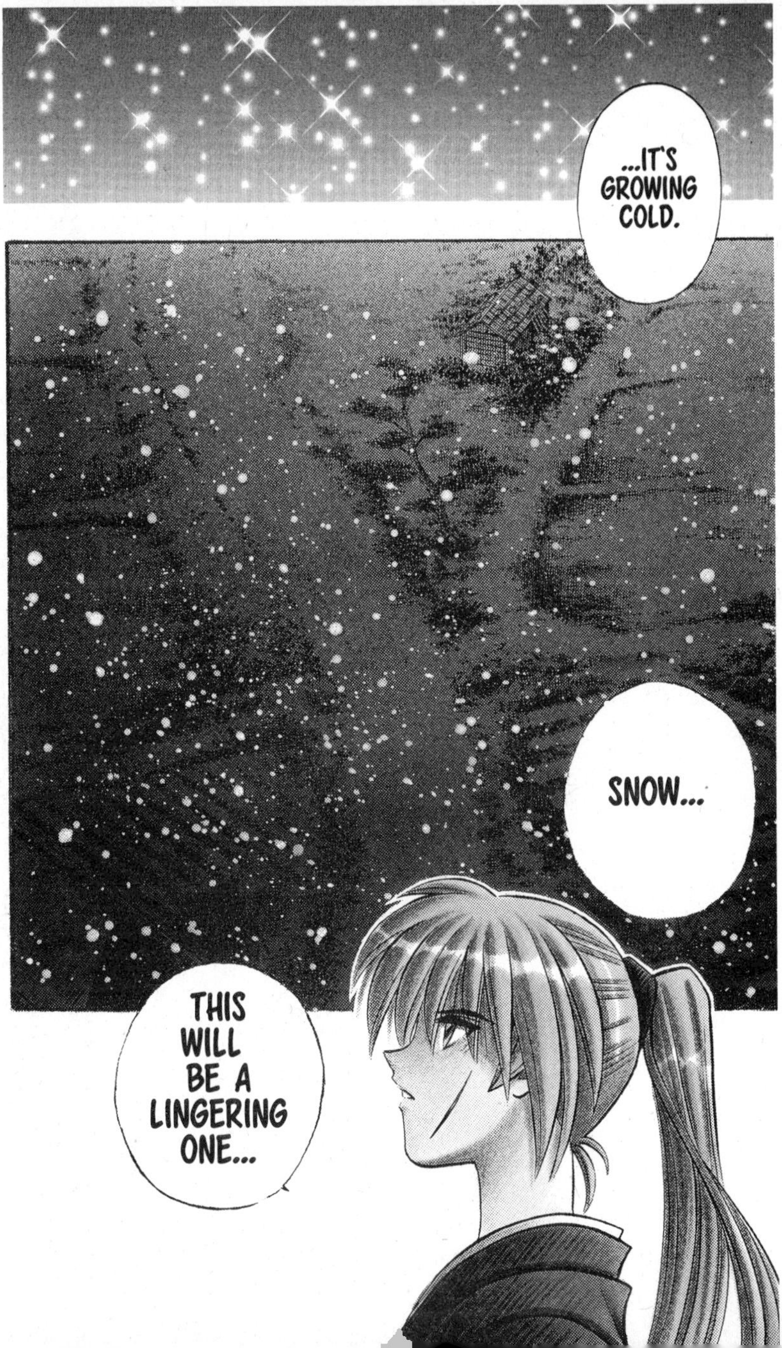
...IT'S GROWING COLD.
SNOW...
THIS WILL BE A LINGERING ONE...

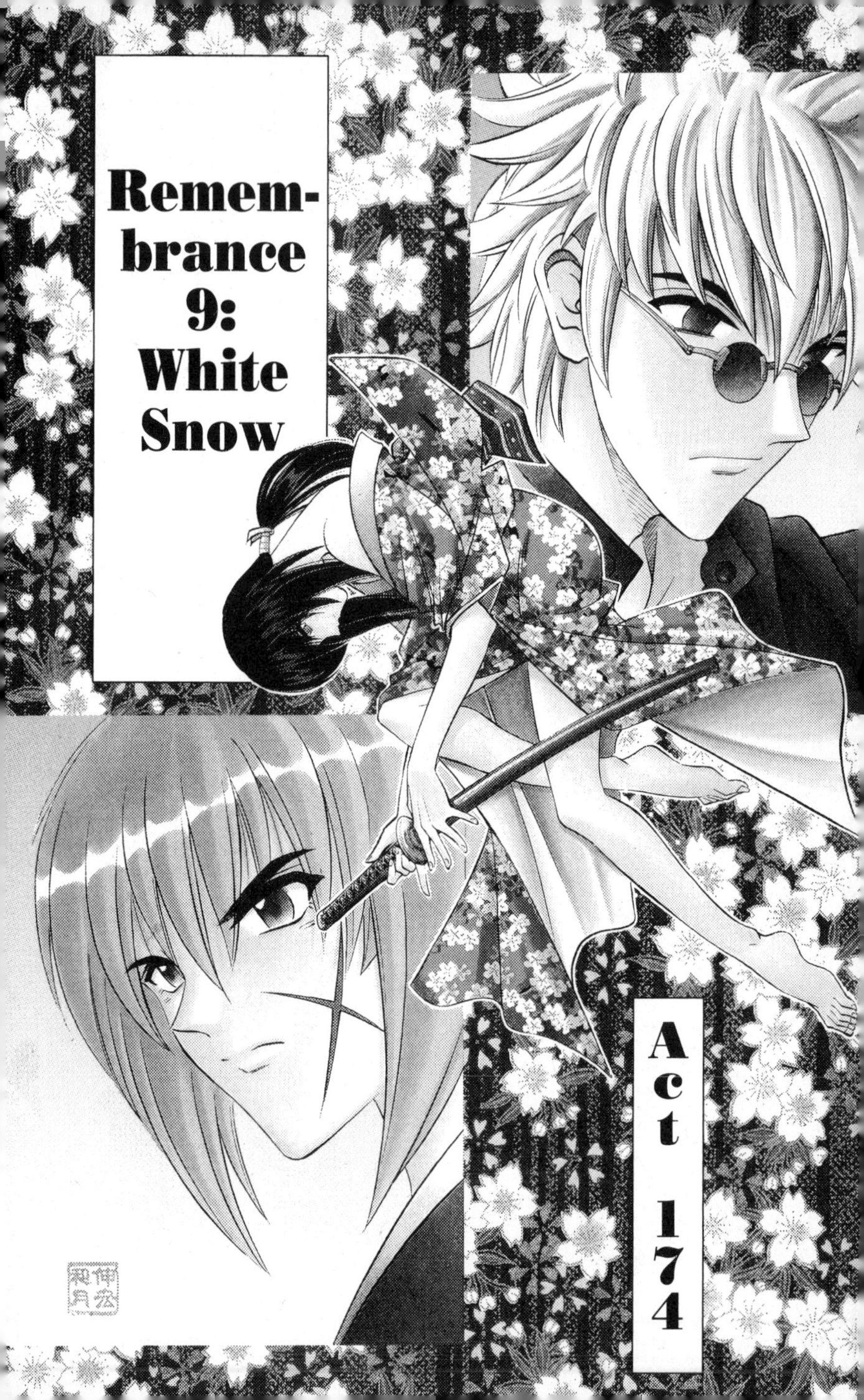
Remembrance 9: White Snow
Act 174

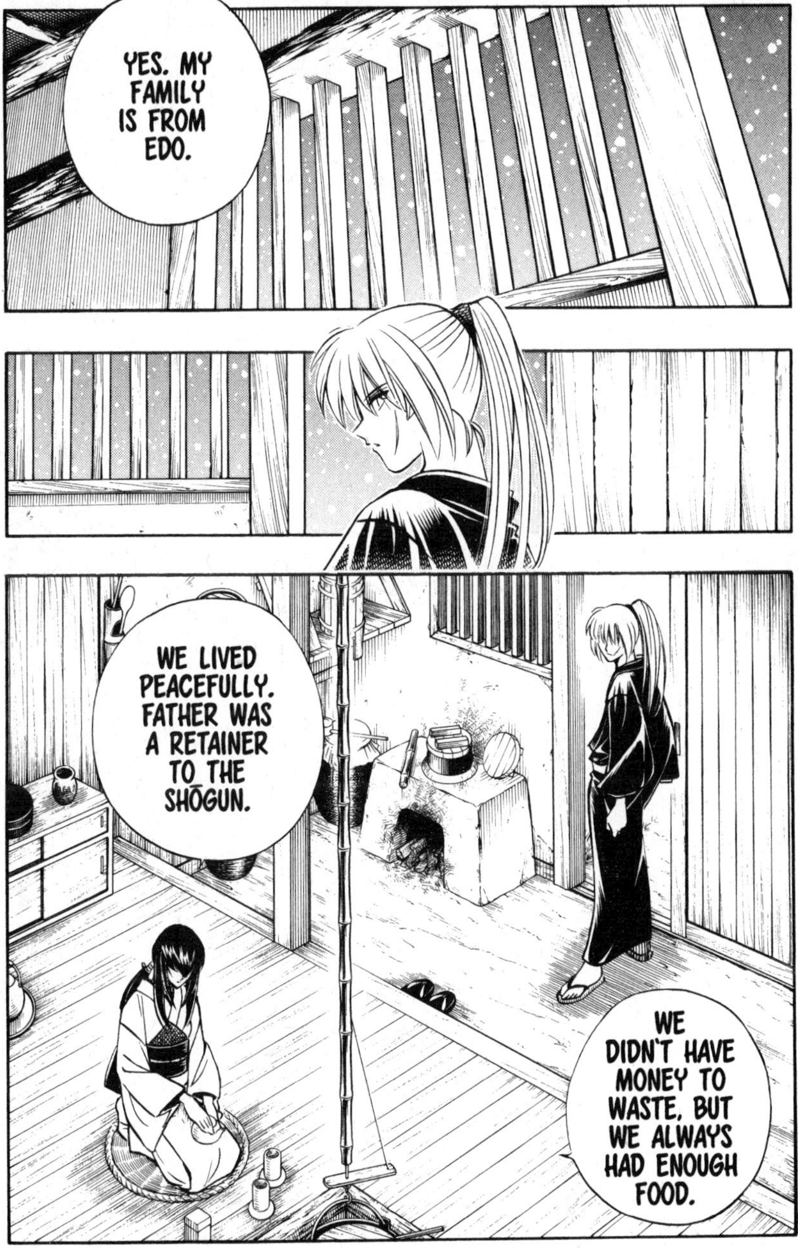
YES. MY FAMILY IS FROM EDO.
WE LIVED PEACEFULLY. FATHER WAS A RETAINER TO THE SHŌGUN.
WE DIDN'T HAVE MONEY TO WASTE, BUT WE ALWAYS HAD ENOUGH FOOD.

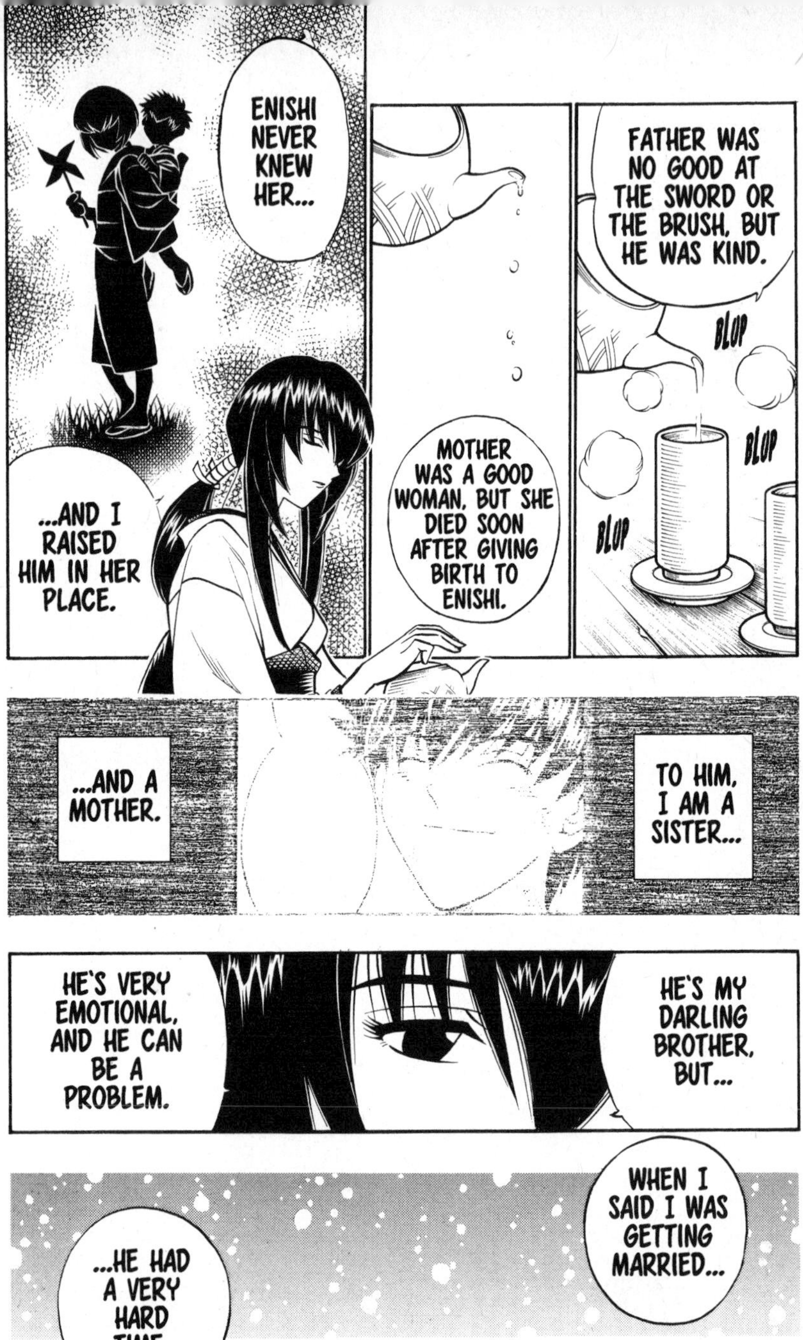
FATHER WAS NO GOOD AT THE SWORD OR THE BRUSH, BUT HE WAS KIND.
BLUP
BLUP
BLUP
MOTHER WAS A GOOD WOMAN, BUT SHE DIED SOON AFTER GIVING BIRTH TO ENISHI.
ENISHI NEVER KNEW HER...
...AND I RAISED HIM IN HER PLACE.
TO HIM, I AM A SISTER...
...AND A MOTHER.
HE'S MY DARLING BROTHER, BUT...
HE'S VERY EMOTIONAL, AND HE CAN BE A PROBLEM.
WHEN I SAID I WAS GETTING MARRIED...
...HE HAD A VERY HARD TIME.

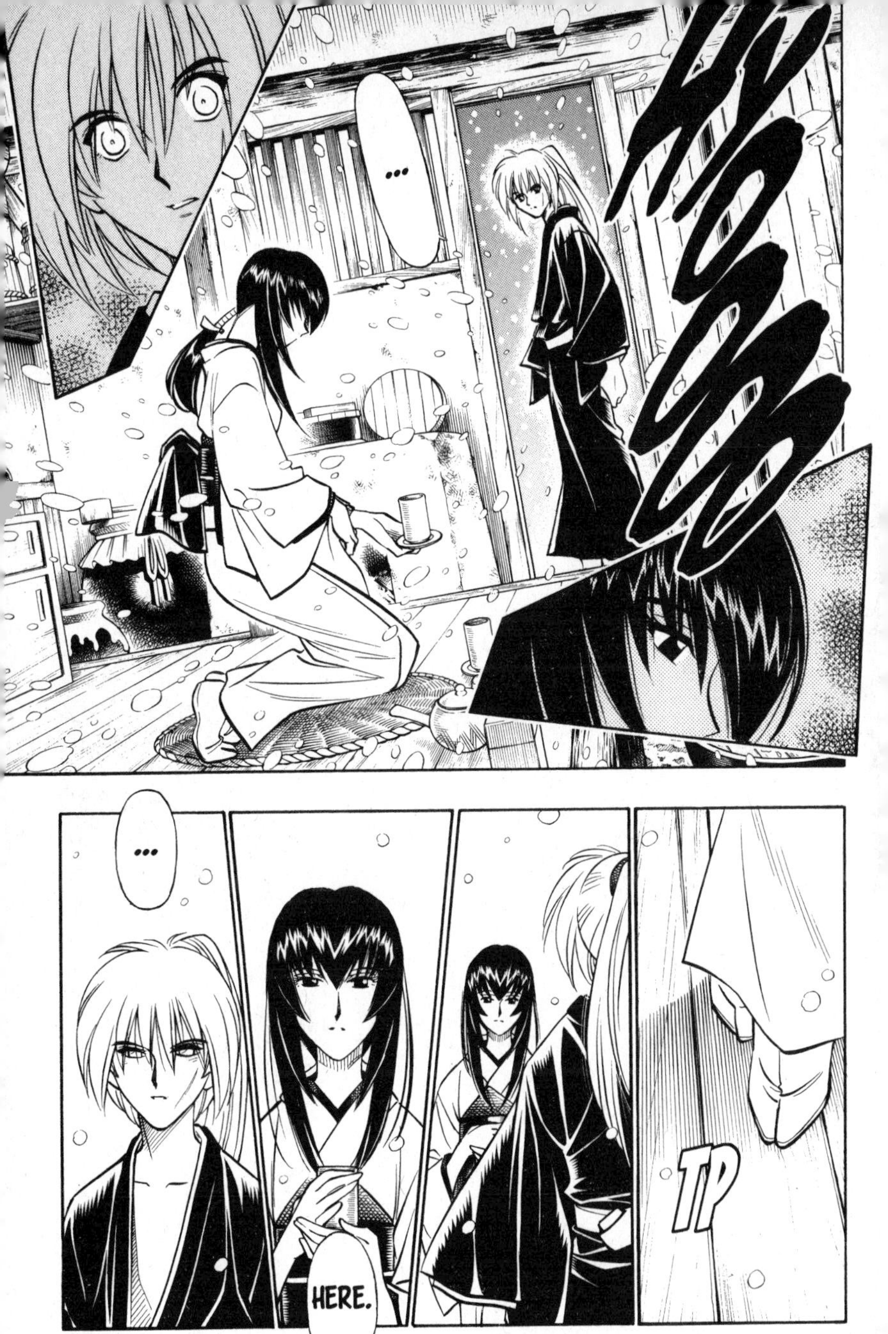
...
TP
HERE.
...

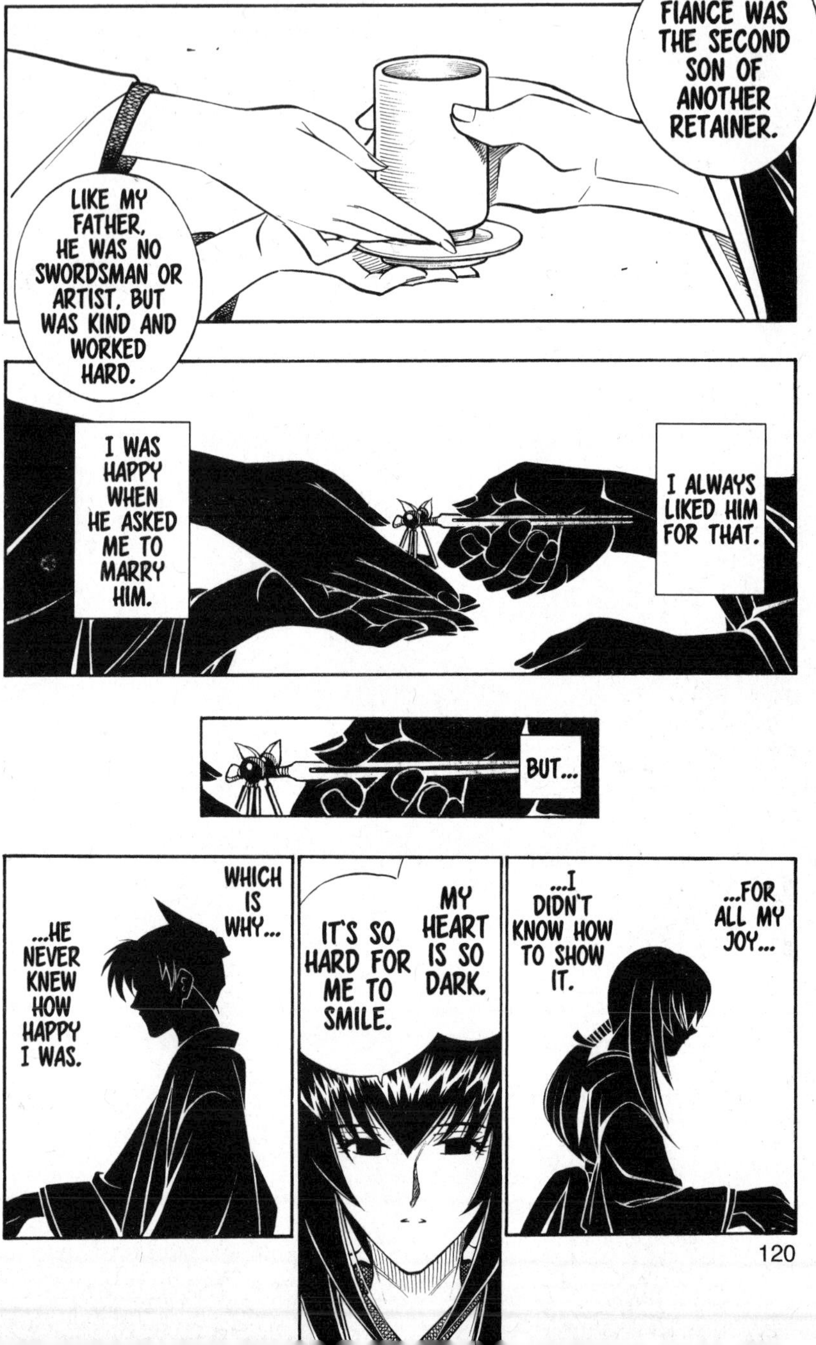
MY FIANCÉ WAS THE SECOND SON OF ANOTHER RETAINER.
LIKE MY FATHER, HE WAS NO SWORDSMAN OR ARTIST, BUT WAS KIND AND WORKED HARD.
I ALWAYS LIKED HIM FOR THAT.
I WAS HAPPY WHEN HE ASKED ME TO MARRY HIM.
BUT...
...FOR ALL MY JOY...
...I DIDN'T KNOW HOW TO SHOW IT.
MY HEART IS SO DARK.
IT'S SO HARD FOR ME TO SMILE.
WHICH IS WHY...
...HE NEVER KNEW HOW HAPPY I WAS.

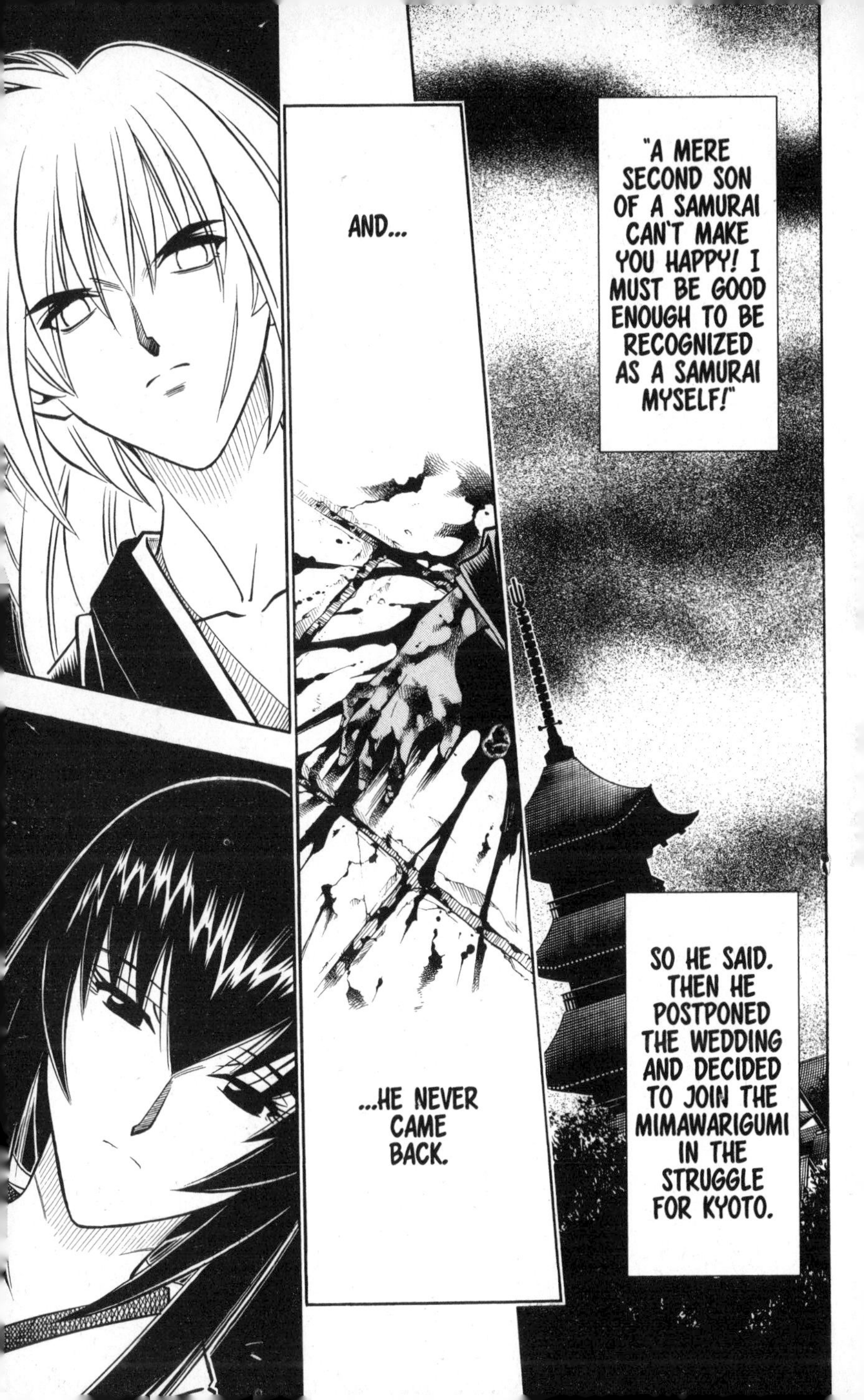
"A MERE SECOND SON OF A SAMURAI CAN'T MAKE YOU HAPPY! I MUST BE GOOD ENOUGH TO BE RECOGNIZED AS A SAMURAI MYSELF!"
SO HE SAID. THEN HE POSTPONED THE WEDDING AND DECIDED TO JOIN THE MIMAWARIGUMI IN THE STRUGGLE FOR KYOTO.
AND...
...HE NEVER CAME BACK.

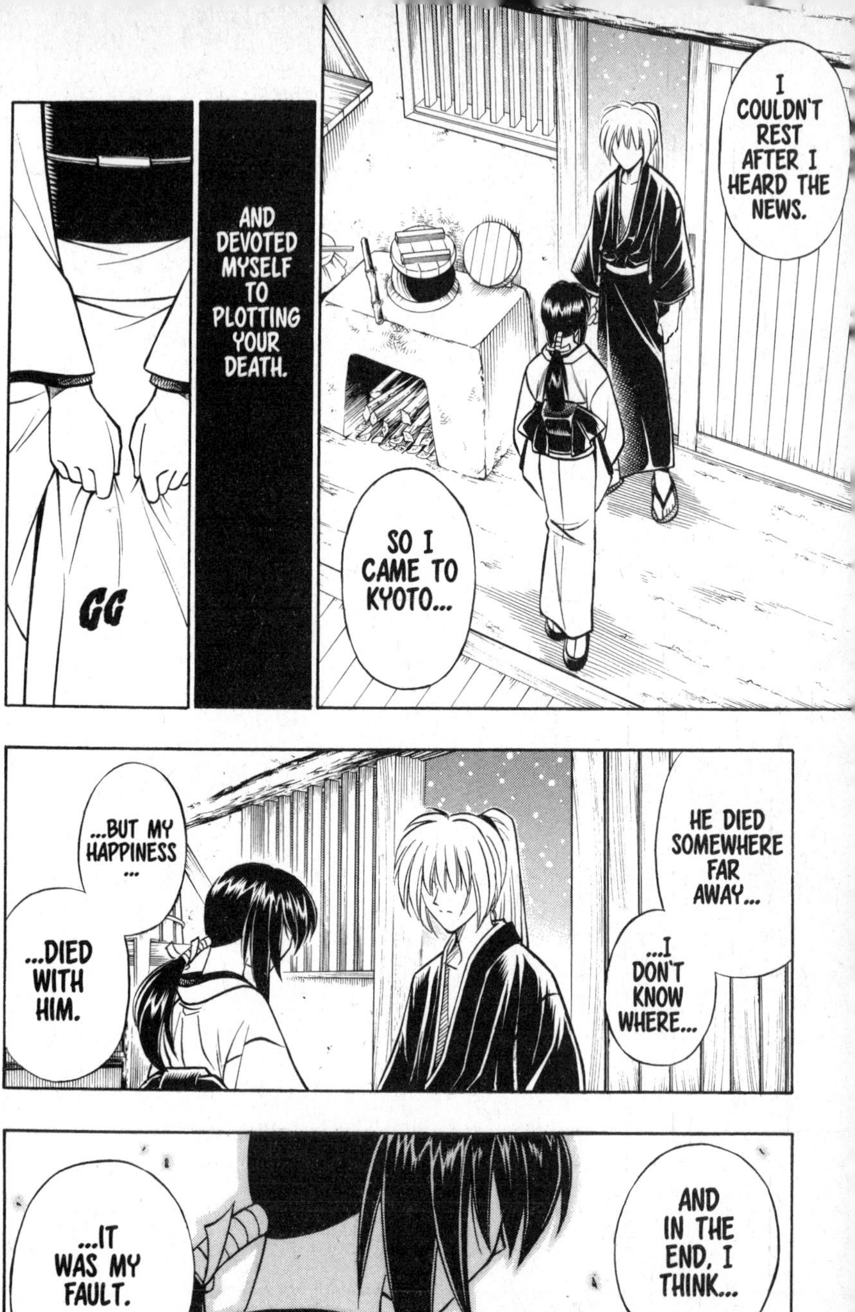
I COULDN'T REST AFTER I HEARD THE NEWS.
SO I CAME TO KYOTO...
AND DEVOTED MYSELF TO PLOTTING YOUR DEATH.
GG
HE DIED SOMEWHERE FAR AWAY...
...I DON'T KNOW WHERE...
...BUT MY HAPPINESS...
...DIED WITH HIM.
AND IN THE END, I THINK...
...IT WAS MY FAULT.

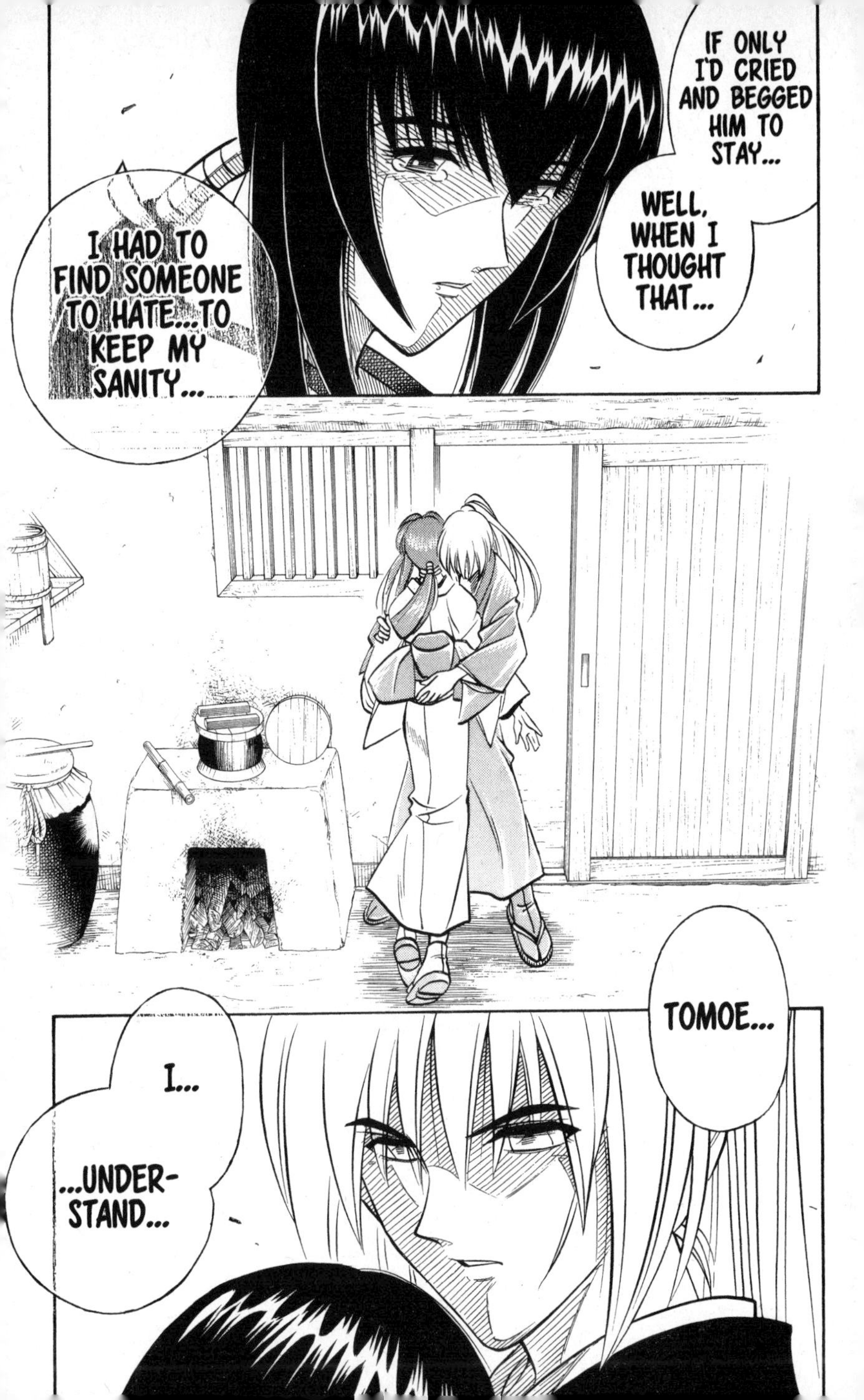
IF ONLY I'D CRIED AND BEGGED HIM TO STAY...
WELL, WHEN I THOUGHT THAT...
I HAD TO FIND SOMEONE TO HATE...TO KEEP MY SANITY...
TOMOE...
I...
...UNDER-STAND...

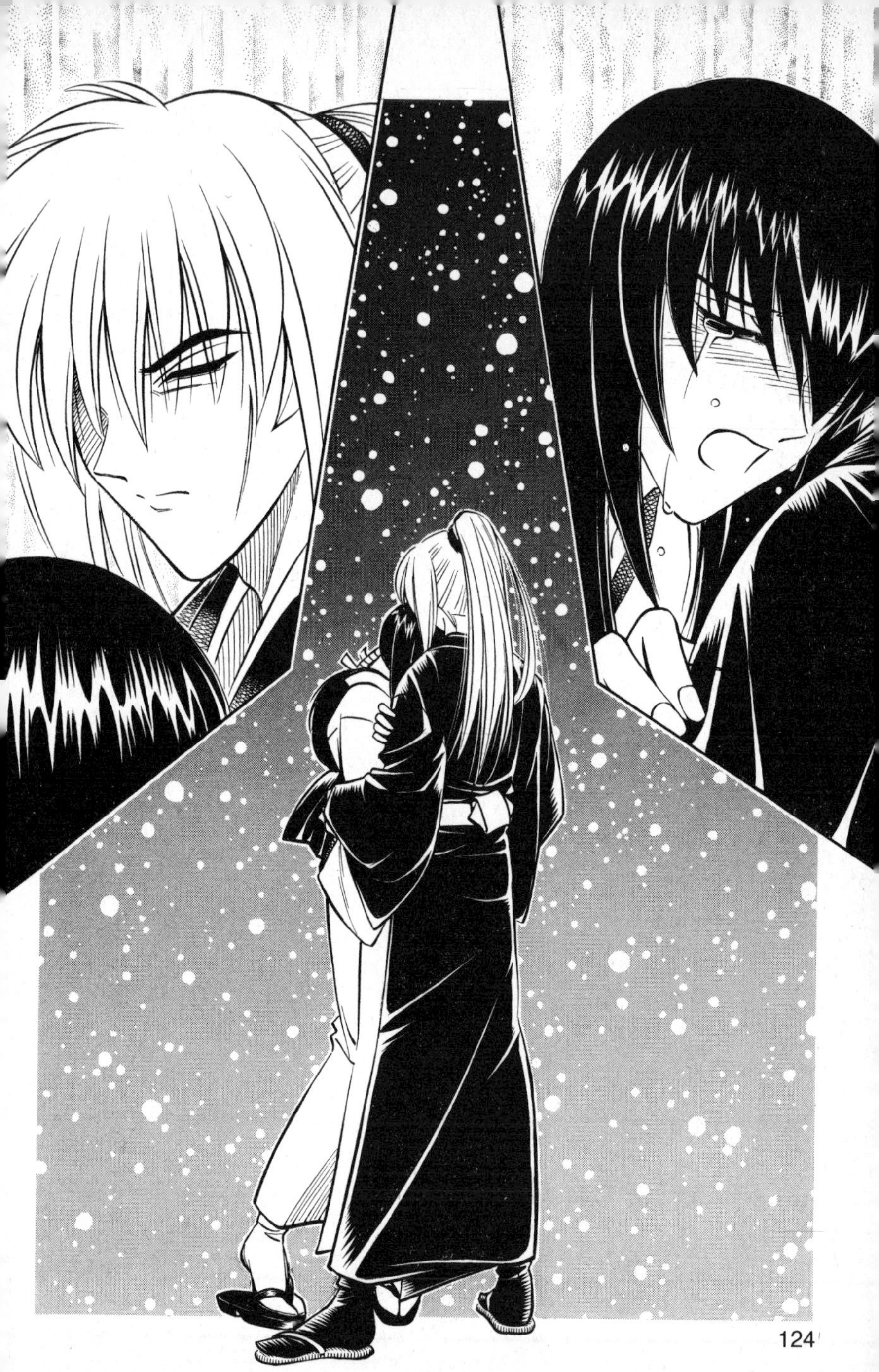

READ THIS WAY

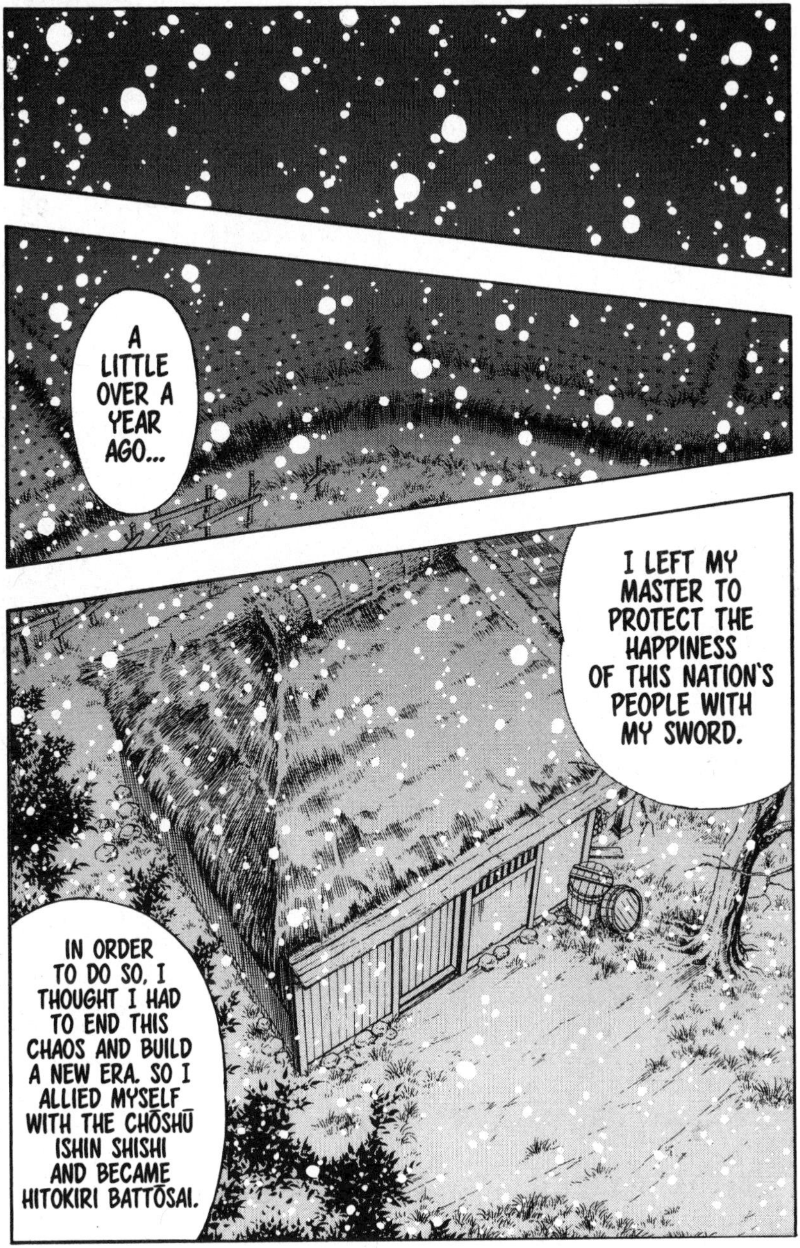
A LITTLE OVER A YEAR AGO...
I LEFT MY MASTER TO PROTECT THE HAPPINESS OF THIS NATION'S PEOPLE WITH MY SWORD.
IN ORDER TO DO SO, I THOUGHT I HAD TO END THIS CHAOS AND BUILD A NEW ERA. SO I ALLIED MYSELF WITH THE CHŌSHŪ ISHIN SHISHI AND BECAME HITOKIRI BATTŌSAI.

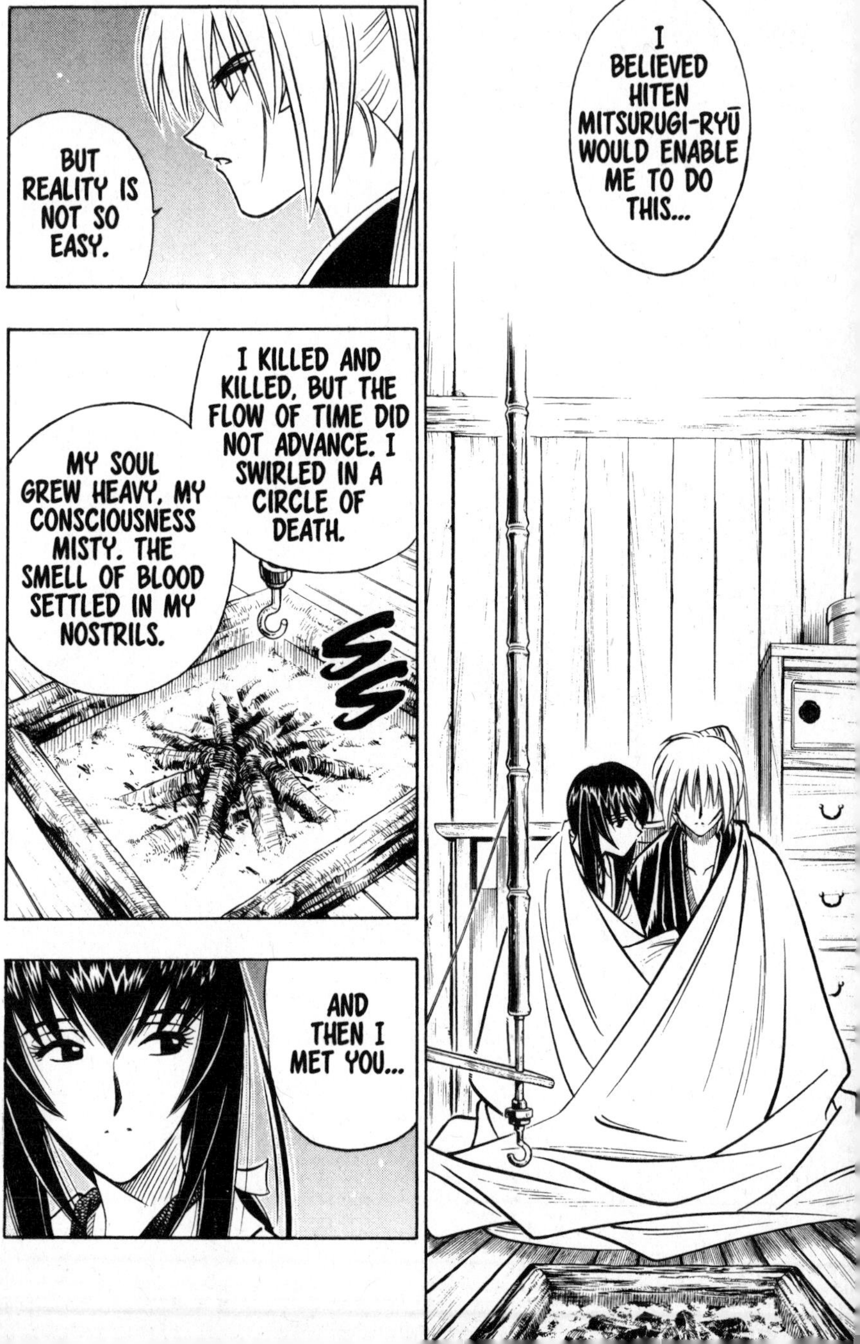
I BELIEVED HITEN MITSURUGI-RYŪ WOULD ENABLE ME TO DO THIS...
BUT REALITY IS NOT SO EASY.
I KILLED AND KILLED, BUT THE FLOW OF TIME DID NOT ADVANCE. I SWIRLED IN A CIRCLE OF DEATH.
MY SOUL GREW HEAVY, MY CONSCIOUSNESS MISTY. THE SMELL OF BLOOD SETTLED IN MY NOSTRILS.
AND THEN I MET YOU...

READ THIS WAY

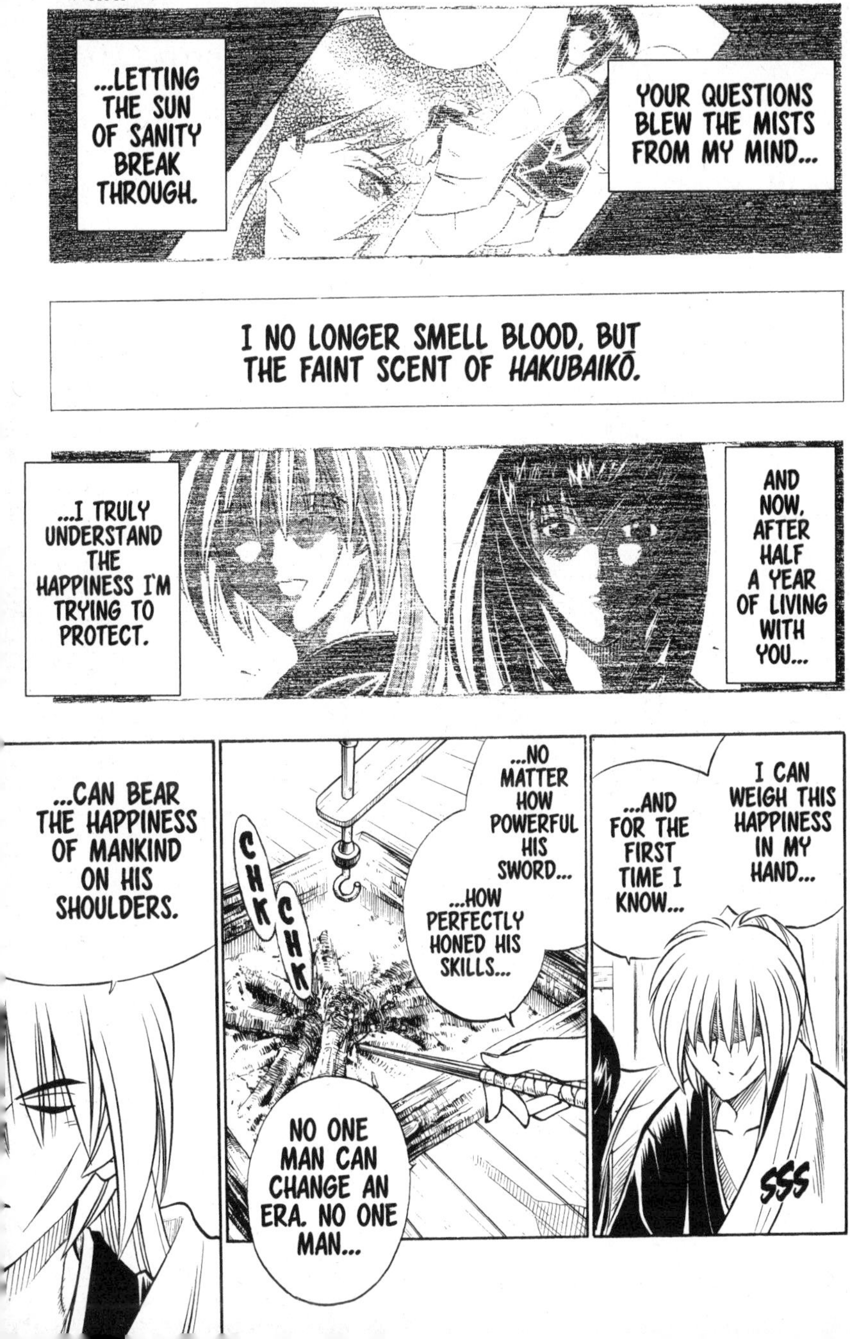
YOUR QUESTIONS BLEW THE MISTS FROM MY MIND...
...LETTING THE SUN OF SANITY BREAK THROUGH.
I NO LONGER SMELL BLOOD, BUT THE FAINT SCENT OF *HAKUBAIKŌ*.
AND NOW, AFTER HALF A YEAR OF LIVING WITH YOU...
...I TRULY UNDERSTAND THE HAPPINESS I'M TRYING TO PROTECT.
I CAN WEIGH THIS HAPPINESS IN MY HAND...
...AND FOR THE FIRST TIME I KNOW...
SSS
...NO MATTER HOW POWERFUL HIS SWORD...
...HOW PERFECTLY HONED HIS SKILLS...
CHK
CHK
NO ONE MAN CAN CHANGE AN ERA. NO ONE MAN...
...CAN BEAR THE HAPPINESS OF MANKIND ON HIS SHOULDERS.

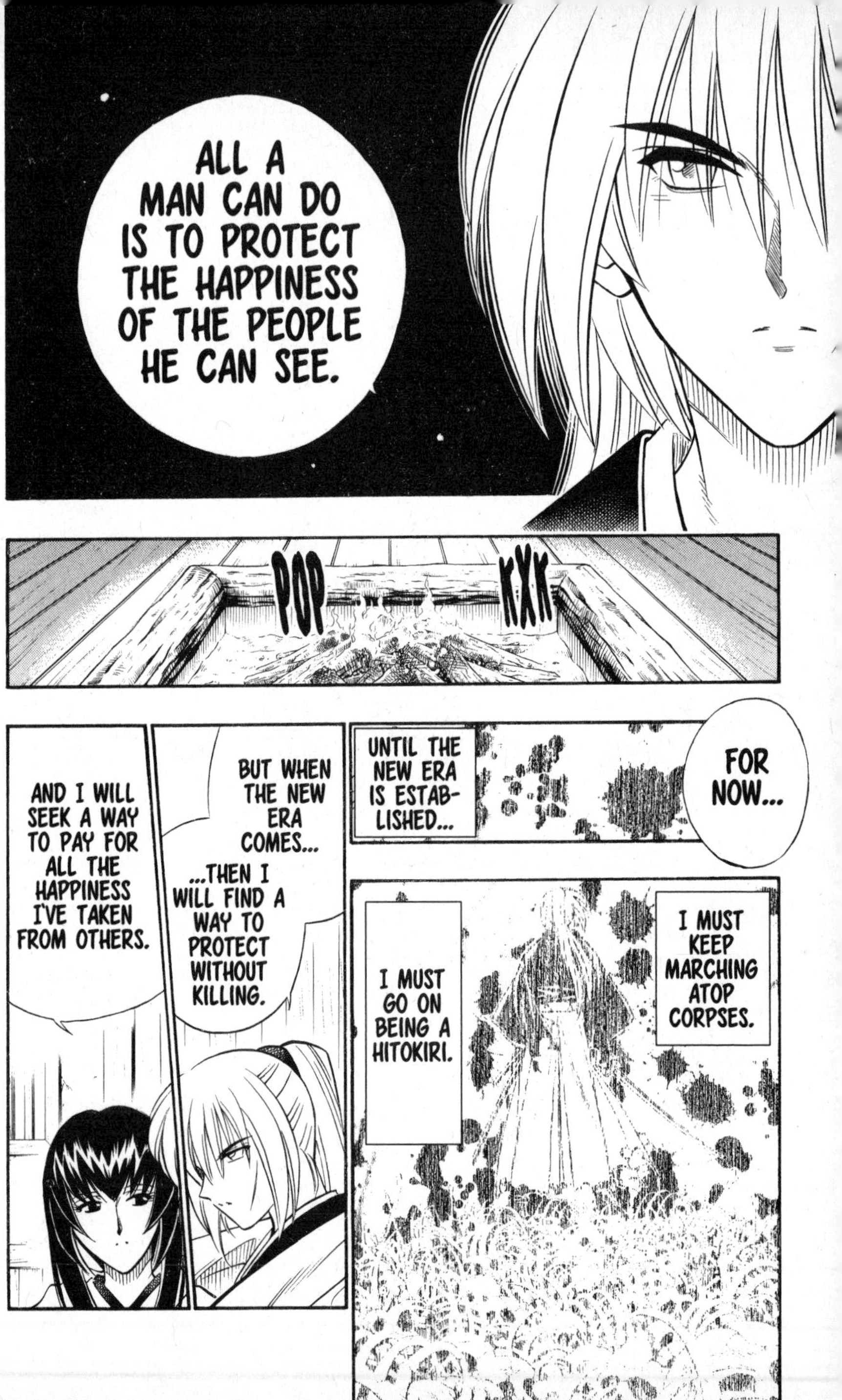
ALL A MAN CAN DO IS TO PROTECT THE HAPPINESS OF THE PEOPLE HE CAN SEE.
KXK
POP
FOR NOW...
UNTIL THE NEW ERA IS ESTAB-LISHED...
I MUST KEEP MARCHING ATOP CORPSES.
I MUST GO ON BEING A HITOKIRI.
BUT WHEN THE NEW ERA COMES...
...THEN I WILL FIND A WAY TO PROTECT WITHOUT KILLING.
AND I WILL SEEK A WAY TO PAY FOR ALL THE HAPPINESS I'VE TAKEN FROM OTHERS.

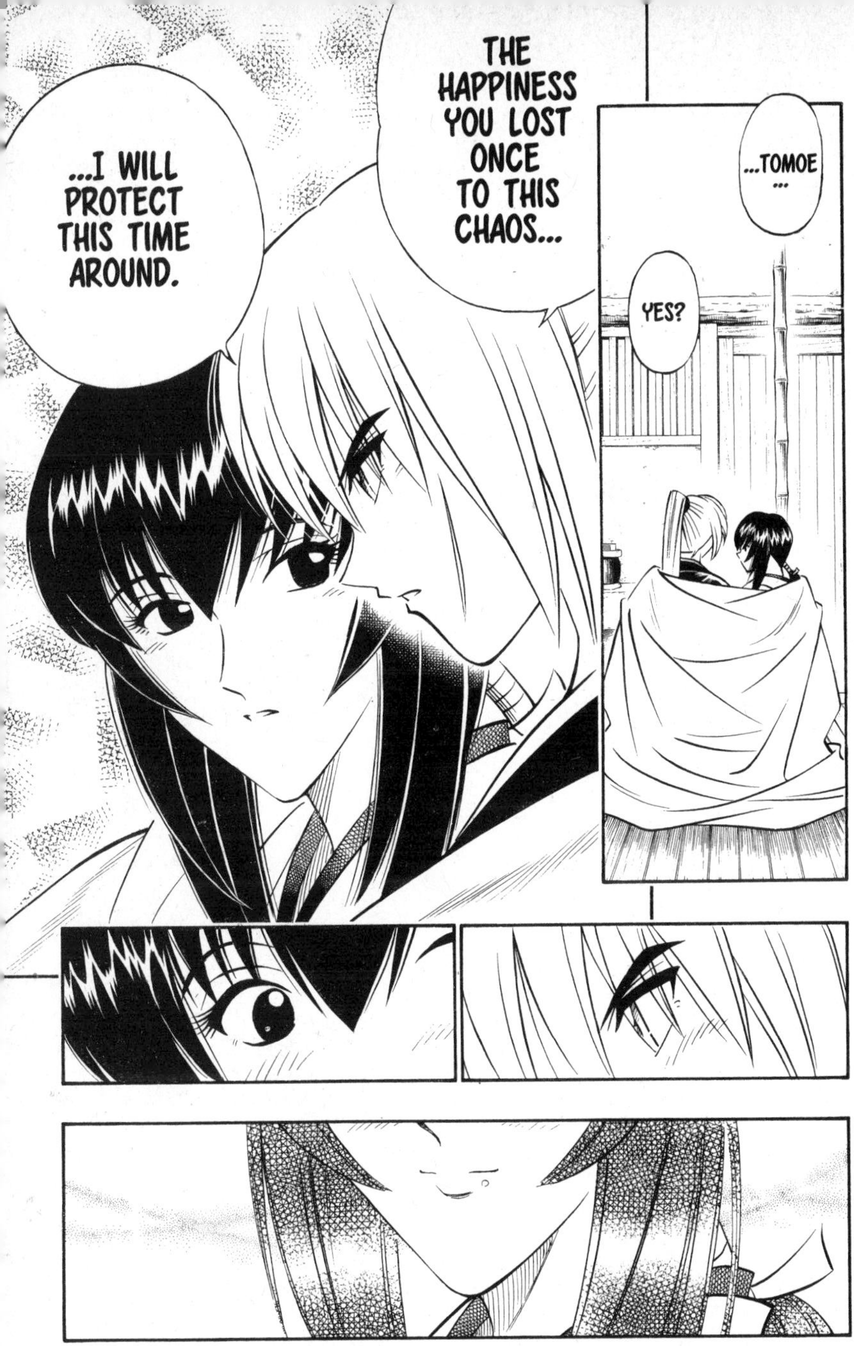
...TOMOE ...
YES?
THE HAPPINESS YOU LOST ONCE TO THIS CHAOS...
...I WILL PROTECT THIS TIME AROUND.

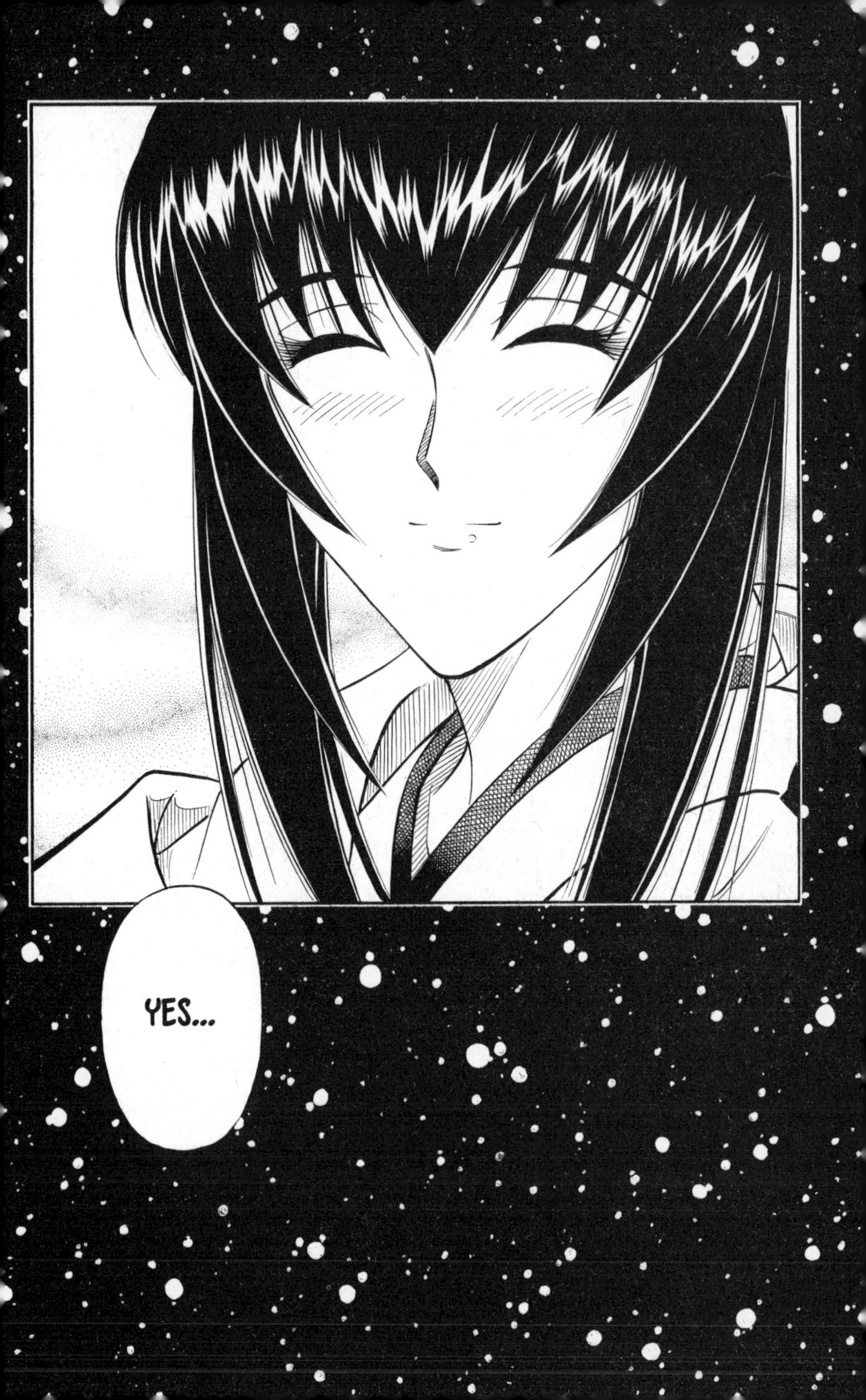
YES...

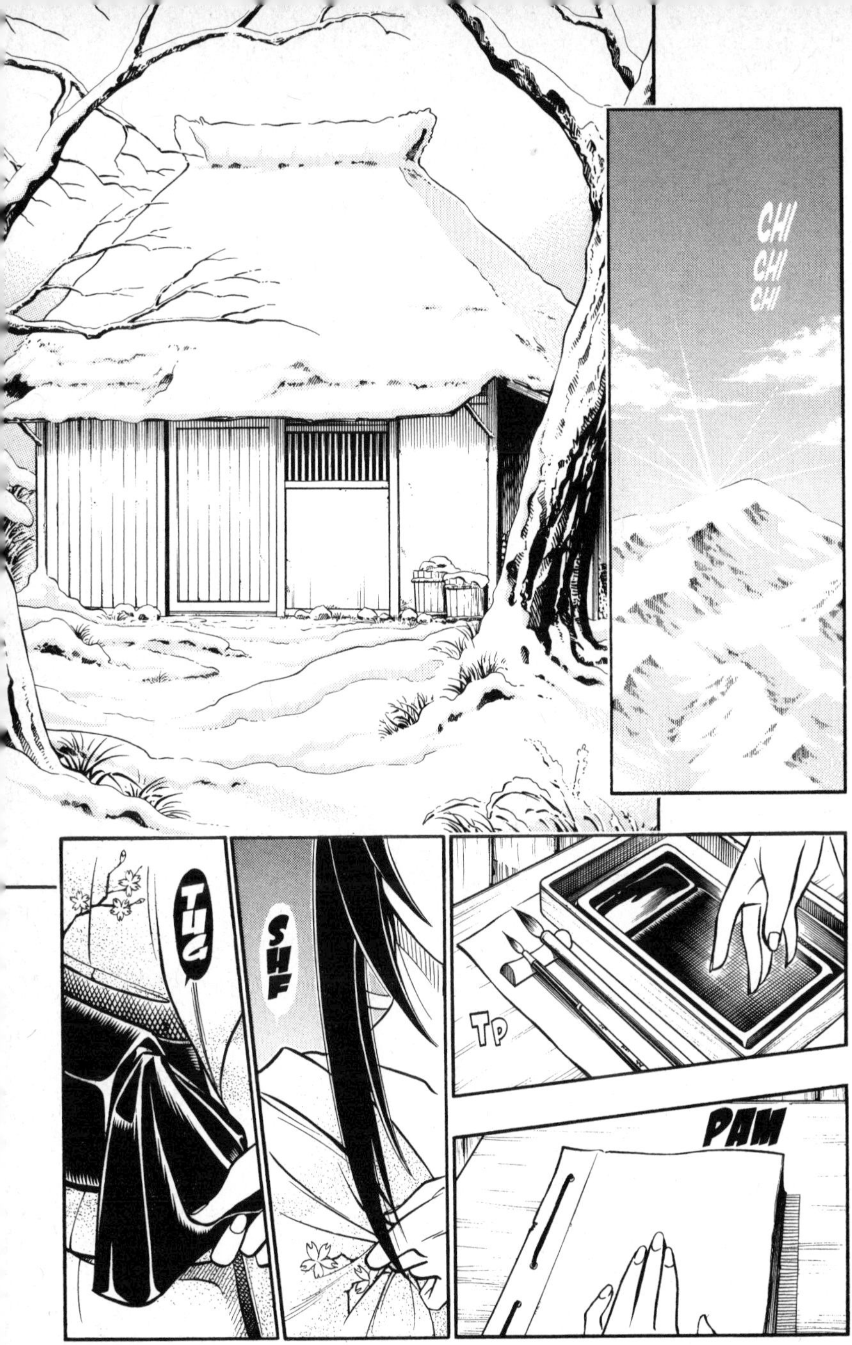
CHI
CHI
CHI
Tp
PAM
SHF
TUG

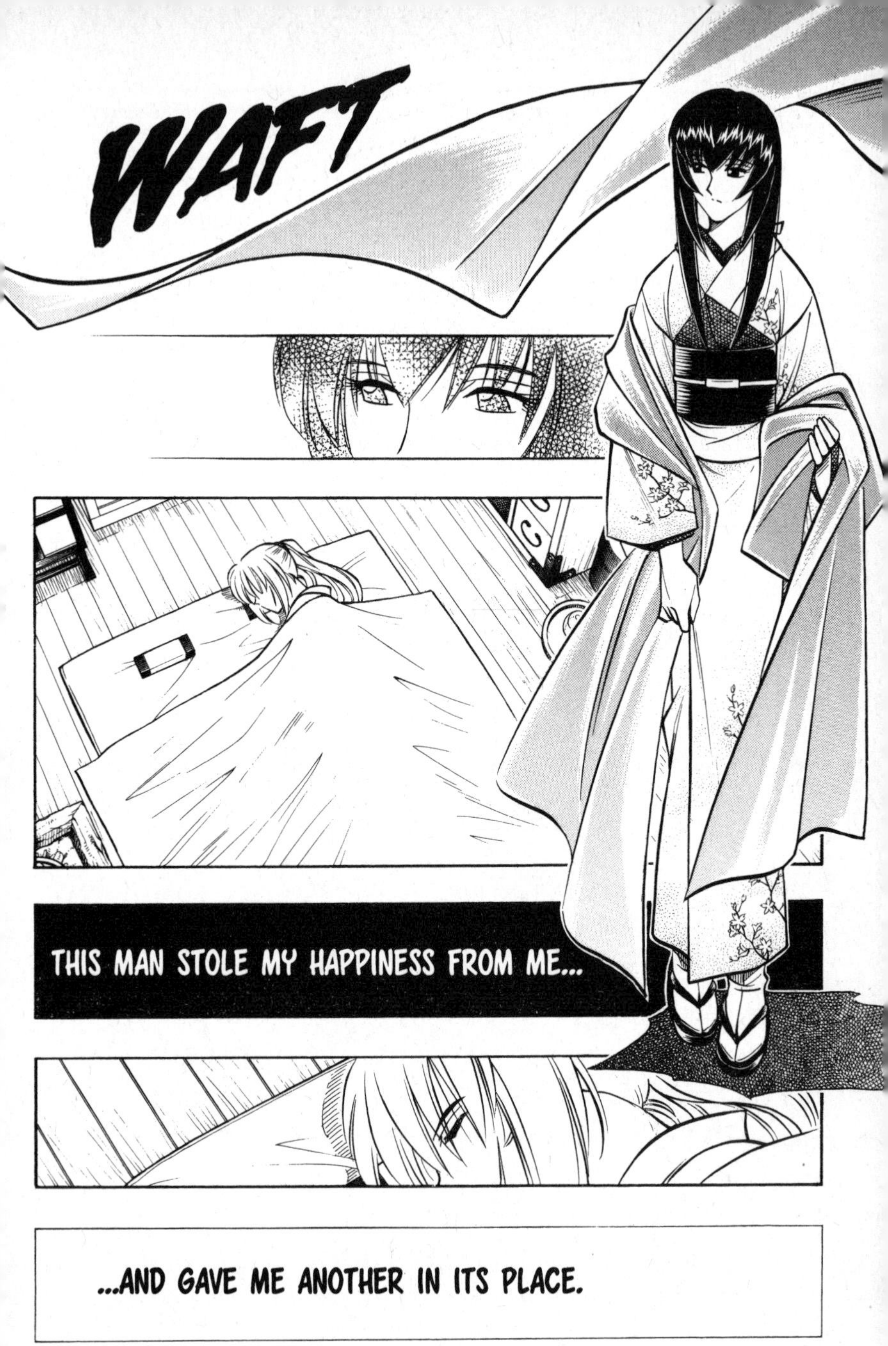
WAFT
THIS MAN STOLE MY HAPPINESS FROM ME...
...AND GAVE ME ANOTHER IN ITS PLACE.

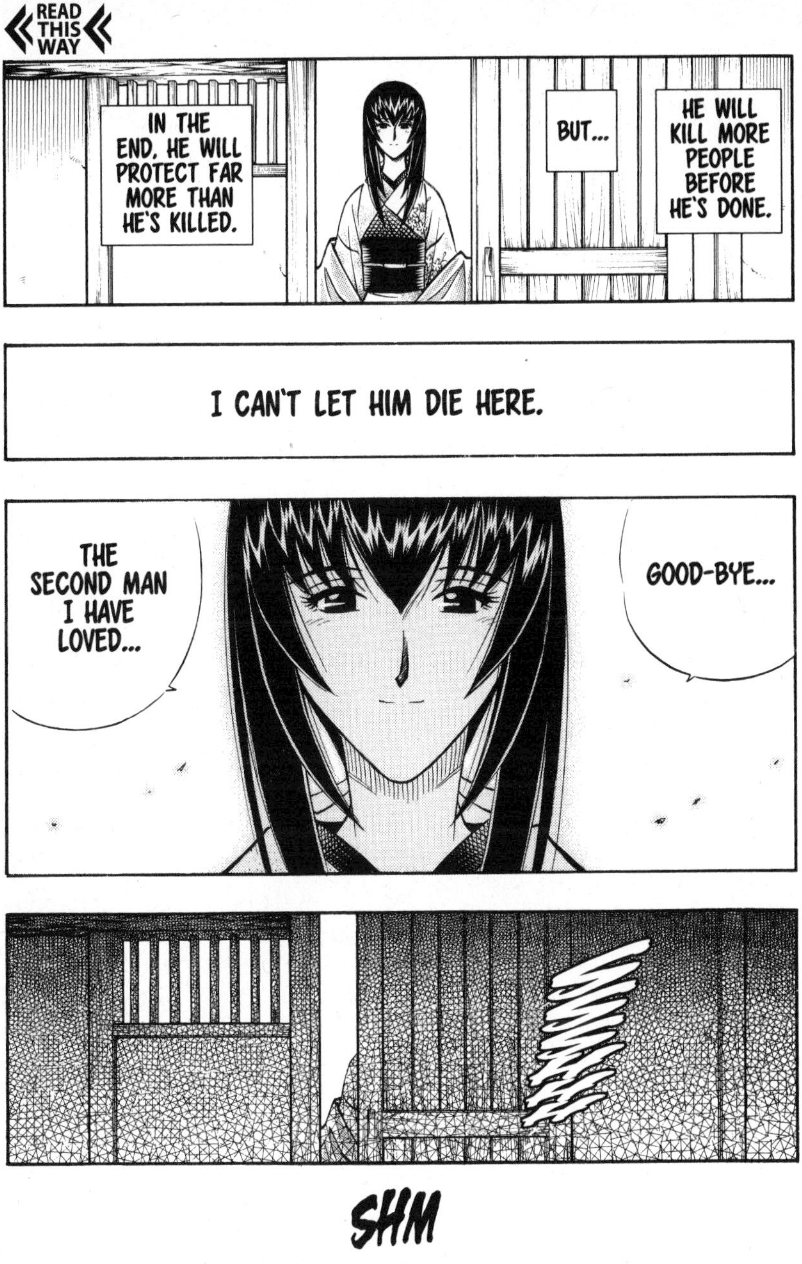
READ THIS WAY
HE WILL KILL MORE PEOPLE BEFORE HE'S DONE.
BUT...
IN THE END, HE WILL PROTECT FAR MORE THAN HE'S KILLED.
I CAN'T LET HIM DIE HERE.
GOOD-BYE...
THE SECOND MAN I HAVE LOVED...
SHM

Rurouni Kenshin

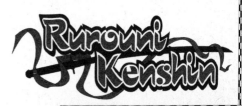

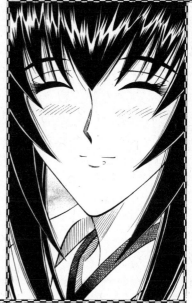

Act 175

Remembrance 10: The Binding Forest

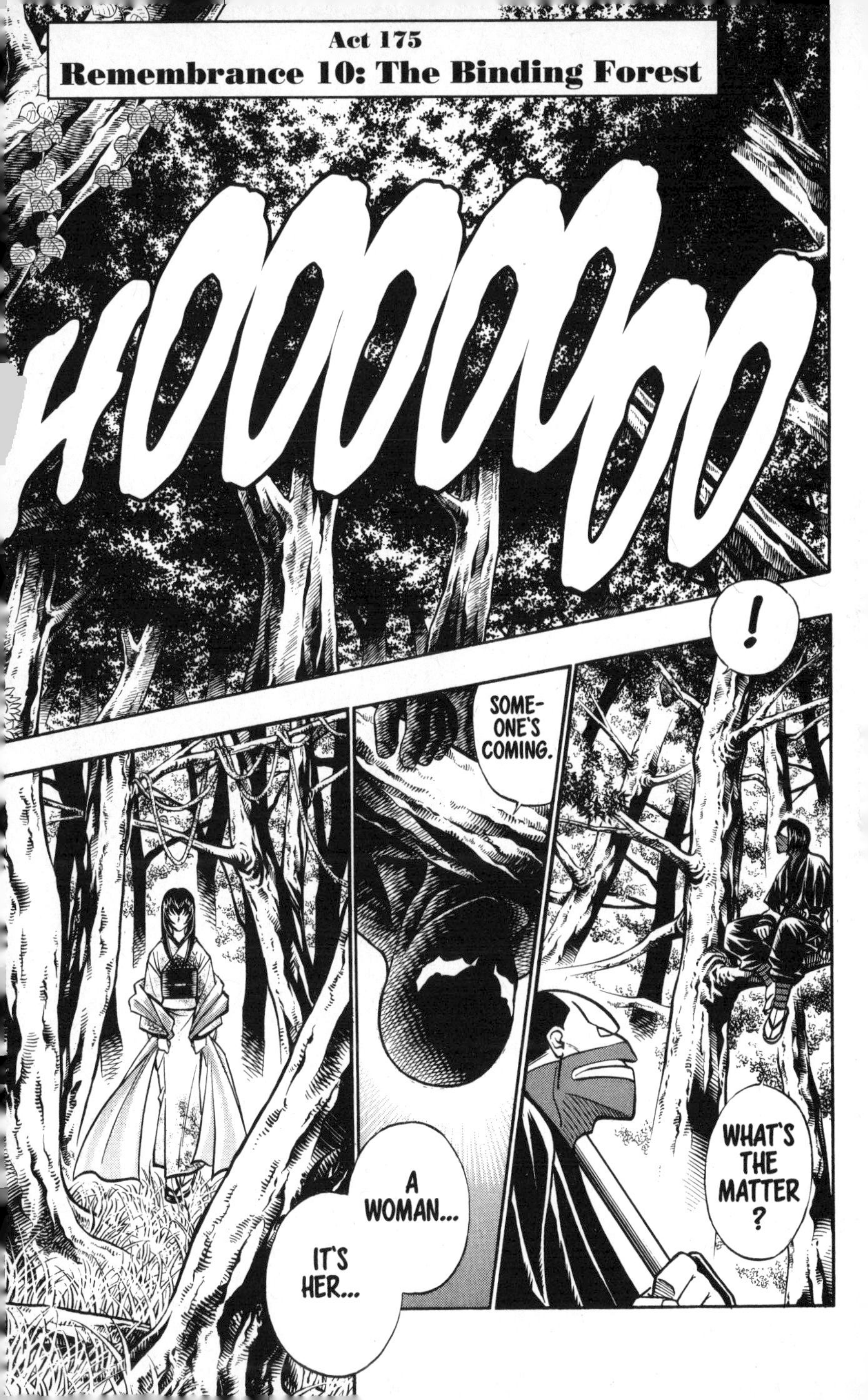
HOOOOOOO
!
WHAT'S THE MATTER?
SOME-ONE'S COMING.
A WOMAN...
IT'S HER...

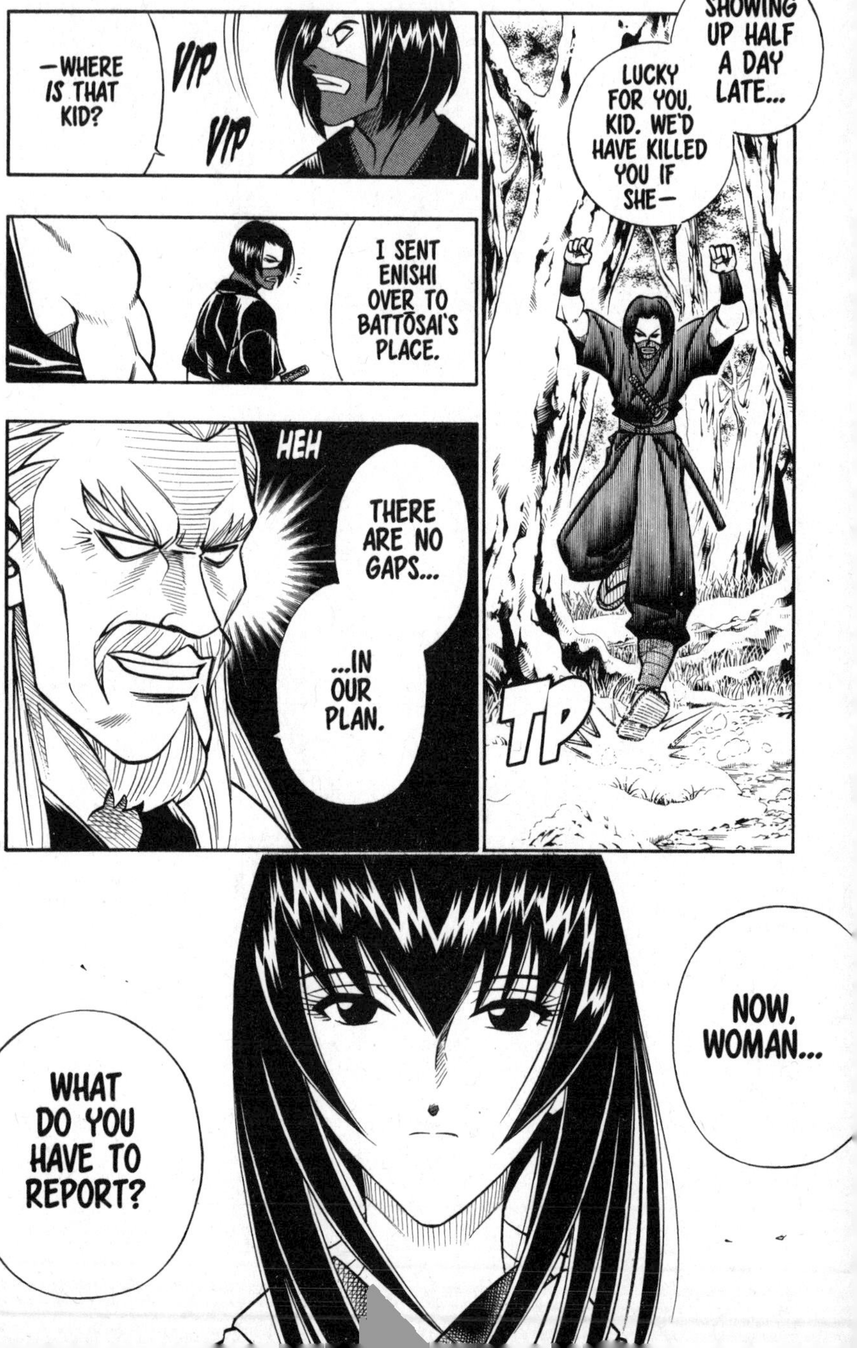
SHOWING UP HALF A DAY LATE...
LUCKY FOR YOU, KID. WE'D HAVE KILLED YOU IF SHE—
TP
VIP
VIP
—WHERE IS THAT KID?
I SENT ENISHI OVER TO BATTŌSAI'S PLACE.
HEH
THERE ARE NO GAPS...
...IN OUR PLAN.
NOW, WOMAN...
WHAT DO YOU HAVE TO REPORT?

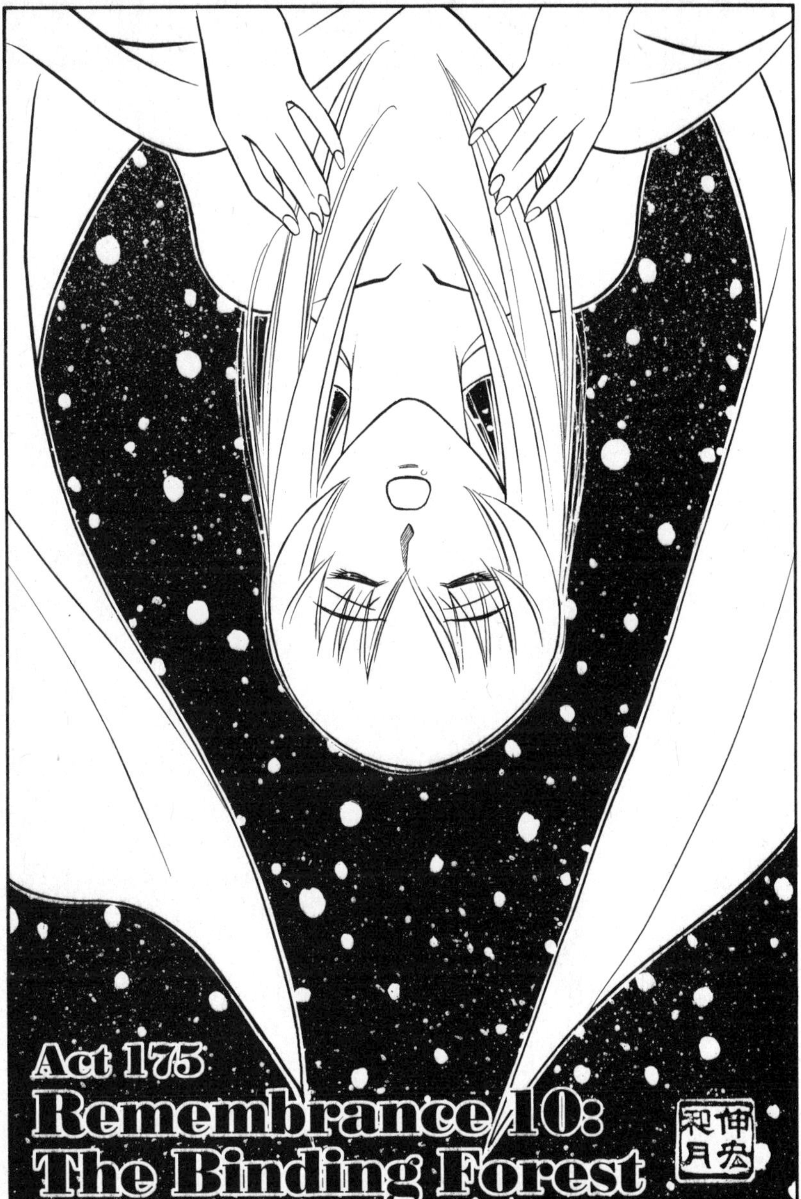
Act 175
Remembrance 10:
The Binding Forest
伸宏
和月

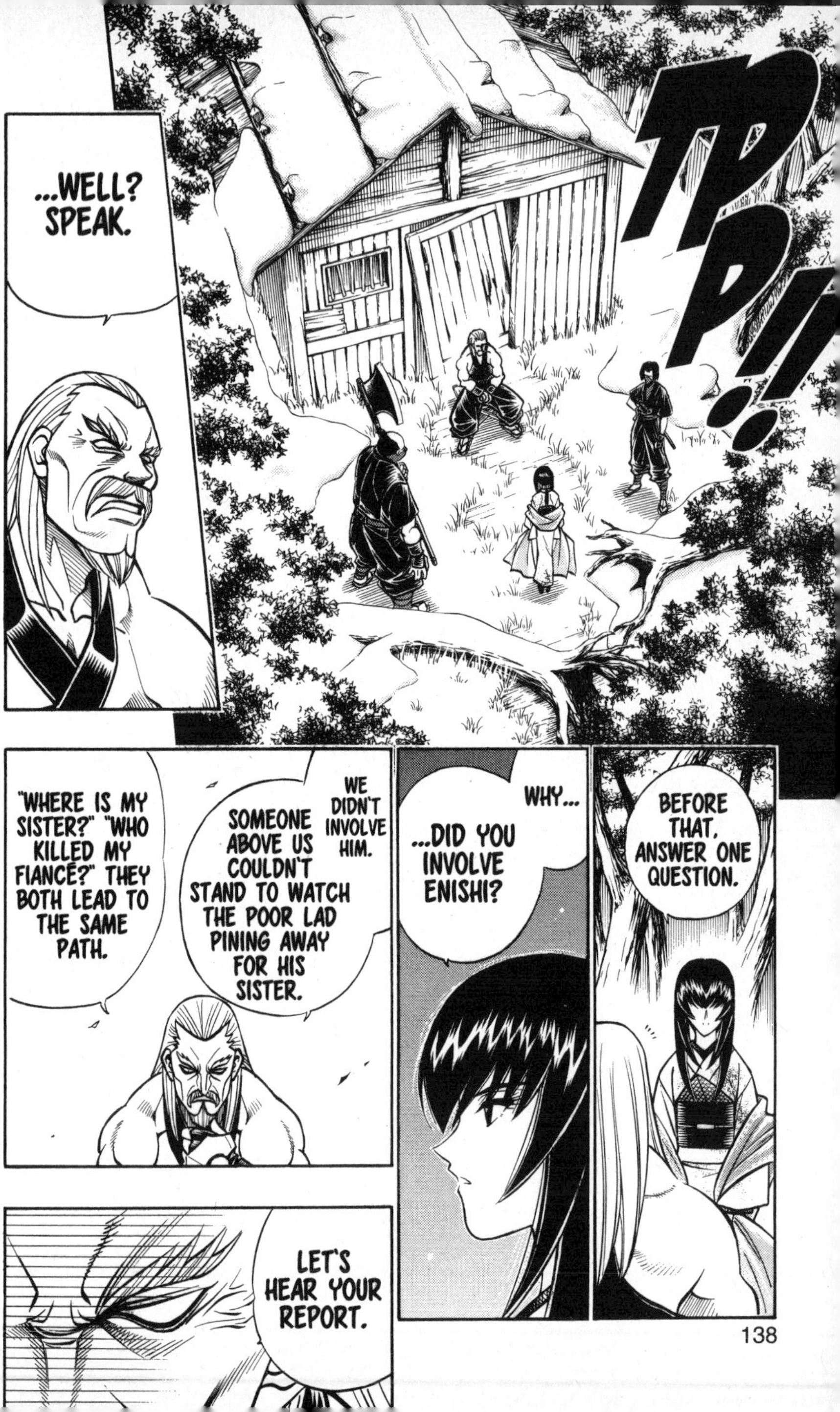
TAP!!
...WELL? SPEAK.
BEFORE THAT, ANSWER ONE QUESTION.
WHY...
...DID YOU INVOLVE ENISHI?
WE DIDN'T INVOLVE HIM.
SOMEONE ABOVE US COULDN'T STAND TO WATCH THE POOR LAD PINING AWAY FOR HIS SISTER.
"WHERE IS MY SISTER?" "WHO KILLED MY FIANCÉ?" THEY BOTH LEAD TO THE SAME PATH.
LET'S HEAR YOUR REPORT.

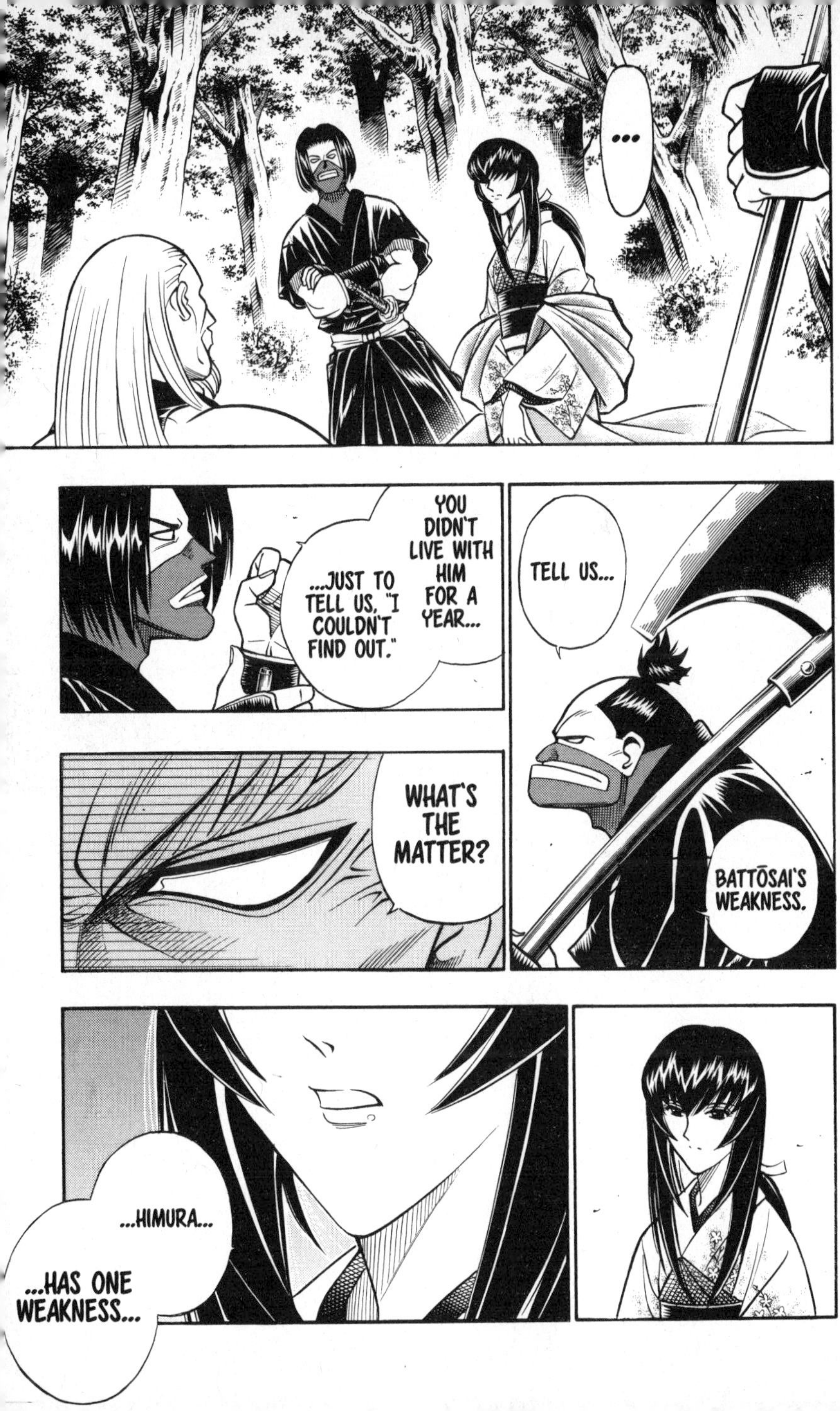
...
TELL US...
BATTŌSAI'S WEAKNESS.
YOU DIDN'T LIVE WITH HIM FOR A YEAR...
...JUST TO TELL US, "I COULDN'T FIND OUT."
WHAT'S THE MATTER?
...HIMURA...
...HAS ONE WEAKNESS...

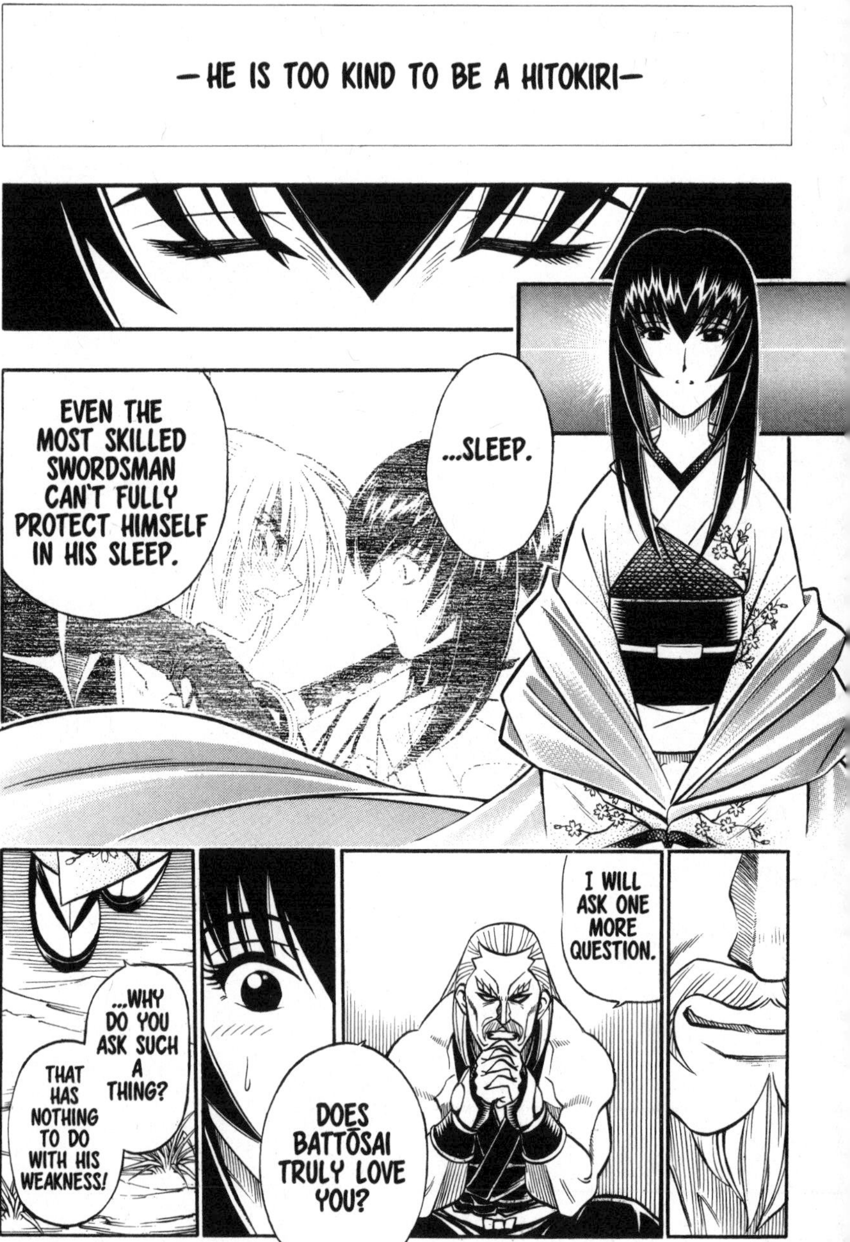
—HE IS TOO KIND TO BE A HITOKIRI—
EVEN THE MOST SKILLED SWORDSMAN CAN'T FULLY PROTECT HIMSELF IN HIS SLEEP.
...SLEEP.
I WILL ASK ONE MORE QUESTION.
DOES BATTŌSAI TRULY LOVE YOU?
...WHY DO YOU ASK SUCH A THING?
THAT HAS NOTHING TO DO WITH HIS WEAKNESS!

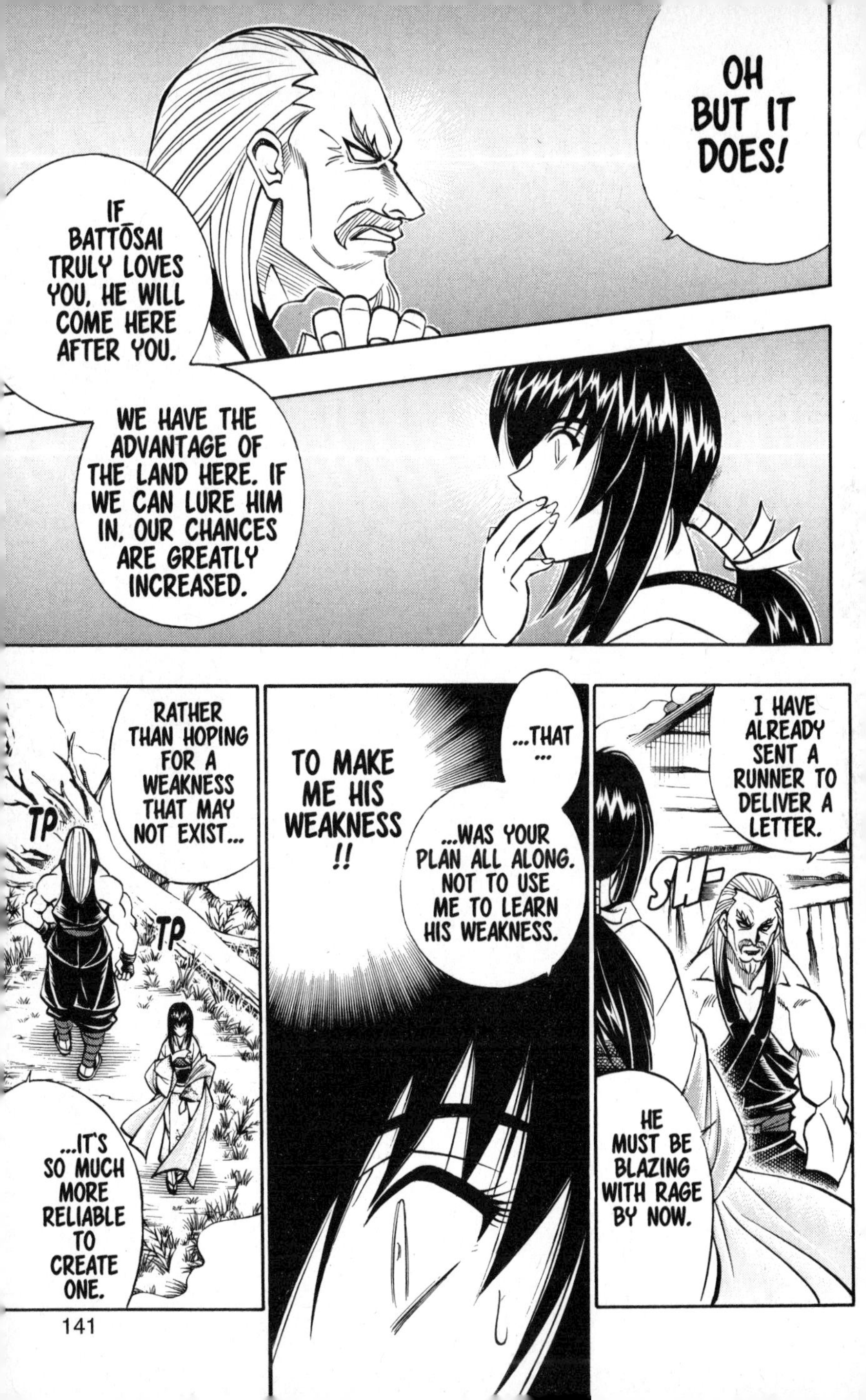
OH BUT IT DOES!
IF BATTŌSAI TRULY LOVES YOU, HE WILL COME HERE AFTER YOU.
WE HAVE THE ADVANTAGE OF THE LAND HERE. IF WE CAN LURE HIM IN, OUR CHANCES ARE GREATLY INCREASED.
I HAVE ALREADY SENT A RUNNER TO DELIVER A LETTER.
SH-
HE MUST BE BLAZING WITH RAGE BY NOW.
...THAT ...
...WAS YOUR PLAN ALL ALONG. NOT TO USE ME TO LEARN HIS WEAKNESS.
TO MAKE ME HIS WEAKNESS !!
RATHER THAN HOPING FOR A WEAKNESS THAT MAY NOT EXIST...
TP
TP
...IT'S SO MUCH MORE RELIABLE TO CREATE ONE.

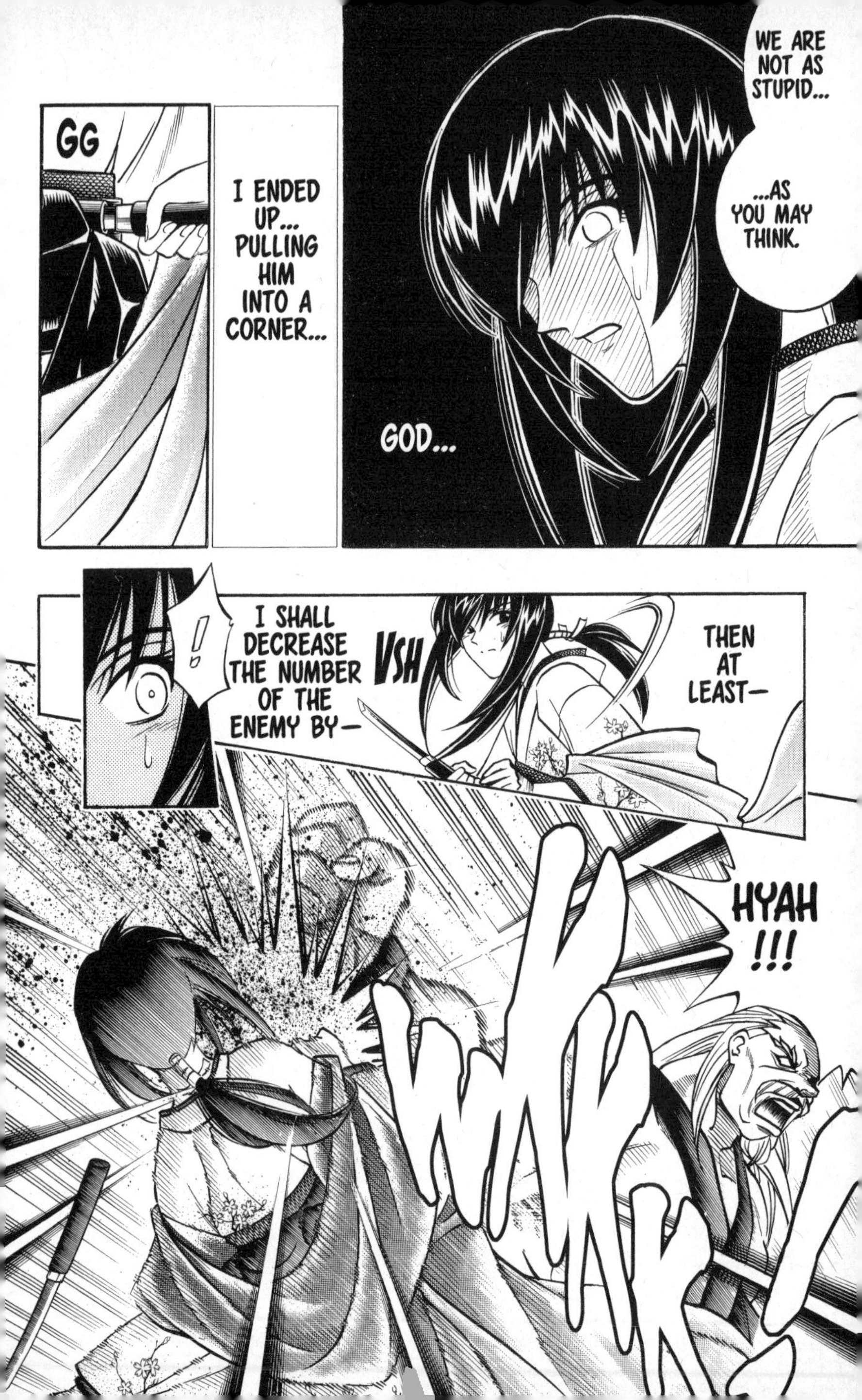
WE ARE NOT AS STUPID...
...AS YOU MAY THINK.
GOD...
I ENDED UP... PULLING HIM INTO A CORNER...
GG
THEN AT LEAST—
VSH
I SHALL DECREASE THE NUMBER OF THE ENEMY BY—
!
HYAH!!!
WHAK

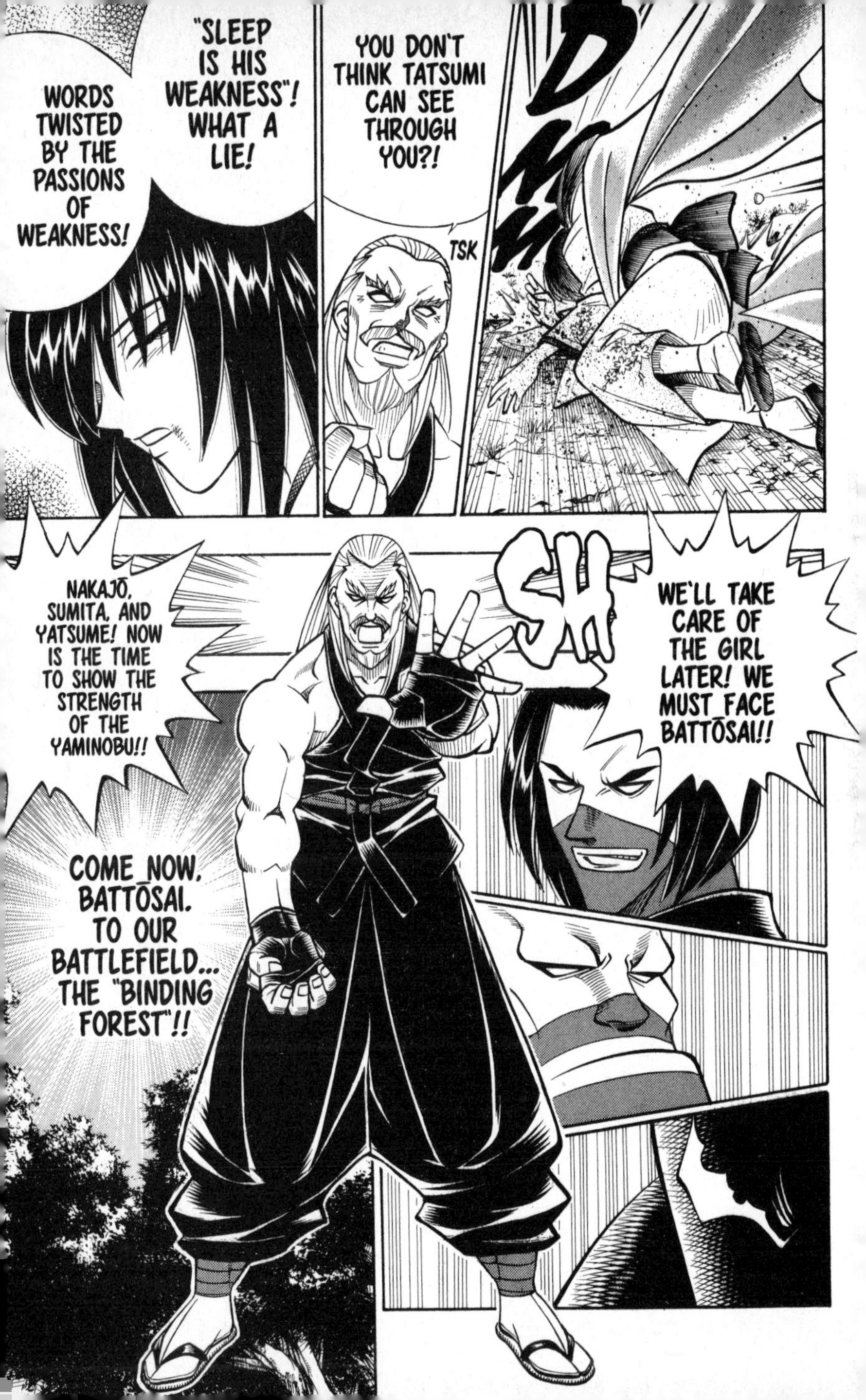
DMM
YOU DON'T THINK TATSUMI CAN SEE THROUGH YOU?!
TSK
"SLEEP IS HIS WEAKNESS"! WHAT A LIE!
WORDS TWISTED BY THE PASSIONS OF WEAKNESS!
SH
WE'LL TAKE CARE OF THE GIRL LATER! WE MUST FACE BATTŌSAI!!
NAKAJŌ, SUMITA, AND YATSUME! NOW IS THE TIME TO SHOW THE STRENGTH OF THE YAMINOBU!!
COME NOW, BATTŌSAI. TO OUR BATTLEFIELD... THE "BINDING FOREST"!!

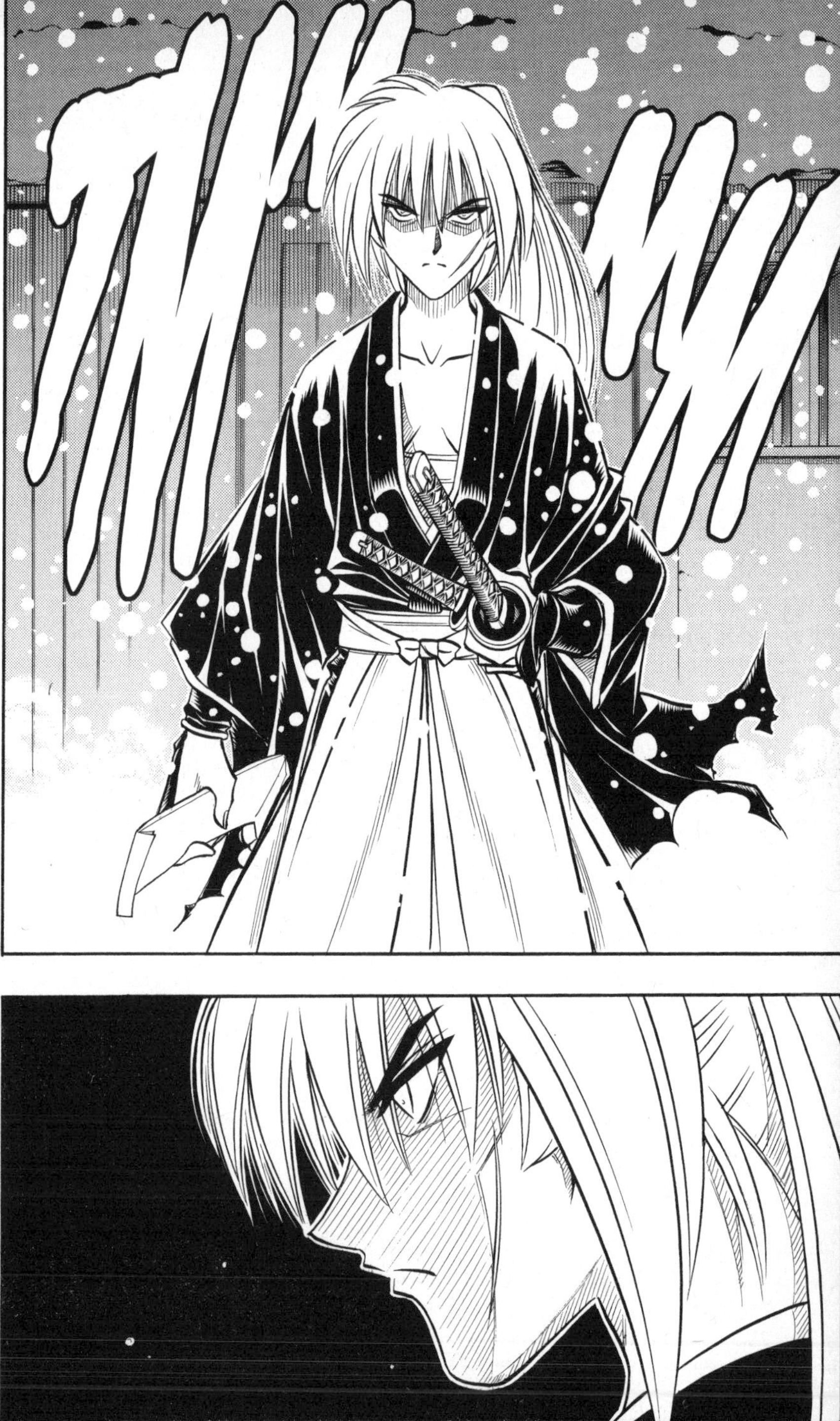

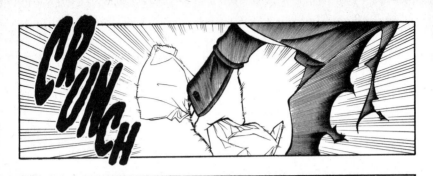

"YOUR TASK, ENISHI, IS TO THROW THIS LETTER INTO BATTŌSAI'S HOME. IF ALL GOES WELL, YOU AND YOUR SISTER CAN GO FREE."

...HE'S MOVING.

WE'RE GOING HOME TO EDO TOGETHER!

NOW, SIS, WE'RE GOING HOME!

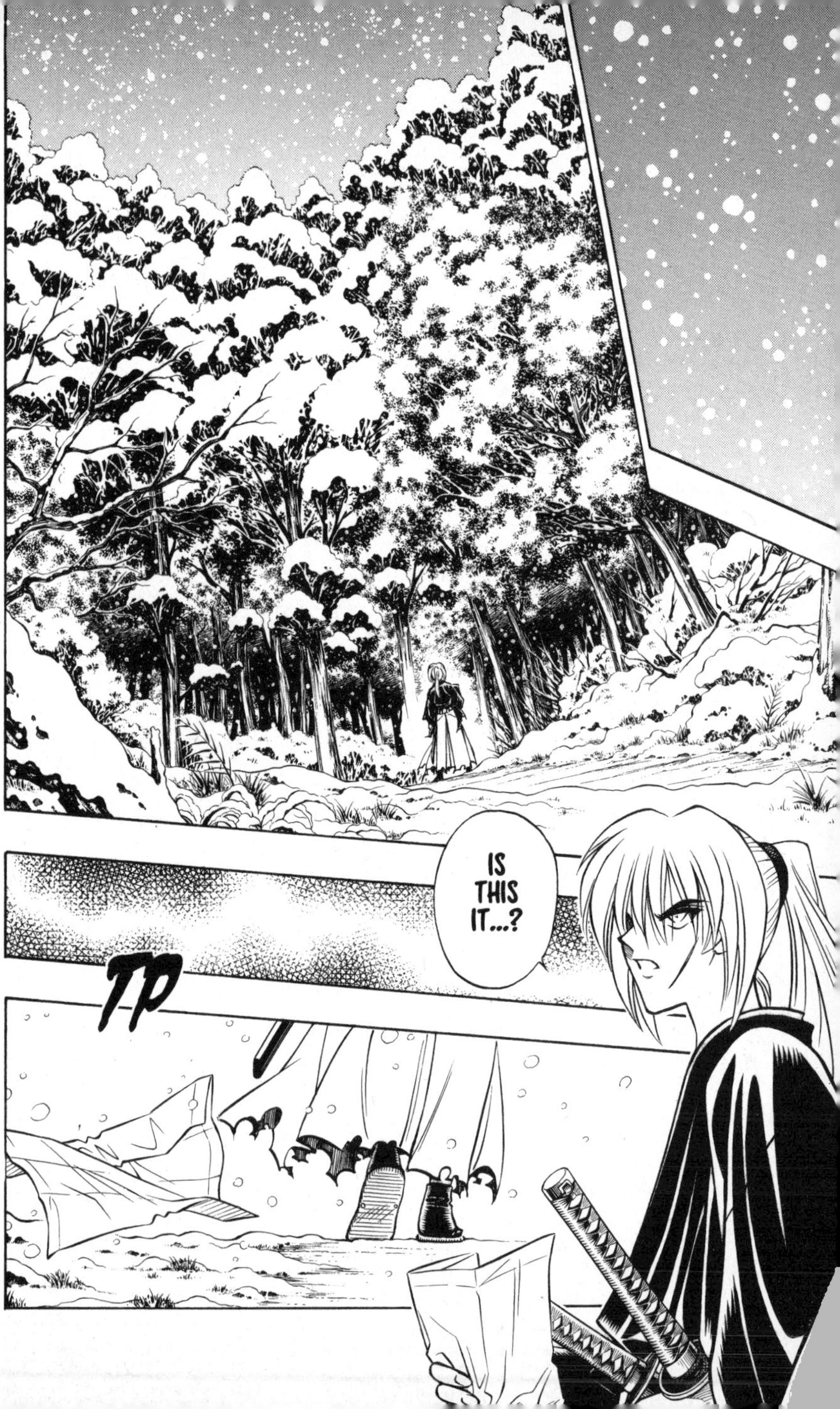
IS THIS IT...?
TP

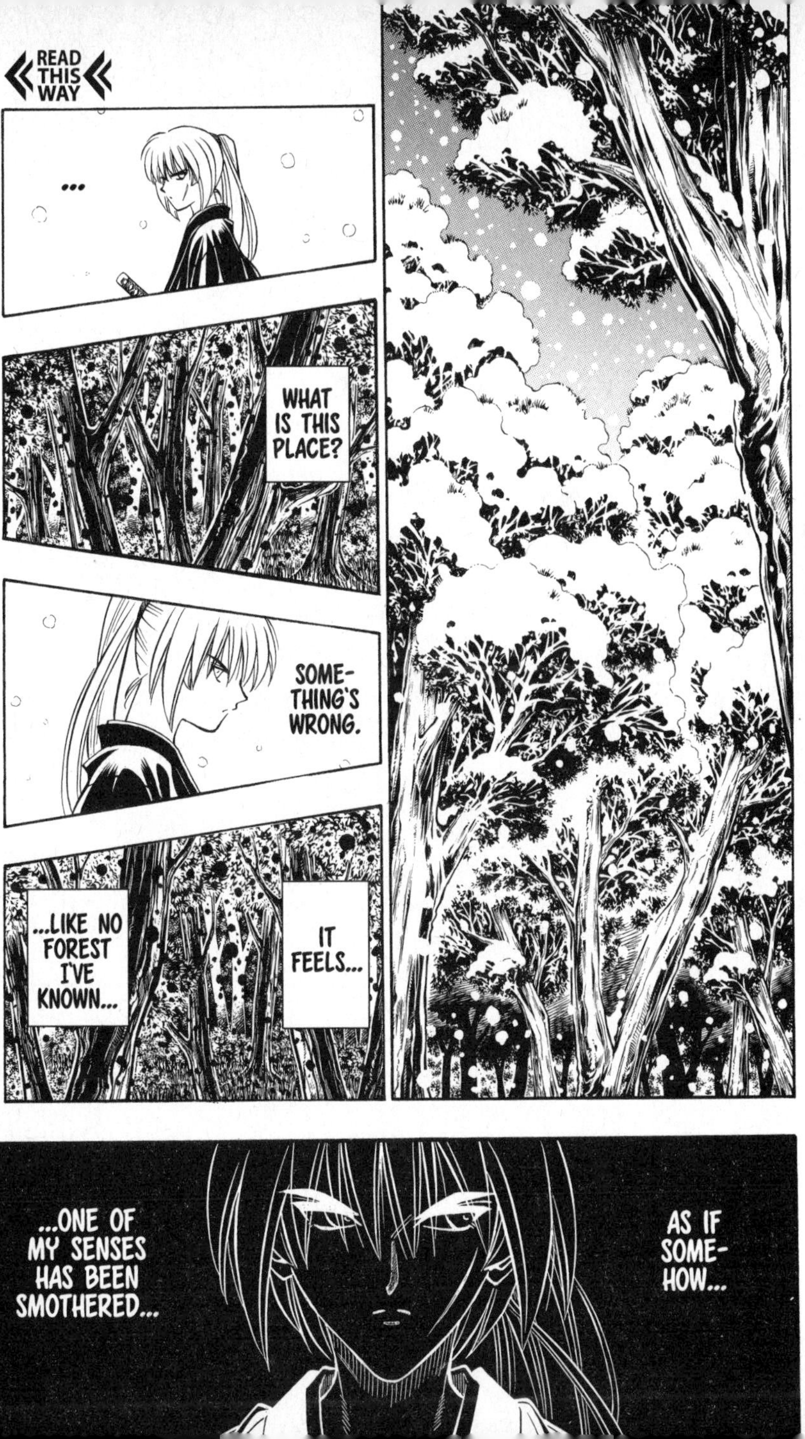
READ THIS WAY
...
WHAT IS THIS PLACE?
SOME-THING'S WRONG.
IT FEELS...
...LIKE NO FOREST I'VE KNOWN...
AS IF SOME-HOW...
...ONE OF MY SENSES HAS BEEN SMOTHERED...

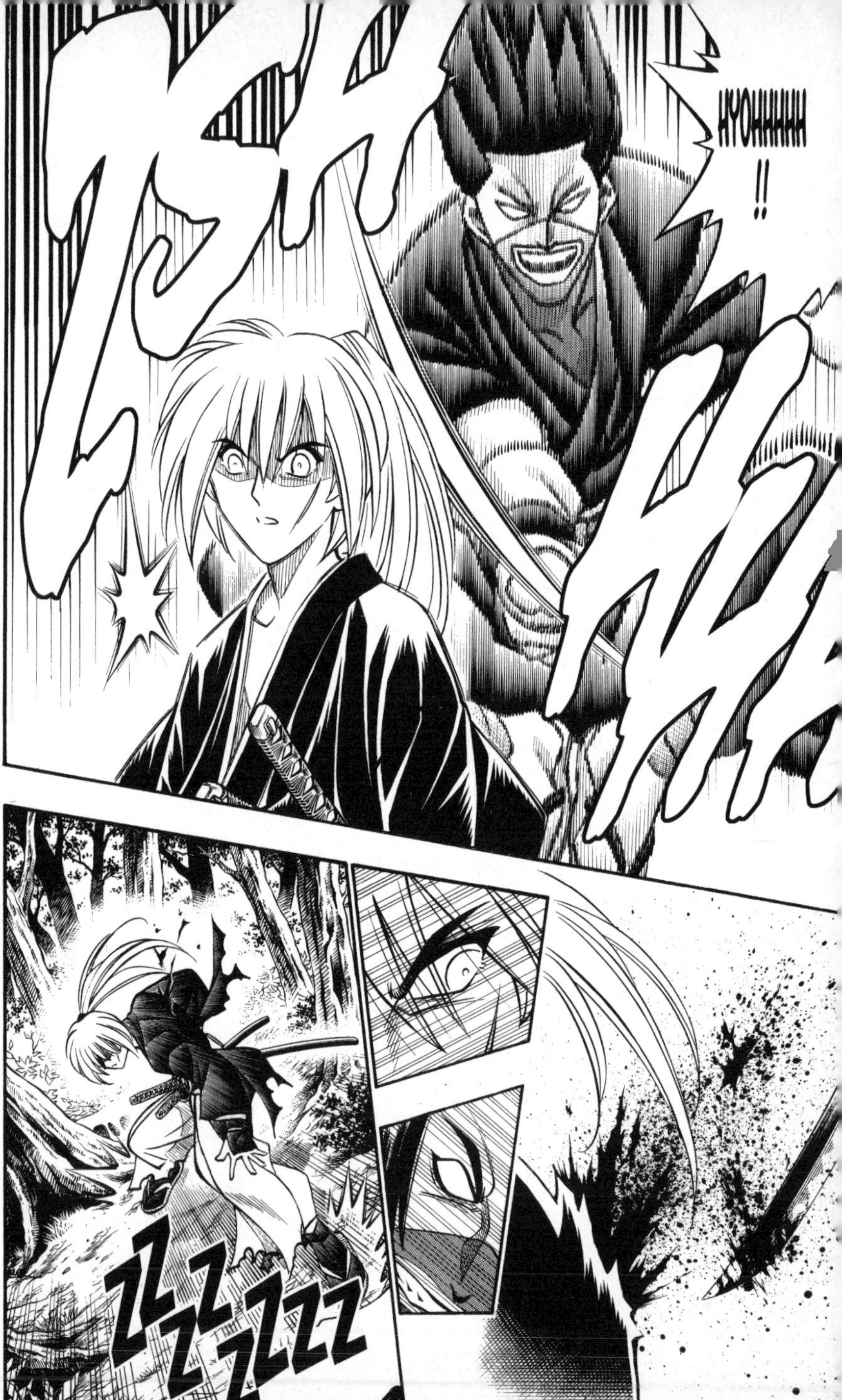
HYOHHHHH !!
ZZZZZZZ

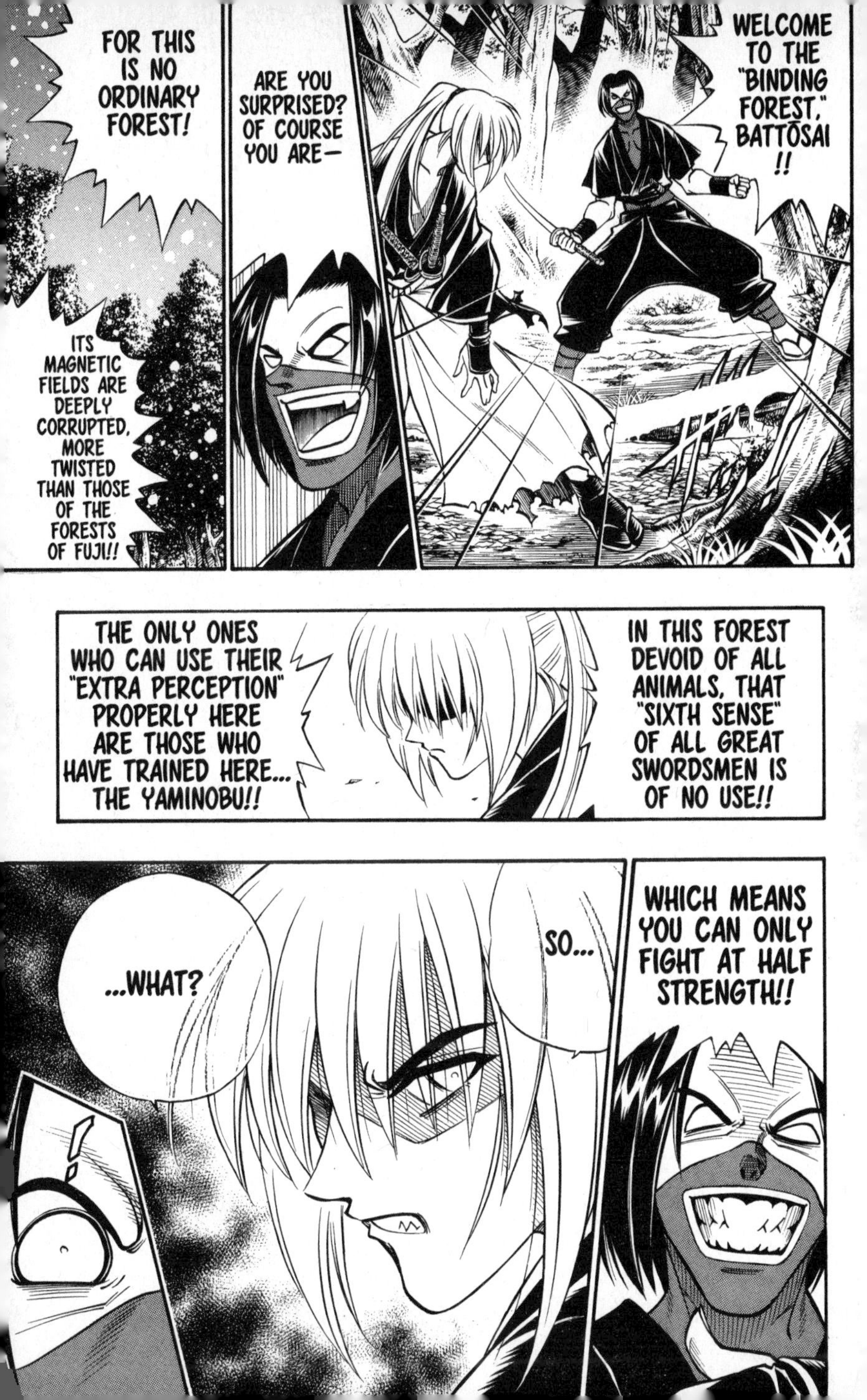
WELCOME TO THE "BINDING FOREST," BATTŌSAI!!
ARE YOU SURPRISED? OF COURSE YOU ARE—
FOR THIS IS NO ORDINARY FOREST!
ITS MAGNETIC FIELDS ARE DEEPLY CORRUPTED, MORE TWISTED THAN THOSE OF THE FORESTS OF FUJI!!
IN THIS FOREST DEVOID OF ALL ANIMALS, THAT "SIXTH SENSE" OF ALL GREAT SWORDSMEN IS OF NO USE!!
THE ONLY ONES WHO CAN USE THEIR "EXTRA PERCEPTION" PROPERLY HERE ARE THOSE WHO HAVE TRAINED HERE... THE YAMINOBU!!
WHICH MEANS YOU CAN ONLY FIGHT AT HALF STRENGTH!!
SO...
...WHAT?
!

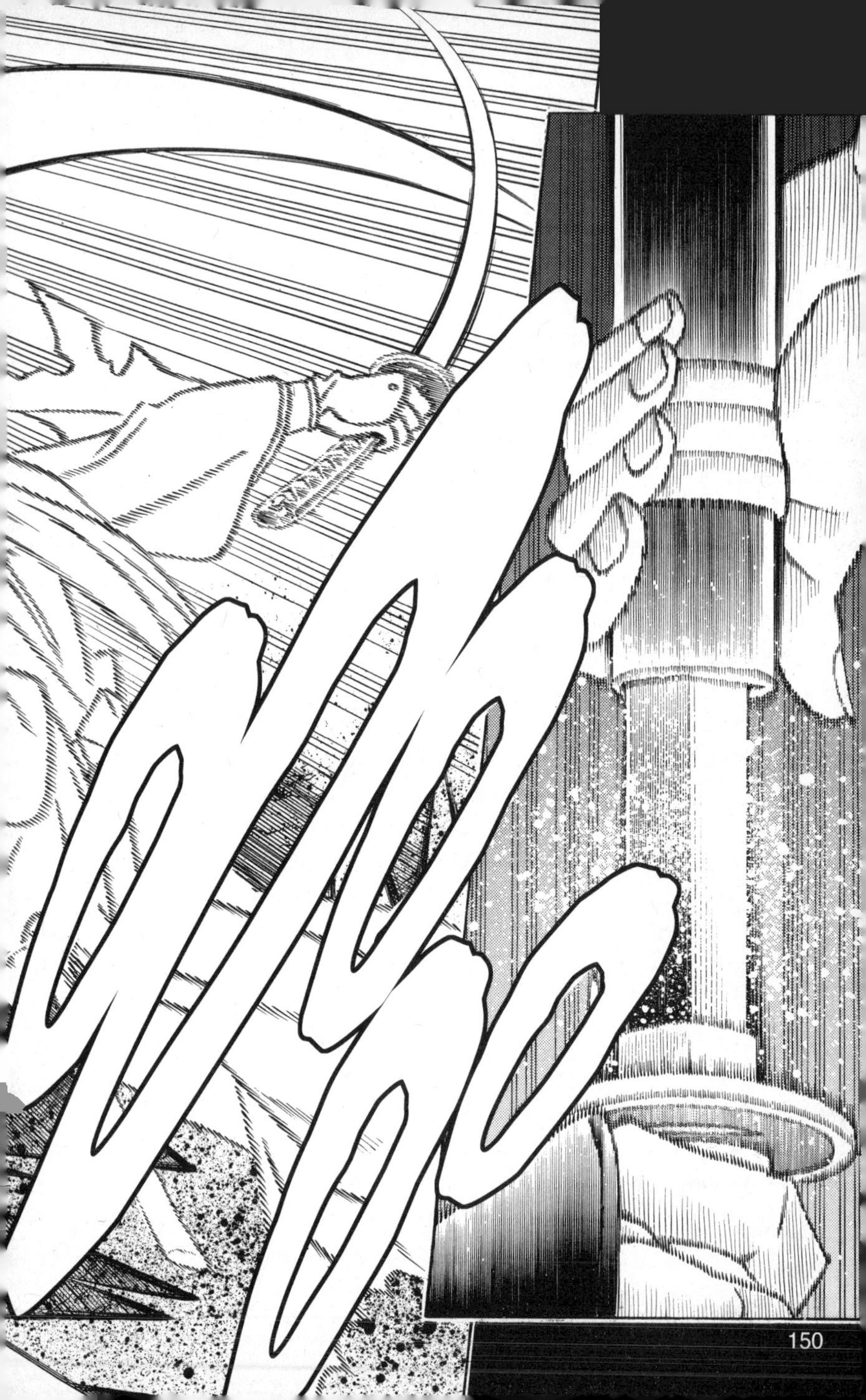

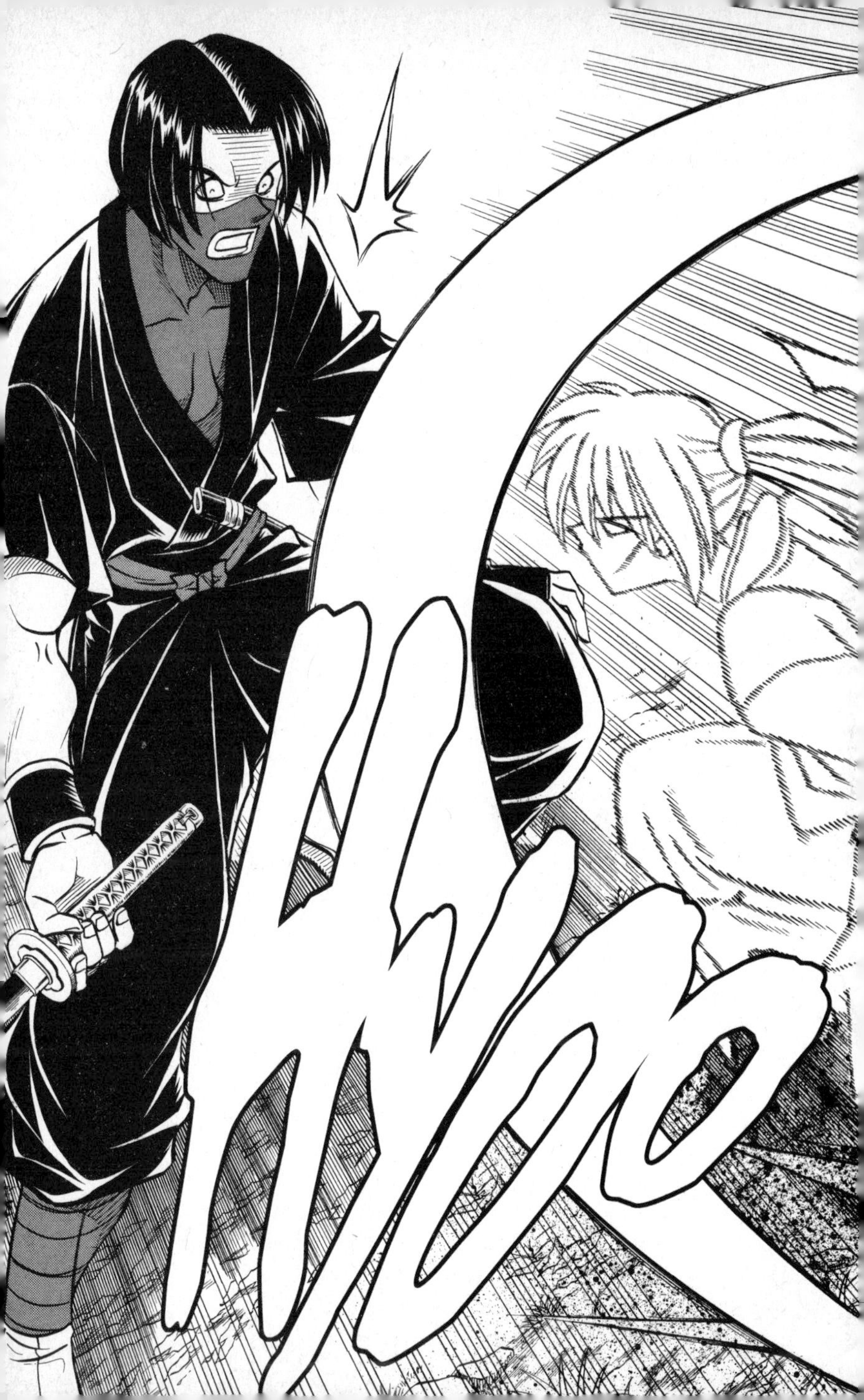
HYOO

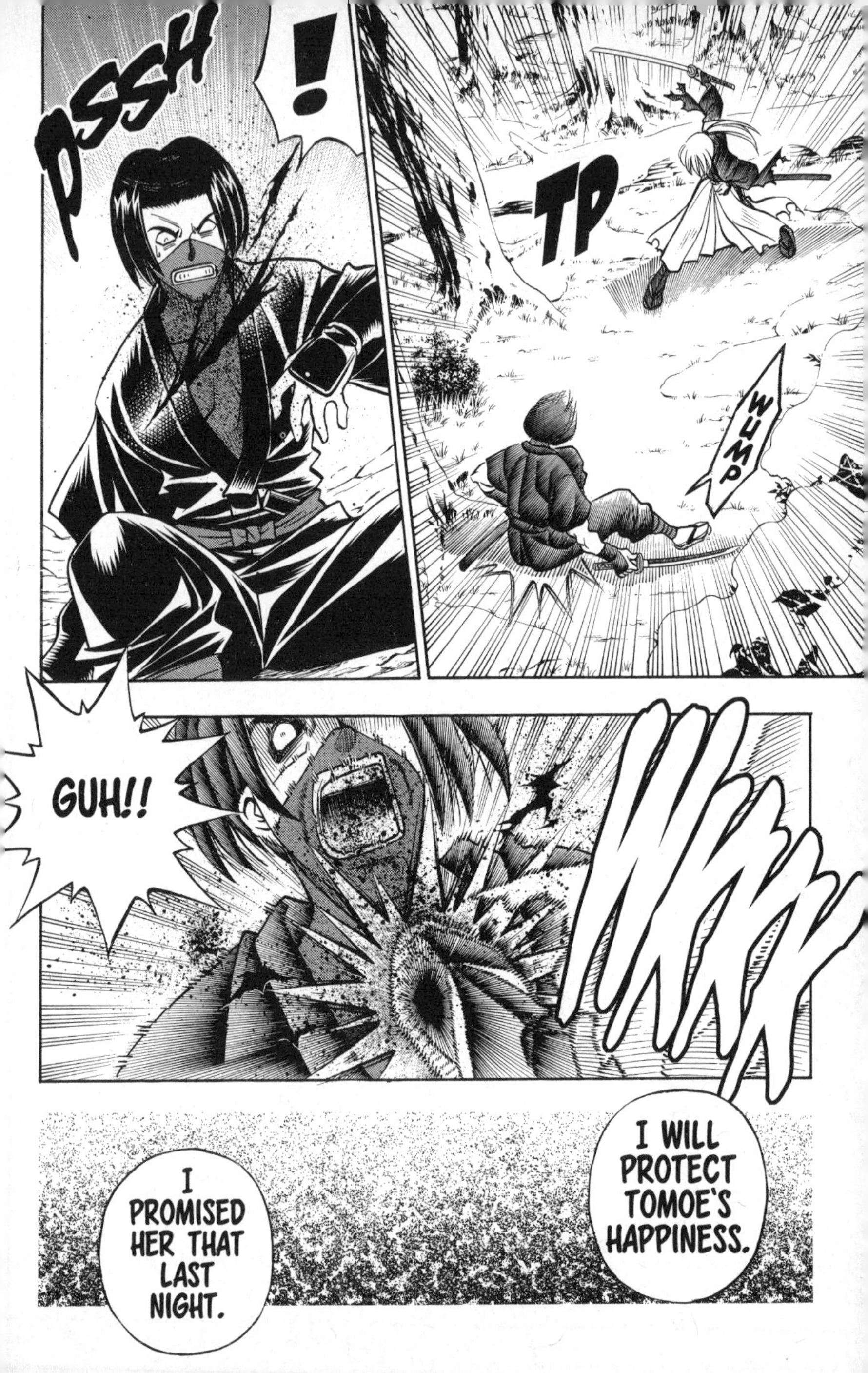
TP
WUMP
PSSH
!
GUH!!
I WILL PROTECT TOMOE'S HAPPINESS.
I PROMISED HER THAT LAST NIGHT.

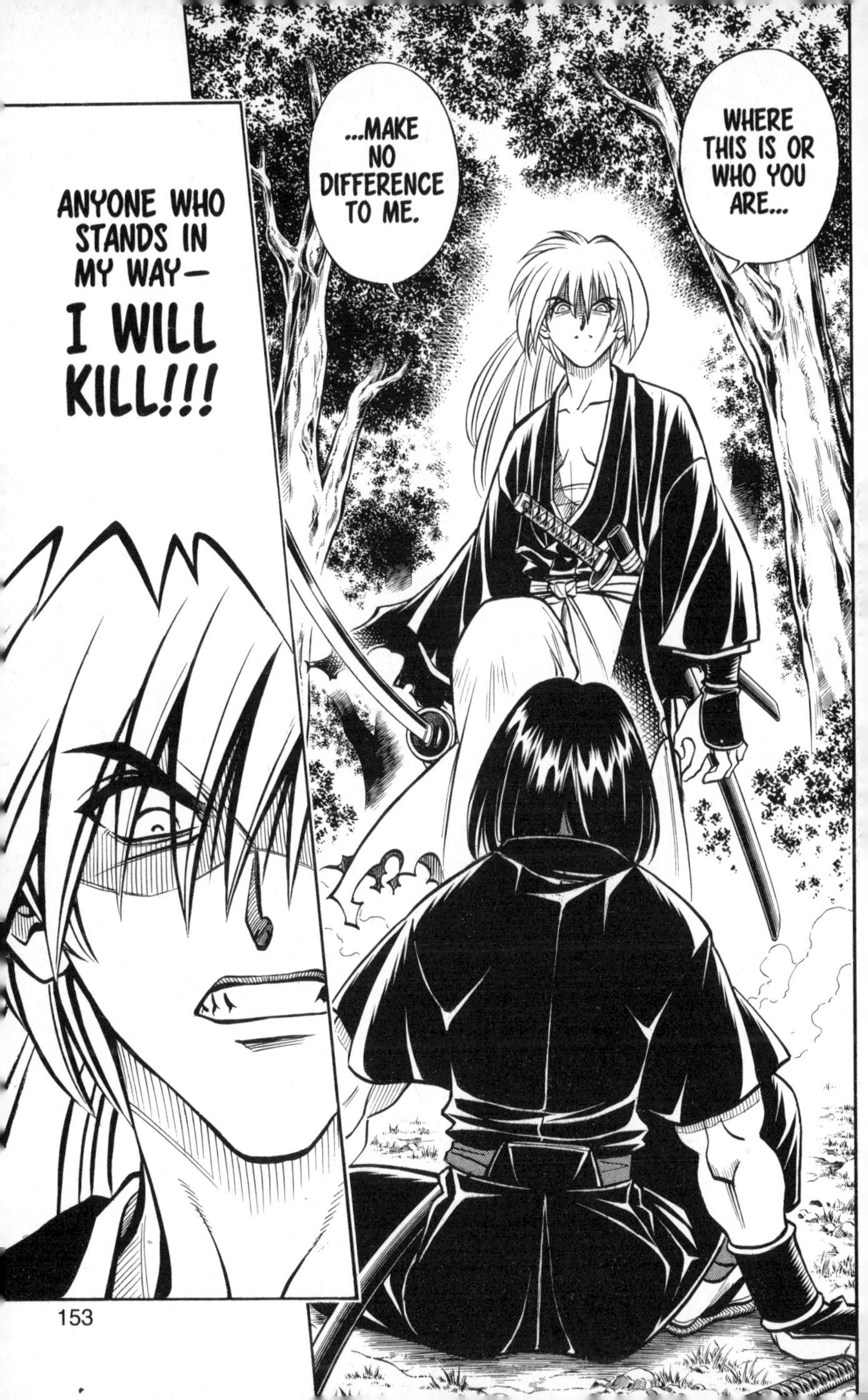
WHERE THIS IS OR WHO YOU ARE...
...MAKE NO DIFFERENCE TO ME.
ANYONE WHO STANDS IN MY WAY— I WILL KILL!!!

Rurouni Kenshin

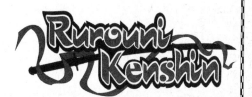

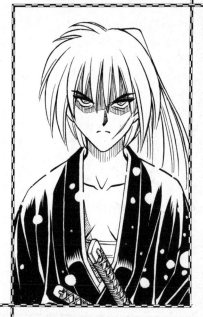

Act 176
Remembrance 11: Shadow Warriors

伸宏
和月

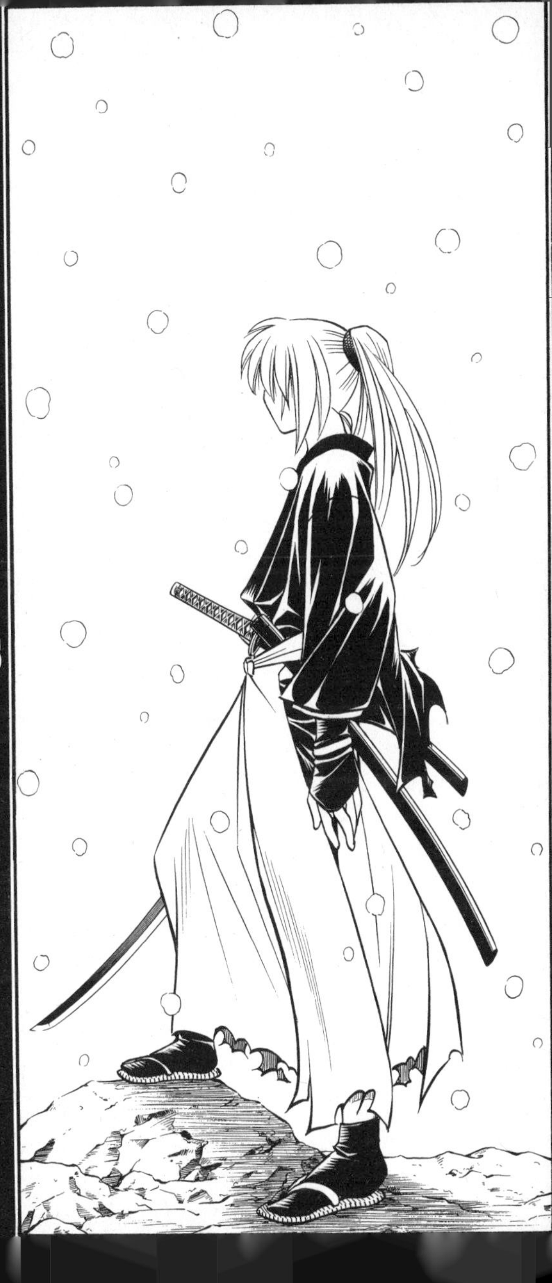

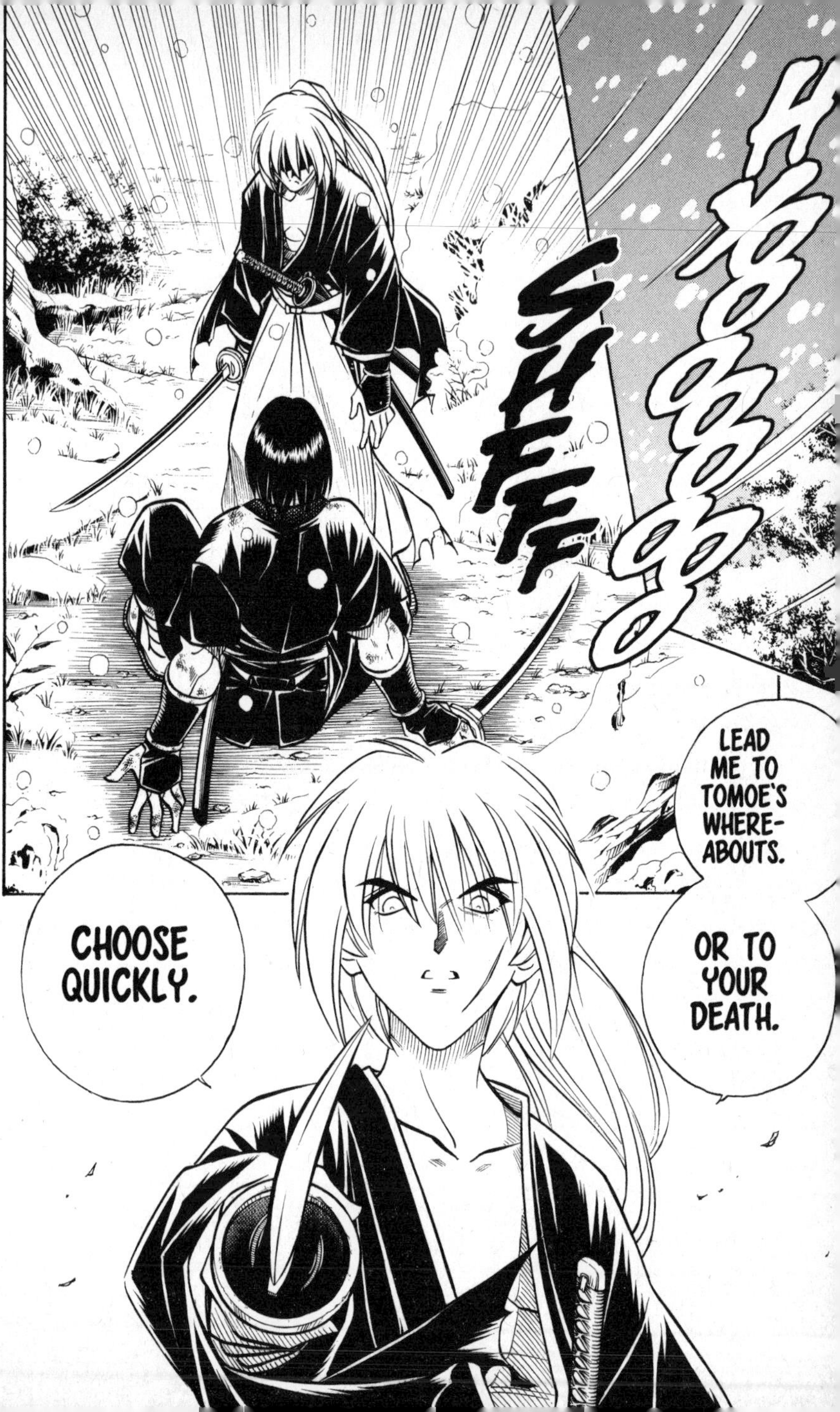
SHFFF
LEAD ME TO TOMOE'S WHERE-ABOUTS.
OR TO YOUR DEATH.
CHOOSE QUICKLY.

READ THIS WAY

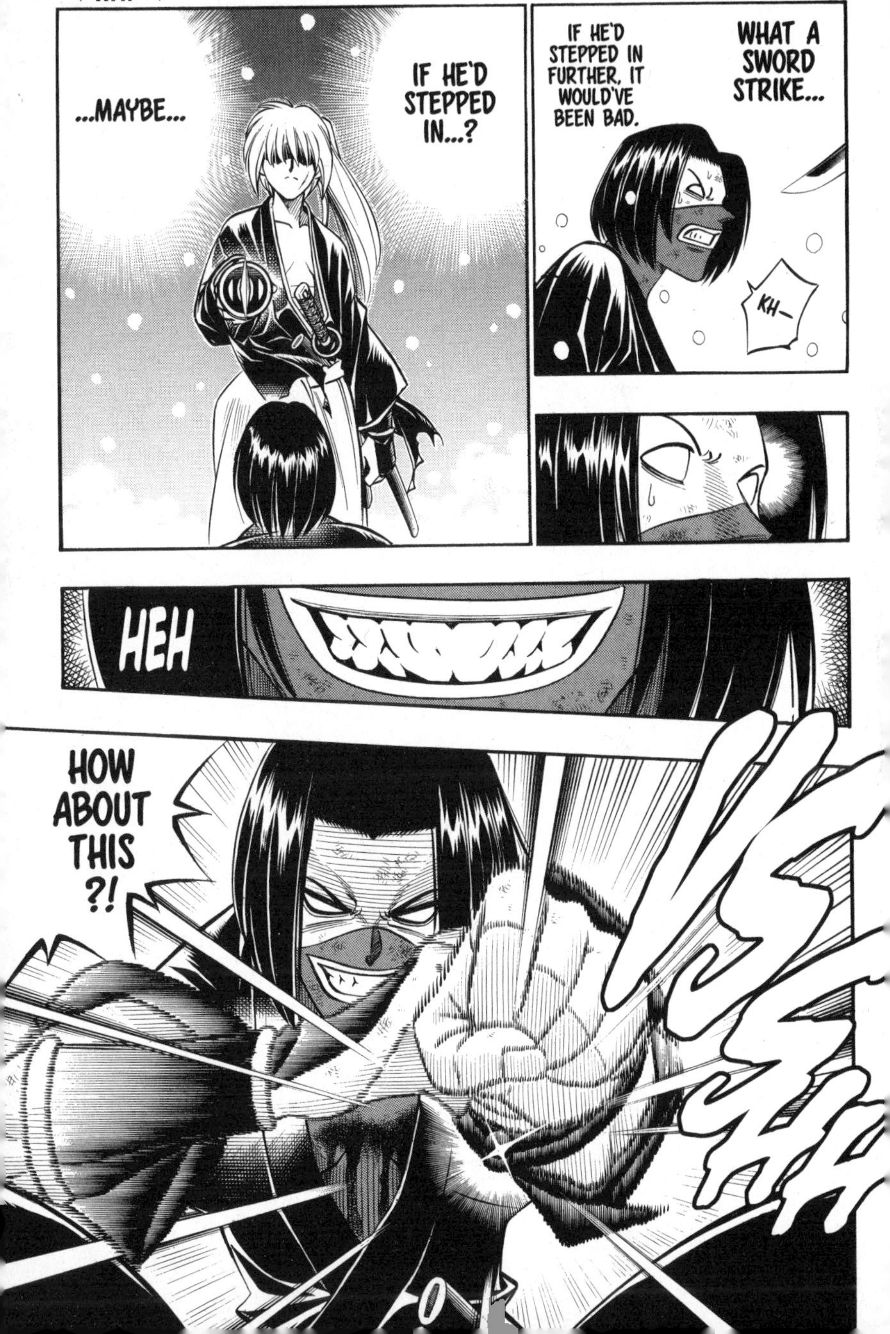
WHAT A SWORD STRIKE...
IF HE'D STEPPED IN FURTHER, IT WOULD'VE BEEN BAD.
KH—
IF HE'D STEPPED IN...?
...MAYBE...
HEH
HOW ABOUT THIS ?!

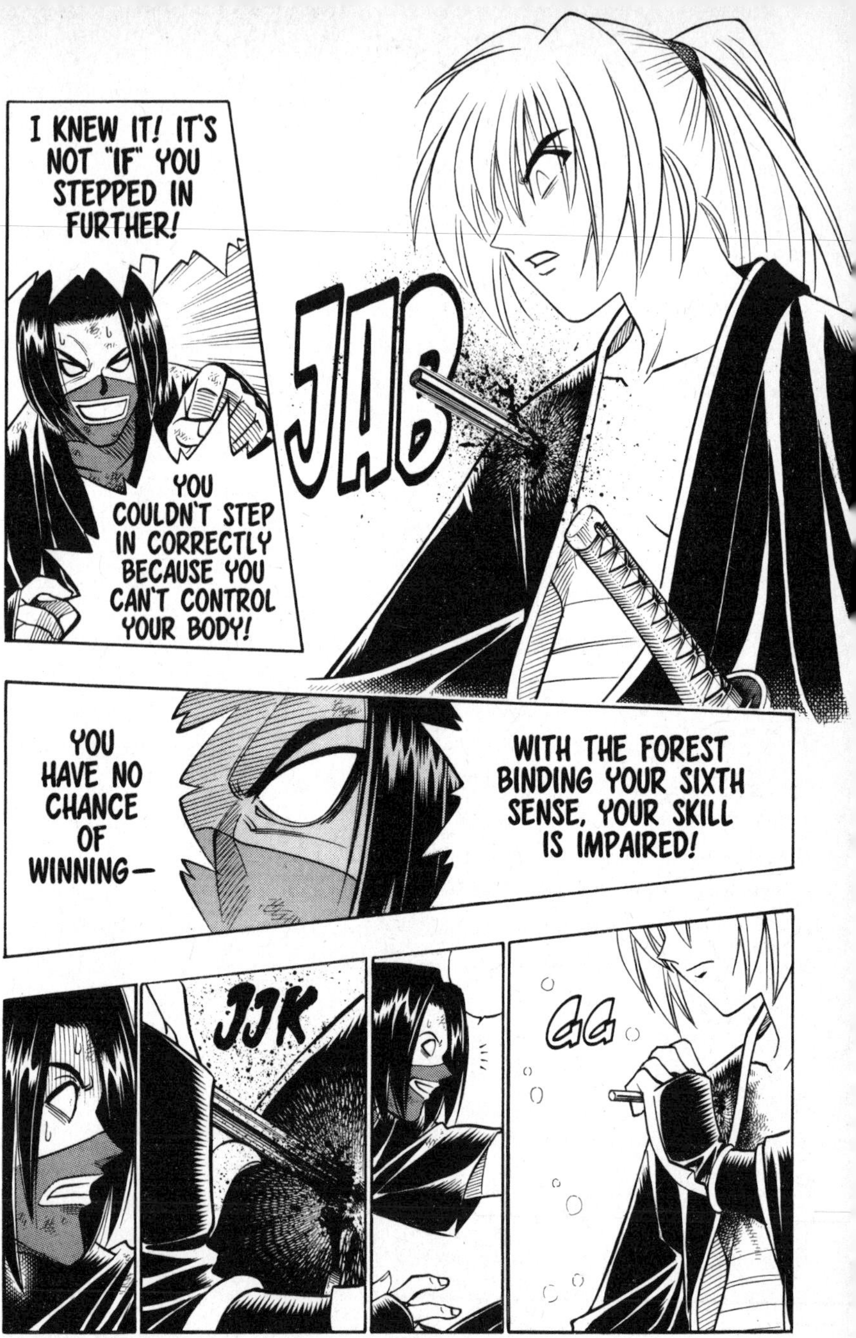

JAB
I KNEW IT! IT'S NOT "IF" YOU STEPPED IN FURTHER!
YOU COULDN'T STEP IN CORRECTLY BECAUSE YOU CAN'T CONTROL YOUR BODY!
WITH THE FOREST BINDING YOUR SIXTH SENSE, YOUR SKILL IS IMPAIRED!
YOU HAVE NO CHANCE OF WINNING—
GG
JJK

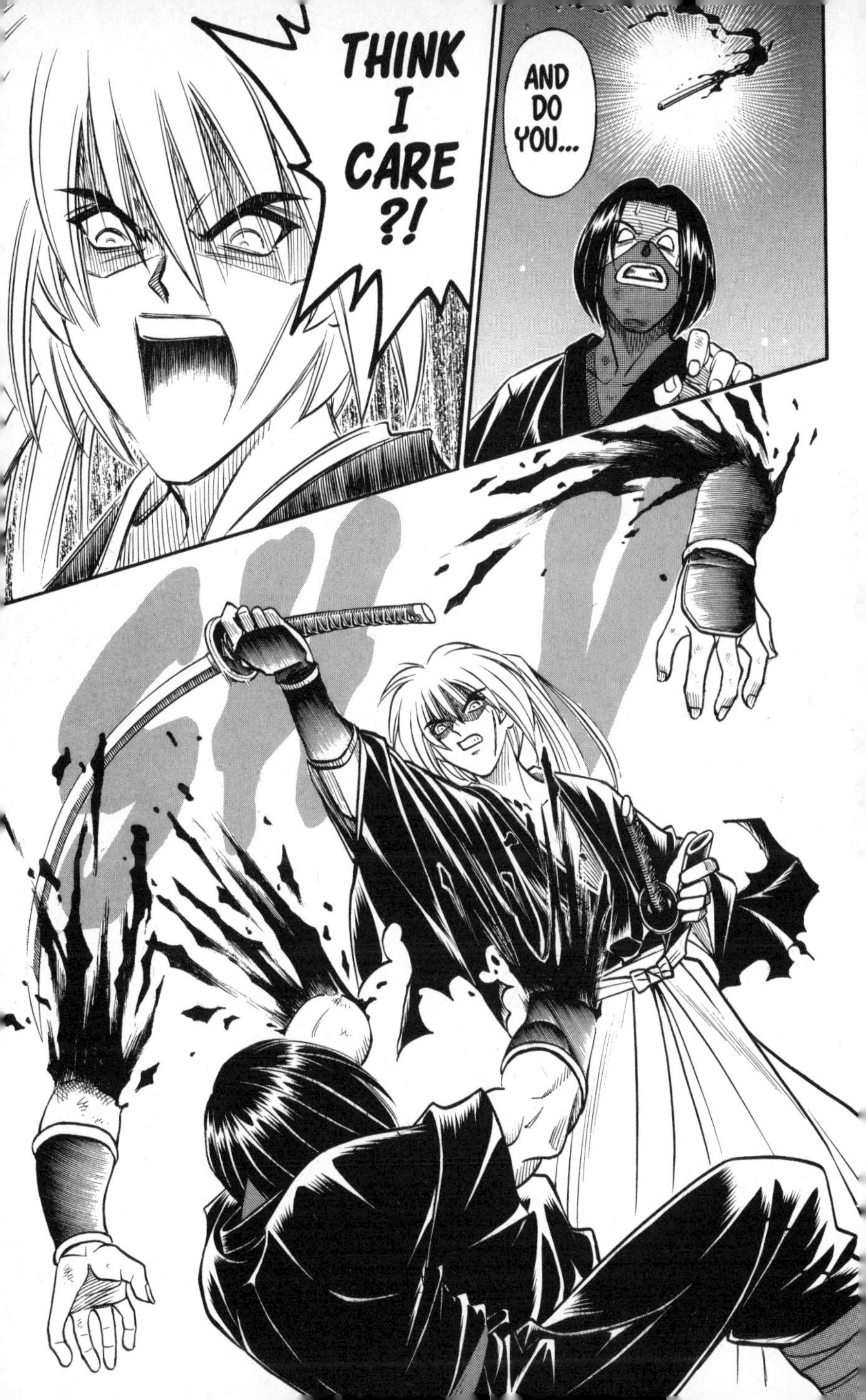
AND DO YOU...
THINK I CARE?!

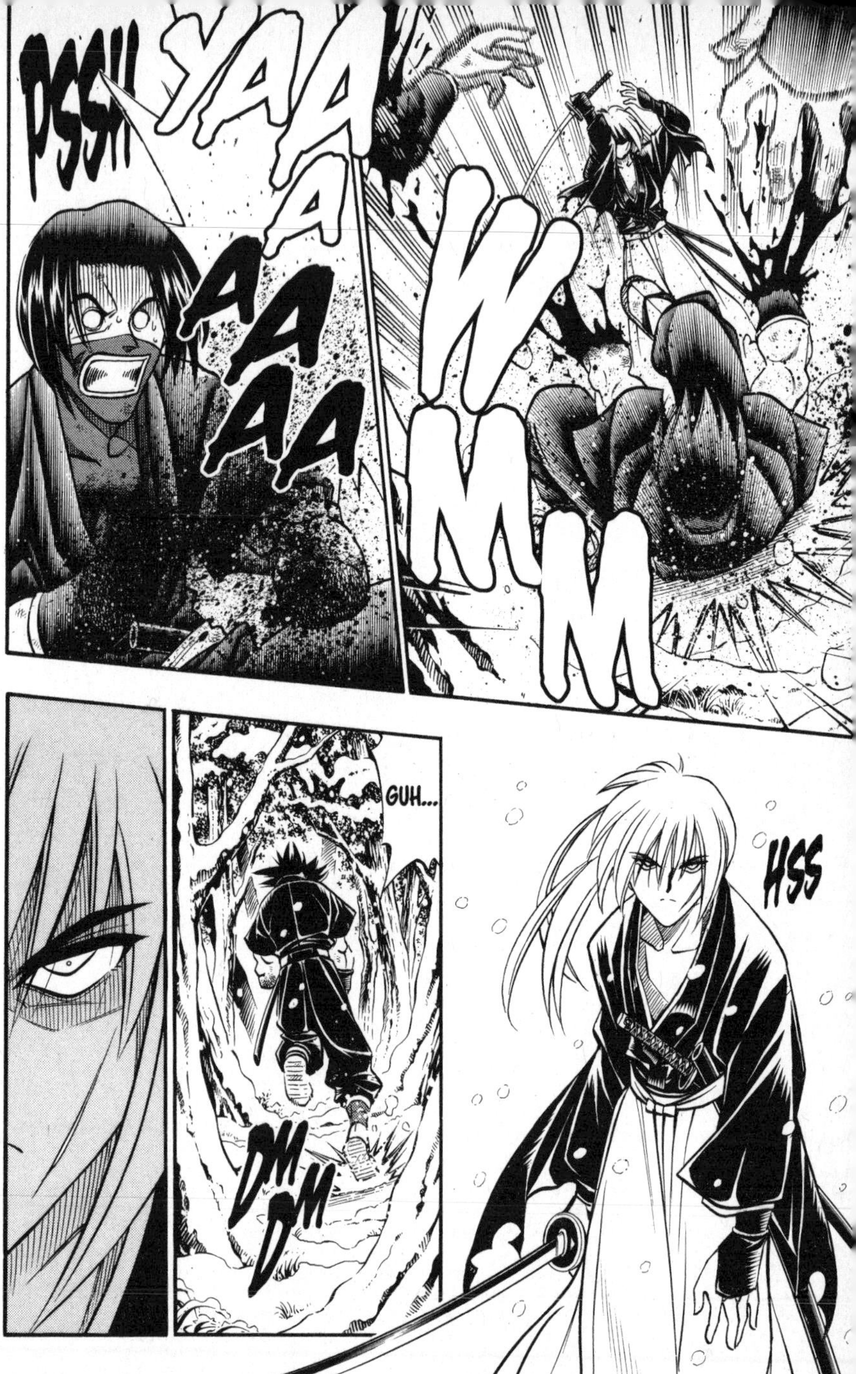
WMM
PSSH
YAAAAAAAA
HSS
GUH...
DM DM

READ THIS WAY

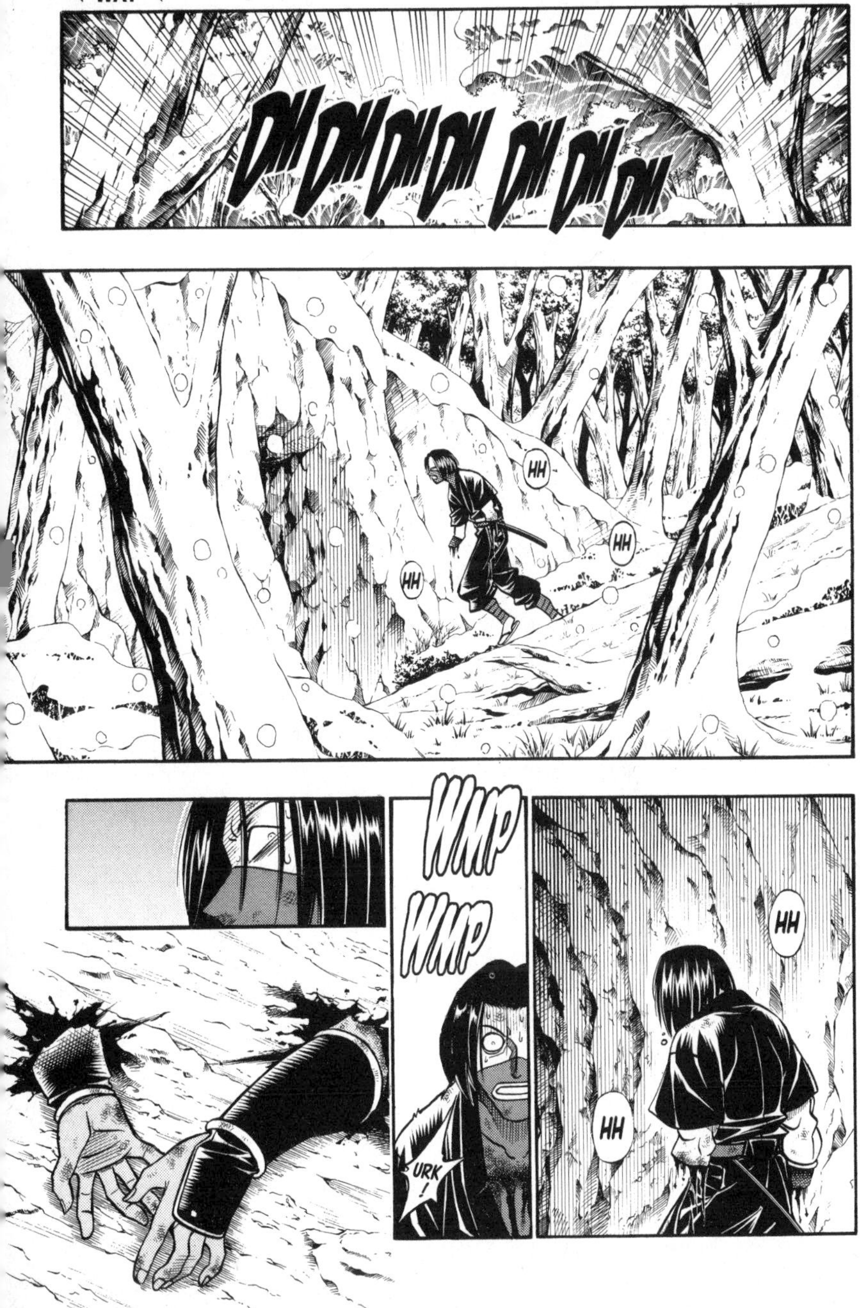
DH DH DH DH DH DH DH
HH
HH
HH
HH
HH
WMP
WMP
URK!

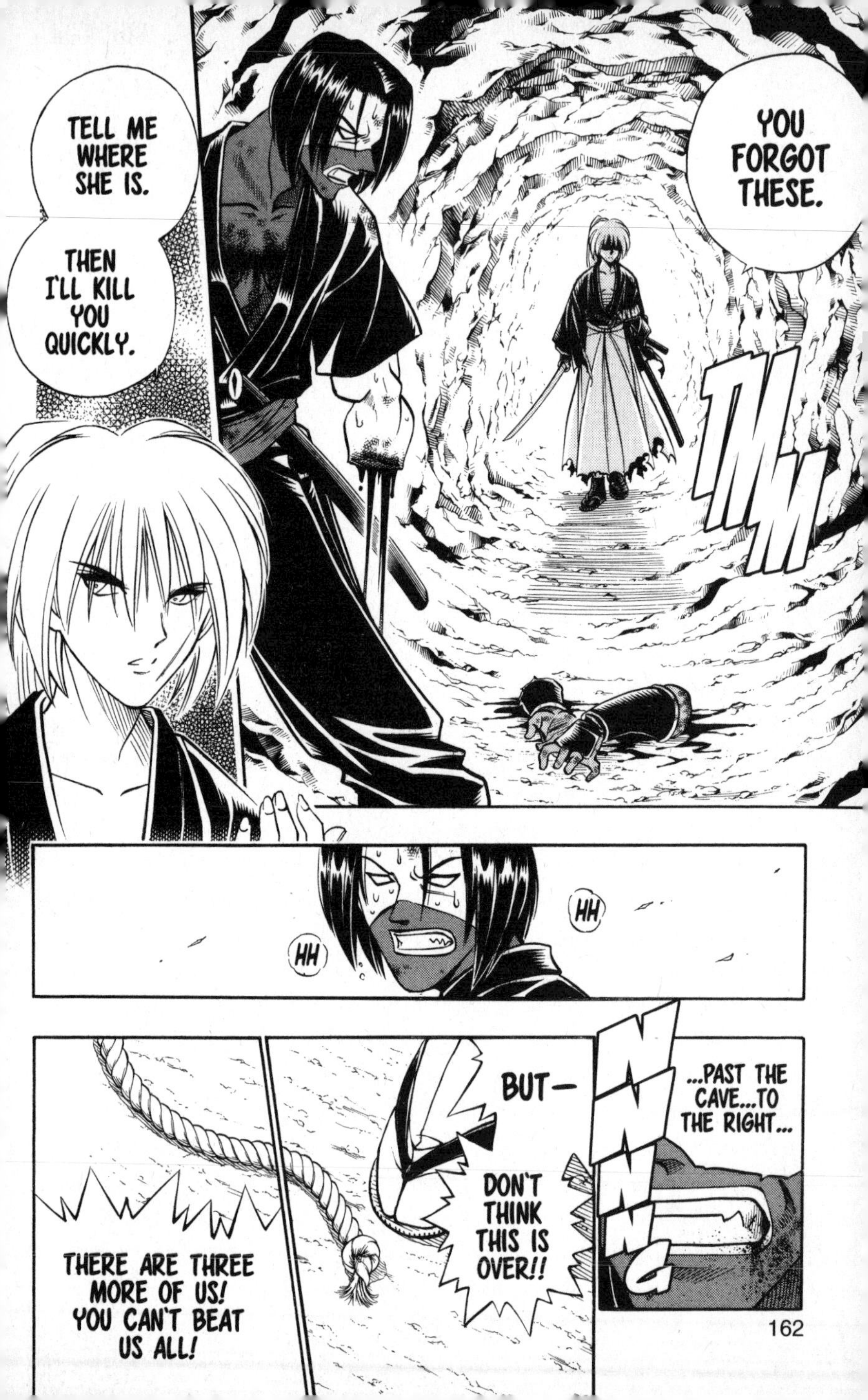
YOU FORGOT THESE.
THM
TELL ME WHERE SHE IS.
THEN I'LL KILL YOU QUICKLY.
HH
HH
...PAST THE CAVE...TO THE RIGHT...
NNNNG
BUT—
DON'T THINK THIS IS OVER!!
THERE ARE THREE MORE OF US! YOU CAN'T BEAT US ALL!

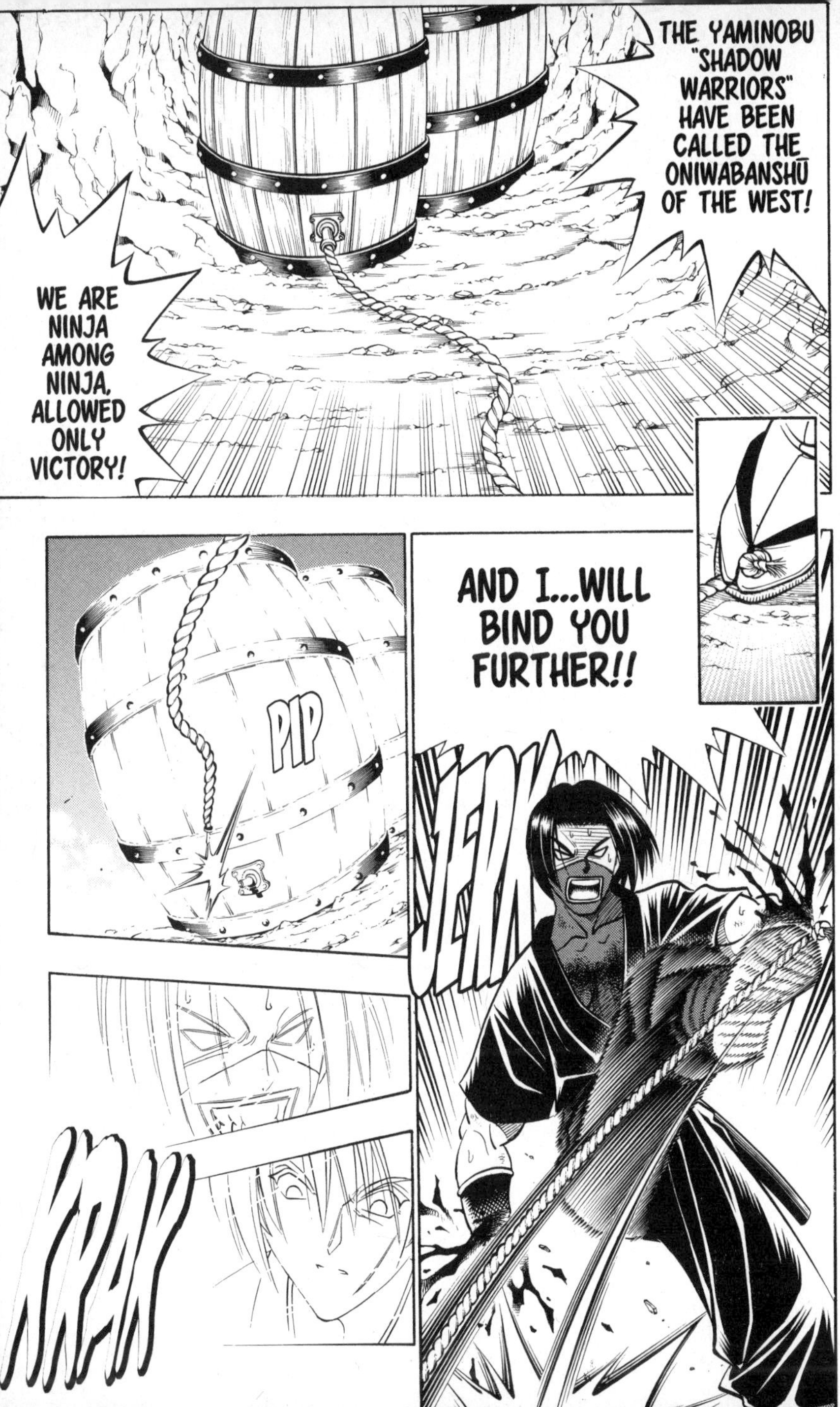
THE YAMINOBU "SHADOW WARRIORS" HAVE BEEN CALLED THE ONIWABANSHŪ OF THE WEST!
WE ARE NINJA AMONG NINJA, ALLOWED ONLY VICTORY!
AND I...WILL BIND YOU FURTHER!!
JERK
PIP

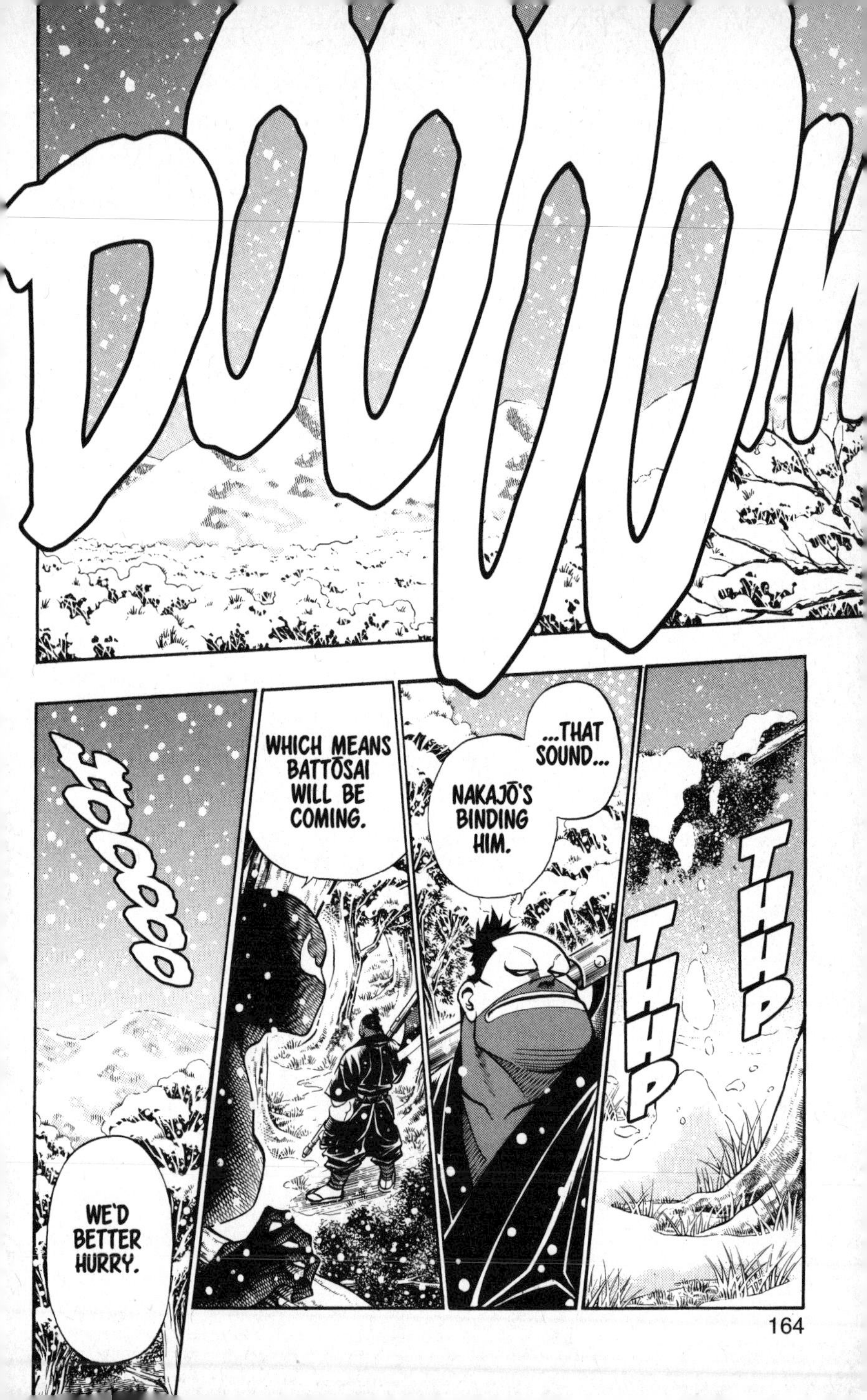
DOOOOOM
THUP THUP
THUP THUP
...THAT SOUND...
NAKAJŌ'S BINDING HIM.
WHICH MEANS BATTŌSAI WILL BE COMING.
HOOOOO
WE'D BETTER HURRY.

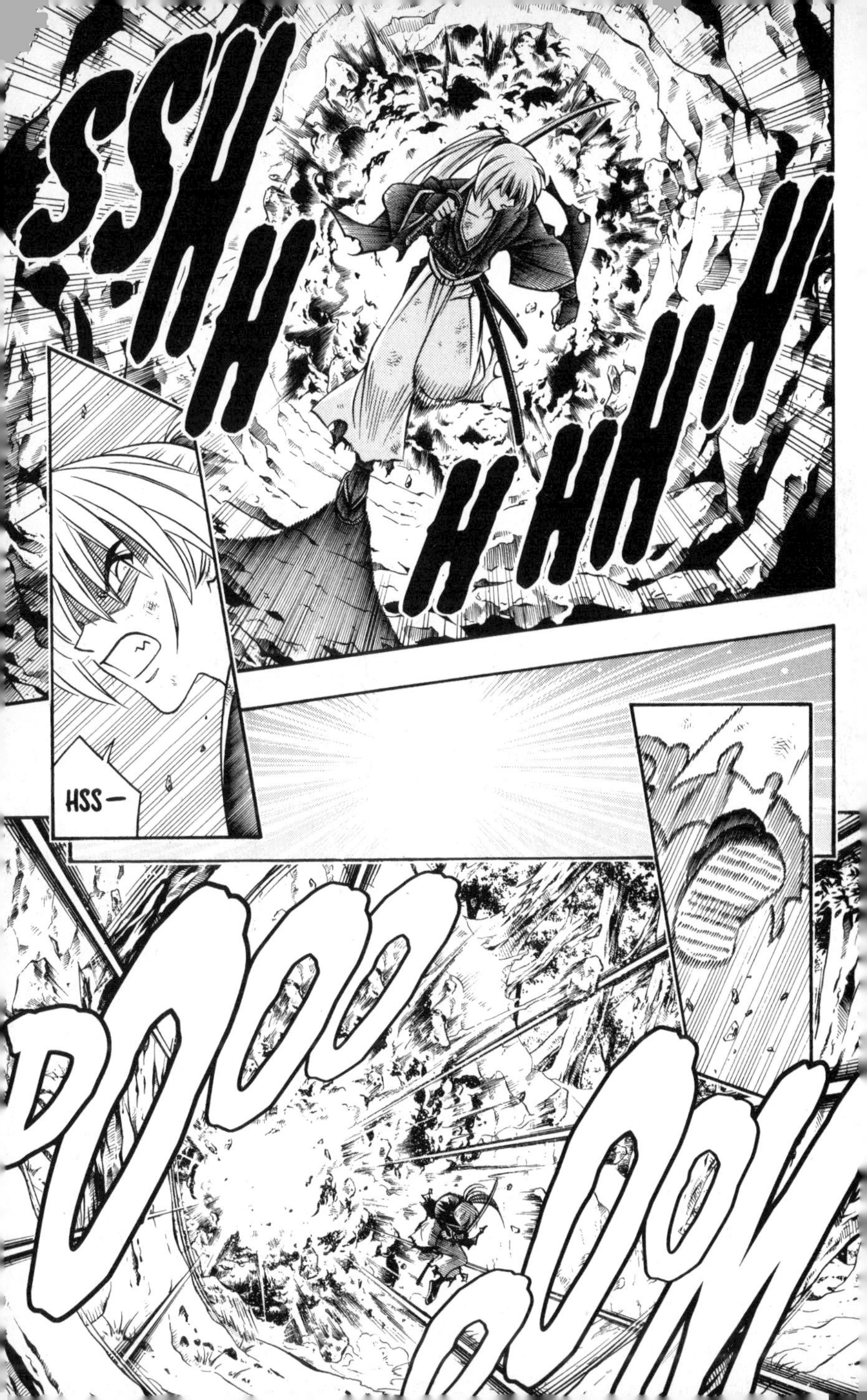
SSHHHHHHHHH
HSS—
DOOOOOOOM

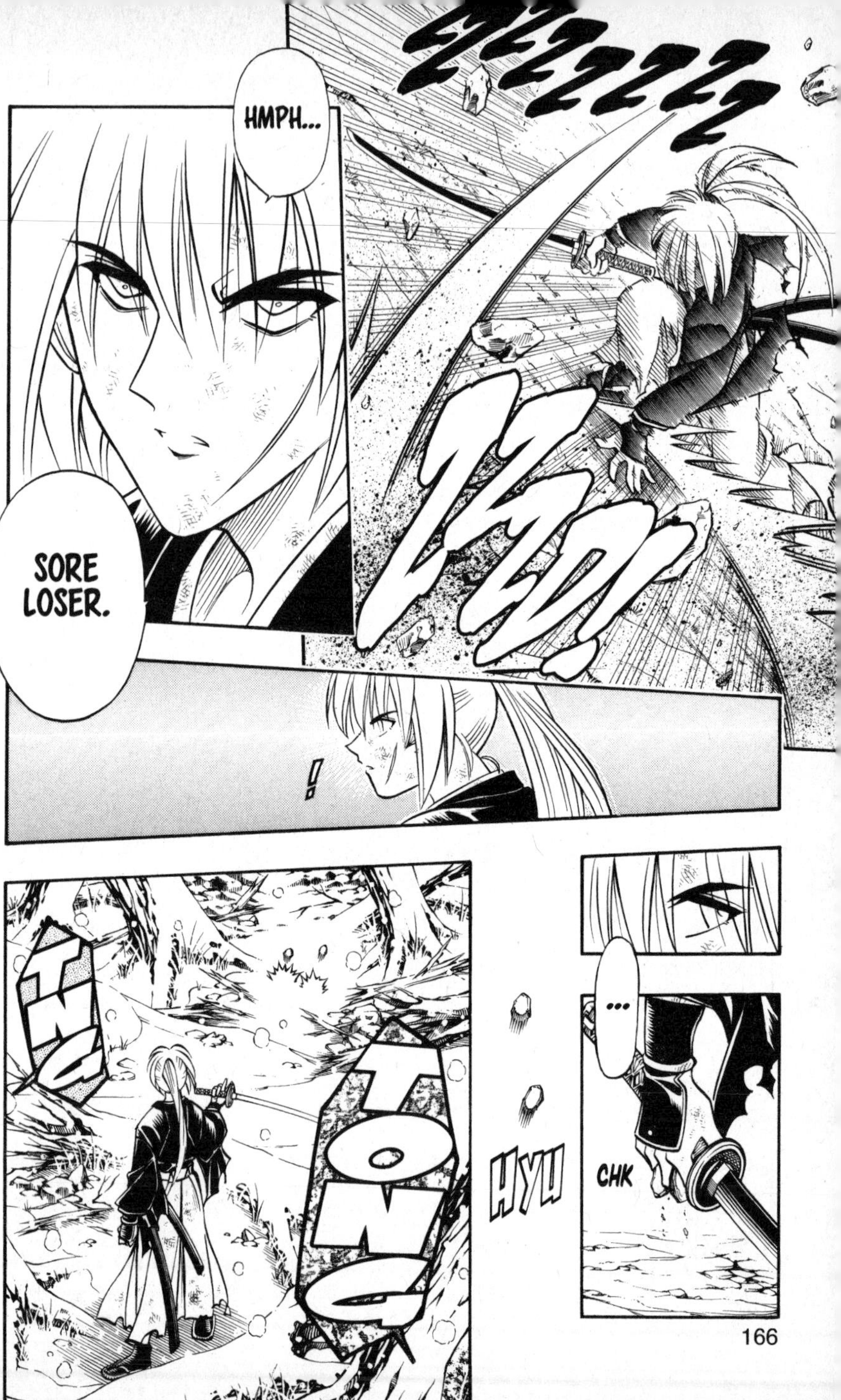
HMPH...
SORE LOSER.
!
...
CHK
HYU
TONG
TING

READ THIS WAY

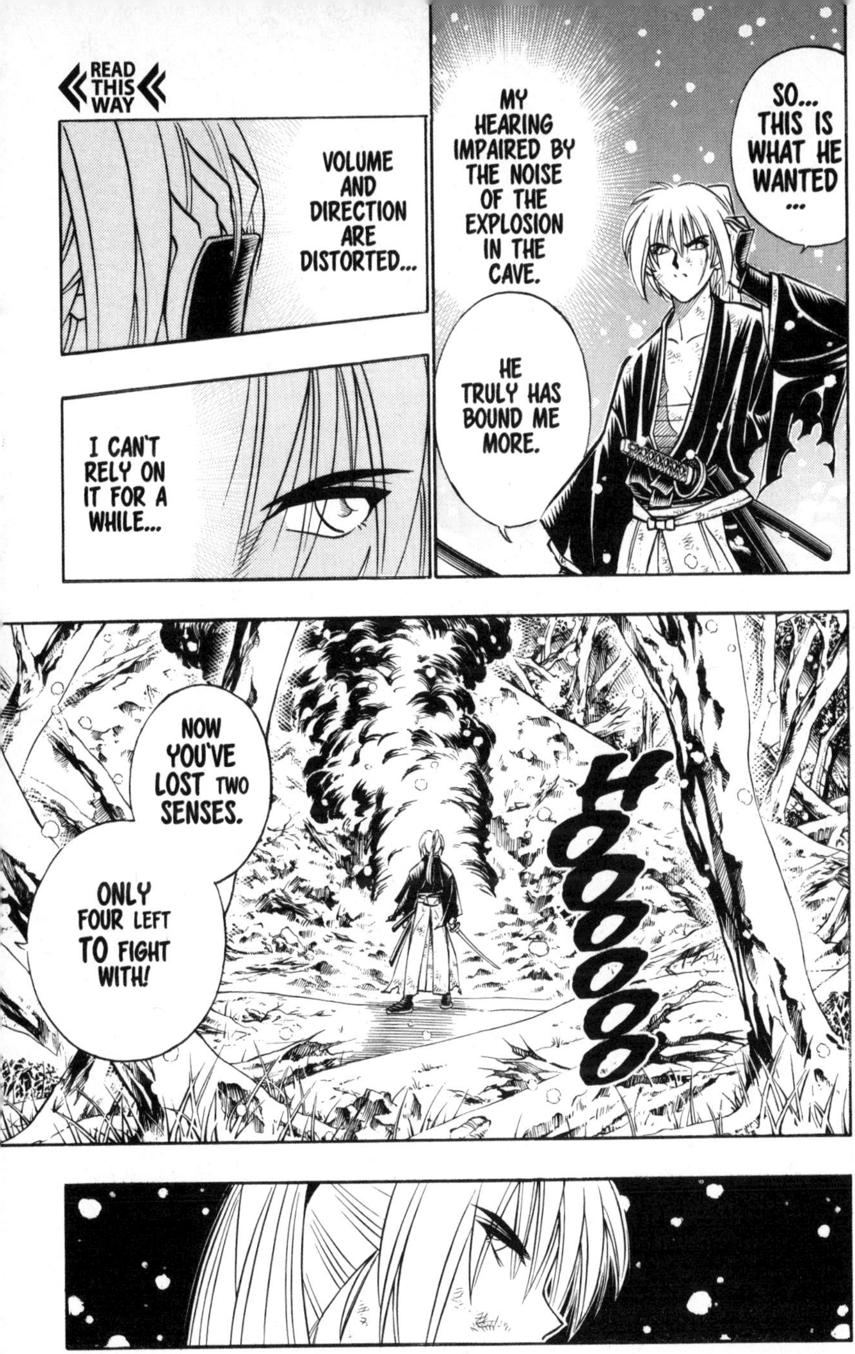
SO... THIS IS WHAT HE WANTED...
MY HEARING IMPAIRED BY THE NOISE OF THE EXPLOSION IN THE CAVE.
HE TRULY HAS BOUND ME MORE.
VOLUME AND DIRECTION ARE DISTORTED...
I CAN'T RELY ON IT FOR A WHILE...
NOW YOU'VE LOST TWO SENSES.
ONLY FOUR LEFT TO FIGHT WITH!
HOOOOOO

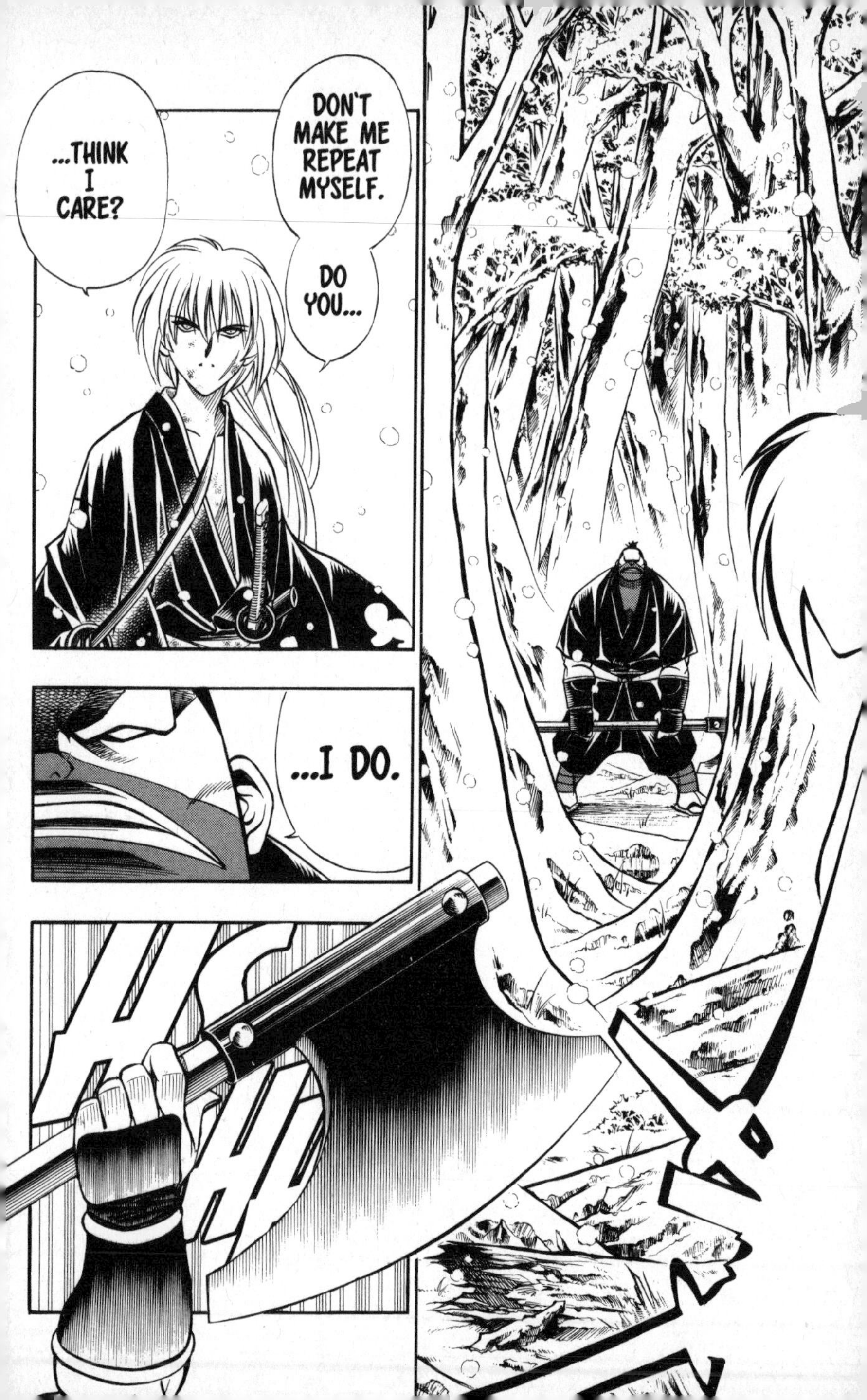
DON'T MAKE ME REPEAT MYSELF.
DO YOU...
...THINK I CARE?
...I DO.

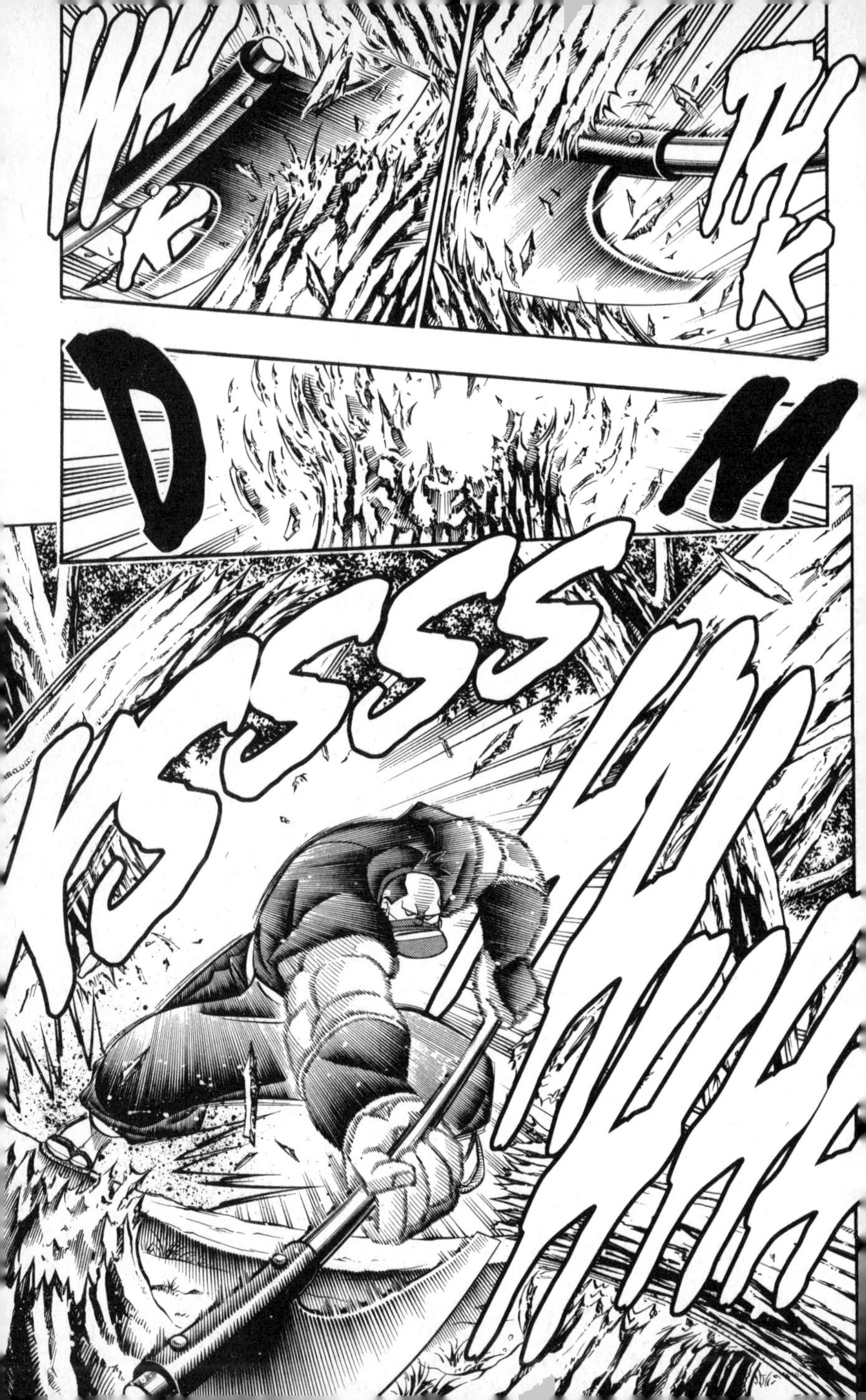
THK
WHK
D M
KSSSSHHHH

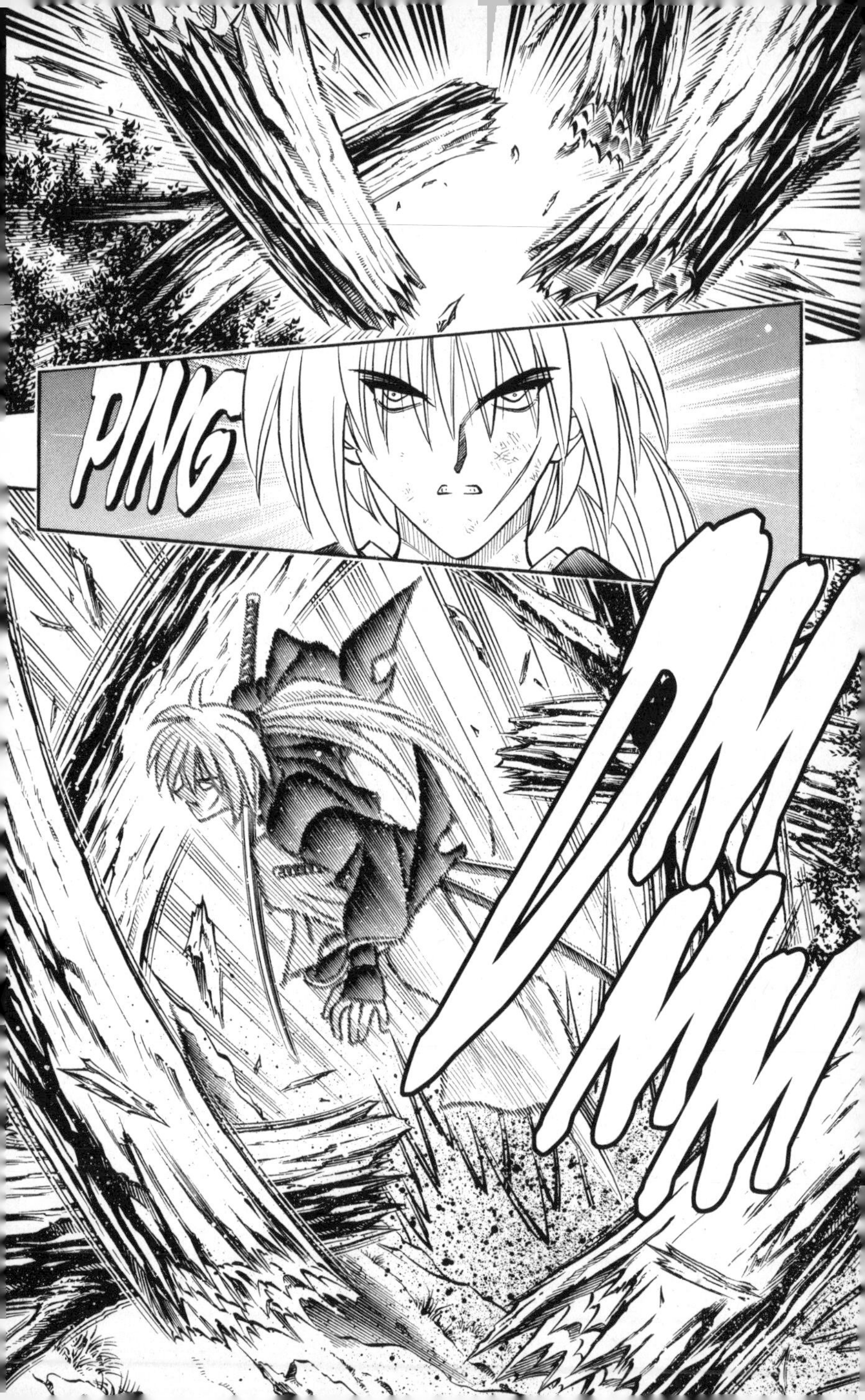
PING

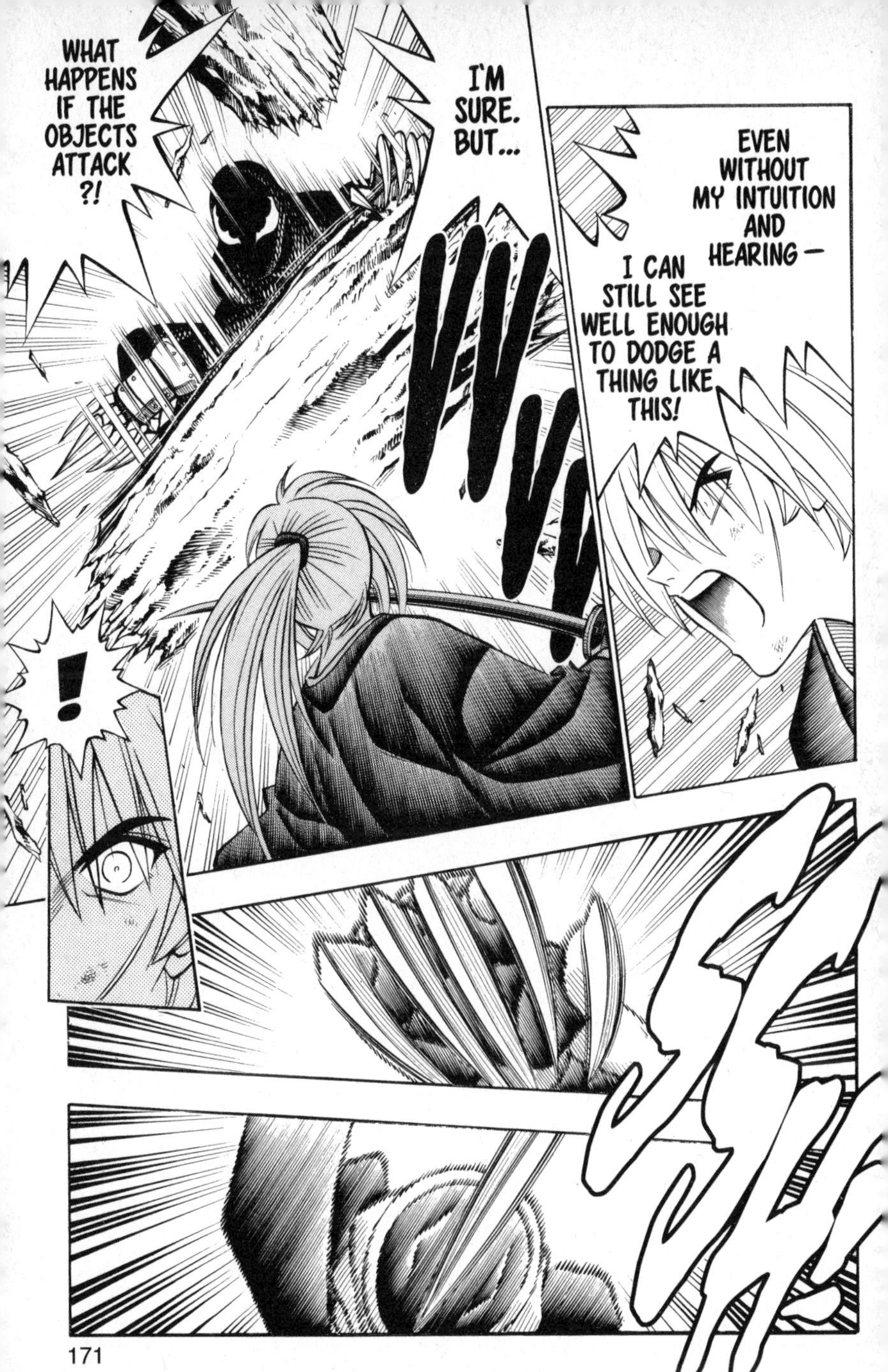
EVEN WITHOUT MY INTUITION AND HEARING—
I CAN STILL SEE WELL ENOUGH TO DODGE A THING LIKE THIS!
I'M SURE. BUT...
WHAT HAPPENS IF THE OBJECTS ATTACK ?!
!

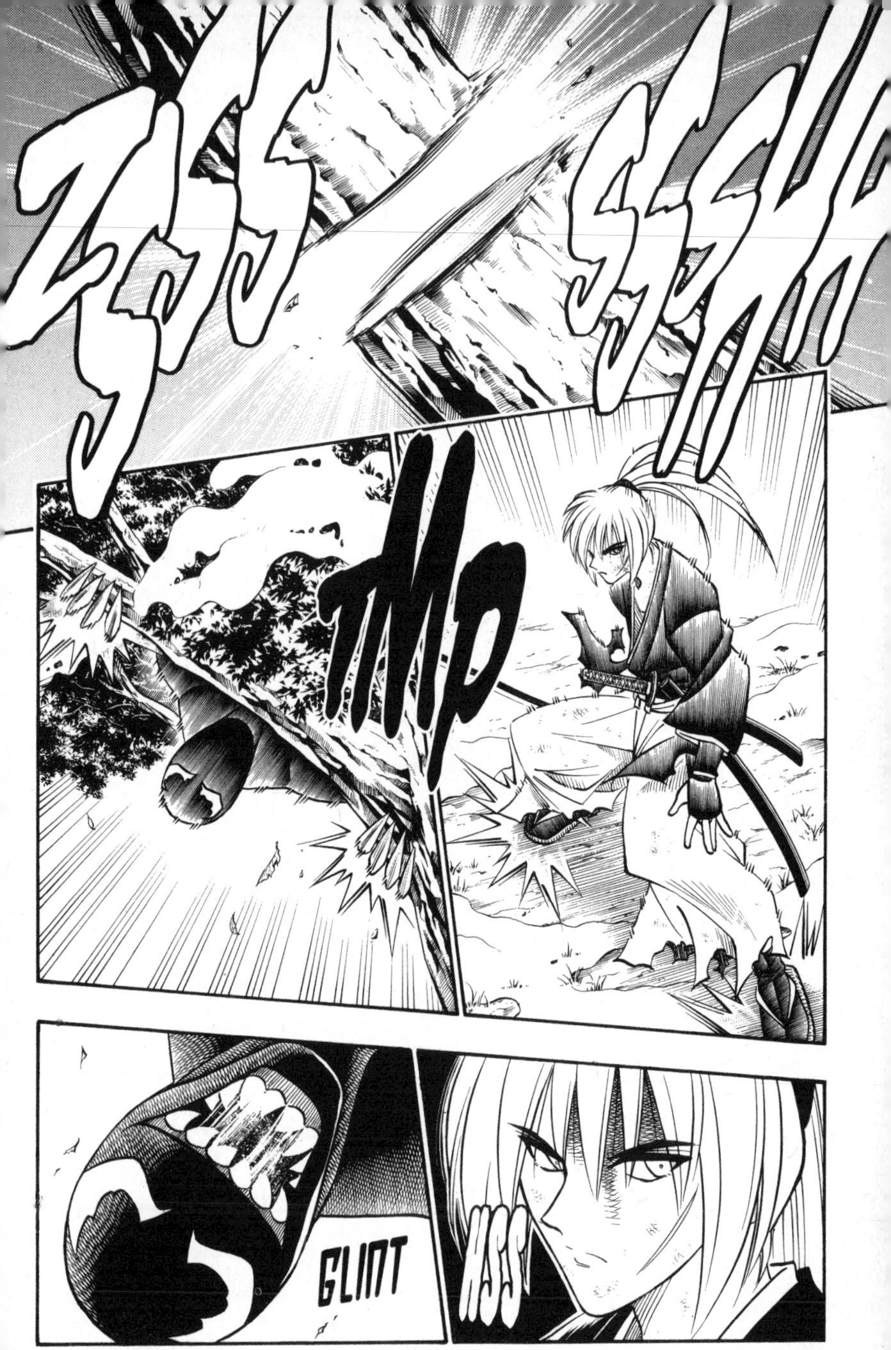
SSSH
ZSSS
HSS
GLINT

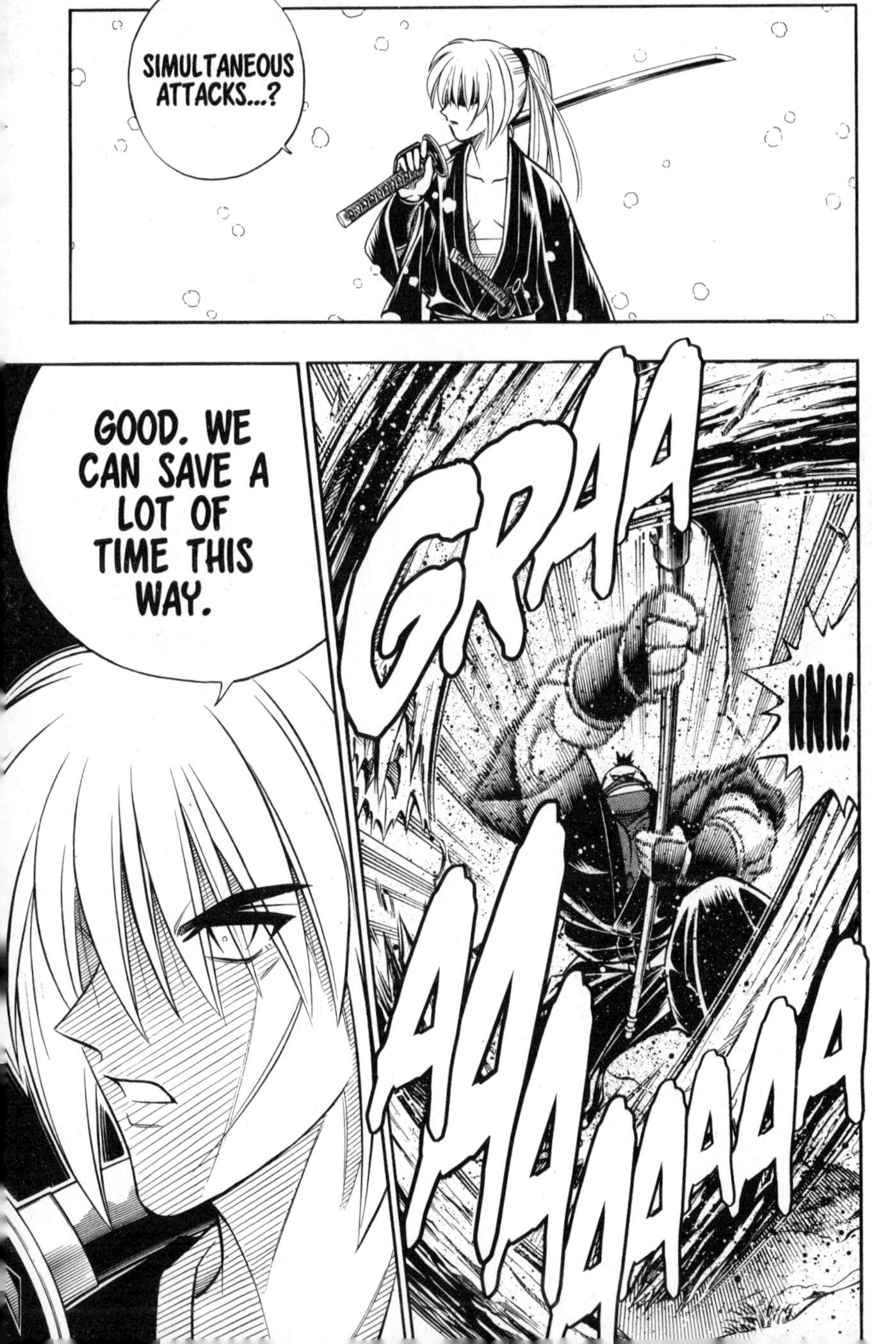
SIMULTANEOUS ATTACKS...?
GRAA
AAAAAAAA
NNN!
GOOD. WE CAN SAVE A LOT OF TIME THIS WAY.

"FREE TALK"

Long time no see! Watsuki here! Watsuki is slightly anxious, since we've yet to find a new workplace, and there is only three months left on our lease. Seriously, what will we do...?

Getting straight to the usual action-figure talk. My favorite figure right now is "Assault Apocalypse" from the *X-Men* series. I personally like the design, but if a normal person looked at it, they'd probably think, "What is this?" I love the gimmick. Basically, when the button on the back is pressed, it shoots missiles out of its chest. It's a pretty basic idea, but five different hatches open instantaneously before the missile is launched! Five hatches, just to shoot a missile!! What stupidity!!! It's great! Gimmicks like that are lacking in the usual McFarlane toys. I'd love them to keep going in that direction.

In terms of games, I haven't been able to play much due to my workload. Even so, I finally beat *Gekka no Kenshi* (SNK) with Washizuka. The ending was exactly the same as I'd imagined, which surprised me. I also got the NeoGeo CD version, so I'd like to take my time and beat the game on all characters. *Samurai Spirits* (SNK) hasn't been installed in the local arcade yet, so I can't play it... I'm looking forward to a console version. One game I think is interesting is *Shiritsu Justice Gakuen* (Capcom). One of my assistants is hooked on it, so I tried it out a little while waiting for *Gekka* and liked it. I was able to enjoy just playing randomly without understanding the system at all. I'll be busy in the near future with the move and all, giving me even less game time than usual, so I hope they put it on a console too.

A new addition to my life, other than figures and games, is a bicycle. That's right, bicycle!! I've always had a bike, but six months ago some shady character messed around with my lock, so I had to get rid of it. I finally decided to spend some big bucks and get a mountain bike. That said, it's actually a fake one with suspension only in the front wheel (the real ones are so expensive I wouldn't want to buy one...). To get back in shape I ride it 15-30 minutes a day when I am not too busy with work. Kichijōji is close enough to ride to, so I can use the time for collecting figures, movies, research, and supplies, killing a few birds with one stone. At least that was plan...but my butt's too sore! I'm staying away from it this week. I should have bought a real one...

For various reasons, I'm thinking of gradually changing my drawing style. I'm hoping to draw in a way the artwork will still look good, without having to draw so many lines. It'll really challenge my sketching and rendering, but I'll try it. (And I do mean gradually, because I won't—and can't—change suddenly). Meanwhile, the story has finally entered the climax of the current episode. There are two climaxes left. After that, there will be a split in the road. Anyway, see you all in the next volume!

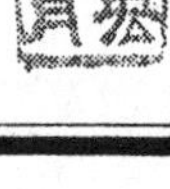

Act 177—Remembrance 12: Fierce Battle

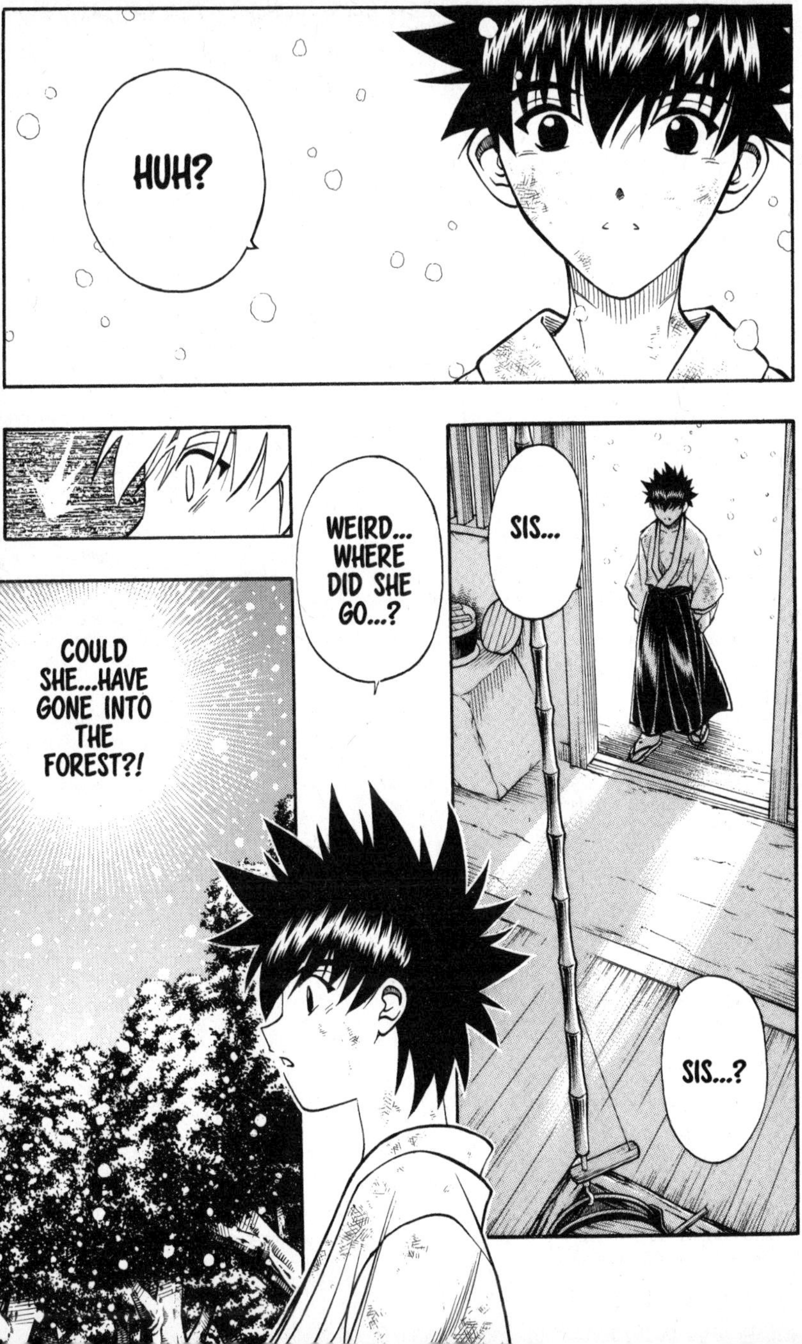
HUH?
SIS...
SIS...?
WEIRD... WHERE DID SHE GO...?
COULD SHE...HAVE GONE INTO THE FOREST?!

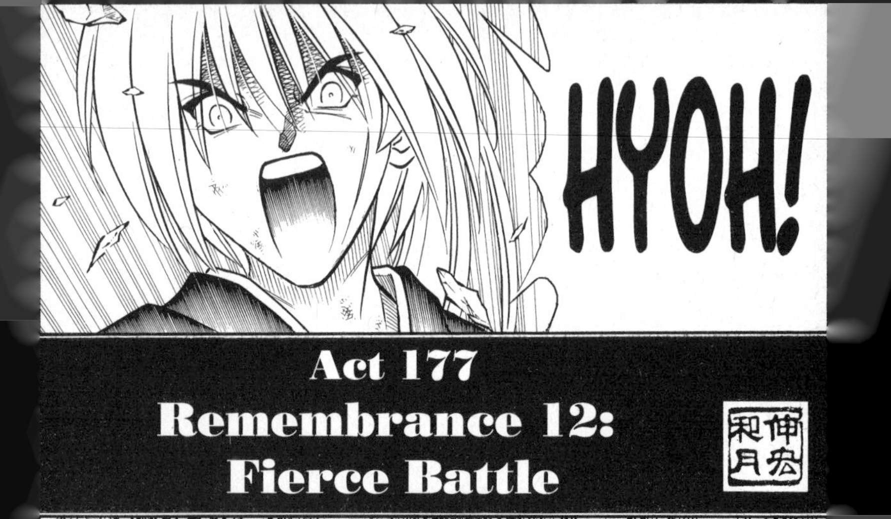
HYOH!

Act 177
Remembrance 12: Fierce Battle

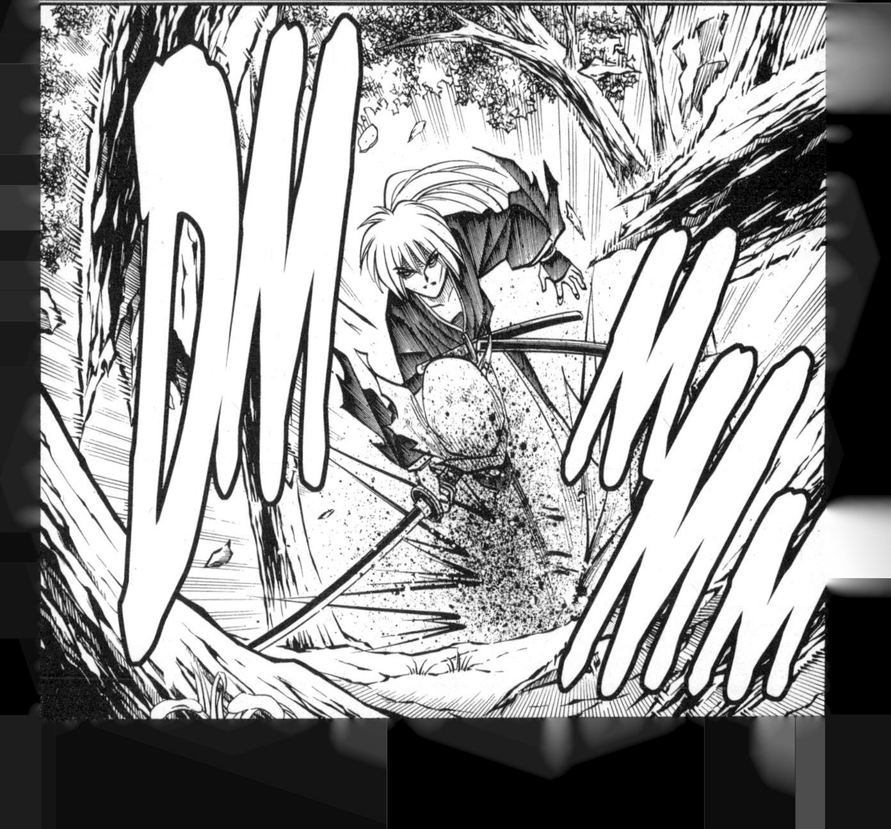

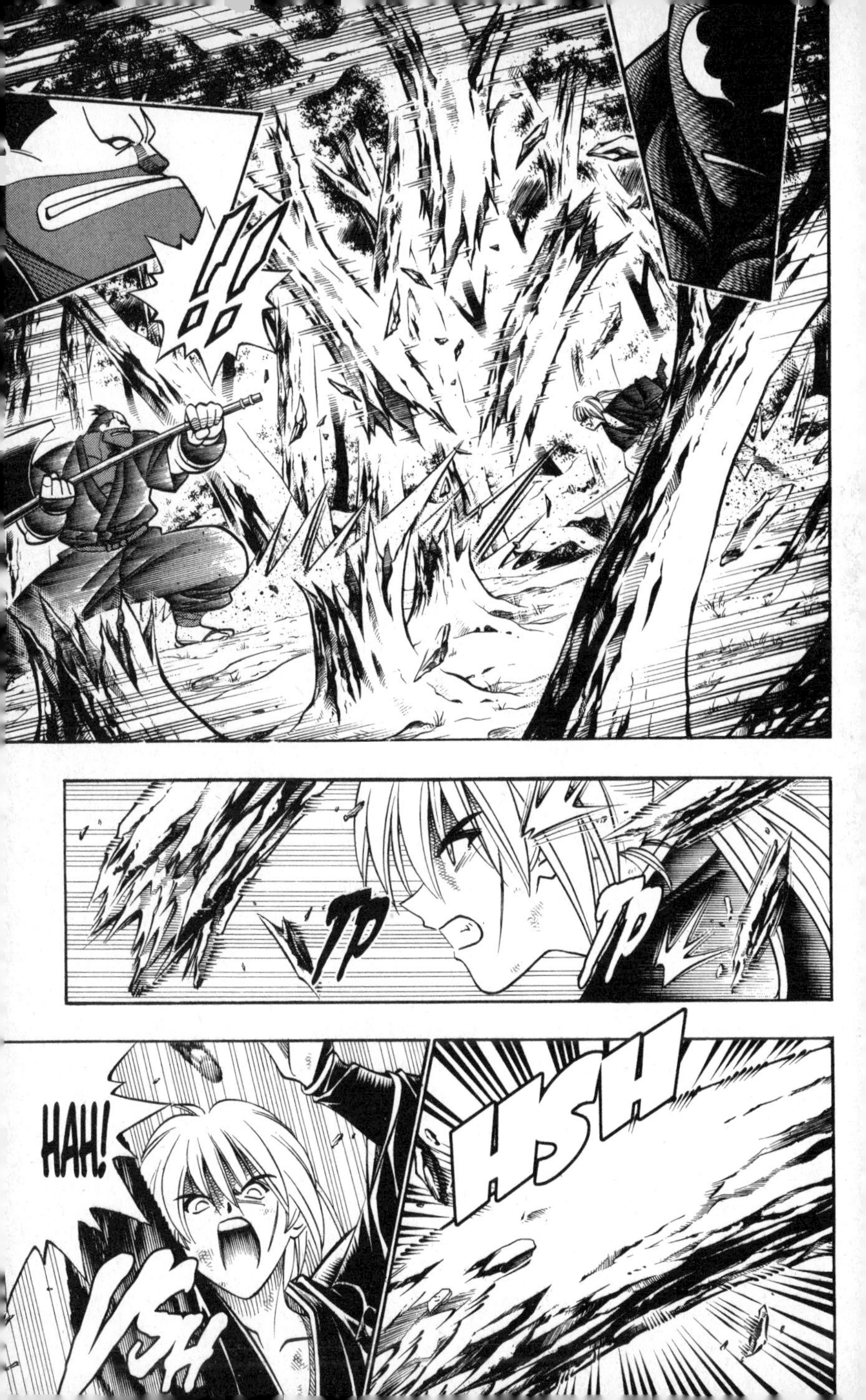
!!
TP
TP
HSH
HAH!
VSH

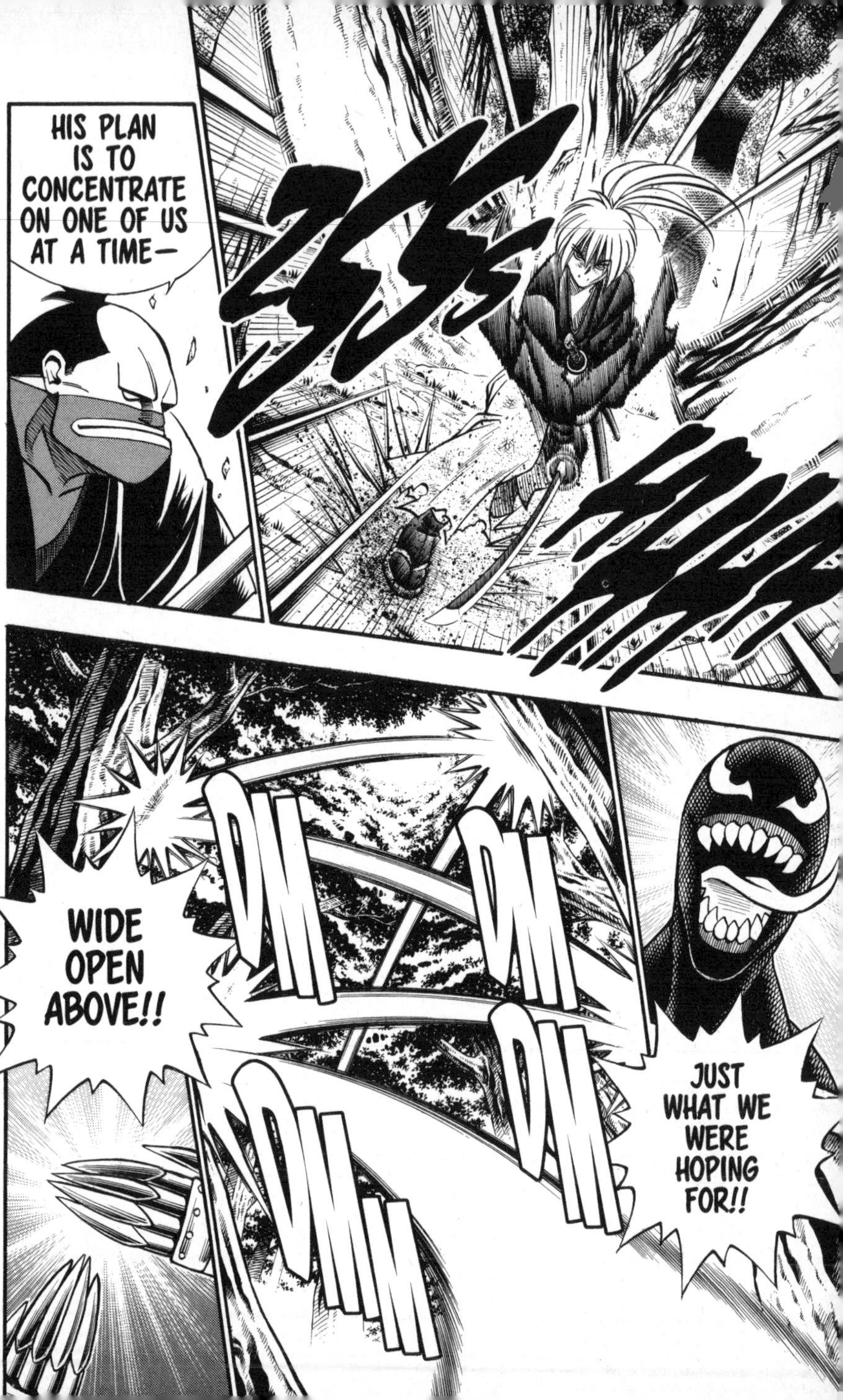
HIS PLAN IS TO CONCENTRATE ON ONE OF US AT A TIME—
JUST WHAT WE WERE HOPING FOR!!
WIDE OPEN ABOVE!!

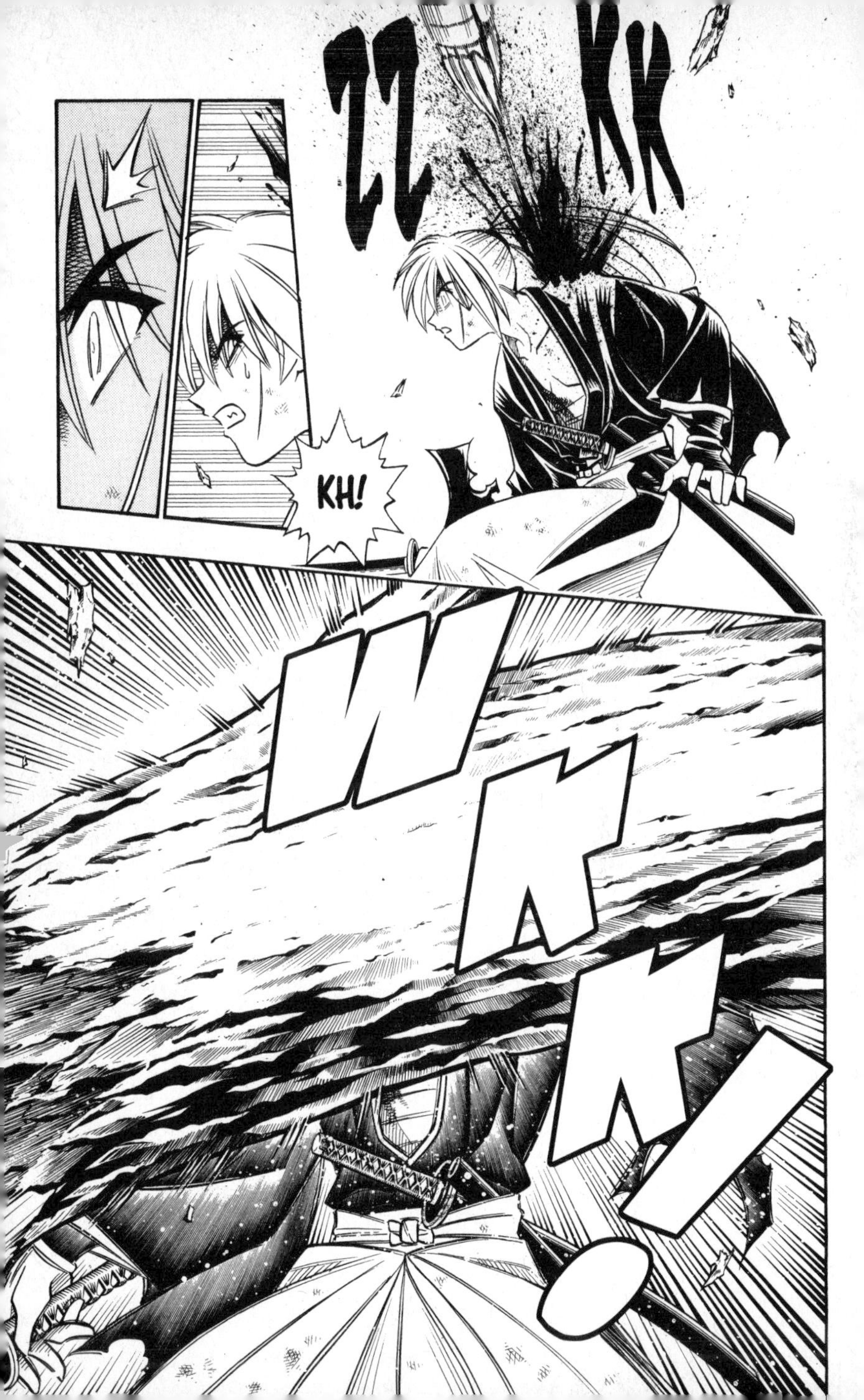
ZZ KK
KH!

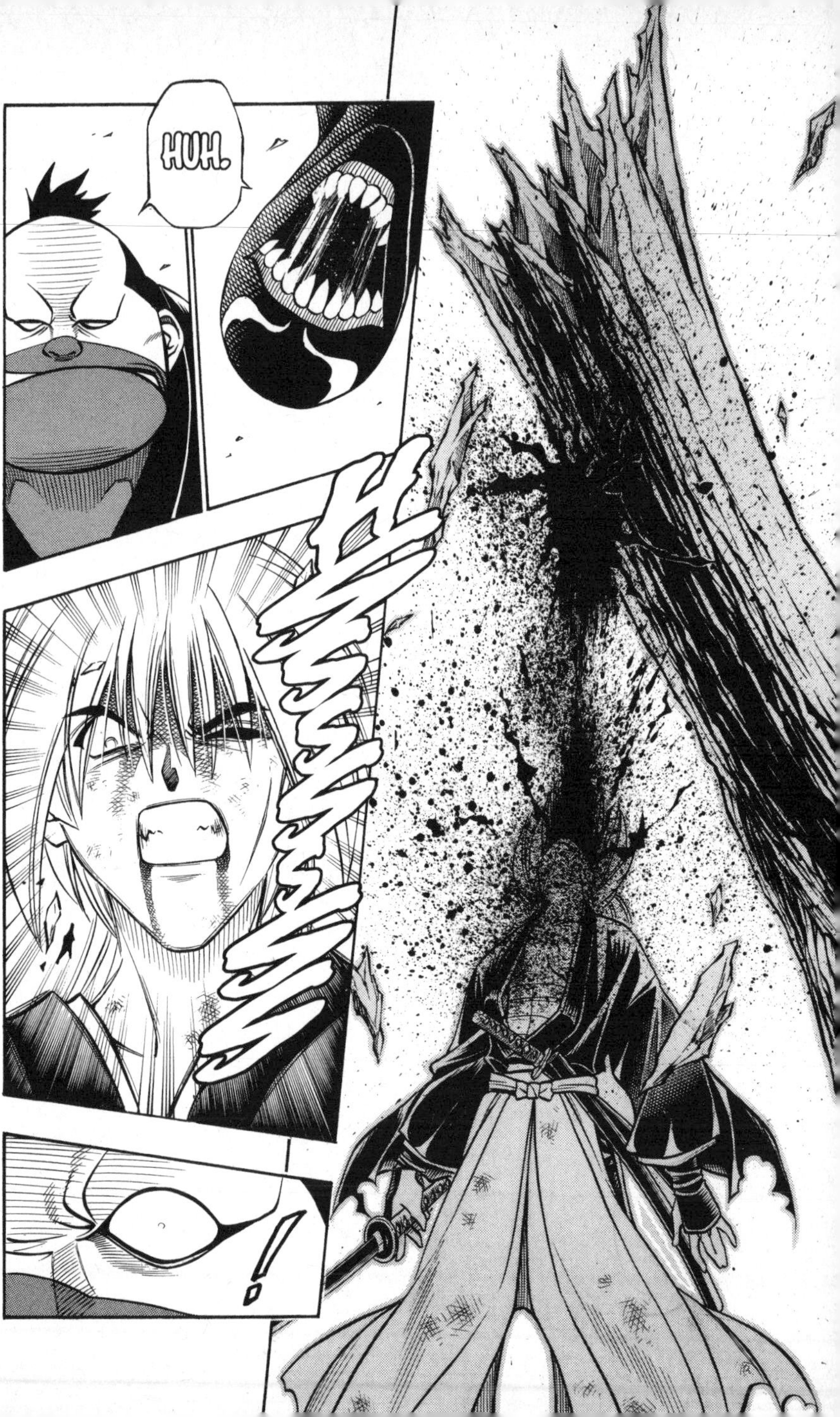
HUH.
HWSSSSSSH
!

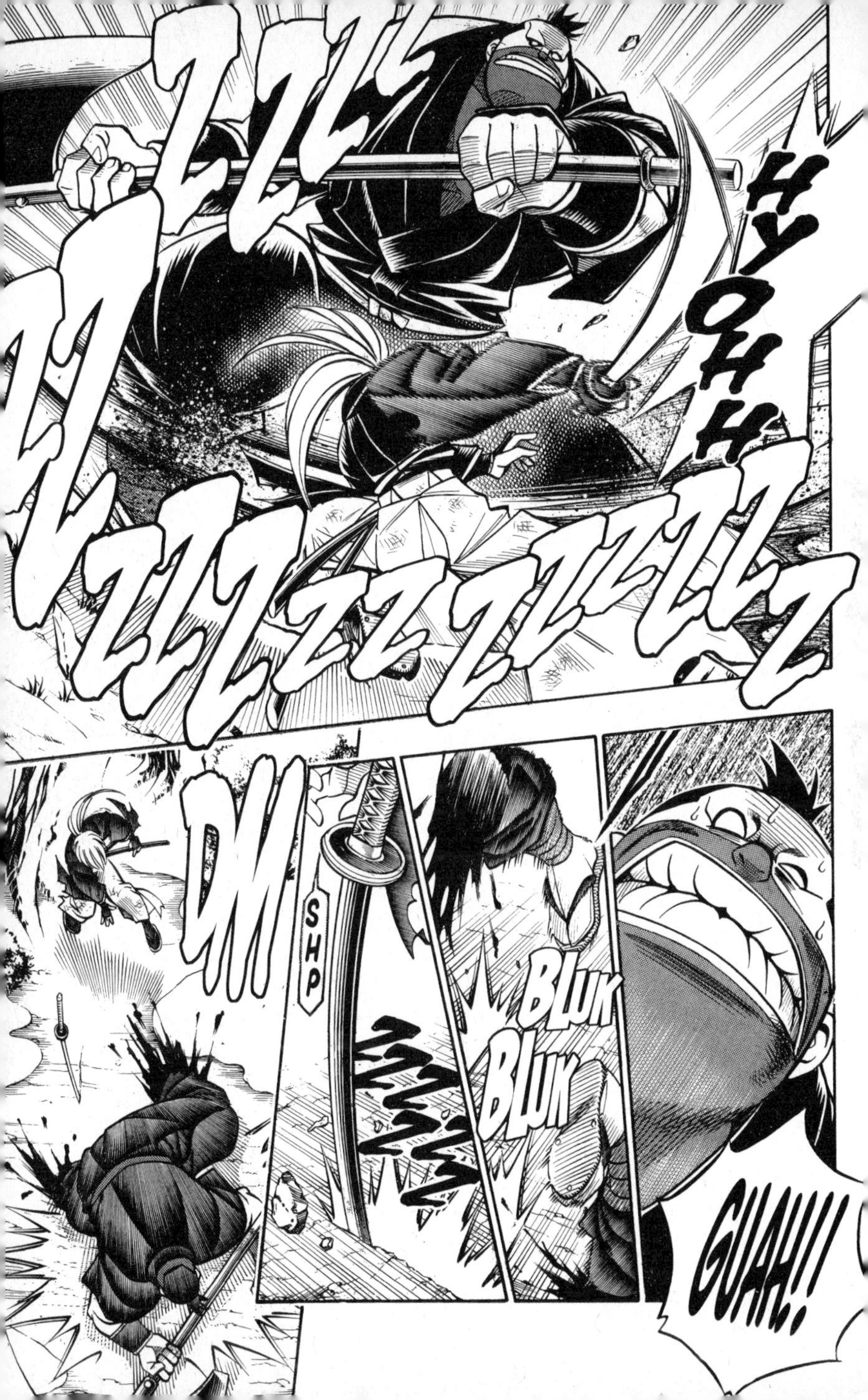
HYOHHH
ZZZZZZZZZZZZZZZ
GUAH!!
BLUK
BLUK
SHP
ZZZZ
DM

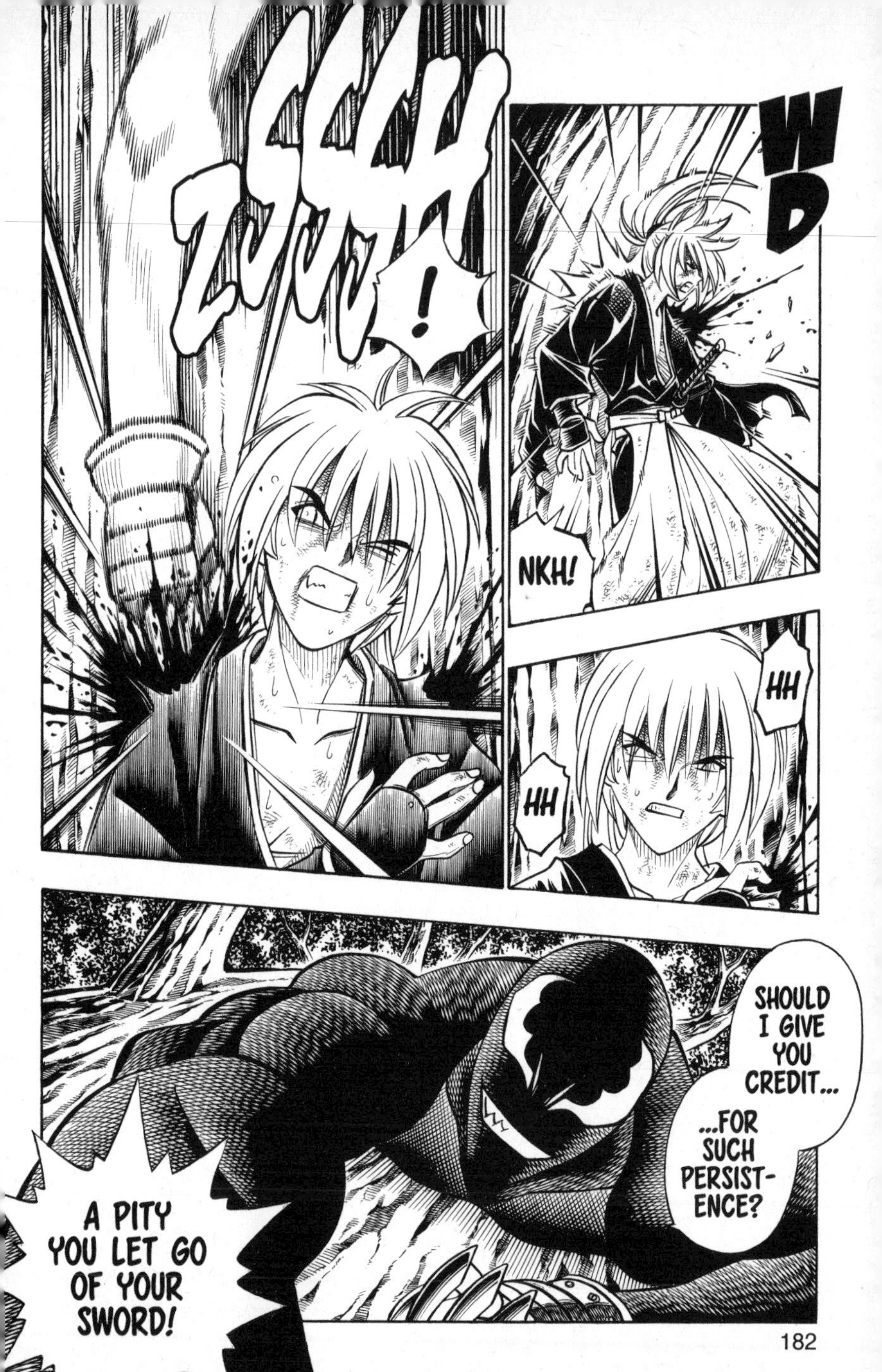
WD
NKH!
HH
HH
SHOULD I GIVE YOU CREDIT...
...FOR SUCH PERSIST-ENCE?
A PITY YOU LET GO OF YOUR SWORD!

READ THIS WAY

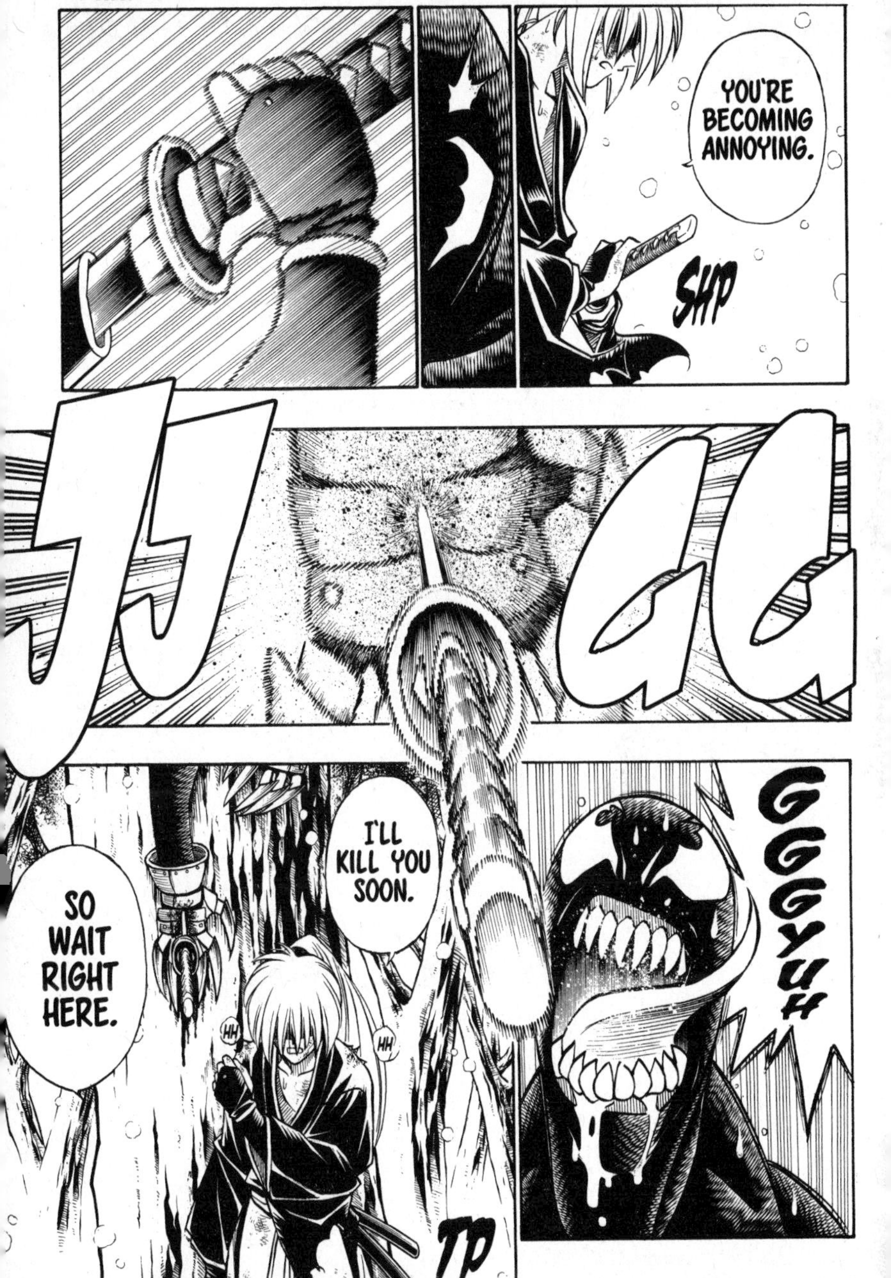
YOU'RE BECOMING ANNOYING.
SHP
JJ
GG
GGGYUH
I'LL KILL YOU SOON.
SO WAIT RIGHT HERE.
HH
HH
TP

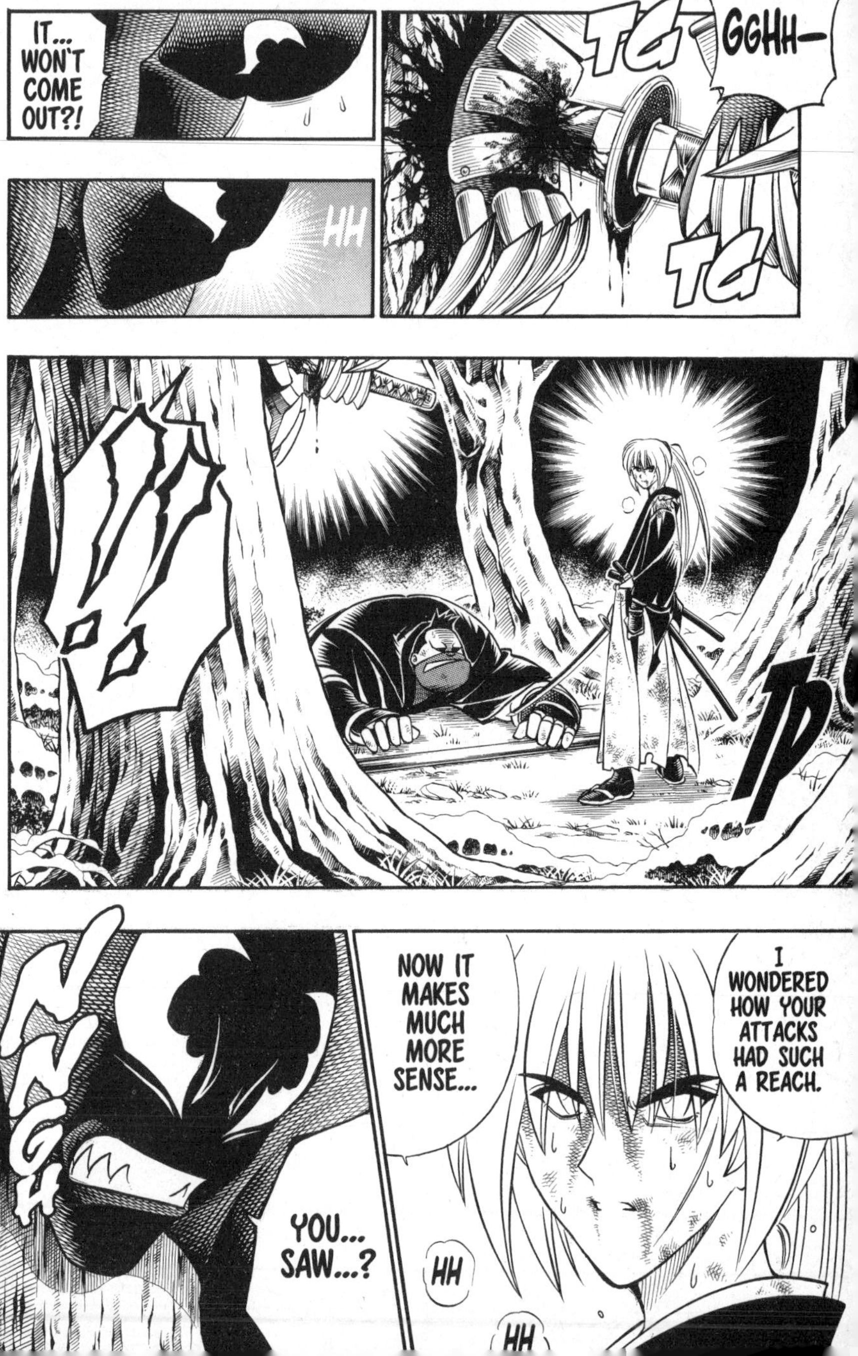
TG
GGHH—
TG
IT... WON'T COME OUT?!
HH
I WONDERED HOW YOUR ATTACKS HAD SUCH A REACH.
NOW IT MAKES MUCH MORE SENSE...
HH
HH
NNGH
YOU... SAW...?

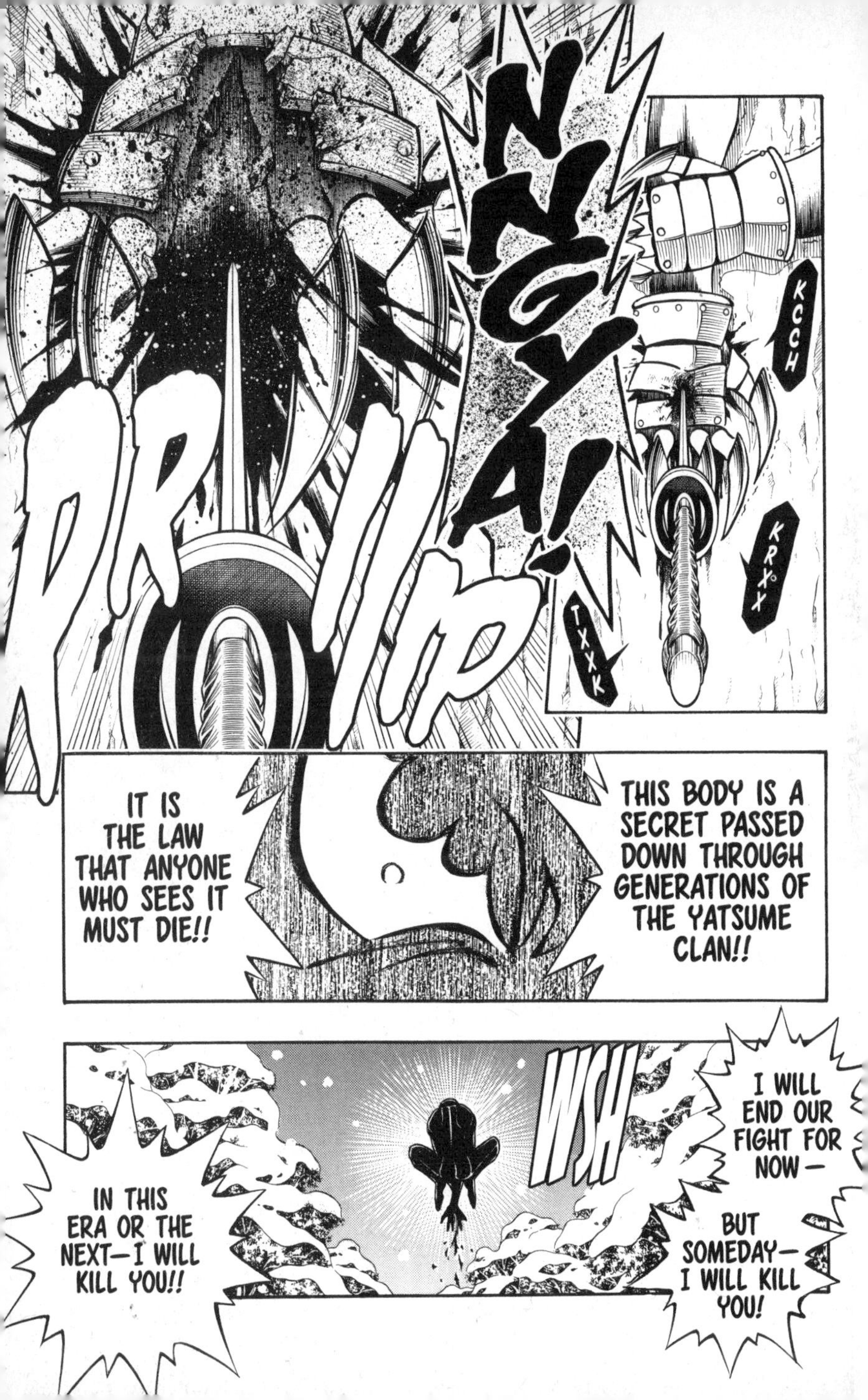
KCCH
KRXX
TXXK
NNGYAA!!
THIS BODY IS A SECRET PASSED DOWN THROUGH GENERATIONS OF THE YATSUME CLAN!!
IT IS THE LAW THAT ANYONE WHO SEES IT MUST DIE!!
I WILL END OUR FIGHT FOR NOW—
BUT SOMEDAY— I WILL KILL YOU!
WSH
IN THIS ERA OR THE NEXT—I WILL KILL YOU!!

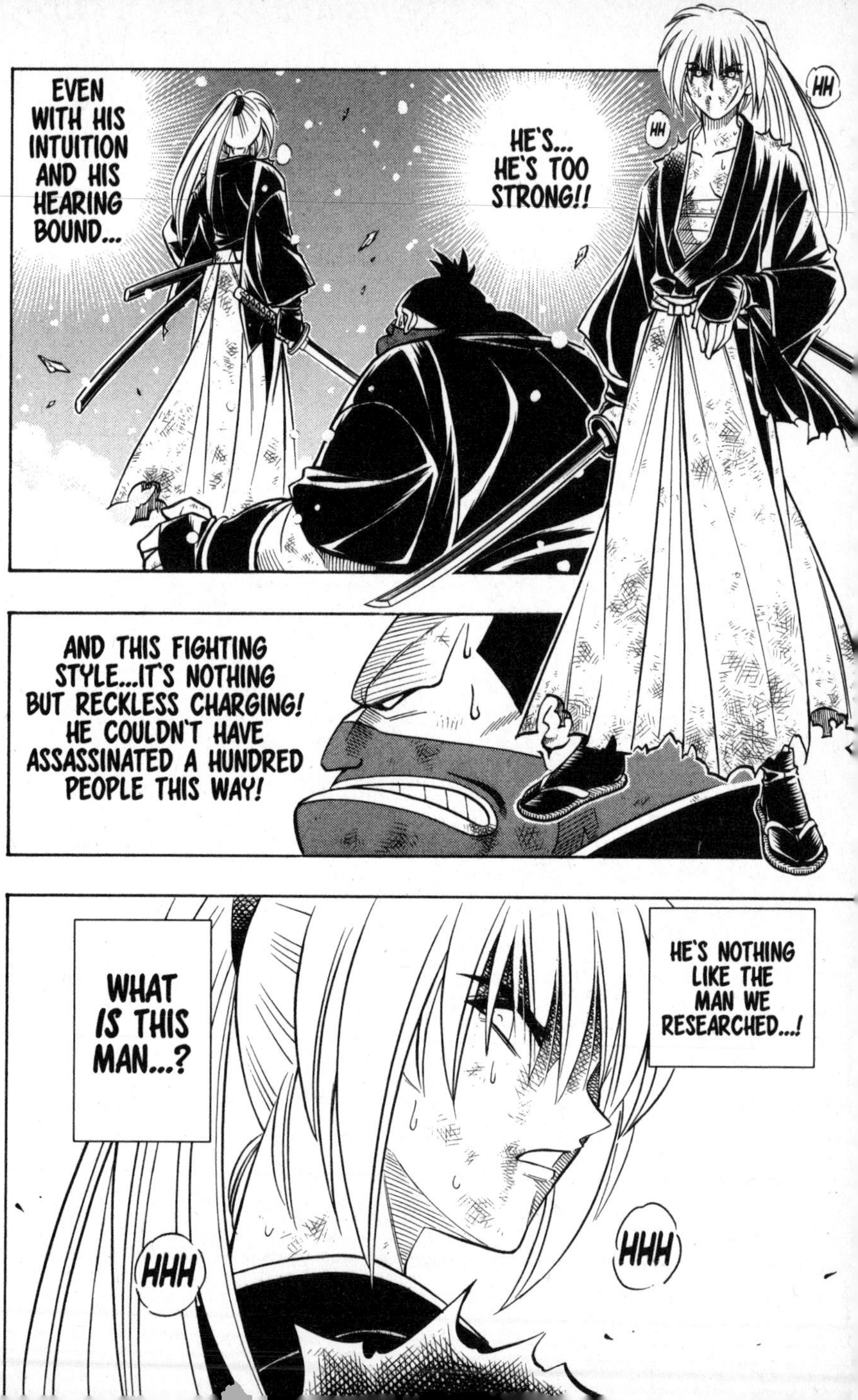
HH
HH
HE'S... HE'S TOO STRONG!!
EVEN WITH HIS INTUITION AND HIS HEARING BOUND...
AND THIS FIGHTING STYLE...IT'S NOTHING BUT RECKLESS CHARGING! HE COULDN'T HAVE ASSASSINATED A HUNDRED PEOPLE THIS WAY!
HE'S NOTHING LIKE THE MAN WE RESEARCHED...!
WHAT IS THIS MAN...?
HHH
HHH

READ THIS WAY

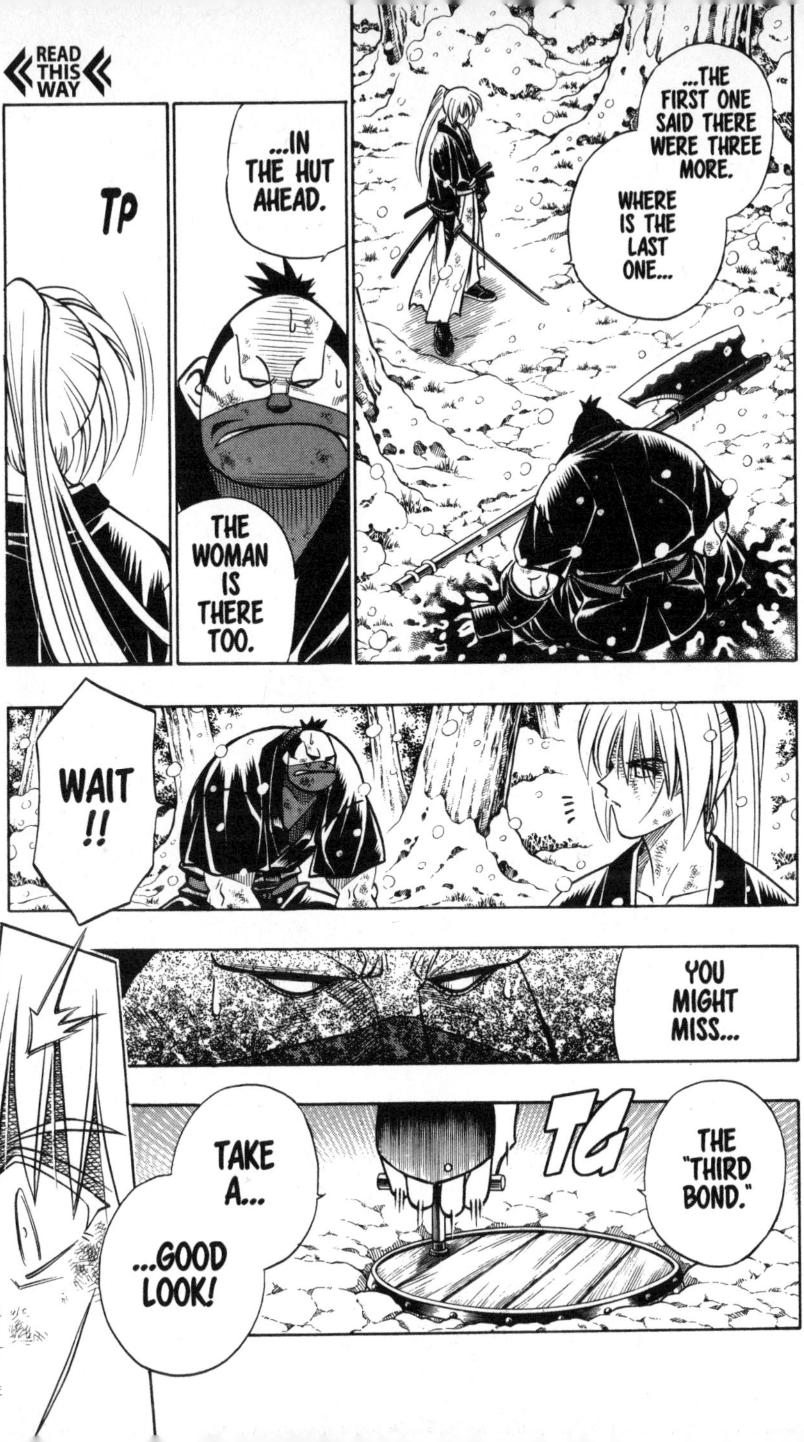

...THE FIRST ONE SAID THERE WERE THREE MORE.
WHERE IS THE LAST ONE...
...IN THE HUT AHEAD.
THE WOMAN IS THERE TOO.
TP
WAIT !!
YOU MIGHT MISS...
THE "THIRD BOND."
TG
TAKE A...
...GOOD LOOK!

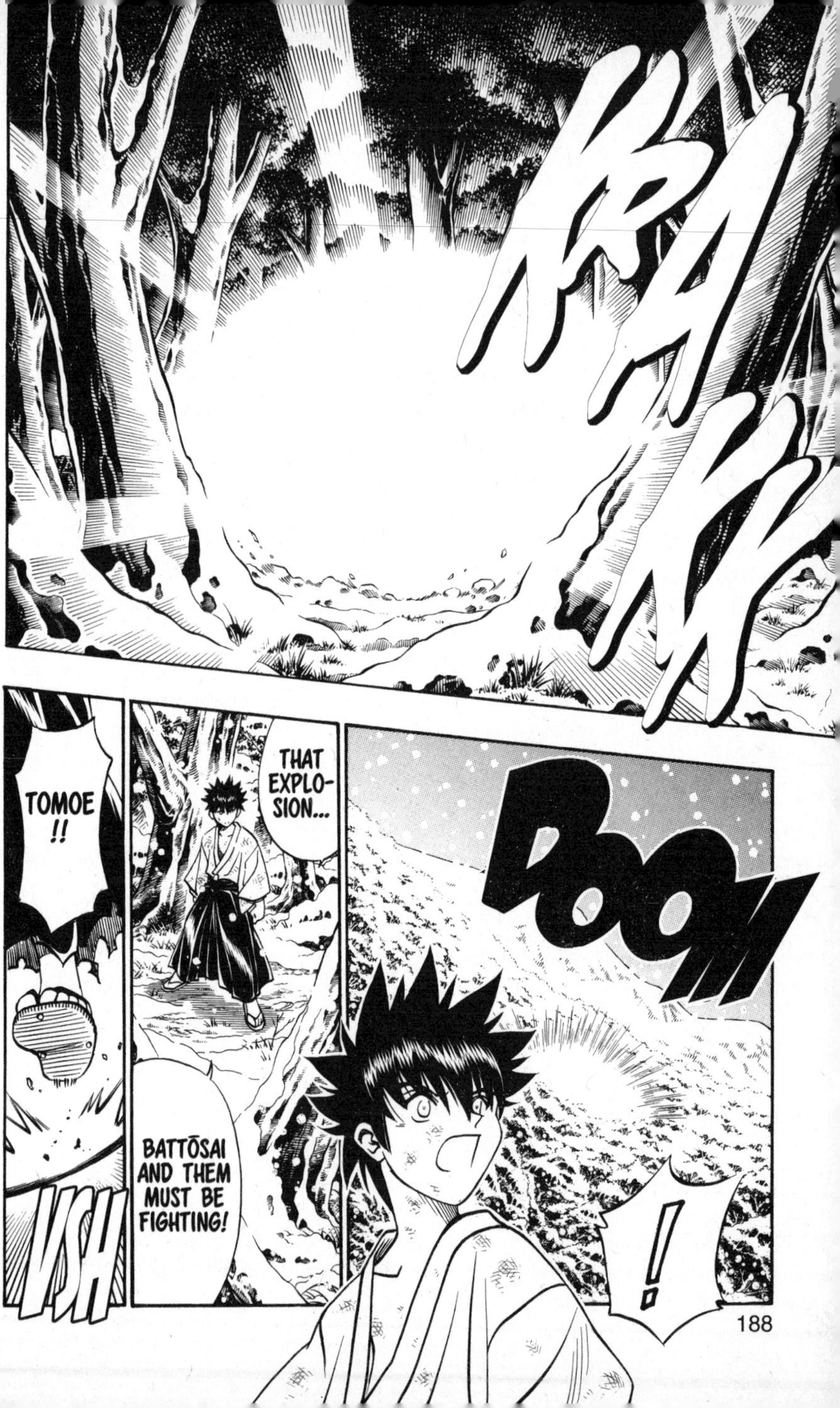
BOOM
!
THAT EXPLOSION...
BATTŌSAI AND THEM MUST BE FIGHTING!
TOMOE !!
VSH

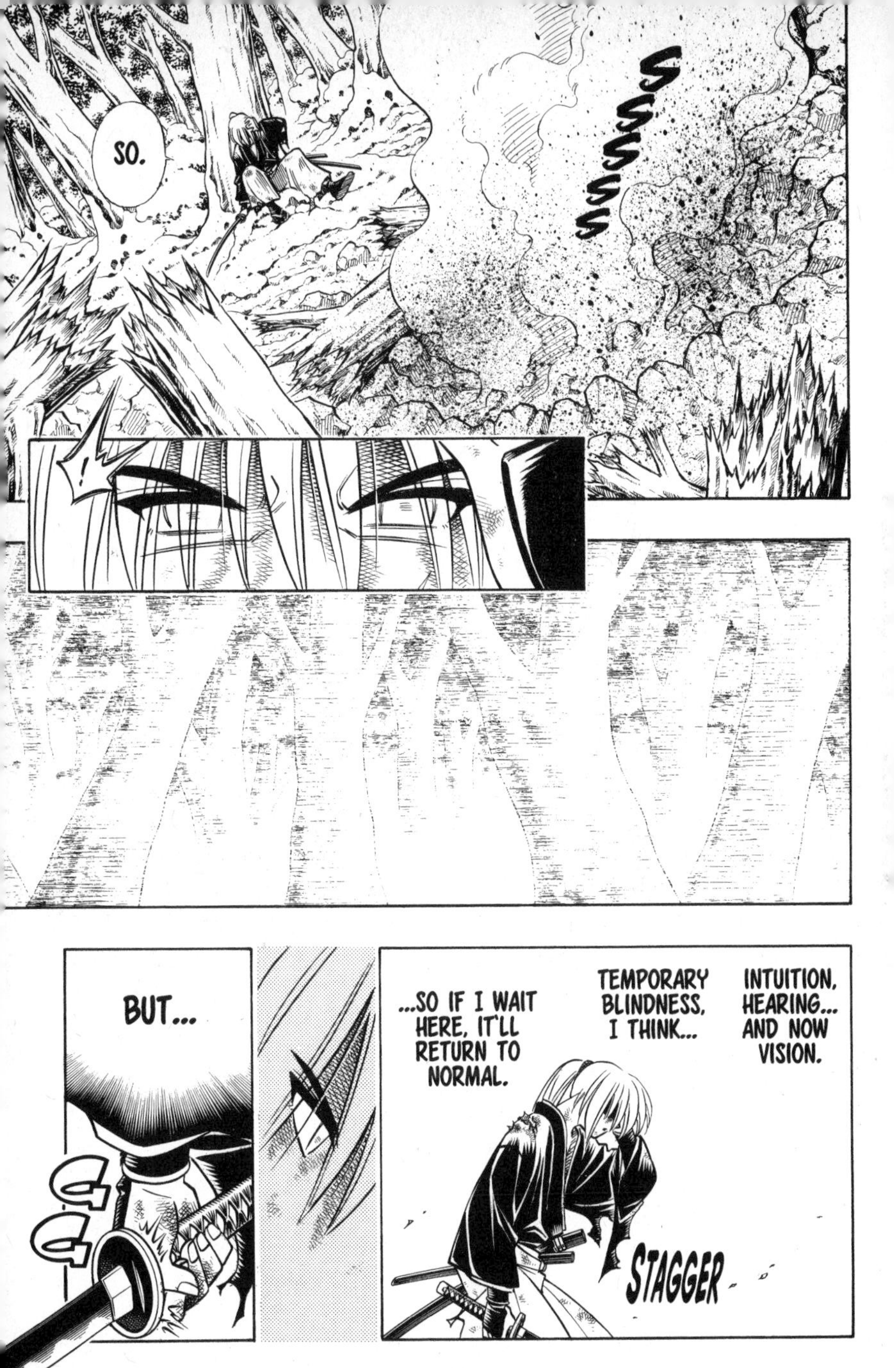
SSSSSS
SO.
!
INTUITION, HEARING... AND NOW VISION.
TEMPORARY BLINDNESS, I THINK...
...SO IF I WAIT HERE, IT'LL RETURN TO NORMAL.
STAGGER
BUT...

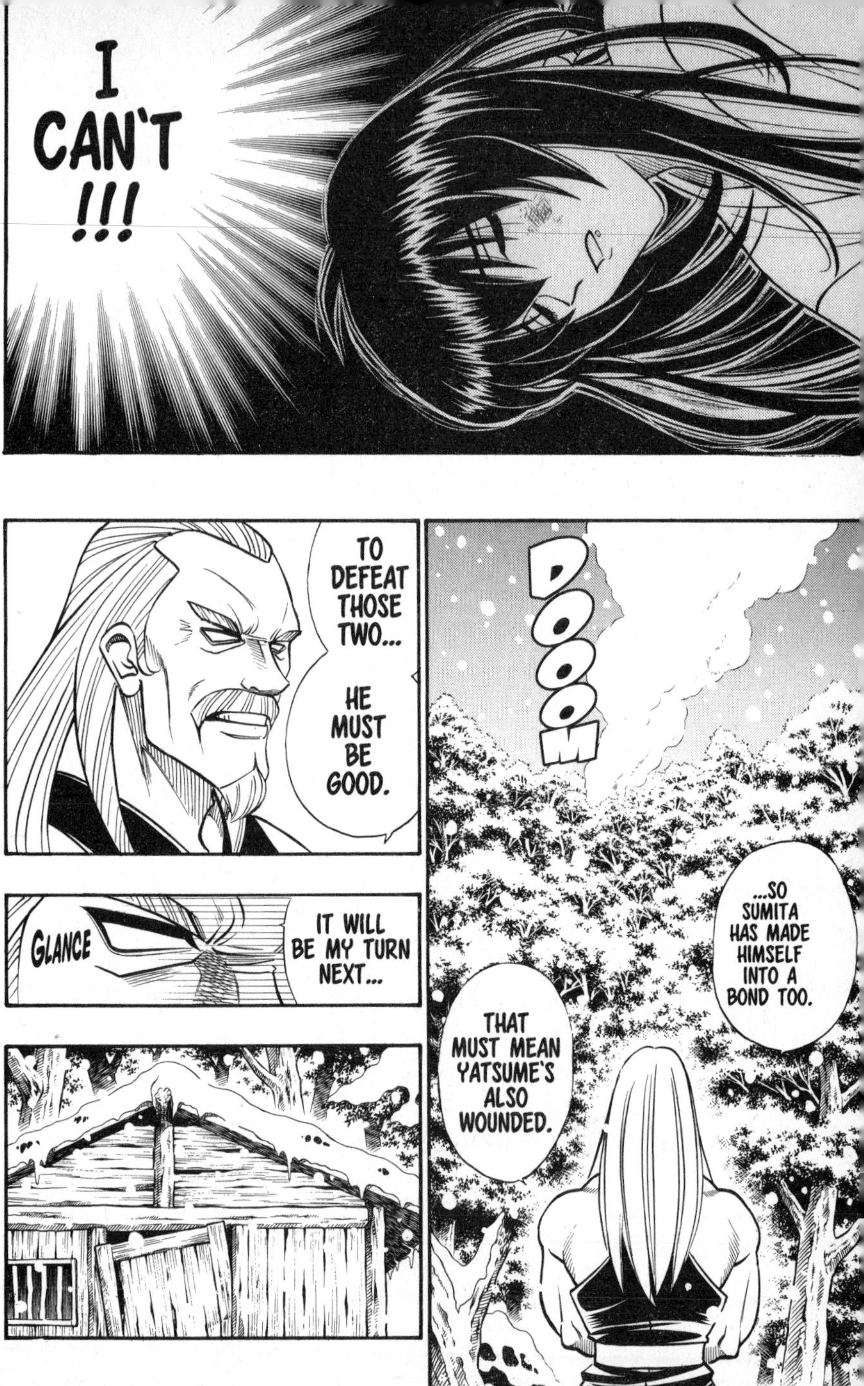
I CAN'T !!!
DOOOOM
...SO SUMITA HAS MADE HIMSELF INTO A BOND TOO.
THAT MUST MEAN YATSUME'S ALSO WOUNDED.
TO DEFEAT THOSE TWO...
HE MUST BE GOOD.
GLANCE
IT WILL BE MY TURN NEXT...

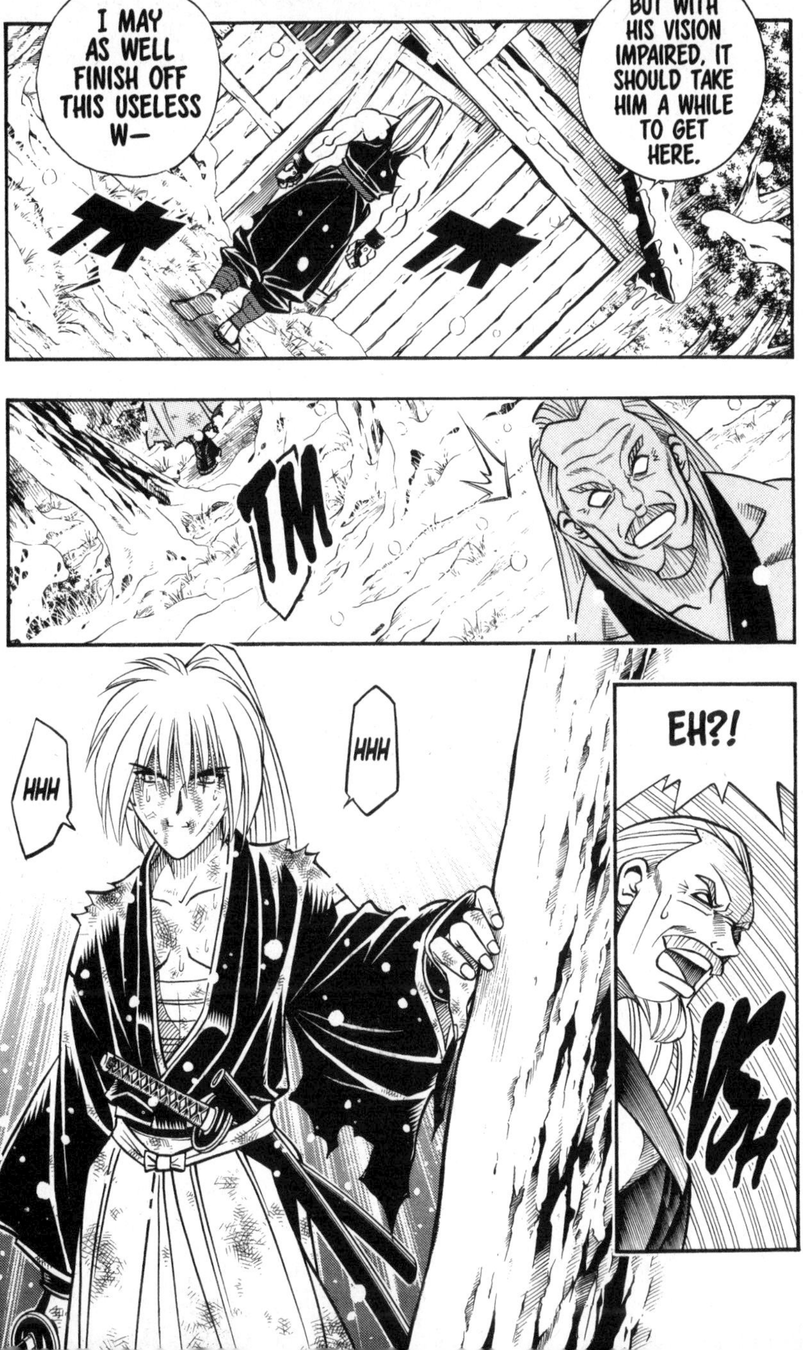
BUT WITH HIS VISION IMPAIRED, IT SHOULD TAKE HIM A WHILE TO GET HERE.
I MAY AS WELL FINISH OFF THIS USELESS W—
TM
EH?!
VSH
HHH
HHH

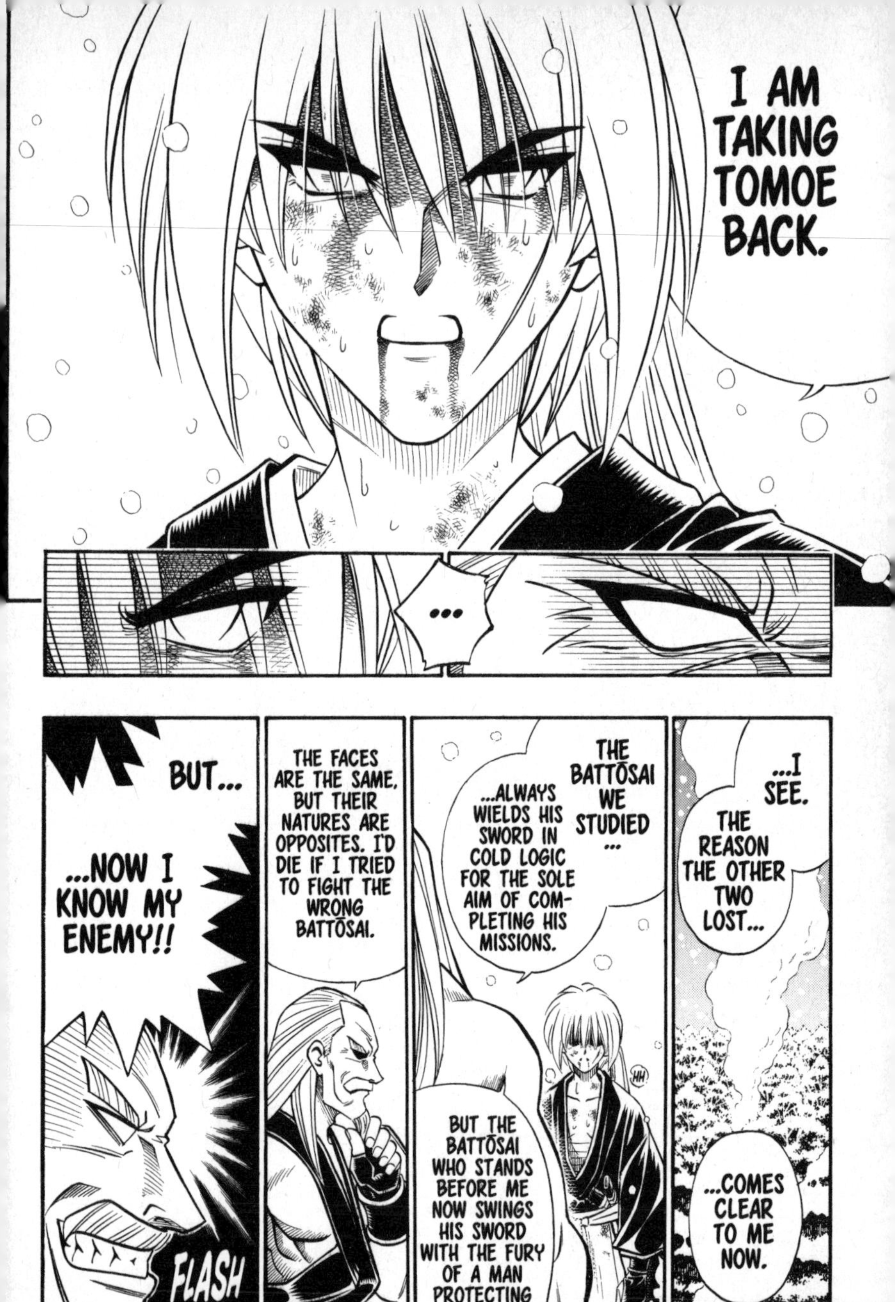
I AM TAKING TOMOE BACK.
...
...I SEE.
THE REASON THE OTHER TWO LOST...
...COMES CLEAR TO ME NOW.
THE BATTŌSAI WE STUDIED...
...ALWAYS WIELDS HIS SWORD IN COLD LOGIC FOR THE SOLE AIM OF COMPLETING HIS MISSIONS.
HH
BUT THE BATTŌSAI WHO STANDS BEFORE ME NOW SWINGS HIS SWORD WITH THE FURY OF A MAN PROTECTING HIS WOMAN.
THE FACES ARE THE SAME, BUT THEIR NATURES ARE OPPOSITES. I'D DIE IF I TRIED TO FIGHT THE WRONG BATTŌSAI.
BUT...
...NOW I KNOW MY ENEMY!!
FLASH

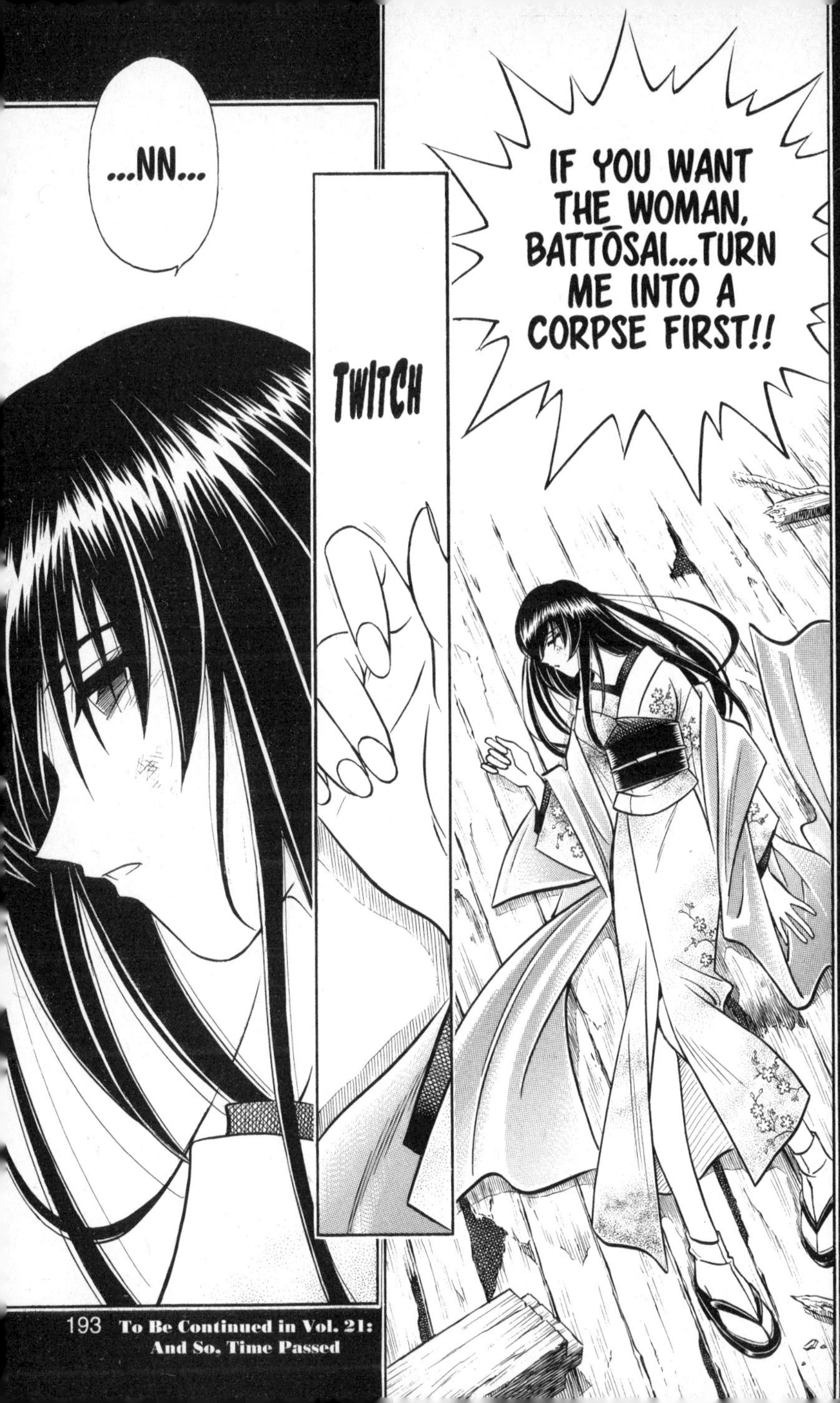
IF YOU WANT THE WOMAN, BATTŌSAI...TURN ME INTO A CORPSE FIRST!!
TWITCH
...NN...

 To Be Continued in Vol. 21: And So, Time Passed

GLOSSARY of the RESTORATION

A brief guide to select Japanese terms used in **Rurouni Kenshin**. *Note that, both here and within the story itself, all names are Japanese style—i.e., last or "family" name first, with personal or "given" name following. This is both because* **Kenshin** *is a "period" story, as well as to decrease confusion—if we were to take the example of Kenshin's sakabatô and "reverse" the format of the historically established assassin-name "Hitokiri Battôsai," for example, it would make little sense to then call him "Battôsai Himura."*

genpuku
A ceremony commemorating a young samurai becoming an adult and usually occurring between the ages of 12 and 18. A samurai could not be married before the **genpuku** occurred.

hakubaikô
The fragrance of white plum blossoms

Himura Kenshin
Kenshin's "real" name, revealed to Kaoru only at her urging

Hiten Mitsurugi-ryû
Kenshin's sword technique, used more for defense than offense. An "ancient style that pits one against many," it requires exceptional speed and agility to master.

hitokiri
An assassin. Famous swordsmen of the period were sometimes thus known to adopt "professional" names—**Kawakami Gensai**, for example, was also known as "Hitokiri Gensai."

Ishin Shishi
Loyalist or pro-Imperialist **patriots** who fought to restore the Emperor to his ancient seat of power

Kawakami Gensai
Real-life, historical inspiration for the character of **Himura Kenshin**

Bakumatsu
Final, chaotic days of the Tokugawa regime

Boshin War
Civil war of 1868-69 between the new government and the **Tokugawa Bakufu**. The anti-*Bakufu*, pro-Imperial side (the Imperial Army) won, easily defeating the Tokugawa supporters.

-chan
Honorific. Can be used either as a diminutive (e.g., with a small child—"Little Hanako or Kentarô"), or with those who are grown, to indicate affection ("My dear...").

-dono
Honorific. Even more respectful than -**san**; the effect in modern-day Japanese conversation would be along the lines of "Milord So-and-So." As used by Kenshin, it indicates both respect and humility.

Edo
Capital city of the **Tokugawa Bakufu**; renamed **Tokyo** ("Eastern Capital") after the Meiji Restoration

sakabatô
Reversed-edge sword (the dull
edge on the side the sharp
should be, and vice versa); car-
ried by Kenshin as a symbol of
his resolution never to kill again

-sama
Honorific. The respectful equiva-
lent of **-san**, **-sama** is used prima-
rily in addressing persons of
much higher rank than one's
self...or, in a romantic sense, in
addressing those upon whom
one is crushing, wicked hard.

-san
Honorific. Carries the meaning of
"Mr.," "Ms.," "Miss," etc., but
used more extensively in
Japanese than its English equiv-
alent (note that even an enemy
may be addressed as "**-san**").

shôgun
Feudal military ruler of Japan

shôgunate
See **Tokugawa Bakufu**

Toba Fushimi, Battle at
Battle near **Kyoto** between the
forces of the new, imperial government and the fallen **shôgunate**. Ending with an imperial
victory, it was the first battle of
the **Boshin War**.

Tokugawa Bakufu
Military feudal government
which dominated Japan from
1603 to 1867

Tokyo
The renaming of "**Edo**" to
"**Tokyo**" is a marker of the start
of the **Meiji Restoration**

-kun
Honorific. Used in the modern
day among male students, or
those who grew up together, but
another usage—the one you're
more likely to find in *Rurouni
Kenshin*—is the "superior-to-infe-
rior" form, intended as a way to
emphasize a difference in status
or rank, as well as to indicate
familiarity or affection.

Kyoto
Home of the Emperor and imperial court from A.D. 794 until
shortly after the **Meiji
Restoration** in 1868

loyalists
Those who supported the return
of the Emperor to power; **Ishin
Shishi**

Meiji Restoration
1853-1868; culminated in the col-
lapse of the **Tokugawa Bakufu**
and the restoration of imperial
rule. So called after Emperor
Meiji, whose chosen name was
written with the characters for
"culture and enlightenment."

Mimawarigumi
Like the *Shinsengumi*, the
Mimawarigumi also patrolled
the streets of Kyoto

Oniwabanshû
Elite group of *onmitsu* or "spies"
of the **Edo** period, also known as
ninja or *shinobi*

rurouni
Wanderer, vagabond

IN THE NEXT VOLUME...

As Kenshin's tortured past comes more and more into focus, casting new light and understanding on his days as a famous (and feared) *hitokiri*, one question is on the minds of everyone at Kamiya Dojo: what will happen when the allotted ten days are up and Enishi's warriors come for them? Will Enishi succeed in exacting his *Jinchû* against Kenshin and his friends? For time continues to flow, from the Bakumatsu into Meiji, and anything is now possible.

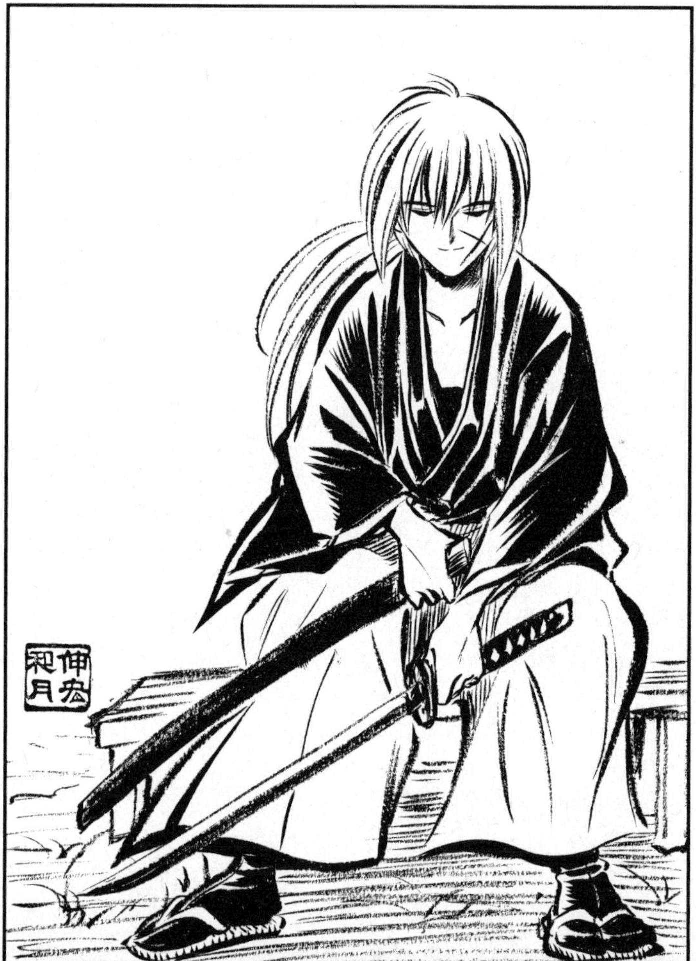
伸宏
和月

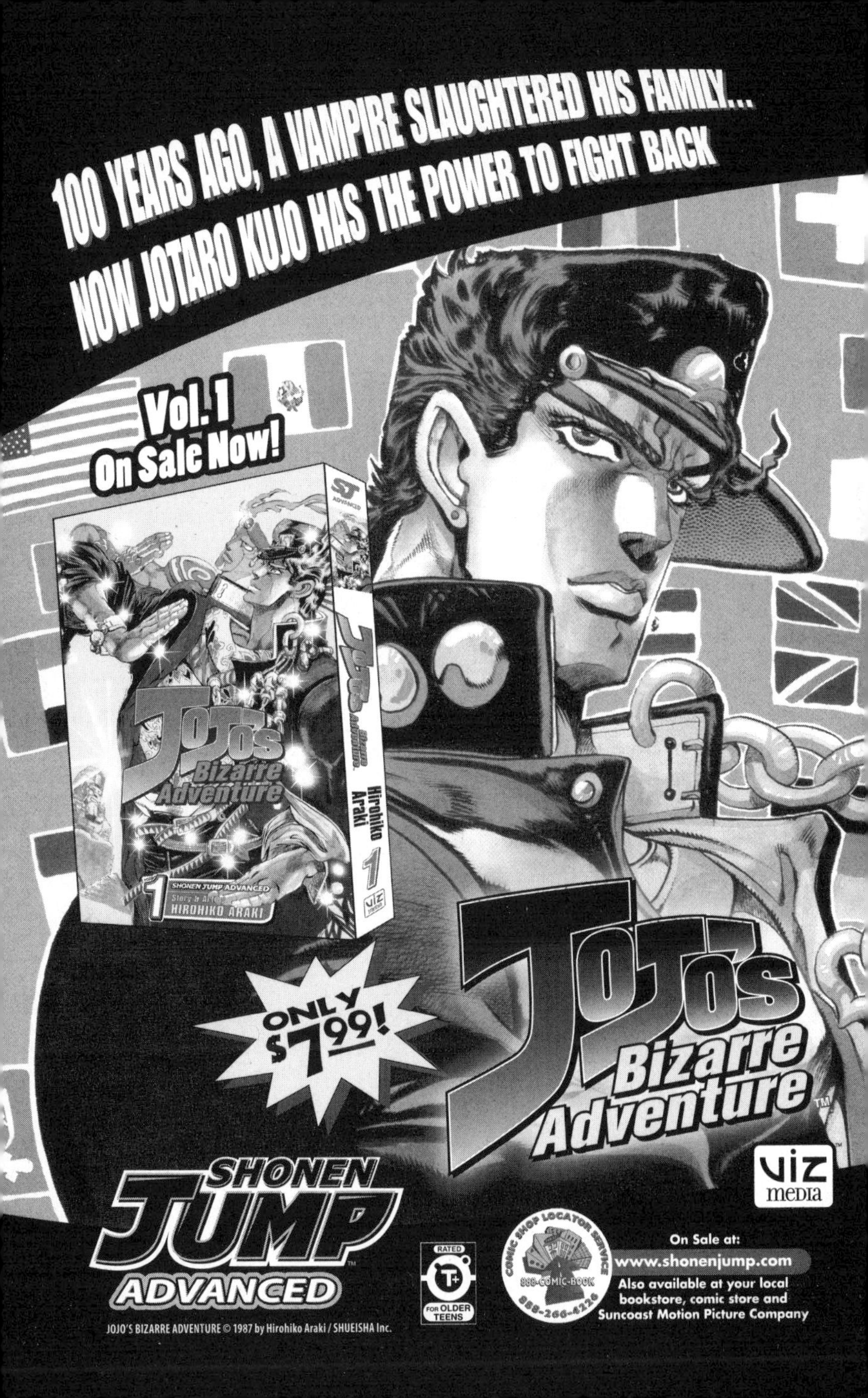
100 YEARS AGO, A VAMPIRE SLAUGHTERED HIS FAMILY...
NOW JOTARO KUJO HAS THE POWER TO FIGHT BACK
Vol. 1
On Sale Now!
JoJo's Bizarre Adventure
SHONEN JUMP ADVANCED
Story & Art by HIROHIKO ARAKI
Hirohiko Araki
ONLY $7.99!
JoJo's Bizarre Adventure™
VIZ media
SHONEN JUMP ADVANCED
RATED T+ FOR OLDER TEENS
COMIC SHOP LOCATOR SERVICE
888-COMIC-BOOK
888-266-4226
On Sale at:
www.shonenjump.com
Also available at your local bookstore, comic store and Suncoast Motion Picture Company
JOJO'S BIZARRE ADVENTURE © 1987 by Hirohiko Araki / SHUEISHA Inc.

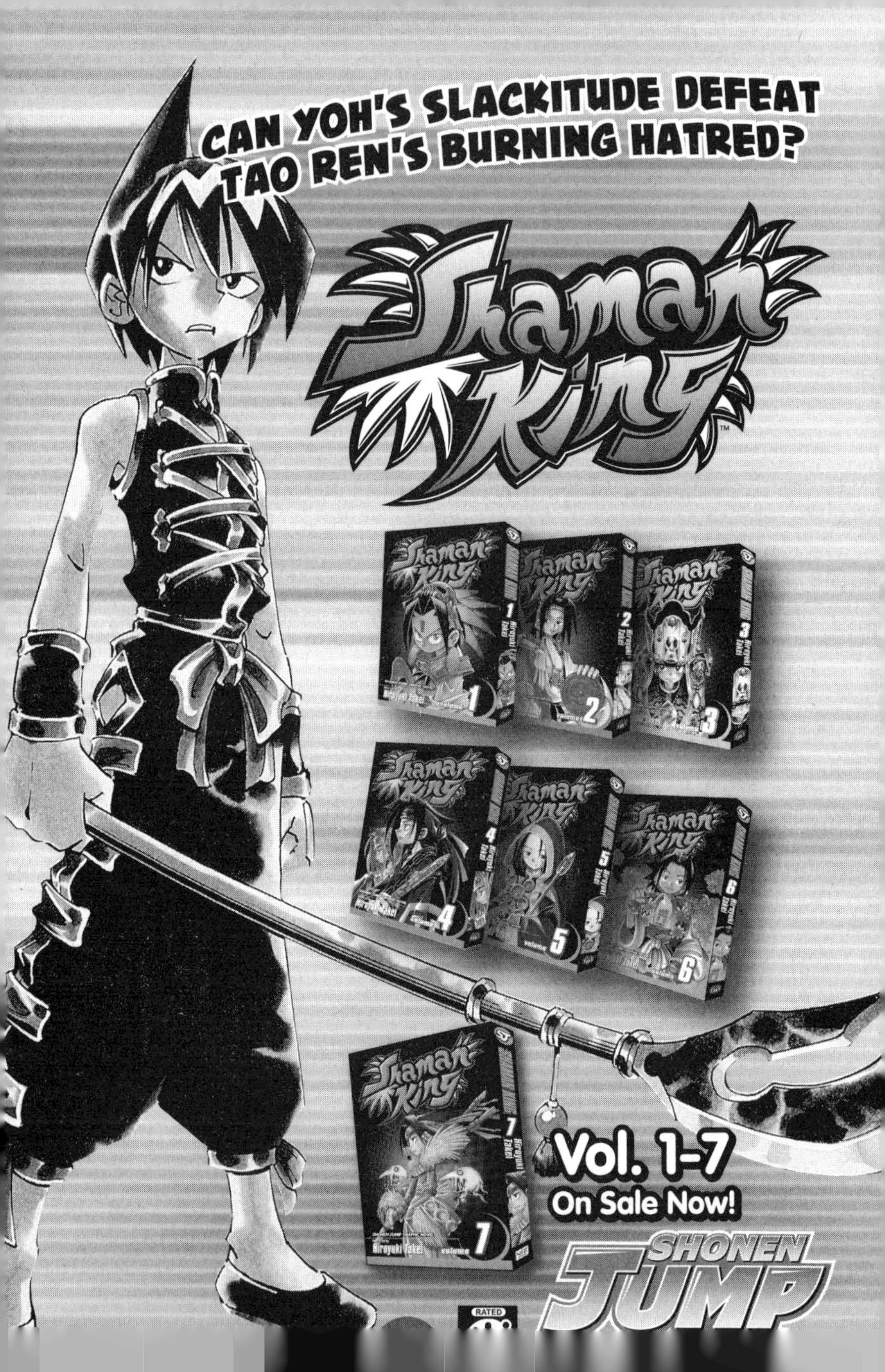
CAN YOH'S SLACKITUDE DEFEAT
TAO REN'S BURNING HATRED?
Shaman King™
Vol. 1-7
On Sale Now!
SHONEN JUMP
RATED

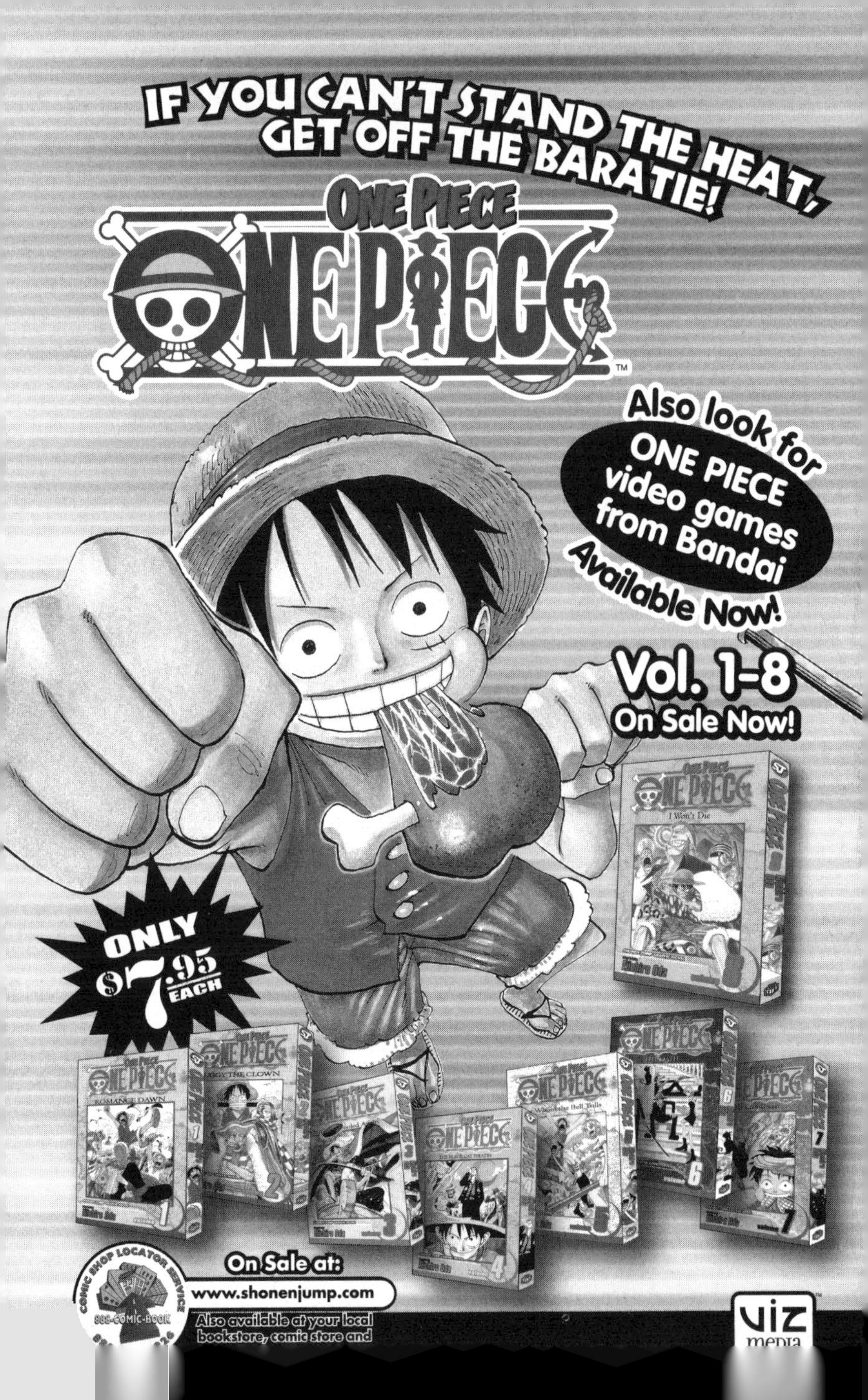
IF YOU CAN'T STAND THE HEAT, GET OFF THE BARATIE!
ONE PIECE
ONE PIECE™
Also look for ONE PIECE video games from Bandai Available Now!
Vol. 1-8 On Sale Now!
ONLY $7.95 EACH
On Sale at:
www.shonenjump.com
Also available at your local bookstore, comic store and
COMIC SHOP LOCATOR SERVICE
888-COMIC-BOOK
viz media

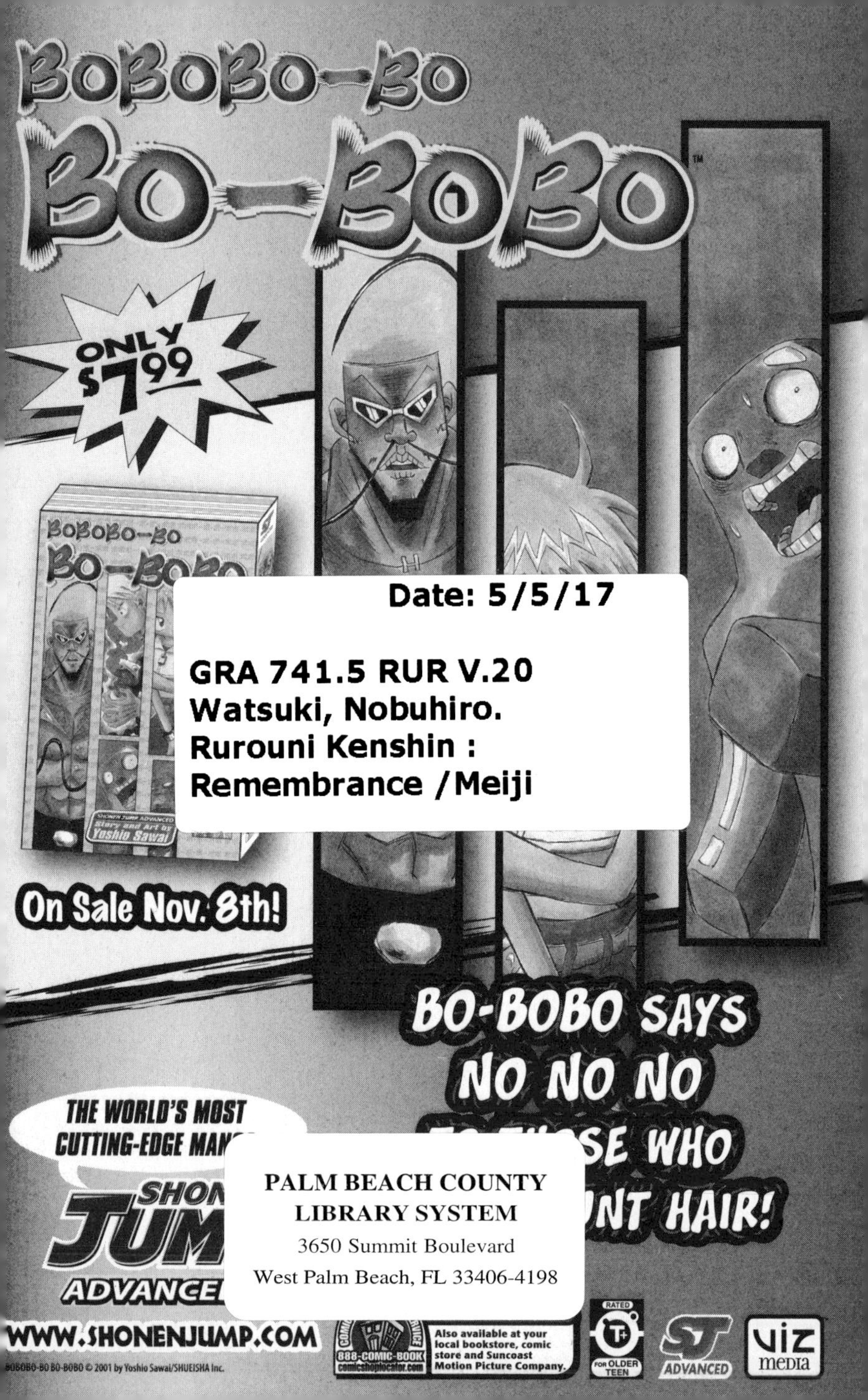
BOBOBO-BO BO-BOBO™
ONLY $7.99
BOBOBO-BO BO-BOBO
Story and Art by Yoshio Sawai
On Sale Nov. 8th!
BO-BOBO SAYS
NO NO NO
SE WHO
NT HAIR!
THE WORLD'S MOST
CUTTING-EDGE MAN
ADVANCE
WWW.SHONENJUMP.COM
BOBOBO-BO BO-BOBO © 2001 by Yoshio Sawai/SHUEISHA Inc.
888-COMIC-BOOK
comicshoplocator.com
Also available at your local bookstore, comic store and Suncoast Motion Picture Company.
RATED T+ FOR OLDER TEEN
SJ ADVANCED
viz media

Check us out on the web!

www.shonenjump.com

NO POSTAGE NECESSARY IF MAILED IN THE UNITED STATES

BUSINESS REPLY MAIL
FIRST-CLASS MAIL PERMIT NO. 113 MT MORRIS IL

POSTAGE WILL BE PAID BY ADDRESSEE

SHONEN JUMP™ THE WORLD'S MOST POPULAR MANGA

SUBSCRIPTIONS SERVICE DEPT.
PO BOX 509
MT. MORRIS IL 61054-7763

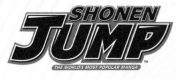

COMPLETE OUR SURVEY AND LET US KNOW WHAT YOU THINK!

SHONEN JUMP™ THE WORLD'S MOST POPULAR MANGA

☐ Please do NOT send me information about VIZ Media and SHONEN JUMP products, news and events, special offers, or other information.

☐ Please do NOT send me information from VIZ Media's trusted business partners.

Name: ______________________________

Address: ______________________________

City: ____________ **State:** ______ **Zip:** ____________

E-mail: ______________________________

☐ **Male** ☐ **Female** **Date of Birth** (mm/dd/yyyy): ___/___/_____ (**Under 13? Parental consent required.**)

1 Do you purchase SHONEN JUMP Magazine?

☐ Yes ☐ No

If **YES**, do you subscribe?

☐ Yes ☐ No

If **NO**, how often do you purchase SHONEN JUMP Magazine?

☐ 1-3 issues a year ☐ 4-6 issues a year ☐ more than 7 issues a year

2 Which SHONEN JUMP Manga did you purchase this time? (please check only one)

☐ Beet the Vandel Buster ☐ Bleach ☐ Bobobo-bo Bo-bobo
☐ Death Note ☐ Dragon Ball ☐ Dragon Ball Z
☐ Dr. Slump ☐ Eyeshield 21 ☐ Hikaru no Go
☐ Hunter x Hunter ☐ I"s ☐ JoJo's Bizarre Adventure
☐ Knights of the Zodiac ☐ Legendz ☐ Naruto
☐ One Piece ☐ Rurouni Kenshin ☐ Shaman King
☐ The Prince of Tennis ☐ Ultimate Muscle ☐ Whistle!
☐ Yu-Gi-Oh! ☐ Yu-Gi-Oh!: Duelist ☐ Yu-Gi-Oh!: Millennium World
☐ YuYu Hakusho ☐ Other ______________

Will you purchase subsequent volumes?

☐ Yes ☐ No

3 How did you learn about this title? (check all that apply)

☐ Favorite title ☐ Advertisement ☐ Article
☐ Gift ☐ Read excerpt in SHONEN JUMP Magazine
☐ Recommendation ☐ Special offer ☐ Through TV animation
☐ Website ☐ Other ______________

4 Of the titles that are serialized in SHONEN JUMP Magazine, have you purchased the paperback manga volumes?

☐ Yes ☐ No

If **YES**, which ones have you purchased? (check all that apply)

☐ Hikaru no Go ☐ Naruto ☐ One Piece ☐ Shaman King
☐ Yu-Gi-Oh!: Millennium World ☐ YuYu Hakusho

If **YES**, what were your reasons for purchasing? (please pick up to 3)

☐ A favorite title ☐ A favorite creator/artist ☐ I want to read it in one go
☐ I want to read it over and over again ☐ There are extras that aren't in the magazine
☐ The quality of printing is better than the magazine ☐ Recommendation
☐ Special offer ☐ Other

If **NO**, why did/would you not purchase it?

☐ I'm happy just reading it in the magazine ☐ It's not worth buying the manga volume
☐ All the manga pages are in black and white, unlike the magazine
☐ There are other manga volumes that I prefer ☐ There are too many to collect for each title
☐ It's too small ☐ Other _____

5 Of the titles NOT serialized in the magazine, which ones have you purchased?
(check all that apply)

☐ Beet the Vandel Buster ☐ Bleach ☐ Bobobo-bo Bo-bobo ☐ Death Note
☐ Dragon Ball ☐ Dragon Ball Z ☐ Dr. Slump ☐ Eyeshield 21
☐ Hunter x Hunter ☐ I"s ☐ JoJo's Bizarre Adventure ☐ Knights of the Zodiac
☐ Legendz ☐ The Prince of Tennis ☐ Rurouni Kenshin ☐ Ultimate Muscle
☐ Whistle! ☐ Yu-Gi-Oh! ☐ Yu-Gi-Oh!: Duelist ☐ None
☐ Other _____

If you did purchase any of the above, what were your reasons for purchasing?

☐ A favorite title ☐ A favorite creator/artist
☐ Read a preview in SHONEN JUMP Magazine and wanted to read the rest of the story
☐ Recommendation ☐ Other

Will you purchase subsequent volumes?

☐ Yes ☐ No

6 What race/ethnicity do you consider yourself? (please check one)

☐ Asian/Pacific Islander ☐ Black/African American ☐ Hispanic/Latino
☐ Native American/Alaskan Native ☐ White/Caucasian ☐ Other

THANK YOU! Please send the completed form to: VIZ Media Survey
42 Catharine St.
Poughkeepsie, NY 12601

VIZ media

All information provided will be used for internal purposes only. We promise not to sell or otherwise divulge your information.